# CHARITIES:
# LAW AND PRACTICE

**AUSTRALIA**
LBC Information Services
Sydney


**CANADA and USA**
Carswell
Toronto, Ontario


**NEW ZEALAND**
Brooker's
Auckland


**SINGAPORE and MALAYSIA**
Thomson Information (S.E. Asia)
Singapore

# CHARITIES: LAW AND PRACTICE

## THIRD EDITION

## ELIZABETH CAIRNS
**Solicitor**

**LONDON     SWEET & MAXWELL     1997**

First Edition 1988
Second Edition 1993
Third Edition 1997

Published in 1997 by
Sweet and Maxwell Limited of
100 Avenue Road, London NW3
Typeset by Tradespools Limited
Printed and bound in Great Britain by Butler and Tanner Ltd,
Frome and London


No natural forests were destroyed to make this product:
only farmed timber was used and replanted


**A CIP catalogue record for this book is available from the
British Library**


ISBN 0 421 56190 4

# PREFACE

In the three years which have passed since the second edition of this book most of the Charities Act 1992 has been implemented. The restrictions on professional fund-raisers contained in Part II of the Act came into force in March 1995 and the new regime for charity accounts applies for accounting periods commencing on or after 1st March 1996. The only part of the 1992 Act which has not yet come into force is Part III, which will provide a unified regulatory system for public and house-to-house collections. This is not now expected until summer 1998.

The De-Regulation Task Force has achieved some minor victories for smaller charities in raising the financial thresholds for accounting, audit and independent examination and allowing groups of charities to be registered under one umbrella charity and simplifying and streamlining regulations in a number of areas relevant to the work of charities.

The Charity Commission has undergone substantial structural changes as part of the continuing process of meeting the criticisms made of it in the Woodfield Report. It now provides much more information than formerly about its policies and practice through the twice-yearly publication *Decisions of the Charity Commissioners*, a number of new leaflets on important points of practice and revised versions of existing leaflets. A regular newsletter is also issued.

As before this book is intended as a practical guide to the law and practice relating to charities and a point of reference for those who wish to do further research. I hope that it achieves this modest aim, but I would always like to hear from readers who have suggestions for improvements.

References throughout to the Charities Act are to the Charities Act 1993.

Elizabeth Cairns
September 1996

# CONTENTS

# TABLE OF CASES

# TABLE OF STATUTES

# 1 WHAT IS A CHARITY?

## Origins

The legal concept of charity has been developed by the courts over several centuries. There is no statutory definition of charity and the courts have refrained from attempting to provide one. Before both the Charities Act of 1960 and the Charities Act 1992 were passed there was some discussion as to whether a definition of charity should be formulated but it was decided that the benefit of flexibility, which allowed the scope of charity to keep pace with changes in society, outweighed the advantages of certainty and clarity which a statutory definition might be expected to provide. It has even been suggested that the advantages of a definition could be illusory in that it might result in "a fresh spate of litigation and provide a set of undesirable distinctions" (Sachs L.J. in *Council of Law Reporting v. Att.-Gen.*[1]) The arguments against a statutory definition are still persuasive and the Charities Act does not contain one although there are a number of eminent lawyers who still argue in favour. Whether it is wise to continue to define a charitable purpose in so abstruse a way now we are part of the Single European Market is questionable. It will undoubtedly inhibit the spread of charitable organisations on the British model in Europe.

The word "charity" is derived from the Latin "caritas," meaning care and in ordinary contemporary usage the term may mean no more than generosity to the poor and needy. The legal meaning of the word is wider than this, in that it encompasses many other purposes which are for the benefit of the community as a whole.

The courts have adopted the practice of referring to an Elizabethan statute (which has now been repealed) for guidance as to what purposes should be regarded as charitable in law. The **Statute of** preamble to the Charitable Uses Act 1601 (usually referred to as **Elizabeth I** the Statute of Elizabeth I) contained a list of purposes which were at that time considered to be charitable in the following terms:

> "The relief of aged, impotent, and poor people; the maintenance of sick and maimed soldiers and mariners, schools of learning, free schools and scholars of universities; the repair of bridges, ports, havens, causeways, churches, sea banks and highways; the education and preferment of orphans; the relief, stock or maintenance of houses of correction; the marriages of poor maids; the supportation, aid and help of young tradesmen; handicraftsmen and persons decayed; the relief or redemption of prisoners or captives; and the aid or ease of any poor inhabitants concerning payments of fifteens, setting out of soldiers, and other taxes."

[1] *Incorporated Council of Law Reporting for England and Wales v. Att.-Gen.* [1972] Ch. 73 at 94.

From this rag-bag of purposes the modern concept of charity has evolved. Although not the earliest, the most influential classification of charitable purposes was made by Lord MacNaughton in the case of *Income Tax Special Purposes Commissioners v. Pemsel*[2]:

> "Charity in its legal sense comprises four principal divisions: trusts for the relief of poverty; trusts for the advancement of education; trusts for the advancement of religion; and trusts for other purposes beneficial to the community not falling under any of the preceding heads."

This classification has traditionally been used as a basis for discussion of charitable purposes.

The courts have not regarded the Elizabethan list as exhaustive but have taken it as providing general guidance as to the kind of purpose which should be regarded as charitable. This broad approach has allowed the concept of charity to be modified as times and conditions changed to include not only purposes similar to those set out in the preamble but also purposes which are considered to be within the spirit of the statute.

Two different but complementary approaches have been adopted by the courts. The first, and more restrictive of the two, **Argument from** is to ascertain whether a purpose has sufficient resemblance to **analogy** one of the original examples or to some earlier decided case to be considered charitable. This is known as the argument from analogy or the stepping-stones approach. Using this approach the provision of lifeboats has been held to be charitable by analogy with the maintenance of sea banks referred to in the preamble, both being for the protection of human life. In another case the provision of a crematorium was considered charitable by analogy with the provision of burial grounds which was charitable by analogy with the upkeep of churchyards which itself was held charitable by analogy with the repair of churches mentioned in the preamble.

The second approach is more flexible and has been favoured in a number of modern decisions. It permits the court to consider if the purpose which is under scrutiny is "within the spirit and intendment" or "within the equity" of the statute. This enables the court to hold purposes to be charitable which cannot be directly connected to one of the original purposes listed in the preamble. It has been suggested[3] that in considering purposes coming under the fourth head (purposes beneficial to the community) any purpose which is established to be for the benefit of the public should be regarded as charitable unless it is a purpose which could not have been intended by the draftsman of the Elizabethan statute even if he had been aware of the changes which had taken place in society since 1601. On this **The wider test** argument, to say that a purpose must be within the spirit of the statute, is to provide a long stop against possible abuse rather than a standard which all charitable purposes must meet. It will permit the court to reject a purpose even though it may be

---

[2] [1891] A.C. 531.
[3] *Incorporated Council of Law Reporting for England and Wales v. Att.-Gen.* [1972] Ch. 73 at 88, *per* Russell L.J.

beneficial to the public if it is clearly outside the contemplation of the statute as, for example, a political purpose would be.

Both approaches are employed in the decided cases but the wider test of what is charitable has been compared favourably with the "stepping stones" approach, which has been described as artificial. The wider test was described by Sachs L.J. in the *Council of Law Reporting* case[4] as having "an admirable breadth and flexibility which enables it to be reasonably applied from generation to generation to meet changing circumstances." However, in considering applications for registration as a charity, the Charity Commissioners will normally reject this test in favour of the argument from analogy. Their role being to give effect to the existing law rather than to make new law, they incline to a cautious approach although they stated in their Annual Report for 1985 that they would try to act "constructively and imaginatively" and would be "robust" in seeking analogies.

# The four heads of charity

## 1. The relief of poverty and human suffering and distress

**"Aged"**
**"impotent"**
**"poor"**

Lord MacNaughton's first category, trusts for the relief of poverty, is perhaps the least satisfactory. Basing it upon the reference in the preamble to "the relief of aged, impotent and poor people" ("impotent" meaning here weak or helpless) it is possible that Lord MacNaughton did not consider the possibility of trusts for the benefit of aged or impotent people who were not poor, perhaps because most persons who were in need of relief at that time would indeed have been poor. However, it was decided in the case of *Re Glyn's Will Trusts*[5] that the phrase "aged, impotent and poor people" should be construed disjunctively and that the relief of the aged (in that case a trust to build cottages for old women) was charitable without reference to poverty. Following this decision it was held in *Re Resch's Will Trusts*[6] that a private hospital for the relief of the sick (who are included in the expression "the impotent") was charitable even though fees were charged which would have excluded the poor from benefit.

A number of other purposes cited in the preamble do not fit conveniently into any of Lord MacNaughton's categories; for example "the education and preferment of orphans," "the supportation, aid and help of young tradesmen, handicraftsmen and persons decayed" and "the relief or redemption of prisoners or captives" and it has been persuasively argued that the relief of poverty should be regarded as a subdivision of a wider class comprising the relief of human suffering and distress generally (see the judgment of Slade J. in *McGovern v. Att.-Gen.*[7]). For convenience this approach will be followed here.

---

[4] *Ibid.* at 94.
[5] [1950] 2 All E.R. 1150n.
[6] [1969] A.C. 514 (P.C.).
[7] *McGovern v. Att.-Gen.* [1982] Ch. 321, *per* Slade J.

**Relief of poverty**   There are many charities of great antiquity still in existence which were established for this purpose. The forms that relief could take were various, including the provision of clothing, fuel and food as well as the giving of alms or doles. These forms of relief are of little value in modern society and the Charity Commissioners will now readily make schemes to

**Modernisation of outdated trusts**   modernise them so that the income may be applied at the trustees' discretion for the relief of need generally (see Chapter 11). It is widely thought, particularly in better-off parts of the country, that there is no longer any need for charities for the poor in modern society and the trustees of many such charities now restrict their activities to making cash payments to pensioners at Christmas without reference to their actual needs. This view would be strongly contested by any working among the less well off who maintain that even in affluent areas and despite the welfare state there is a useful role for charities for the relief of poverty which can give help in emergencies and in ways not provided for by the state. Homeless young people certainly qualify as deprived and several charities aim to provide them with shelter and financial support.

**The meaning of "poor"**   "Poor" does not necessarily mean destitute. Poverty is a comparative term and the concept may vary in different social conditions. An element of deprivation must be present but in assessing whether this is or is not the case regard may be had to the individual's background and the standard of life to which he had been accustomed.[8]

Few new charities for the relief of poverty in the United Kingdom are now established to provide relief in these traditional ways. There has, however, been a resurgence of interest in almshouses many of which had fallen into decay in the years following the Second World War but have now been restored and revived because of the encouragement and

**Almshouses**   inspiration of the National Association of Almshouses, (see Appendix E). Many ancient almshouses which would otherwise have decayed beyond hope of repair have been saved. A recent unusual case decided by the Commissioners[9] concerned a trust which provided loans either interest free or at low rates for poor people to enable them to buy their own homes. Despite objections from the Revenue that the beneficiaries might derive a profit at the expense of the charity the trust was registered.

Modern charities coming under the heading of the relief of poverty are concerned less with providing financial assistance or

**Deprivation**   benefits in kind and more with attempting to remedy the effects of deprivation. Organisations such as those which provide training for young people to enable them to find work or give assistance to those setting up in business on their own can be regarded as coming under this head as can those concerned to help "latch-key" children whose parents are obliged to work to support them. The Commissioners have agreed to register a foundation which would establish a "fair trade mark" for third world products, guaranteeing that the product had been produced under good working conditions and that part of the

---

[8] *Re Coulthurst* [1951] Ch. 661.
[9] Charity Commissioners' Annual Report for 1990.

price would be used to maintain or improve conditions for workers.[10] Organisations which aim to support and help people who have suffered as a result of crime, drug or sexual abuse, violence or homelessness or simply through living in decaying inner city areas or run-down housing estates all seek to combat deprivation in different guises and have been registered as charities under this heading. The provision of community facilities in impoverished areas may also be charitable under this wider definition of poverty. A number of charities have been set up recently to counsel and help the victims of domestic violence.

**Unemployment**       The relief of unemployment by, for example, the provision of work for unemployed but otherwise able-bodied people is not regarded as charitable. The relief of poverty among the unemployed on the other hand is charitable whether through the provision of direct financial relief or, more indirectly, by training individuals so that they are able to earn a living or helping them to find work.

Both direct and indirect methods may be used to relieve poverty. A law centre is charitable under this head since it provides legal advice for those who cannot afford to consult a solicitor. The Commissioners have accepted that the improvement of agriculture and provision of public works in the Third World may indirectly be for the relief of poverty so long as it can be shown that the poor will indeed benefit as a result.

**Relief of sickness**   Although the relief of the sick is not specifically mentioned in the preamble (unless it can be said to be included in the reference to the relief of impotent, *i.e.* weak or **Hospitals**   powerless people), the provision of hospitals and care of the sick has traditionally been regarded as charitable. Before the National Health Service was established, voluntary hospitals were established as charities, and now hospitals outside the National Health Service which are not run for profit but are open to any patient able and willing to pay the fees are charitable. Funds to provide extra comforts and facilities (*e.g.* toys for sick children) at National Health Service hospitals and the Friends of various hospitals are also considered to be charitable as are nursing homes and hospices for the terminally ill. It is only a small step from charities like these to organisations devoted to improving the standard of care of the sick. The promotion of high standards of nursing has been held charitable[11] as has the provision of a home for nurses on the grounds that a comfortable place to live would improve their **Medical research**   efficiency. Medical research and the promotion and encouragement of the study and practice of surgery have also been held to be charitable both as promoting the relief of sickness and as advancing education. Sickness is not limited to **Mental illness**   physical ailments. The relief of those suffering from mental disorders is accepted by the Charity Commissioners as charitable as is the treatment of drug and alcohol addiction. Half-way houses for persons who have undergone treatment for mental conditions or addiction have been

[10] *Decision of the Charity Commissioners*, Vol. 4, pp. 1–7.
[11] *Royal College of Nursing v. St. Marylebone Borough Council* [1959] 1 W.L.R. 1077.

established as charities.

**Indirect relief of sickness**
Methods of relief which indirectly relieve the suffering of sick people or aid their recovery are acceptable. In their leaflet on Charities for the Relief of Sickness (CC6) the Charity Commissioners list a number of ways in which charities for the general relief of sickness might distribute their funds. These include the provision of items such as bedding, heating appliances, wheelchairs and food for special diets, payment for services such as help in the home, meals on wheels, shopping and laundry and help for the relatives of the sick by arranging for them to visit patients in hospital or providing temporary relief for those who care for sick people at home. Physical and mental illnesses have adverse social effects on the sufferers and their families. The amelioration of these can also be a charitable purpose and several charities have been registered in this area. Examples are the provision of recreational facilities for the mentally ill, the rehabilitation of people who have had limbs amputated and counselling for the families of babies who have died from cot death syndrome and other ailments. Counselling is not itself a good charitable purpose but it may be a means of promoting a charitable purpose such as the relief of sickness (see the recent Charity Commission leaflet INF10 on Counselling).

The relief of sickness has also been extended to include the promotion of health. Family planning clinics which are accepted as charitable under this head as being concerned to protect the health of women and their children, and clinics providing services such as screening for cervical cancer and the provision of uncontaminated blood for transfusions in countries where it is not normally available are other examples.

**Methods of relief of the aged**
**Relief of the aged**    In an era when there is a rapidly ageing population the relief of the aged is of increasing importance. The relief provided should be directed specifically at the infirmities and disabilities of old age and gifts of money are often inappropriate. Many of the services for the sick mentioned above are also helpful to the aged. In addition the provision of sheltered accommodation and housing associations for the aged meet a specific need of old people. Organisations such as Help the Aged and Age Concern provide help and care for old people in a number of ways which are well accepted as being charitable. These are concerned not only with alleviating the physical infirmities of old age but also with the loneliness and isolation which so often attends it and range from chiropody and the provision of household aids to visitors' services and the organisation of social gatherings, holidays and outings.

**The disabled**
**Relief of the impotent**    The relief of people who are physically weak or helpless covers a wide area from the prevention of cruelty to children (which may also be charitable under the fourth head) to the care of the blind and other persons suffering from physical disabilities. Workshops for the disabled, training guide dogs and the provision of facilities like the speaking book service also come within this subdivision. Organisations which provide counselling and support for the victims of rape and other crimes, and for the families of missing

children and young women are also regarded as charitable as are refuges for women who have suffered domestic violence and an emergency telephone service for children who are suffering physical or sexual abuse at home.

**Trade apprentices**    Trusts to enable poor persons to become apprenticed to a trade have long been considered charitable. Modern organisations with broadly similar aims are now accepted as charitable. These provide training and rehabilitation for the handicapped or for those who have not received any proper training in order to fit them for work and carry on a charitable tradition going back for several centuries.

## 2. The advancement of education

**Schools and universities**    The origins of Lord MacNaughton's second head of charity are found in the references in the preamble to the Elizabethan statute to "schools of learning, free schools and scholars of universities." It is well established that education need not be provided free of charge in

**Fee paying schools**    order to be charitable (see *The Abbey Malvern Wells Ltd. v. Ministry of Local Government and Planning*[12]). Education is itself charitable whether the beneficiaries are rich or poor and whether or not fees are paid. Consequently schools in the private sector which charge fees may be charitable provided they are not run for profit. There are many schools within the state education system which were originally established by private individuals or churches during the great expansion of education in the nineteenth century. These are now maintained to a greater or lesser degree by the local education authority as voluntary

**State schools**    controlled schools or voluntary aided schools. All the running costs of a voluntary controlled school are met by the local education authority. Only the school site itself is held upon charitable trusts. A voluntary aided school on the other hand is funded in part (at least 15 per cent of its capital and running costs) from a charitable endowment and is allowed a greater degree of autonomy than a controlled school. Many voluntary aided schools were originally Church of England or Catholic foundations and continue to provide education within a religious framework.

Recently two new kinds of educational charities within the state sector have been set up. The Education Reform Act 1988 established City Technology Colleges to provide education with an emphasis on technology in urban areas. It also provided a mechanism for any primary or secondary school to opt out of local education authority control and become a grant-maintained school established as an educational charity. Gifts for purposes connected with both independent and state schools such as the provision of equipment and facilities at the school, the establishment of scholarships and prize funds and funds to provide extra-curricular educational activities may be charitable. Many state schools have set up fund-raising trusts to provide additional financial support. Such trusts may be eligible for registration as charities but if they are registered their activities

[12] [1951] Ch. 728.

will be limited to supplementing what is provided by the state because the Charity Commissioners consider that it is not charitable to relieve the taxpayer by discharging obligations which should properly be borne by the state.

**Universities**    Universities and colleges are charitable as are funds for a wide variety of purposes subsidiary to the university itself such as scholarships, the endowment of lectureships or chairs in specific studies, libraries and funds for the provision of equipment and the maintenance of buildings. The provision of accommodation for students is charitable. Almost certainly universities and colleges will be "exempt" charities—(see the Second Schedule to the Charities Act and page 47 below).

A students' union will also be charitable if its primary purpose is to support the educational purposes of the university.[13] Part II of the Education Act 1944 requires the governing body of every educational establishment to which it applies (which includes universities and colleges of further education) to ensure that student unions operate in a fair and democratic manner and to bring to the attention of all students at least once a year any restrictions imposed by charity law on the activities of student unions. The Department of Education and Employment has published a leaflet entitled "Students' Unions: A Guide" which explains clearly and in some detail what is and is not permissible for a charitable students' union. A union may operate a bar or catering facilities for the benefit of its members and profits will form part of the union's funds. If members of the public have access the profits may be taxable. A union may publish a newspaper, hold debates and encourage clubs and societies, all of which are considered to promote the development of the mental and physical potential of the students. However, it is not permissible for unions to engage in political campaigns unless these directly concern the students

**Students' unions**    themselves and it will certainly be outside the proper scope of a union's activities to support a political cause in a foreign country or an industrial dispute.

Education is not confined to the provision of formal instruction. It was held in *Re Koeppler's Will Trusts*[14] that the concept of education is wide enough to cover the promotion of conferences at which intensive discussions took place on a variety of academic subjects between people of influence in their own countries who would both learn from the process and instruct the other participants.

**Physical and recreational education**    The concept of an educational charity has been greatly extended by the courts since 1601 and is not limited to instruction in academic subjects at educational establishments.

**Sport**    The promotion of sport is not in itself considered to be charitable[15] but trusts to promote sport at schools and universities have been held to be charitable. In *Re Mariette*[16] a trust to build fives courts and provide prizes for sports at a boys'

[13] *Att.-Gen. v. Ross* [1986] 1 W.L.R. 252.
[14] *Re Koeppler's Will Trusts* [1986] Ch. 423.
[15] *Re Nottage* [1895] 2 Ch. 649 and see page 16 below.
[16] [1915] 2 Ch. 284.

school was upheld, the court deciding that education involved more than the promotion of learning alone and that the promotion of the students' physical development was an essential part of the educational process. The encouragement of sports at schools and universities generally was held to be charitable in *I.R.C. v. McMullen*[17] which concerned a trust to provide facilities for football and other sports for pupils at schools and universities. There are now a number of registered charities for the promotion of single sports among schoolchildren and young people. It was emphasised in the *McMullen* case that the concept of education changes as social values change and that an activity which a century ago would not have been regarded as forming an integral part of the educational curriculum may well be so regarded now.

Other recreational activities for young people may also be charitable. City farms provide an insight into country life for children brought up in urban surroundings. Trusts to promote a chess tournament and provide a schoolchildren's outing have been held to be charitable but doubts have been expressed as to the limits which should be placed on such trusts and it seems **Hobbies** likely that a trust promoting a hobby which had little or no educational value would not be upheld.

Education includes not only academic training but more generally the wider development of the character and **Character** personality. The purposes of the Boy Scouts Association, **development** namely the instruction of boys in the principles of discipline, loyalty and good citizenship, are charitable as are those of the Outward Bound Trust Ltd, which provides mental and physical character training and education for boys and girls.

**The arts**   Education need not involve any actual teaching or instruction. Museums, art galleries, concert halls and libraries for the benefit of the public generally may be charitable as providing facilities for education provided tat they are not run **Aesthetic** for profit. Trusts to advance public knowledge of and interest in **education** the arts and to promote artistic taste are charitable. Trusts to provide a theatre for performance of the plays of Shakespeare[18] and to advance public knowledge of the works of Delius[19] have been held to be charitable and the Charity Commissioners have registered as charities organisations devoted to promoting knowledge of the works of certain poets and writers such as Keats and Shelley and artists such as William Morris. It is thought that registration would be refused in a case where the **Artistic merit** works to be promoted were clearly without artistic merit although it is difficult to say where the line would be drawn in practice. In *Re Pinion, Westminster Bank Ltd. v. Pinion*[20] a collection of furniture and bric-a-brac was described by the judge as "rubbish" and a claim that its preservation was a charitable purpose was dismissed. On the other hand a trust to educate the public in the works of Dorothy L. Sayers has been registered as a charity presumably on the basis of her religious

[17] *I.R.C. v. McMullen* [1981] A.C.1.
[18] *Re Shakespeare Memorial Trust* [1923] 2 Ch. 398.
[19] *Re Delius* [1957] Ch 299.
[20] [1965] Ch. 85.

**Festivals**

works and her authoritative work on Dante rather than the detective novels for which she is now better known. Arts festivals may also be charitable since these are directed to the education of the public by promoting artistic activities but not carnivals which are concerned with amusement or entertainment rather than education. A public memorial to an important individual or an historic event may be charitable if it can be said to have an educational value although a religious monument which does not serve an educational purpose will not be.[21]

**Conservation**   Although the National Trust and other trusts for the preservation of the national heritage have been held to be charitable under the fourth head a number of bodies concerned with the conservation of wildlife and the environment have been registered as educational charities. Zoos are charitable on account of their educational value. Bird sanctuaries which **Rare and** facilitate the study of ornithology, trusts to promote the **endangered** breeding and protection of rare or endangered species of plants, **species** birds, (the barn own for example) and animals such as elephants and rhinoceroses and trusts for the preservation of rare breeds of domestic animals have all been accepted as promoting education in its widest sense. Concern for the preservation and protection of the environment has resulted in a number of new charities some of which will come under the head of education, some under the fourth head and some under both. Examples of educational charities in this category include charities to conserve the rain forests and their fauna and flora, research into waste recycling, education in the value of clean air and the causes and consequences of pollution and education in the ecological importance of trees. Trusts for the preservation of steam railways have also been registered as charities as have trusts to preserve in working order such relics of the recent past as windmills. Industrial museums, collections of such things as toys, musical instruments and vintage cars are of educational value in enhancing public understanding of the past. In order to **Public benefit** qualify as educational there must be educational benefits to the public either through public access or through the publication of the results of study and research conducted by the charity. The amount of access which must be permitted in order to satisfy this requirement varies with the nature of the property and may be minimal in some cases (such as rare habitats) where the sites would be damaged or destroyed by unrestricted access by the general public.

**Research**   The conditions which should be met if a trust to undertake research is to be charitable were explained by Wilberforce J. in *Re Hopkins Will Trusts*.[22] The research

> "must either be of educational value to the researcher, or must be so directed as to lead to something which will pass into the store of educational material, or so as to improve the sum of communicable knowledge in an area which

---

[21] *Murray v. Thomas* [1937] 4 All E.R. 545 and Charity Commissioners' Report for 1989.
[22] *Re Hopkins Will Trusts* [1965] Ch. 669.

education may cover: education in this context extending to the formation of literary taste and appreciation."

**Pure research** Research may therefore be charitable even when it is unconnected with any formal teaching and many organisations and learned societies concerned with medical, scientific, historical and literary research are registered as charities. On the other hand research which is undertaken solely for private purposes or for the personal interest of the researcher alone will not be charitable. Difficult cases may arise in the field of commercial research where for example the principal beneficiaries are those engaged in a particular trade. The Charity Commission normally requires the objects of a research **Publication of** charity to include a requirement that the useful results of its **results** work should be published in order that public, rather than private, benefit is assured. (See the recently issued Charity Commision leaflet on Research Trusts, INF1)

**Propaganda or** **What is education?** There is an important distinction between education and what might be described as propaganda. **education** In the case of *Re Bushnell (decd.)*[23] the judge distinguished between, on the one hand, the education of the public to enable them to choose for themselves whether or not to support a particular theory by providing them with neutral information, and on the other, the promotion of that theory. Only the former is education in the charitable sense. In another case an organisation established to foster good relations between Sweden and the United Kingdom was held not to be charitable because its purpose was to promote a particular attitude of mind.[24] If the activities are genuinely educational it is immaterial that the underlying aims and aspirations of the organisation are to promote certain attitudes or opinions and it may still be charitable.[25] For example a number of charities have been registered whose aims are to educate the public in the history and culture of foreign countries, the indirect result of whose **Promoting an** activities may well promote understanding between peoples. It is **attitude of mind** necessary in every case to asses whether on balance the purpose is to educate or to proselytise. Presumably those organisations engaged in "peace studies" which have been registered as charities are engaged in genuine programmes of research into methods by which disputes between nations may be resolved peacefully and educating the public in the study of peace and are not directed towards the promotion of any particular theory or political programme. The distinction between an educational organisation and a pressure group may sometimes be difficult to discern from their stated objects but if the Charity Commissioners or the Inland Revenue consider on the basis of the past or proposed activities of an organisation that it will in practice be promoting a particular theory or view or will be **Pressure groups** acting as a pressure group, registration will be refused. It is sometimes possible to "hive off" to a charitable trust activities

---

[23] [1975] 1 W.L.R. 1596.
[24] *Anglo-Swedish Society v. I.R.C.* (1931) 16 T.C. 34 and see *Re Shaw* [1957] 1 W.L.R. 729.
[25] *Re Koeppler's Will Trusts* [1986] Ch. 423.

which are genuinely educational where other aspects of an organisation's work are regarded as political or polemical. This arrangement has been adopted by Friends of the Earth, Greenpeace and Amnesty International to name only a few and has the advantage that the overall work of the organisation is not restricted by the educational charity straitjacket but the benefits of charitable status are still available to a limited extent.

**Manual skills**

In an income tax case education was distinguished from training in manual skills.[26] The latter was said not to be education which is necessarily concerned with training the mind. Nonetheless, where training in manual skills is combined with the provision of guidance and help in developing the necessary self-confidence to enable unemployed people to find work the organisation may be charitable. A number of organisations have been registered, the objects of which are to educate young people to develop their skills so as to develop their full potential as members of society. Such organisations may also be charitable under the first head.

## 3. The advancement of religion

Two elements are required for a valid religious charity to be established, first that the religion concerned must be of a kind which is accepted by the courts as a religion and secondly that the activities of the charity will tend to promote or advance that religion.

**What is religion?**   Religion is defined in the Oxford Dictionary as "recognition on the part of man of some higher unseen power as having control of his destiny and as being entitled to obedience, reverence and worship" or more simply as "a particular system of faith and worship." In *Re South Place Ethical Society*[27] the view that a system of belief which did not

**Belief in God**   involve faith in a deity could constitute a religion was rejected. Dillon J. said:

> "Religion, as I see it, is concerned with man's relations with God and ethics are concerned with man's relations with man. The two are not the same and are not made the same by sincere inquiry into the question, what is God. If reason leads people not to accept Christianity or any known religion but they do believe in the excellence of qualities such as truth, beauty, and love, or believe in the platonic concept of the ideal, their beliefs may be to them the equivalent of a religion but viewed objectively they are not religion."

The position of Buddhism, which is generally accepted to be a religion but may not involve a belief in God, is perhaps to be regarded as an exception (see *Re South Place Ethical Society*). Hinduism, although polytheistic, would almost certainly be regarded as a religion for the purposes of charity.

[26] *Barry v Hughes* [1973] 1 All E.R. 537.
[27] [1980] 1 W.L.R. 1565.

**Worship**          The nature of worship was considered in *Reg. v. Registrar-General, ex p. Segerdal*,[28] a case which concerned a claim by the Church of Scientology that a chapel used by the Church should be exempt from rates as a place of worship. Buckley L.J. said: "Worship I take to be something which must have some at least of the following characteristics: submission to the object worshipped, veneration of that object, praise, thanksgiving, prayer or intercession." The claim that Scientology was a religion was rejected.

All the main world religions and many individual sects are accepted as complying with these two criteria. The courts have adopted a tolerant approach and provided that there is belief in a Supreme Being and some form of worship they will not be concerned with the merits of the beliefs which are being promulgated. In *Thornton v. Howe*[29] the doctrines in question were described by the court as incoherent and confused but not contrary to religion and their promotion charitable. This case was followed more recently in *Re Watson*.[30]

**The advancement of religion**    Donovan J. in *United Grand Lodge v. Holborn Borough Council*[31] (a rating case) considered whether the activities of freemasons could be said to advance religion. He said: "To advance religion means to promote it, to spread its message ever wider among mankind; to take some
**Positive steps**   positive steps to sustain and increase religious belief; and these
**required**        things are done in a variety of ways which may be comprehensively described as pastoral and missionary." He concluded that although freemasonry required its members to have faith in God and to believe in good works it did not advance or promote any particular religious beliefs and therefore was not itself a religion in the charitable sense. In *Cocks v. Manners*[32] a gift for the benefit of an order of nuns who devoted their lives to prayer and contemplation was held not to be charitable. One of the essential characteristics of a religious charity, that it should tend directly or indirectly towards the instruction or edification of the public, was not present (see also page 23 below).

Religion may be advanced in a number of different ways:
**Upkeep of**        The maintenance of places of worship is charitable and this
**Churches**         includes the upkeep of churchyards, and the provision of furniture and ornaments in the church as well as the maintenance of the structure itself. The provision of a tomb or memorial is not charitable, however, since this is a private rather than a public purpose unless the memorial forms part of the structure of the church in which case it can be interpreted as a gift for the upkeep of the building itself (for non-religious memorials see page 10 above). The building need not be used solely for worship although it seems that the non-religious activities should be ancillary to the main religious purpose.[33]

[28] [1970] 2 Q.B. 697.
[29] (1862) 31 Beav. 14.
[30] *Re Watson dec'd.*; *Hobbs v. Smith* [1973] 1 W.L.R. 1472.
[31] [1957] 3 All E.R. 281.
[32] *Cocks v. Manners* (1871) L.R. 12 Eq. 574.
[33] *Neville Estates v. Madden* [1962] Ch. 832.

**Provision of music**
**Support of clergy**

The promotion of music in a church such as the provision of an organ or the support of a choir is charitable. Gifts for the benefit of clergy such as the provision or repair of a minister's residence, the education of candidates for holy orders, and payment of a stipend to a priest, sexton or organist, are charitable although gifts of this nature for the benefit of Church of England clergy are now added to diocesan funds under the control of the Diocesan Board of Finance.

**Missionary purposes**

The active spread of religion both at home and overseas is charitable but a gift for "missionary purposes" alone will be void since it may include non-charitable purposes, unless it can be inferred that missionary work in connection with a particular religion was intended.[34] A gift for a Sunday School will be charitable as will be a gift for the publication of religious works and the distribution of Bibles and prayer books.

Care must be taken in drafting gifts for religious purposes. A gift to a vicar of a parish for parish work has been held not to be charitable since parish purposes may include purposes which are not charitable.[35] But a gift to the holder of an office whose duties are charitable for purposes which are unspecified will be interpreted as a gift for those charitable purposes.[36]

## 4. Other purposes beneficial to the community

The majority of new charities come within the fourth head which has provided the greatest scope for the development of charity law to meet the changing needs of society. The attitude of the courts in taking a broad approach to the preamble to the Elizabethan statute has assisted this process. Russell L.J. in *Incorporated Council of Law Reporting for England and Wales v. Att.-Gen.*:[37] considered that where any purpose is shown to be beneficial to the community the correct approach is to consider it to be prima facie charitable. However, the courts have

**Flexibility of the fourth head**

reserved a line of retreat based on the "equity" of the statute, in case the purpose is of a kind so different from the examples given in the preamble that it could not have been within the contemplation of the legislators even had they foreseen the circumstances in which their words would be applied. The question to be asked, therefore, in each case is whether there are any grounds for holding a particular purpose to be outside the equity of the statute.

This generous approach has not been followed in every recent case and (as was mentioned earlier in this chapter) the Charity Commissioners, while trying always to act constructively and to favour charity, have preferred in novel cases to adopt the stricter approach and base their decisions on analogy and precedent though in their 1985 Annual Report they stated that their "general approach would be to favour charity" (para. 27). This general approach was confirmed in *Decisions of the Charity Commission*, Vol. 2 (pages 5–10)

[34] *Re Rees* [1920] 2 Ch. 59
[35] *Farley v. National Westminster Bank* [1939] A.C. 430.
[36] *Re Garrard* [1907] 1 Ch. 382.
[37] [1971] Ch. 626.

The wide scope of the fourth head will be apparent from the brief summary that follows.

**Purposes of public utility**   The repair of bridges, ports, havens, causeways and highways was included in the preamble to the Elizabethan statute. Such public works are now provided from public funds but modern charities of this class include

**Public halls and reading rooms**   trusts to provide public amenities such as libraries and museums (which would also constitute educational charities), public and village halls, reading rooms, park benches and bus shelters. The publication of law reports has been held to be charitable in that it facilitates the proper administration of the law and by analogy the Charity Commissioners have registered family conciliation services on the footing that if parties are persuaded to settle their differences the courts will be relieved of the burden of dealing with such matters. A gift for the general benefit of the inhabitants of a particular locality is charitable. A trust formed to promote high standards and efficiency among civil servants and public sector employees by educating them about private sector organisations and practice has been registered as a charity.[38]

**Protection of the public**   The support of the armed forces is

**Armed forces and police**   charitable. Most army regiments have regimental funds which provide a variety of benefits for the officers and men of the regiment such as mess funds, libraries and other facilities which promote the well-being and *esprit de corps* of the regiment and therefore its efficiency. Promoting reunions of ex-servicemen is not a charitable purpose since this cannot be said to improve the efficiency of the current members of the forces. Organisations such as the British Legion are not therefore charitable although the relief of ex-members of the armed forces who are in need will be charitable under the first head. Training civilians in rifle shooting was considered to make people more efficient if called upon to serve in the army and therefore charitable and rifle shooting is an exception to the rule that the promotion of sport is not charitable.[39] The Charity Commissioner's present view is that circumstances have changed radically since the decision in *Re Stephens*. They do not consider rifle clubs to be established for the purpose of contributing to the defence of the realm (which they accept is a good charitable purpose) and have refused to register two clubs.[40] (See below p. 40) The Charity Commissioners have registered as charities a number of organisations established to train young people in seamanship and navigation and the promotion of the efficiency of the police is also a good charitable purpose (*I.R.C. v. City of Glasgow Police Athletic Association*).[41]

**Public safety**   A voluntary fire brigade was held by the court to be charitable[42] and the encouragement of road safety and high standards of driving has been accepted by the Charity

---

[38] Charity Commissioners' Report for 1990.
[39] Re Stephens, *Giles v. Stephens* [1892] 8 T.L.R. 792.
[40] *Decisions of the Charity Commissioners*, Vol. 1, pp. 4–13
[41] [1953] A.C. 380.
[42] *Re Wokingham Fire Brigade Trust* [1951] Ch. 373.

Commissioners as charitable. The lifeboat service is also
charitable.

**Sports and recreation**   It is a curious anomaly that even
though sport plays such a large and important part in the life of
the country and is generally regarded as being beneficial to both
participants and spectators the promotion of competitive sport
is not a charitable purpose unless it is linked with education (see
p. 8). The rule originates with the case of *Re Nottage*[43] where it
was held that a trust to provide a prize for a yacht race was not
charitable since it promoted "mere sport" and benefited only the
competitors. The Commissioners have recently[44] refused to
register an athletics club on the grounds that its primary purpose
was the promotion of competitive sport and that it existed for
the benefit of its members rather than the public at large. The
Commissioners did not accept that the main object of the club
was to promote physical education and health, which would
have been charitable.[45]

On the other hand, the provision of an area for general
public recreation has for long been regarded as a charitable
purpose and many village and town halls are held in part for
recreational purposes. The decision of the House of Lords in the
case of *I.R.C. v. Baddeley*[46] raised doubts as to whether a
number of organisations established for recreational purposes
were indeed charitable and the Recreational Charities Act 1958

**Recreational**   was passed in order to put the matter beyond doubt. The Act
**Charities Act**   provides that it is charitable "to provide or assist in the provision
**1958**   of facilities for recreation or other leisure time occupation, if the
facilities are provided in the interests of social welfare." The
requirement that the facilities should be provided in the interests
of social welfare will only be satisfied if—

"(a)   they are provided with the object of improving the
**Social welfare**        conditions of life of those for whom they are primarily
           intended; and
(b)   (i)   those persons need the facilities by reason of their
             youth, age, infirmity or disablement, poverty or
             social and economic circumstances; or
      (ii)  the facilities are available to the members or the
             female members of the public at large."

Consequently recreational facilities, the use of which is
restricted only to men who have no specific need for the
facilities, will not qualify under the Act. Recreational
facilities for the benefit of a specific racial group may be
charitable.[47]

A large number of public playing fields are registered as
**Playing fields**   charities. A standard form of declaration of trust has been
agreed with the Charity Commissioners and the Inland Revenue
and advice and assistance can be obtained from the National

---

[43] [1895] 2 Ch. 649.
[44] Charity Commissioners' Report for 1988.
[45] *Re Hadden* [1932] 1 Ch. 133; *Re Morgan* [1955] 1 W.L.R. 738.
[46] [1955] A.C. 572.
[47] *Decisions of the Charity Commissioners*, Vol. 4, pp. 18–21, and see model clause
   in App. B.

Playing Fields Association. Many village greens and commons are held on charitable trusts (often originating from Inclosure Acts passed in the eighteenth and nineteenth centuries) to provide a place of recreation for the inhabitants of the locality. Others are common land now registered under the Commons Registration Act 1965. Land held upon charitable trusts was not eligible for registration under the Act.

**Commerce and agriculture**   The promotion of industry, commerce and art was held to be charitable in *Crystal Palace Trustees v. Minister of Town and Country Planning*[48] following the decision in *I.R.C. v. Yorkshire Agricultural Society*[49] that the promotion of agriculture was charitable. The court held that these purposes were for the general benefit of the public rather than the benefit of individuals engaged in industry and commerce and therefore came within the fourth head. More recently Business in the Community has been registered as a charity.[50] Its work in supporting individuals in establishing small businesses, monitoring local employment prospects and recommending action to improve them was considered to promote industry and commerce generally and to be directed to the benefit of the community as a whole. The promotion of horticulture is charitable and the preservation of rare breeds of domestic animals has been accepted by the Charity Commissioners as promoting agriculture by facilitating the breeding of improved stock.

The Charity Commissioners have registered as charities organisations to improve standards of design and to promote standards of fine craftsmanship. Training persons who are or will be employed in a particular industry has been held without argument to be charitable.[51]

**Protection of the heritage**   The purposes of the National Trust, namely, "promoting the permanent preservation for the benefit of the nation of lands and tenements (including buildings) of beauty or historic interest and as regards lands for the preservation (so far as practicable) of their natural aspect features and animal and plant life" were held to be charitable in *Re Verrall*.[52] A number of charities for the preservation of land and buildings of historic or aesthetic interest and the protection of the countryside have since been registered as charitable. The public benefit will only be secured in each case if the public is given reasonable access to the property. What is reasonable will depend upon its nature and location.

Although the majority of charities concerned with conservation of wildlife are registered as educational charities some may also fall under the fourth head.

The preservation of the environment generally has been accepted as a charitable purpose under the fourth head and, in

**Promoting Industry**

**Design and craftsmanship**

**National Trust**

**Preservation of buildings**

**Protection of environment**

---

[48] [1951] Ch. 132.
[49] [1928] 1 K.B. 611.
[50] Charity Commissioners' Annual Report for 1988.
[51] *Construction Industry Training Board v. Att.-Gen.* [1973] Ch. 173.
[52] [1916] 1 Ch. 100.

particular, protection from pollution and the promotion of efficient methods of disposing of waste.

**Animal charities**

**Mental and moral improvement** Trusts for the prevention of cruelty to and the protection of animals have been accepted as charitable under the fourth head since, in the words of Swinfen Eady L.J. in *Re Wedgewood*[53]

> "A gift for the benefit and protection of animals tends to promote and encourage kindness towards them, to discourage cruelty, and to ameliorate the condition of the brute creation, and thus to stimulate humane and generous sentiments in man towards the lower animals, and by these means promote feelings of humanity and morality generally, repress brutality, and thus elevate the human race."

**Requirement of public benefit**

The public benefit will not be served, however, if the moral improvement is outweighed by other adverse consequences to mankind. This was one reason for the decision in *National Anti-Vivisection Society v. I.R.C.*[54] that a trust for the suppression of vivisection was not charitable. Similarly a trust to provide a sanctuary for the protection of birds and animals from man[55] was held not to be charitable, there being no discernible benefit to man. Purposes as diverse as the establishment of humane slaughterhouses, homes for stray dogs and cats, animal hospitals and sanctuaries for animals that have suffered cruelty or neglect both in the United Kingdom and abroad have been registered as charitable. The Commissioners have decided[56] that it is not charitable to prevent the exploitation of animals.

*Re South Place Ethical Society*[57] finally established clearly that the mental or moral improvement of the public by means other than the prevention of cruelty to animals is a good charitable object. The relevant purposes of the society in that case were "the study and dissemination of ethical principles and the cultivation of a rational religious sentiment." The court held that the society was not established for the advancement of religion, the necessary elements of faith and worship being lacking, but that by analogy with earlier cases none of which provided conclusive authority on the point the objects were charitable within the fourth head as well as being educational.

**Humanism**

Since this decision the Charity Commissioners have registered the British Humanist Association, the objects of which are the mental and moral improvement of the human race by means of the advancement of humanism. They have also decided that trusts to promote racial harmony may be charitable and it was on this basis that a trust established primarily to protect and support the Jewish community from racial harrassment was registered in 1994.[58] The promotion of

---

[53] [1915] 1 Ch. 113.
[54] [1948] A.C. 31.
[55] *Re Grove-Grady* [1929] 1 Ch. 557.
[56] *Decisions of the Charity Commissioners*, Vol. 2, pp. 1–4, in which the law on animal charities is reviewed.
[57] [1980] 1 W.L.R. 1565.
[58] *Decisions of the Charity Commissioners*, Vol. 4, pp. 8–12.

ethical standards in business was held to be charitable by the Commissioners.[59]

**Sex equality**      The promotion of equality of women with men in political and economic opportunity has been held to be charitable as leading to an advance in thinking and education in ideas of general benefit to the community.[60]

[59] *Decisions of the Charity Commissioners,* Vol. 2, pp. 5–10.
[60] *Halpin v. Seear* referred to in the Commissioners Annual Report for 1977, paras. 34–36.

# 2 MATTERS AFFECTING CHARITABLE STATUS

## The requirement of public benefit

A charity must be established for the benefit of the public or a sufficiently important section of the public rather than for the benefit of private individuals. This is the main justification for the legal and fiscal concessions granted to charities. The dividing line between private and public benefit and the measure of the benefit which should be conferred varies with each of the four heads of charity.

### The relief of poverty

**Private class**

The relief of poverty is considered to be anomalous in that the relief of a very small class of beneficiaries, such as the residents of a particular street, the occupants of particular cottages, and people who are connected by some private or personal link may be charitable. A gift for the poor employees of a company was held to be charitable in *Dingle v. Turner*[1] and a trust for relations of the donor's son and daughter who were in needy circumstances has also been upheld (*Re Scarisbrick*).[2] The poor on a particular estate have been held to be a sufficiently wide class as have the poor members of particular trades or professions. But it must be clear that the gift is not for the benefit of particular individuals since a gift for the benefit of individuals, however great their need, is a private rather than a public purpose and therefore not charitable. A gift for immediate distribution to the donor's next of kin will be interpreted as a gift for individuals and will not be charitable.

**Named individuals**

**Next of kin**

### The relief of the sick and aged

There is no authority as to whether gifts for the relief of a similarly restrictive class of the sick or aged should be regarded as charitable. Since the courts have consistently held trusts for the relief of poverty to be anomalous, it must be doubtful.

### Trusts for the advancement of education

**Benefit to the community**

The subject-matter of an educational trust must be of sufficient value to benefit the community if it is to be charitable and this is a question to be decided on the facts of each case. The leading

---

[1] [1972] A.C. 601.
[2] [1951] Ch. 622.

case on this point is *Re Pinion*[3] where the testator left his pictures, furniture and other objects to trustees to be maintained as a collection. Most of the items were of poor quality and the court decided that since there was no evidence that the gift would benefit the public it was not charitable.[4] The Charity Commissioners will want to be satisfied as to the educational value of the subject-matter when considering an application for registration and may require evidence that the field of study is of sufficient importance to confer a clear educational benefit on the public. Where the work of an educational organisation is concerned with subjects outside the conventional areas of education, such as the study of the teachings of obscure philosophers or writers, it may be necessary to produce expert evidence as to its value.

A related point concerns the nature of education. In the case of *Re Shaw*[5] the court was concerned with the will of George Bernard Shaw which contained a bequest for the purpose of conducting research into the advantages of his revised alphabet and informing the public. It was held that it was insufficient merely to increase the sum of human knowledge by informing the public of the benefits of the new system. There must also be an element of public education involved and this was not achieved by persuading the public that the new alphabet was "a good thing". The trust was held not to be charitable.

While individuals may derive benefits from an educational charity the main purpose of the charity must be for the benefit of the public. Scholarship funds, for example, exist primarily to encourage high standards of learning, which is clearly of public benefit, the advantage to the recipient being incidental to the primary purpose. There have been a number of cases concerning the balance which must be struck between individual and public benefit; between promoting the interests of individuals and education in the charitable sense. The distinction was explained by Lord Devlin in *Chartered Insurance Institute v. London Corporation*[6]:

**Benefits to individuals**

> "I think that the advancement of education means the advancement of education for its own sake in order that the mind may be trained ... On the other hand education in a particular aptitude is primarily designed for the acquisition of some professional advantage."

In that case the balance of benefit was in favour of the individual members of the Institute which was therefore held not to be charitable.

A rather stricter interpretation of what is a sufficient section of the public applies to educational purposes than to those under the first head. Beneficiaries may be confined to a restricted class such as the followers of certain religious doctrines or the daughters of missionaries but if they are personally linked to a particular individual or company the trust will be considered to be for the benefit of a private class rather

[3] [1965] Ch. 85.
[4] And see *Re Hummeltenberg* [1923] 1 Ch. 237.
[5] [1957] 1 All E.R. 745.
[6] [1957] 1 W.L.R. 867.

**Private and public class**

than for public benefit. Consequently, a scholarship fund for the benefit of the descendants of certain individuals was not charitable[7] nor was an educational fund for the benefit of the children of the employees of a substantial public company despite the considerable number of potential beneficiaries. Even where the class is numerous the single link will mean that the class will not be a section of the public. In the case of *Oppenheim v. Tobacco Securities Trust Co. Ltd*[8] a settlement established to provide education for the children of a company employing more than 110,000 people was held not to be a charity but a private trust. The illogicalities which result were pointed out by Lord Denning in *I.R.C. v. Educational Grants Association Ltd.*[9]

**Company employees**

"The inhabitants of a named place are a section of the community for this purpose: but the employees of a particular company or companies are not. It follows that if a man sets up a trust *for the children of the inhabitants of Bournville,* it will be held to be for the public benefit. But if he sets up a trust for the *children of those employed by Cadburys Ltd at Bournville,* it will be held to be for private benefit. In each case the beneficiaries will probably be identical, but in point of law the one trust is charitable and the other is not."

**Preference for private class**

Apart from the anomalous case of ancient trusts for the education of the founder's kin at a school or college which have for centuries been regarded as charitable there is only one possible exception to the rule. It has been held[10] that a gift for public educational purposes is charitable even though the trustees were directed to give preference to employees of a particular company. Doubts have been cast on the correctness of this decision. The Commissioners have stated in their Annual Report for 1978 that they consider a preference for the members of a private class will only be acceptable if it is expressed in permissive rather than mandatory terms. They also point out, on the authority of the Educational Grants Association case, that even if the stated purposes of the organisations are charitable the trustees will be acting outside their powers if they apply a substantial part of the funds of the charity for the benefit of the members of the private class. What proportion may properly be applied in this way is unclear.

**Research**

The Commission's view on research as a charitable activity will be set out in a leaflet, "Charities and Research".[11] The research should be of benefit to the public, which means that the subject must be of real value and calculated to enhance knowledge of the natural and social world. It should not be undertaken for private purposes and the intention should be to publicise the useful results. Where research is funded or sponsored by a non-charitable organisation the results should still be available to the public within a reasonable time.

---

[7] *Davies v. Perpetual Trustee* [1959] A.C. 439.
[8] [1951] A.C. 297.
[9] [1967] Ch. 993 at 1009.
[10] *Re Koettgen's Will Trusts* [1954] Ch. 252.
[11] Due out in late 1996. See also Charity Commission Information Sheet 1.

## Trusts for the advancement of religion

**Religious tendency**

It is assumed that a gift for the advancement of religion is beneficial to the public and the courts will not consider the merits of the beliefs which are to be promoted provided that they have a religious tendency and do not undermine morality or religion. In *Re Watson*,[12] for example, a gift to publish and disseminate certain religious works which the court held to be of no intrinsic merit was held to be charitable.

**Enclosed orders**

The necessary element of public benefit has, however, been found lacking in some cases. A private chapel would not be charitable since it would benefit only the private class attending. A gift for the benefit of an enclosed contemplative order of nuns has been held not to be charitable because the institution lacks the necessary element of instruction or edification of the public. In *Gilmour v. Coats*[13] the argument that the nuns set an example to the public of self-denial and that their prayers benefited the public was rejected by the court. Recently the court and the Commissioners have been more ready to find that a benefit to the public is present in such cases. The Commissioners were prepared to accept that a trust for the benefit of a contemplative order of nuns was charitable because, as the outward expression of their dedication, the nuns provided spiritual counselling for the public.[14] In the unreported case of *Re Hetherington's Will Trusts* [1988] the court decided that a gift for masses for the soul of the testatrix was charitable. The masses were to be said in public and this provided the necessary element of public benefit.[15] The erection or maintenance of a private tombstone or memorial is for the benefit of the donor or his family rather than the public generally and is not charitable. If, however, the monument forms part of the fabric of the church itself its upkeep may properly be provided for out of funds devoted to the maintenance of the church. A diocesan retreat house to which individuals may go for a period of religious contemplation has been held to be for the benefit of the individuals but not for the benefit of the public generally.[16] It could be argued, however, that in contrast with a closed monastic order an indirect benefit is derived by the public in their contact with those who attend a retreat and who later return to their normal lives. This was the basis of the decision in *Neville Estates v. Madden*,[17] which concerned a synagogue open only to members—a private class. It was decided in that case that the synagogue was a charitable institution.

**Tombstones**

**Retreats**

## Trusts for the general benefit of the public

**Benefit not assumed**

The benefit to the public under the fourth head may be utilitarian or it may be a mental or moral benefit (see Chapter 1) but in each case the benefit to the public must be demonstrated.

[12] [1973] 1 W.L.R. 1472.
[13] [1949] A.C. 426.
[14] Charity Commissioners' Report for 1989.
[15] Charity Commissioners' Report for 1988.
[16] *Re Warre's Will Trusts* [1953] 1 W.L.R. 725.
[17] [1962] Ch. 832.

The donor's belief that the purposes are beneficial is not in itself sufficient (see *Re Hummeltenbery*[18]—a case concerning the training of spiritualist mediums). In *National Anti-Vivisection Society v. I.R.C.*[19] a gift for the suppression of vivisection was held not to be charitable because this would impede medical research. Gifts simply for the benefit of the inhabitants of a particular locality or a section of them such as a particular town, parish or borough have been upheld as charitable. In *Re Christchurch Inclosure Act*[20] a trust for the benefit of the occupiers of certain cottages was held to be charitable. Presumably the class of beneficiaries, though small in number, was considered to be a sufficiently large section of the public.

## Overseas purposes

Purposes which fall within one of the first three heads of charity will be charitable whether the beneficiaries live in the United Kingdom or abroad. Many examples could be cited. Charities devoted to the relief of poverty and suffering are active in Africa and other Third World countries; registered charities support schools, colleges and the arts throughout the world and Christian organisations carry on missionary work far from home. The position of organisations coming within the fourth head is not so straightforward. The Charity Commissioners' stated view[21] used to be that some benefit, direct or indirect, to the community in the United Kingdom must be demonstrated **Benefit to UK** in every case if the purposes are to be regarded as being for the **community** public benefit. This approach was based on remarks made by the judge in the case of *Camille and Henry Dreyfus Foundation v. I.R.C.*,[22] who considered that some purposes which would be charitable under the fourth head if executed in the United Kingdom, such as the promotion of the efficiency of the armed forces, could, if carried on in a foreign country, be contrary to the interests of the community at home.

Recent cases in Canada and Australia have adopted a less insular approach and the courts there have held that purposes which would be regarded as charitable within the particular **Recent decisions** jurisdiction will also be charitable if carried out abroad provided that there is a clear benefit to the community where the trust is to be carried out.[23] The Commissioners have now revised their opinion on this point and fourth head purposes carried on overseas will be accepted as charitable provided they would not be charitable if carried on in the United Kingdom and they are not likely to be inimical to the interests of the inhabitants of this country.[24] The promotion of the efficiency of the armed services of a foreign country is an obvious example of a purpose which would not be regarded as charitable.

---

[18] [1923] 1 Ch. 237.
[19] [1948] A.C. 31.
[20] (1888) 38 Ch.D. 520.
[21] Charity Commissioners' Report for 1963.
[22] [1956] A.C. 39.
[23] See "The charitable nature of overseas purpose trusts" by G. Kodilinye, *Trust Law & Practice*, Vol. 4, No. 2, p. 74.
[24] Charity Commissioners' Report for 1992, paras. 73–76.

# Non-charitable activities

Most charities engaged in activities which are not strictly charitable but which further their main purposes such as fund-raising, the administration of the charity's assets and the employment of people to carry out the work for which the charity is established. This does not cause any difficulty when it is subordinate to the charity's objects but occasionally the non-charitable activity assumes so important a part in the charity's overall operations that the inevitable conclusion is that the purposes of the charity are not restricted to those which are exclusively charitable. Cohen L.J. in *Tennant Plays Ltd v. I.R.C.*[25] put the point in the following way: "I think the principle that one must look only at the main or dominant purpose of the company must be taken with a little reserve. I feel some doubt that a company can be said to be established for charitable purposes only if it carried on a substantial non-charitable purpose, for instance . . . a public house in order to produce

**Trading to raise funds** funds for its charitable purposes." In such a case it could be argued that the company was established not solely for charitable purposes but also for profit. If the non-charitable activity is to be substantial or a permanent feature of the charity's activities it should be carried on by a separate non-charitable organisation in order to safeguard tax relief and charitable status (see Chapter 8). All charity shops, Christmas card sales, property development, sales of alcohol and similar undertakings which are carried on more than occasionally should be organised in this way.

**Trading in furtherance of objects** In contrast some charities carry out their objects by means of activities which are not in themselves charitable. An example of this was considered in *Falkirk Temperance Cafe Trust v. I.R.C.*[26] In that case the Trust pursued its primary purpose of promoting temperance through running a cafe where only non-alcoholic drinks were served. The cafe was undoubtedly a trade but this activity was nonetheless held to be acceptable. The purpose of the Trust was to promote temperance and not to make a profit. Theatres and art galleries may be in a similar position. Provided that the balance of the activities is towards charity rather than profit, the conduct of the trade is acceptable but it is a point to be decided on the particular facts of each case. Similar principles apply in cases where the non-charitable activities are inseparable from the primary purposes of the charity such as the sale of goods made by disabled people in the charity's workshops, or the sale of Bibles and religious literature by charities established to advance the Christian religion.

**Advice of Charity Commissioners** Where non-charitable activity is proposed which is either substantial, for example property development, or is intended to be permanent, it is advisable for guidance to be sought from the Charity Commissioners in advance in order to avoid problems arising later over the availability of tax relief and the charitable status of the organisation.

[25] [1948] 1 A.C. 506.
[26] (1927) 11 T.C. 395.

**Individuals
deriving benefit**

Rather different questions arise where individuals derive benefits from the activities of the charity. Several cases have dealt with this point in relation to professional organisations which, in promoting high standards of practice, which is accepted as being in the interests of the public, also confer benefits on their members. If these benefits are merely incidental to the charitable objects, they are acceptable but if members are the primary beneficiaries then the organisation will not be charitable. Again it is a question of balance. In *Royal College of Nursing v. St. Marylebone B.C.*[27] the objects of the College were stated to be the promotion of the science and art of nursing and the better education and training of nurses. The question before the court was whether the College was for the benefit of nursing generally, which would be charitable as indirectly relieving the sick, or for the benefit of the nurses themselves. In that case, it was held that the wording of the Charter of the College implied that its main purpose was to benefit the sick and any benefits to the nurses were incidental. A similar point was raised in *Incorporated Council of Law Reporting for England and Wales v. Att.-Gen.*[28] It was held that the benefits to individual lawyers of the activities of the Council in publishing law reports were ancillary to its main purpose which was to facilitate the free and accurate dissemination of knowledge of the law. In other cases, however, the balance of benefit has been found to be in favour of the individuals. This was so in the case of *I.R.C. v. Glasgow (City) Police Athletics Association.*[29] This case concerned a sports club which was accepted as promoting the efficiency of the police force through providing members with facilities for relaxation and keeping fit but was, nonetheless, held not to be charitable. Lord Normand said[30] that if the organisation was to be charitable it must be shown that "viewed objectively the association is established for a public purpose, and that the private benefits to members are the unsought consequences of the pursuit of the public purpose, and can therefore be regarded as incidental."

It is difficult to generalise as to where the dividing line falls between activity which is incidental to the main charitable purposes, and activity which will render the organisation non-charitable. Each case depends very much upon its particular facts and the general flavour of the institution. Where the

**Division of
organisation**

activities have fallen on the wrong side of the line it may be possible for the "trade union" or other activities directed to the benefit of individuals to be conducted by a separate non-charitable organisation and for the charity to engage only in activities which are clearly for the benefit of the public.

[27] [1959] 1 W.L.R. 1077.
[28] [1972] Ch. 73.
[29] [1953] A.C. 380.
[30] *Ibid.* at 396.

# Political activity

## Political purposes

Increasingly, charities engage in high profile campaigning. They promote changes in the law sometimes by means of emotive advertisements; they lobby M.P.s; they publicise their views of what government policy should be and seek to persuade the public to support them. There is some general concern that a few charities may go too far in engaging in such activities and confusion as to what activities are permissible for a charity. As is so often the case in charity law there is no clear line of demarcation between what is and what is not allowed. Each case will turn on its own particular facts. Although the principles are clear enough and have been established for some time their application in individual cases leaves ample room for doubt and uncertainty.

Briefly, the rule is that while a charity may engage in political activity in order to promote its charitable purposes a purpose which is political cannot be charitable.

The reasons why no political purpose can be charitable were put by Slade J. in *McGovern v. Att.-Gen.*[31] in the following way:

**Political purposes not charitable**

> "The court will not regard as charitable a trust of which a main object is to procure an alteration of the law of the United Kingdom for one or both of two reasons: first, the court will ordinarily have no sufficient means of judging as a matter of evidence whether the proposed change will or will not be for the public benefit. Secondly, even if the evidence suffices to enable it to form a prima facie opinion that a change in the law is desirable, it must still decide the case on the principle that the law is right as it stands, since to do otherwise would usurp the functions of the legislature."

For similar reasons the following purposes are to be regarded as political and therefore not charitable: the furtherance of the interests of a particular political party; the procurement of changes in the law of a foreign country; and the procurement of the reversal of government policy or of particular decisions of government or other authorities in this country or in a foreign country.[32]

## Power to engage in political activity

**Ancillary powers**

Although a political purpose may not be charitable it is clear that political activity may be permissible if it is undertaken in furtherance of some charitable purpose. It is, however, often a difficult question of construction to determine whether a power to engage in political activity such as promoting or influencing legislation is, strictly speaking, ancillary to the good charitable objects or if, in reality, it should be interpreted as a purpose rather than a power. If the latter, the organisation will not be

**Suggested test**

charitable. It is thought that if the political activity is an essential

[31] [1982] 1 Ch. 321 at 336.
[32] *Ibid.*, at 340.

element in the achievement of the purposes of the organisation or will form a substantial part of its activities, then the organisation will not be charitable. If, on the other hand, the political activity is subordinate and incidental to the main charitable purposes of the organisation, then the charitable status of the organisation should not be in danger. It was said in *National Anti-Vivisection Society v. I.R.C.*[33] that if the dominant purpose had been the abolition of vivisection and the alteration of the law merely a means of achieving this then the Society could have been charitable. In that case, however, the court held that the main purpose of the Society was to secure a change in the law.

The distinction between powers and purposes has caused considerable difficulties recently when some charities, for example those for the relief of poverty abroad, have not been content to limit their activities to alleviating poverty and suffering directly, believing that more could be achieved by attacking the underlying causes of poverty which may lie in the social structure of the countries concerned or in the policies of their governments. This may be acceptable where the campaign is clearly in furtherance of the principal charitable purpose and is limited to providing information and well-reasoned advice, recommending changes in the law and informing the public in a responsible way of the proposals it advocates. It should not seek to pressurise governments, local, national or foreign nor should it overstep the boundary between education and propaganda. A balanced and rational approach should be observed.

**Charity Commission guidelines**     The Charity Commission revised their guidelines in 1995 (Charity Commission leaflet CC9) on the type of activity which it considers a charity may properly engage in without the trustees running the risk of committing a breach of trust or the organisation losing its charitable status. These are summarised as follows:

> "a charity can engage in political activity if:
> * there is a reasonable expectation that the activity concerned will further the stated purposes of the charity, and so benefit its beneficiaries, to an extent justified by the resources devoted to the activity;
> * the activity is within the powers which the trustees have to achieve those purposes;
> * the activity is consistent with these guidelines;
> * the views expressed are based on a well-founded and reasoned case and are expressed in a responsible way."

**Campaigning**     The Charity Commission confirms in its guidance that it is permissible for charities to campaign on issues relevant to their work and can make a valuable contribution to public debate on important issues by doing so. But the manner in which they conduct a campaign must be carefully controlled. Charities should not support one particular political party and if their views coincide with those of one party they should make their independence clear. All information provided to the public should be clear and accurate. Where the nature of the campaigning activity makes it impractical to provide a full

[33] [1948] A.C. 31.

reasoned account of the charity's position a simple statement of its conclusions is permissible provided that this can be rationally justified if necessary. Campaigns which appeal to the emotions and sympathies of the public are not forbidden but again they must be capable of rational explanation.

**Permissible political activities** Charities are allowed to comment on proposed legislation, support, oppose or promote legislation, comment on public issues and advocate changes in the law provided that these activities are likely to promote their charitable purposes. In paragraphs 23 to 31 of its leaflet the Commission gives examples of some of the kinds of political activity which are or are not permissible in furtherance of the purposes of a charity:

"23. A charity may seek to influence government or public opinion through well-founded, reasoned argument based on research or direct experience on issues either relating directly to the achievement of the charity's own stated purposes or relevant to the wellbeing of the charitable sector.

24. A charity may provide information to its supporters of the public on how individual Members of Parliament or parties have voted on an issue, provided they do so in a way which will enable its supporters or the public to seek to persuade those Members or parties to change their position through well-founded, reasoned argument rather than merely through public pressure.

25. A charity may provide its supporters, or members of the public, with material to send to Members of Parliament or the government, provided that the material amounts to well-founded, reasoned argument.

26. A charity may organise and present a petition to either House of Parliament or to national or local government, provided that the purpose of the petition is stated on each page.

27. A charity must not base any attempt to influence public opinion or to put pressure on the government, whether directly or indirectly through supporters or members of the public, to legislate or adopt a particular policy on data which it knows (or ought to know) is inaccurate or on a distorted selection of data in support of a preconceived position.

28. A charity must not participate in party political demonstrations.

29. A charity must not claim evidence of public support for its position on a political issue without adequate justification.

30. Except where the nature of the medium being employed makes it impracticable to set out the basis of the charity's position, a charity must not seek to influence government or public opinion on the basis of material which is merely emotive.

31. A charity must not invite its supporters, or the public, to take action in support of its position without providing them with sufficient information to enable them to decide

whether to give their support and to take the action requested. In particular, a charity must not invite its supporters or the public to write to their Members of Parliament or the government without providing them with sufficient information to enable them to advance a reasoned argument in favour of the charity's position."

**Local charities**   The Commission has issued separate guidance on local charities and political activities.[34] While much of the material it contains is similar to that in leaflet CC9 summarised above it helpfully clarifies some points of particular concern to community centres and village halls. There is no objection to a local charity allowing its premises to be used by the local member of parliament for surgeries and meetings with constituents or in using them for voting. Village halls and community centres may also be used for political meetings and fund-raising events by political parties provided that there is no discrimination between different parties because of their views or policies. Use of the facilities may be refused on grounds of safety or public order but only very exceptionally will it be proper to deny an organisation use of the property because of the fear of alienating its other beneficiaries. The Commission recommends trustees to ask for its advice before making a decision in these circumstances.

Another point which is clarified in the guidance is the position of local authority representative trustees. It is quite common for a local authority to have the right to nominate representatives to be trustees of local charities. Once appointed those individuals, like their co-trustees, must act in the interests of the charity. It is improper for them to take decisions for political reasons or in the interests of the authority they represent.

It was held in *Re Strakosch dec'd; Temperley v. Att.-Gen.*[35]

**Race relations**   that a trust "to strengthen the bonds of unity between the Union of South Africa and the Mother Country and which incidentally will conduce to the appeasement of racial feeling between the Dutch and English speaking sections of the South African community" was not charitable. The appeasement of racial feeling was held to be a political purpose. The Charity Commissioners now consider that the passing of the Race Relations Act 1976 means that the promotion of good race relations in this country has been judged by the legislature to be for the benefit of the public and has therefore been taken out of the political arena. Gifts for this purpose may therefore be charitable (see Charity Commissioners' Annual Report, 1984).

[34] ("Political Activities and Campaigning by Local Community Charities, CC9a issued 1996)
[35] [1949] 1 Ch. 529.

# 3 THE CHARITY COMMISSION

## The Constitution of the Charity Commission

The Charity Commission was established in 1853 to provide an inexpensive and simple means of dealing with problems encountered by charities which, until then, had to be resolved by the Court of Chancery. The expenses and delay involved in court proceedings put any remedy effectively beyond the reach of many charities. The constitution of the Charity Commission is now governed by the Charities Act 1993. Their jurisdiction originally extended only to England and Wales but their supervisory powers now apply to Scottish charities which are managed or controlled wholly or mainly in or from England and Wales.[1] Charities in Northern Ireland are the concern of the Northern Ireland Office. Responsibility for the Charity Commission was transferred from the Home Office to the Department of National Heritage in 1996. The Voluntary and Community Division of the Department now deals with charity issues.

**Charity Commissioners**
Until recently there have been three full-time Charity Commissioners appointed by the Secretary of State but these may be reduced to two. Two commissioners are required to be lawyers. The Chief Commissioner is not usually legally qualified and most incumbents have been transferred from other government departments. Recently, applications have been sought from outside the civil service though the present incumbent came from the Home Office. For the last few years part-time Commissioners drawn from among people with practical experience in the charitable sector have been appointed in addition to the permanent Commissioners. The Charity Commissioners act as a Board rather than individually and they are seldom personally involved with particular cases.

The Commissioners are deemed to be civil servants and they and the staff of the Commission are paid by the Treasury. Their terms of employment and scales of pay are the same as in government departments. Although the Secretary of State Department of National Heritage represents the Charity Commissioners and answers questions in relation to charity matters in Parliament he has no jurisdiction over them and has no power to direct them in the conduct of their duties. If the Charity Commission is criticised in Parliament the Secretary of State is not himself responsible and can only advise and influence them to take whatever remedial action is necessary.

The Commissioners are not a corporate body but paragraph 4 of the First Schedule to the Charities Act provides that they may sue and be sued in the name of the Charity Commissioners for England and Wales rather than as

[1] Charities Act 1993, s.80 and see below, p. 52.

individuals and that any proceedings will not be affected by a change in their membership.

The Commissioners are subject to the jurisdiction of the High Court in the exercise of their quasi-judicial powers and appeals from their decisions may be made to the High Court. This remedy is seldom used because of the expense involved and in practice there is no realistic method of obtaining a review of the Charity Commissioners' decisions except in the few cases where the money at stake is sufficiently substantial to warrant an appeal to the Court.

**Appeal from Commissioners' decisions**

# The Structure of the Charity Commission

The Charity Commission has a staff of approximately 580 divided between its offices in London, Taunton and Liverpool. The addresses of the three offices are given at the end of the book. At the end of 1995 there were 154,500 main charities and a further 26,967 subsidiary charities on the register. During the 1980s many complaints were expressed about the efficiency and effectiveness of the Charity Commission and in particular about the delays in dealing with correspondence, the length of time taken to register new charities and the lack of effective supervision and control over charities once they were registered. These concerns eventually led to the Woodfield Report in 1988,[2] many of the recommendations of which have now been adopted. In particular the resources allocated to the supervision and control of charities have been substantially increased and there is increased emphasis on providing guidance and information on practice and policy. A regular newsletter is produced and some of the Commission's decisions are published. Information is also available on the Internet (see Appendix E).

**The Operational Divisions**

There are six principal divisions in the Charity Commission with which those involved in charities may come in contact. These are the Charities Support division which provides advice and assistance; the Legal division providing legal support on casework, developing guidance to charities and holding surgeries in legal topics; the Official Custodian's division; the Monitoring division which sifts the information provided in charities' annual reports and accounts and ensures that these are received: and the Investigation division which conducts inquiries where malpractice is suspected; the Registration division which deals with questions of charitable status and the Policy division. In the last few years the way in which the Charity Commission is organised has been changed substantially and it is no longer run primarily by lawyers. A new database is to be established in 1996, which will give a more coherent classification of charities on the register by reference to both their stated objects and their activities.

**Regional Offices**

For the most part the work of the various divisions of the Charity Commission are divided geographically between the three offices as set out below. Local charities are allocated on the

[2] *Efficiency Scrutiny of the Supervision of Charities* (HMSO) under the Chairmanship of Sir Philip Woodfield, K.C.B., C.B.E.

basis of the area of benefit of the charity (*i.e.* where the beneficiaries are located). National and overseas charities are allocated according to where their main office is located.

## LONDON OFFICE

Local charities in:

| | |
|---|---|
| Bedfordshire | Hertfordshire |
| Buckinghamshire | Kent |
| Cambridgeshire | Norfolk |
| East Sussex | Northamptonshire |
| Essex | Suffolk |
| Greater London | Surrey |
| | West Sussex |

National charities based in all the Greater London Boroughs

## TAUNTON OFFICE

Local national and overseas charities based in:

| | |
|---|---|
| Avon | Hereford & Worcester |
| Berkshire | Isle of Wight |
| Cornwall | Mid Glamorgan |
| Devon | Oxfordshire |
| Dorset | Somerset |
| Dyfed | South Glamorgan |
| Gloucestershire | West Glamorgan |
| Gwent | Wiltshire |
| Hampshire | |

and national and overseas charities based in:

| | |
|---|---|
| Bedfordshire | Kent |
| Buckinghamshire | Surrey |
| East Sussex | West Sussex |
| Hertfordshire | |

## LIVERPOOL OFFICE

Local, national and overseas charities based in:

| | |
|---|---|
| Cheshire | Merseyside |
| Cleveland | North Yorkshire |
| Clwyd | Northumberland |
| Cumbria | Nottinghamshire |
| Derbyshire | Powys |
| Durham | Shropshire |
| Greater Manchester | South Yorkshire |
| Gwynedd | Staffordshire |
| Humberside | Tyne & Wear |
| Lancashire | Warwickshire |
| Leicestershire | West Midlands |
| Lincolnshire | West Yorkshire |

and national and overseas charities based in:

| | |
|---|---|
| Cambridgeshire | Northamptonshire |
| Essex | Suffolk |
| Norfolk | |

The exceptions to these allocations are:

The registration of national or overseas charities is dealt with by the office responsible for the area in which the applicant lives;

Welsh charities which operate in Wales alone are the responsibility of the Liverpool office;

All National Health Service charities are dealt with by the Liverpool office and

All charities connected with the armed forces are the responsibility of the Taunton office.

Information on the distribution of the work of the Charity Commission can be found in leaflet CC 50 Getting in Touch with the Charity Commission.

Each regional office now has a regional operations officer in charge of all the work of the office and heads of each of the registration, Charity Support, Monitoring and Investigations divisions in that office.

**Registration division**   The Registration division is divided between London, Taunton and Liverpool. Much of the routine and preliminary work in the registration division which deals with applications for charitable status is dealt with by staff who are not legally qualified. They have a large number of precedents for guidance and will conduct a preliminary correspondence with the applicants and request any further information which may be required. Cases in which a model trust deed or constitution has been agreed with the Inland Revenue will be entirely processed by the administrative staff. Other cases will usually be referred to Legal division who will decide whether or not to register after consultation with the **Charities Support division**   Inland Revenue. The procedure for an appeal against a decision not to register is outlined in Chapter 4.

The Charities division has general responsibility for providing advice and help to existing local and small national charities. Routine matters such as the operation of sections 74 and 75 of the Act (winding up and amalgamating small charities), appointing new trustees and vesting property in trustees, authorising the expenditure of capital, making schemes to amalgamate local charities and modernise the trusts of small ancient charities are dealt with in this division which is staffed by non-legally qualified personnel. Unusual points will be referred to the legal division for advice. Where consent to disposals of land is required under s.36, this will now be dealt with by the Charities Support Division. Within the Charities Support Division in the London office a special unit has been established recently with responsibility for large charities with its annual income of £10 million or assets of £100 million.

## Official Custodian's division

The functions of the Official Custodian for charities are being progressively wound down as investments other than land are returned to individual charity trustees.[3] This process was nearly

---

[3] See below, p. 46.

completed by the end of 1995. The Official Custodian is an official appointed by the Charity Commissioners.

## The legal division

Much of the work of the Charity Commission has a legal dimension and although many problems arise regularly and increasingly the practice of the Commission is being standardised more unusual or complex points will be referred to a lawyer. The advice of the legal division will often be required in connection with the registration of new charities on questions of charitable status and the drafting of the governing instrument.

## Investigations division

This division has been separated from the Monitoring Division. There are now about 40 staff whose function is to investigate complaints and allegations involving the misuse of charitable funds and misconduct in the administration of charities and fund-raising and evidence of abuse which may arise as a result of an examination of a charity's accounts or information passed to the Commissioners by the Inland Revenue under Finance Act 1986, s.33. Cases of poor management or neglect are now dealt with by Charities Support division, allowing Investigations division to concentrate on cases where charitable funds are at risk.

## Monitoring division

The monitoring division is responsible for scrutinising the annual returns and accounts which charities are now required to submit each year to the Commission and ensuring compliance. Any possible problems are referred to Investigations or Charities Support divisions as appropriate. The installation of a new database in 1996 will enable charities to be categorised according to objects, activities and areas of operation and it is intended that larger charities will be required to provide more details about their activities which will increase the information available to the public from the register. Smaller charities will still need only to provide basic information.

## Policy division

This division is composed of lawyers and senior administrators and is responsible for representing the views of the Charity Commission to other departments and developing constructive policies to meet the needs of the voluntary sector. One of the most frequent complaints made about the Charity Commission in the past has been that conflicting rulings are often given by different individual officers. It is hoped that this problem will eventually disappear and more consistent decisions will be made in future.

# The functions of the Charity Commissioners

**Charities Act, s.1**    Section 1 of the Charities Act provides that the general function of the Charity Commission shall be to promote the effective use of charitable resources by encouraging the development of better methods of administration, by giving charity trustees information or advice on any matter affecting the charity, and by investigating and checking abuses.

Their general object is to act so as best to promote and make effective the work of each charity in carrying out its stated purposes. They are specifically precluded from themselves acting in the administration of a charity[4] and, therefore, although they may advise the trustees on the ways in which the management may be improved they may not intervene directly. It is only when the conduct of those running the charity amounts to a breach of their duty that the Commissioners may themselves take action. Even in these circumstances, however, their powers are limited to removing the defaulting trustees and appointing new ones, appointing a receiver or manager, making a scheme for the administration of the charity or taking steps to preserve the assets of the charity.

**Educatioinal charities**    The Education Act 1973 transferred to the Charity Commissioners the similar duties originally given to the Minister for Education in relation to educational charities.

The work of the Charity Commissioners can, broadly speaking, be divided into four separate categories:

(i)    the registration of new charities and maintenance of the Central Register of Charities;
(ii)   giving advice and assistance to trustees;
(iii)  giving consent as required by status to certain transactions and
(iv)   supervising the administration of charities.

## Registration

The Commissioners are required (s.3 of the Charities Act) to maintain a register of charities which is open to the public and which contains such information as the Commissioners decide. They may remove from the register organisations which appear no longer to be charities, which cease to exist or no longer operate.

The number of new charities registered each year increased dramatically after the implementation of the Charities Act 1992. In 1995, 8,752 new charities were registered, down from 11,616 in the previous year. It is likely that the numbers will level off in future.

**Charities not required to register**    It should be noted however that many charities are not required to register. Exempt charities and charities excepted by regulation (which are considered in detail later in this chapter[5]) need not register. A further group comprises charities having neither permanent endowment nor income of more than £1,000

---

[4] Charities Act, s.1(4).
[5] See below, pp. 47–48.

from any source per year nor the use and occupation of land.[6] Finally, places of worship (without restriction as to the religion which is practised) need not register.

All other charities are required to register although there are no sanctions if they fail to do so.

A charity is defined in section 96 of the Charities Act as "any institution, corporate or not, which is established for charitable purposes and is subject to the control of the High Court in the exercise of the Court's jurisdiction with respect to charities." When considering similar wording in a taxing statute

**Foreign charities**   the court held in *Camille and Henry Dreyfus Foundation v. I.R.C.*[7] that "established" meant established in the United Kingdom and that an organisation established abroad whose activities were solely carried out abroad was not so established. The Commissioners' current practice is to register trusts and unincorporated associations only if a majority of the trustees are resident or property is situated within the jurisdiction. A company registered in England and Wales is eligible for registration regardless of the residence of its directors.

The procedure for registration of a charity is explained in Chapter 4. Once registered an organisation is conclusively presumed to be a charity.[8] The particulars of each registered

**Central Register**   charity are recorded on the Central Register of Charities, which is open to inspection by the public. The Register of Charities was until recently kept manually and since much of the information it contained was based on details provided at the time of registration it tended to be inaccurate and out of date. In 1990 computerised records were introduced and plans made for them to be checked and updated regularly. Initially the details contained in the manual records were transposed on to the computer and consequently errors and out-of-date information has been carried into the new system. The process of improving the accuracy of the Register is still continuing. A new database is to be operational in 1996 and this will allow more information to be available to the public and the Commission. Charities with an income of £10,000 or more will be required to provide additional information about their activities in their annual report required by section 45 of the Charities Act. It is hoped in future that changes in the names and addresses of the correspondents, the trustees and the annual income of the charity will be regularly updated and the Register will become a much more useful tool for those interested in charities than it ever was in the past. The additional information provided by larger charities will enable a more coherent and informative classification of registered charities.

There is no fee for checking the details on screen but there

**Fees**   is a fee of 10 pence per page for copies of entries on the Register and documents.

The information held on the Register includes the objects of the charity, details of the governing instrument including the date when it became operative, the annual income of the charity and the name and address of the person to whom

---

[6] Charities Act, s.3(5).
[7] [1954] 1 Ch. 672.
[8] Charities Act, s.4(1).

correspondence should be sent. Anyone who wishes to read the governing instrument or inspect the latest accounts must ask for the file to be sent for. This cannot normally be done the same day but copies can be sent on payment of a fee.

Information about registered charities can be obtained over the telephone between the hours of 10 a.m. and 4 p.m. Monday to Friday from any of the Commission's offices but it can sometimes be difficult to get through.

**Registration not a "seal of approval"**

Contrary to widely held belief registration does not imply that a charity is either well-run or deserves support. The Commissioners are obliged to register any organisation which is established for charitable purposes (other than those mentioned above) regardless of merit and even where doubts exist as to the good faith of the promoters. Registration therefore implies no more than that the Charity Commissioners are satisfied that the governing instrument fulfils the necessary conditions. Despite the defects and limitations of the registration arrangements the Register provides a useful service to those wishing to give to charity, to the Inland Revenue in processing claims for repayment of tax and in checking abuse and dishonesty in fund-raising.

## Removal from the Register

The Commissioners may remove a registered charity from the Register[9] where

> it no longer appears to the Commissioners to be a charity
> it ceases to exist
> it does not operate
> it was registered in error
> there has been a change of circumstances

6,274 charities were removed from the register in 1995 most of which had ceased to operate or had been wound up.

## No longer a charity

A change in the objects of a charity may have the effect that it is no longer established for exclusively charitable purposes. Such a change would be unusual since normally a power of variation will not extend to the objects clause. A "Time charity" where property is dedicated to charitable purposes for a limited period only is a possible example of a change of objects. Charitable companies may by special resolution alter their objects[10] but such an alteration is ineffective without the prior written consent of the Commissioners[11] and they would be unlikely to give consent to an alteration which may the company non-charitable.

---

[9] Charities Act, s.3(4).
[10] Companies Act, 1985, s.4.
[11] Charities Act, s.64(2).

## Ceases to exist

Where a charity winds up under a power in the governing instrument or no longer has any assets if it is a trust or being a company is dissolved it may be removed from the Register.

## Does not operate

A charity which does not function risks being removed from the Register. If the charity trustees wish to accumulate funds for a specific purpose they should notify the Commissioners of their reasons in the Annual Return. Provided they are acting responsibly they should not encounter problems.

Section 28 of the Charities Act gives the Commissioners new powers to deal with dormant bank accounts where it is impossible to locate the charity or the trustees.[12]

## Registered in error

The Commissioners may rectify an entry on the Register[13] and such an entry is an exception to the rule that registration is conclusive evidence that the organisation was a charity when it was registered.

## Changes of circumstances

The Charity Commissioners may remove from the Register an organisation previously regarded as charitable (section 4(5) of the Charities Act) which allows them to consider the matter afresh where there has been a change of circumstances. Charity law has evolved over the centuries as was explained in Chapter 1. This flexibility is one of the strengths of English charity law. If purposes which could not have been regarded as charitable in earlier times are now so regarded it seems logical that purposes previously considered charitable may cease to be so. The Charity Commissioners appear to think so and are undertaking a clean-up of the Register which may involve removing organisations previously regarded as charitable. They have stated[14] that they do not consider gun clubs to be charitable and will refuse to register them in future. Gun clubs which were registered have been removed from the register. Since there are a number of cases in which the courts have held gun and rifle associations to be charitable the correctness of their stand may be open to doubt,[15] but to date the clubs which have been refused registration have not appealed against the decision. More recently school fees saving trusts were removed and an appeal to the High Court against this decision is pending.

[12] See below, p. 52.
[13] Charities Act, s.4(1).
[14] *Decisions of the Charity Commissioners*, Vol. 1, pp. 4–13.
[15] See Peter Clarke, "The Charitable Status of Rifle Clubs" *Charity Law & Practice Review* Vol. I, Issue 2.

## Later judicial decision

The Commissioners have a similar power to remove an institution from the Register where the law or the received view of the law changes as a result of a later decision of the court. An example of this was the decision in *I.R.C. v. Baddeley*[16] when the House of Lords decided that recreational purposes were not charitable, contrary to the prevailing opinion. The decision was effectively overturned by the Recreational Charities Act 1958. During the progress of the case through the courts a number of institutions were initially treated as being charitable, a view which subsequently had to be revised and then later confirmed.

## Advice and assistance

**Promoting effective use of funds**

Much of the work of the Charity Commission is concerned with promoting the effective use of charitable resources, a duty imposed on them by section 1(3) of the Charities Act. This aspect of their duties covers such matters as making schemes to alter the purposes of the charity where these have become outdated or unsuitable, advising on the powers and duties of the trustees or directors, appointing new trustees where the chain of trusteeship has been broken and there is no one with the power to appoint new trustees and encouraging the amalgamation of small charities. These matters are discussed in detail later in this book. The Charity Commissioners may not interfere in the administration of charities, which is the sole concern of the charity trustees.[17] Their role is limited to encouraging a high general standard in administration and they may take steps to remove trustees where there has been neglect or breach of duty (see below, p. 45 and Chapter 6). Generally speaking, officials at the Charity Commission are helpful and prepared to go to considerable lengths to try to solve problems encountered by those involved in running charities although criticisms are sometimes made about delays and advice which is inconclusive or legalistic. In general the staff have considerable expertise and frequently problems which appear to be insuperable will be found to have a simple solution. If difficulties arise the first step should always be to approach the Charity Commission. Although it may take time to get an answer the service is free of charge and it will be preferable to seek advice at an early stage rather than delay asking for help, which can result in a minor problem being exacerbated.

In the last few years the Commission has issued several guidance notes and leaflets setting out its view on a number of topics and revised its existing leaflets. A full list of publications can be found in Appendix F. Some of these set out the Commission's interpretations of the law such as that on political activity. Others are concerned with promoting good practice like the leaflet on the retention of income reserves.

[16] [1955] A.C. 572 (see p. 16).
[17] Charities Act, s.1(4).

## Advice under section 29 of the Charities Act

Section 29 of the Charities Act empowers the Commissioners to give any charity trustee advice on any matter affecting the performance of his duties. Applications for advice must be made in writing. The circumstances where such advice may be given include occasions where trustees are unclear about the meaning of the governing instrument, where a dispute has arisen among the trustees over the propriety of a certain course of action or a complaint has been made about the way in which trustees exercise their discretionary powers. If charity trustees act in accordance with advice given under section 29 they will be protected from any action for breach of trust provided that the trustees do not know or suspect that the advice was given in ignorance of material facts. Care should therefore be taken to ensure that the Commissioners are given full information before they are asked to advise.

**Protection for Trustees**

The Commissioners are not able to interpret the wording of the governing instrument conclusively. This can only be done by the court. Advice under section 29 cannot provide protection where trustees need guidance as to the meaning of a trust deed or constitution.

## Dealings authorised under section 26 of the Charities Act

Section 26 of the Charities Act enables the Commissioners to authorise an action which is not strictly within the scope of the trustees' powers. The Commissioners must first be satisfied that the action in question is in the interests of the charity. Examples of transactions which may be authorised under this section are making an investment which is not within the scope of the trustees' powers; the use of part of a property for purposes outside the terms of the trusts on which it is held; sharing property with another charity and spending permanent endowment on terms that it is recouped to capital over a period of time.

## Consent to sales

The Commissioners' consent is required under section 36 of the Charities Act to any sale, lease for a term of more than seven years or disposal of land which is to a connected person (*e.g.* a trustee or relative of a trustee) or does not conform to the code of practice set out in the section. Section 38 of the Charities Act contains similar provisions in respect of mortgages. These topics are discussed fully in Chapter 10.

The purpose of these restrictions is to ensure that the best possible terms are obtained by the charity trustees and that deals are not done which benefit individuals more than the charity.

## Supervision of charities

Malpractice on the part of charities can take the form of bad management, breach of trust and improper activities (such as political activities) as well as dishonesty in dealing with the funds of the charity. The failure of the Charity Commission to control charities[18] effectively led eventually to a reform of its supervisory functions and the adoption of a more active approach to monitoring their activities. There are more than 180,000 registered charities and it is impractical to expect the Commissioners to ensure that all are properly administered. Their approach to supervision falls into two categories. First, they will take up and investigate complaints made to them and secondly, problems may be revealed through analysis of a charity's accounts and annual report.

## Response to complaints

Complaints about the activities of a charity are sometimes made by aggrieved beneficiaries or would-be beneficiaries, other charities working in the same field, charity trustees who are concerned about the way their colleagues are running the charity and members of the public who are concerned about aspects of a charity's activities.

**Inland Revenue information**        Since 1986 the Inland Revenue has been able to pass information to the Commissioners which would previously have been regarded as confidential.[19] In consequence the Commissioners will now be made aware of cases of breach of trust or misapplication of funds which are discovered by the Revenue when processing claims for tax relief and will be able to take appropriate action. Section 10 of the Charities Act authorises any government department, local authority, police constable and other public regulatory bodies to disclose any information to the Commissioners in order to help them carry out their functions.

**Charity accounts**        All charities (other than exempt and excepted charities) are now required to submit accounts to the Commissioners each year.[20] These accounts should provide sufficient information to enable a judgment to be made as to whether the charity is being administered properly and efficiently,.and give some information about the activities of the charity. Until recently many charities failed to submit accounts as requested. Less than half the charities included in the National Audit Office survey in 1987 had done so in the previous five years but persistent failure to do so is now a criminal offence punishable by a fine.[21]

The National Audit Office Survey also disclosed that only 4 per cent of accounts submitted to the Commissioners had actually been examined by them. It is unrealistic to suggest that

---

[18] See *Monitoring and Control of Charities in England and Wales* National Audit Office Report 1987 HMSO. Woodfield Report 1987, paras. 70–77 HMSO. Report of House of Commons Committee of Public Accounts 1987 HMSO.
[19] Finance Act 1986, s.33.
[20] Charities Act, s.48.
[21] Charities Act, s.49.

**Scrutiny of accounts** all charity accounts should be examined each year, desirable though this might be, since a small army of bureaucrats would be needed, wholly disproportionate to the number of malpractice cases likely to be brought to light. Accounts are examined by Monitoring Division in Liverpool. The accounts to be scrutinised are selected from among charities of different sizes, a higher proportion of larger charities being checked. Any problems which are identified will be referred to Charities division for action or, in more serious cases, to Investigations division. Special attention is given to those charities which have been identified as potential "problem" charities either from information provided in the course of registration or because of a complaint or where regular monitoring of accounts has been recommended by one of the administrative divisions of the Charity Commission.

The standardisation of charities' accounts and additional disclosure requirements which were brought into force for accounting periods beginning after March 1, 1996,[22] will make it easier to identify problems.

## Treatment of complaints

The Commissioners will in the first instance usually refer any complaint or point arising from consideration of the accounts to the charity trustees for their comments and explanation. Where no satisfactory explanation is provided the Commissioners will wish to investigate further and the case may be referred to Investigations division for evaluation. Where there is no suspicion of fraud or deliberate malpractice the Commission's function will be to ensure that the charity continues to function effectively. They will therefore inform the trustees of their duties and point out where their management has been defective in an effort to promote higher standards and will seek to achieve a solution to any problem by discussion and negotiation.

## Resolution of disputes

Where a dispute has arisen between the trustees the Commission officials will endeavour not to support one side or the other but to achieve a compromise in the interests of the charity. This approach can be frustrating for trustees or individuals who are convinced that there has been maladministration and would like the Commissioners to intervene decisively but it is only when there is adequate evidence of impropriety or maladministration that they will be willing to do so and the matter will then be referred to the Investigations division. As mentioned earlier, Investigations division now concentrates on cases where an initial evaluation has shown serious cause for concern, which needs further examination. Because the Commissioners are not permitted to act in the administration of a charity they are not able to dictate to charity trustees how they should run the charity. In the absence of evidence of misconduct they can only advise.

[22] See Chapter 10.

# Section 8 inquiries

Some cases cannot be resolved in this way. The individuals concerned may not co-operate or there may be substantial indications of wrongdoing. In such cases the Charity Commissioners have considerable powers which can be used to investigate the way in which a charity is run and to protect the charity assets. Section 8 of the Charities Act authorises the Charity Commissioners to institute inquiries into particular

**Procedure** charities or groups of charities. The procedure has been improved recently but it is still somewhat cumbersome and will only be resorted to if it is not practicable to resolve the problems in any other way. If after an initial evaluation there is sufficient cause for concern the Commissioners may appoint an accountant or lawyer or some other person to carry out an inquiry and report back to them but more usually one of their own staff will act. The inquiry will normally be instituted by an order of the Commissioners which sets out its scope and authorises the person conducting the inquiry to require documents and other information to be produced and the attendance of any person to give evidence or produce

**Evidence** documents relevant to the inquiry. Evidence may be taken on oath. The report of the person making the inquiry may be published and will be published if it is desirable to bring his findings to the notice of any person or authority (the police for example) who might wish to take action as a result. 609 inquiries were started in 1995 and of those completed during the year rather less than half were substantiated. The majority of these (204 cases) involved inadequate management and poor financial control. But a sizeable number (124) involved deliberate wrongdoing. The Commissioners do not have power to conduct an inquiry in respect of an exempt charity.[23] If, having instituted an inquiry under section 8, the Commissioners are satisfied either that there has been misconduct or mismanagement, or that action is necessary or desirable to protect the property of the charity or to secure that it is properly applied, they have wide

**Powers of** powers to take remedial action under section 18. They may
**Commissioners** suspend any charity trustee or officer or employee of the charity or appoint additional trustees; the property of the charity may be vested in the Official Custodian for charities without the need for an application by the charity trustees; the assets of the charity may be frozen and restrictions placed upon the transactions which may be entered into on behalf of the charity without the Commissioners' consent and a receiver or manager may be appointed.

## Appointment of receiver or manager

The power to appoint a receiver or manager was recommended in the Woodfield Report[24] and sections 18 and 19 of the

[23] See below, p. 47.
[24] Para. 76.

Charities Act set out the provisions concerning their functions. The Charities (Receiver and Manager) Regulations 1992[25] cover such matters as appointment, remuneration and reports. The person appointed may not be an employee of the Commissioners. The powers and duties of the receiver or manager will be specified by the Commissioners and he may be given any of the powers of the charity trustees. He may be protected by acting on the written advice of the Commissioners under section 29 of the Charities Act in the same way as charity trustees. In 1995 three orders were made appointing a receiver or manager.[26]

## Removal of trustees

**Protection of charity**

If, having instituted an inquiry under section 8, the Commissioners are satisfied both that there has been misconduct or mismanagement and that it is necessary or desirable in order to protect the charity or ensure that the funds are properly applied they may remove a charity trustee, officer, agent or employee who has been responsible for or privy to or facilitated the misconduct or mismanagement or they may make a scheme for the charity without the need for an application from the trustees. This power is used sparingly. In 1995 only nine trustees from two charities were removed.[27]

## Disqualification of trustees

A person who has been removed from the office of charity trustee or trustee for a charity either by the Commissioners under section 18 of the Charities Act or by the court is disqualified from acting as such in future. The Commissioners are required to keep a register of all such persons which is available for public inspection.[28]

The Commission has issued Guidance Notes on the Institution and Conduct of Inquiries into Charities (CC47(a) and (b)).

## Fund-Raising

The function of authorising public charitable collections throughout England and Wales or a substantial part of the country has been given to the Commissioners by section 72 of the Charities Act 1992. The implementation of the new regime regulating public collections has been postponed and is not now likely before summer 1998.[29]

---

[25] S.I. 1992 No. 2355.
[26] Charity Commission Report for 1995, paras. 45–50.
[27] Charity Commission Report for 1995, para. 50.
[28] Charities Act, s.72(6).
[29] See below, Chap. 12.

# The Official Custodian for charities

Section 3 of the Charities Act 1960 (now Charities Act, s.2) established an Official Custodian for charities whose function was to hold, as custodian trustee, land and other property on behalf of charity trustees. The Charity Commissioners designate one of their officials as Official Custodian.

The Official Custodian is a corporation sole with perpetual succession. Consequently, once property is in his name there is no further need to transfer it to new trustees on death or retirement, thus saving trouble and expense. The problems which can arise when property remains vested in the names of persons who are no longer trustees and who may in some cases

**Untraced trustees** be difficult to trace are also avoided. In such cases, where reasonable efforts to identify the persons in whom property is vested have failed, it may be appropriate for it to be vested in the Official Custodian to avoid a similar problem arising again.

**Duties** The Official Custodian acts as custodian trustee of the property vested in him. He may not involve himself in the administration of the property which remains under the control of the trustees nor is he concerned with the management of the charity. He holds the charity property to the order of the trustees and is obliged to comply with their directions in dealing with it and to carry out their instructions, for example as to sales and letting of land and changes of investment. However, before complying with the trustees' directions the Official Custodian must, in exercise of his duties as custodian trustee, satisfy himself that this will be in accordance with the terms of the trust and that the necessary consents have been obtained.

## Divestment

As part of the process of concentrating the work of the Charity Commission more on supervising charities the role of the Official Custodian was considerably reduced. Sections 29 and 30 of the Charities Act 1992 provided for the Official Custodian to divest himself of all property vested in him other than land (including leases and other interests in land) or property vested by virtue of an order of the Commissioners. The process is now almost complete and the Official Custodian now holds investments only where the Commission has exercised its powers to protect charity property.

Charities no longer have the advantage of having the interest and dividends paid to them gross. This will only be available in future in respect of units in a common investment fund or government stocks on the Post Office Register. Land or interests in land belonging to a charity may still be held by the

**Land** Official Custodian and the deeds may be held in the safe keeping of the Official Custodian who will give the appropriate certificate to the Charity's auditors.

The procedure for transferring property to the Official

**Transfer of property to the Official Custodian** Custodian is for the trustees to write to him giving details of the trustees of the charity and of the property. If he agrees to act, the land will be vested in the Official Custodian by order of the Commissioners.

**Dealings in land**

The Official Custodian need not execute any conveyance, transfer, lease or other deed relating to land vested in him which can be executed by the charity trustees in his name. The Official Custodian should be made a party to the deed. The only exception is where the land or interest was vested in the Official Custodian by the Commissioners exercising their protective powers contained in section 18 of the Charities Act after an inquiry instituted under section 8.[30] In such cases the trustees must be authorised to execute the deed by order of the Commissioners.

The service of the Official Custodian are free.

# Limitations on the Commissioners' jurisdiction

Some institutions which are established for charitable purposes are nonetheless subject to the jurisdiction of the Charity Commissioners only to a limited extent. These fall into two groups.

## Exempt charities

**Effect of exemption**

Certain institutions specified in Schedule 2 to the Charities Act are known as exempt charities. They include a number of universities and medical schools, all grant-maintained schools, the British Museum, the Victoria and Albert Museum and the Science Museum, the Royal Botanical Gardens at Kew and registered Friendly Societies. These charities are not subject to the supervisory jurisdiction of the Charity Commissioners but they are subject to the jurisdiction of the court in relation to charities. An exempt charity is not required to be registered nor may an exempt charity register voluntarily.[31] Exempt charities are required to keep proper books of account[32] and to preserve them for six years but they need not comply with the provisions of sections 41 to 45 of the Charities Act which specify the form and contents of accounts and requirements for audit and for an annual report. An exempt charity must, on the written request of any person, provide a copy of the latest accounts of the charity but may charge a reasonable fee for doing so.[33]

An exempt charity is not required to submit an annual report to the Charity Commissioners under Charities Act, s.45.

The Commissioners' powers to institute an inquiry under section 8 of the Charities Act with regard to a charity do not extend to an exempt charity and consequently their powers under section 18 to act for the protection of charities are not available in respect of exempt charities.

[30] Charities Act, s.22(2) and (3).
[31] Charities Act, s.3(2) and (5)(a).
[32] Charities Act, s.46(1).
[33] Charities Act, s.47(2) and (3).

The restrictions on sales, leases, other dispositions and mortgages of land held in trust for a charity imposed by the Charities Acts do not apply to exempt charities.[34]

Although the Commissioners have all the powers to make schemes and orders in respect of exempt charities conferred by sections 13 and 16 of the Charities Act they may only do so on the application of the charity or on an order of the court. Section 16(5) (power to make schemes on application of one or more trustees or person interested) does not apply.

## Excepted charities

**Charities excepted by regulations**

Certain charities are excepted by regulations made from time to time from the requirement to register and to submit an annual report and accounts.

Excepted charities include funds held for Boy Scouts or Girl Guides Associations; voluntary schools within the state sector which have no permanent endowment other than the school site itself; certain charities connected with the Methodist, Baptist and Congregational churches; certain small charities applicable for the promotion of religion (Christian and non-Christian); Church of England charities where the property is vested in a diocesan trust corporation and certain charities connected with the promotion of the efficiency of the armed forces. The general obligation to keep proper accounting records [35] applies to excepted charities as it does to all charities and the requirements of sections 41 and 42 of the Charities Act as to the form and content of accounts and the need for audit or examination of accounts also apply. Excepted charities need not submit their accounts to the Commissioners annually.[36] They may be requested by the Commissioners to prepare an annual report containing information on the charity's activities and trustees of officers.[37]

Although the accounts of a charity which is excepted by regulation from the need to register are not open to public inspection a copy of the most recent accounts may be obtained on payment of a reasonable fee by writing to the charity.[38]

**Exempt charities contrasted**

An excepted charity is fully subject to the restrictions on sales, leases, mortgages and other dispositions of land held in trust for the charity. In contrast to exempt charities, excepted charities are also subject to the supervisory functions of the Charity Commissioners. Inquiries under section 8 of the Charities Act may be instituted and all the protective powers contained in section 18 are available in respect of excepted charities. The Commissioners also have all the powers to make schemes and orders contained in sections 13 and 16 of the Charities Act.

[34] Charities Act, ss.36(10) and 38(7).
[35] Charities Act, s.46(1).
[36] Charities Act, s.46(4).
[37] Charities Act, s.46(5).
[38] Charities Act, s.47(2).

## Small charities

Charities which have neither

> permanent endowment
> the use or occupation of land or
> an income of more than £1,000 a year

are not required to be registered and like charities excepted by regulation are excepted from the requirement to submit an annual report and accounts to the Commission, though they may provide a copy of their most recent accounts to any person who asks for them and pays a reasonable fee.[39]

## Foreign element

Where there is a foreign element the proper law of the charity will govern such matters as whether the court or the Charity Commissioners have power to settle a scheme for the administration of the charity or to vary its purposes *cy-près*. As mentioned above in connection with registration, jurisdiction will not be assumed unless property is situated or a majority of the trustees are resident within the jurisdiction or the charity is constituted as an English company. Where trustees are resident within the jurisdiction the court will be prepared to make a scheme to vary the purposes even when the purposes are to be carried out wholly abroad.[40]

## Administration and contentious matters

The Charities Act imposes two further restrictions on the Commission's powers. First they are not permitted to "act in the administration of a charity".[41] They may not therefore direct trustees how to run their charity though they can and do advise and encourage them to adopt good practices. Recently the Commission has issued a number of leaflets setting out their views on a variety of administrative matters which have given rise to difficulties in the past such as the retention of reserves of income, handling cash and campaigning by charities. Much of the work of the Charities Support division is to help charity trustees to run their charities more effectively. The Commission is only empowered to take any positive action when the trustees have committed a breach of trust or duty or have been guilty of maladministration or dishonesty.

**Questions of title**   The second limitation is that in exercising their powers under section 16 (to make schemes for the administration of a charity, appoint or remove charity trustees and vest or transfer property) in any case, which, because of its contentious nature or any question of law or fact which it may involve, is best decided by the court.[42] They may not, for example, decide questions of title to property.

[39] Charities Act s.46(3) and (4) and s.47(2).
[40] *The Colonial Bishoprics Fund* [1935] Ch. 148.
[41] Charities Act, s.1(4).
[42] Charities Act, s.16(10).

# Orders of the Charity Commissioners

**Enforcement**

Orders of the Charity Commissioners requiring the production of documents or other information made under sections 8 or 9 of the Charities Act or made under sections 16 or 18 requiring property to be transferred or payments made are enforceable as if they are orders of the High Court. A person disobeying such an order may therefore be committed for contempt of court and his property may be seized (Charities Act, s.88).

Section 87 of the Charities Act allows the Commissioners to issue directions to a person who fails to comply with the requirements of the Charities Act (the duty to submit accounts for example) and the Charitable Trustees Incorporation Act 1872 and breach of the directions will be punishable in the same way.

The Commissioners' hands have recently been further strengthened by introducing a number of new criminal offences punishable by a fine. Offences are committed where documents issued by a charity do not bear the information required by section 5 or there is persistent default in compliance with the accounting requirements (section 49) (see Chapter 10); where a person acts as a charity trustee or trustee for a charity while disqualified under section 73 (see Chapter 6); where misleading or false information is provided to the Commissioners knowing or recklessly or a document which a person is liable to produce is destroyed (section 11) or an order made under section 18 for the protection of a charity is breached.

The consent of the Director of Public Prosecutions is required by section 94 before proceedings may be instituted.

## Fees

At present the services of the Commissioners are free. The only charges made are for copying documents. Section 85 of the Charities Act 1992 paves the way for charging for the discharge of the Commissioners' functions and for inspection of the Central Register of Charities. Charges for registering new charities are still under consideration. It seems likely that if and when charges are introduced charities using a model governing instrument will be charged less than those using their own precedents.

## Appeals

**Commissioners' certificate**

An appeal against an order made by the Charity Commissioners under section 16 establishing a scheme for the administration of a charity or appointing or removing a trustee or renting or transferring property must be brought within three months in the High Court. The Attorney-General may be a party either as appellant or as defendant representing the Commissioners, depending upon his assessment of the merits of the appeal. An appeal against an order may only be made with a certificate from the Charity Commissioners that it is a proper case for appeal or

with the leave of a judge of the Chancery Division.[43] If a
certificate is refused an application to the court for leave must be
made within 21 days, the Attorney-General being the

**Who may appeal**  respondent. An appeal may be brought by the charity, any of the
charity trustees or any person who has been removed as an
officer or employee. Where the appeal is against an order
establishing a scheme any person interested[44] in the charity may
appeal and in the case of a local charity any two inhabitants of
the locality or the parish council (s.16(11) to (13)).

**Registration**  Appeals against a decision to register or not to register an
**decisions**  organisation as a charity or to remove an organisation from the
Register do not require the Commissioners' certificate nor is
there any time limit. However, the Attorney-General is still
required to be a party and it is always wise to consult his office at
an early stage to ascertain if he would be prepared to support the
appeal. An appeal may be brought by the Attorney-General if he
can be persuaded to take the case up, by the trustees of the
organisation or by any person whose objection to registration
has been overruled.[45]

**Duty of care**  While the Commissioners have a duty to take care when
exercising their powers, that duty is not owed to any individual
or charity. An action brought against the Commissioners
claiming damages for negligence failed in the case of *Mills and
Others v. Winchester Diocesan Board of Finance and others*.[46]

**Judicial review**  Orders of the Commissioners may be subject to judicial
review.

## Charity Names

The Commissioners are given power by section 6 of the
Charities Act to direct a registered charity to change its name
where its name is the same or too like that of another charity
**Similar name**  (registered or unregistered). They may also direct a change if
they consider the name to be misleading as to the charity's
purposes or activities or implying wrongly that it is connected
with any body or person or is offensive. The Commission has
given details of its practice in implementing its powers under s.6
in Vol. 4 of Decisions of the Charity Commissioners, pp. 22–25.
They consider that the section applies to a working name as well
as to the formal name of a charity. The use of a term such as
"society", "trust" or "foundation" will not be enough to
distinguish a charity having an otherwise similar name, nor will
the sole use of a word describing the work of the charity such as
**Misleading name**  "cancer relief" unless this is linked with another identifying
word. The Commissioners may also direct a change of name
where the name includes any of the words or expressions
specified in the Charities (Misleading Names) Regulations
1992[47] where they consider the inclusion of the word or
expression is likely to mislead the public. The Regulations

[43] Charities Act, s.16(13).
[44] See below, Chap. 10.
[45] Charities Act, s.4(3) and (4).
[46] [1989] Ch. 428.
[47] S.I. 1992 No. 1901.

specify such words as Authority, Church, European, Her
Majesty, National, Official, Royal, School and University.

## Dormant bank accounts

The Commissioners have power to direct a financial institution
such as a bank or building society to transfer cash held by them
to one or more other charities where the institution, after
making reasonable inquiries, is unable to locate the charity or
any of the trustees (Charities Act, s.28). In its report for 1995
the Commission disclosed that they had only identified 82
dormant charities the assets of which would be distributed
during 1996.

# Scottish charities

There is no equivalent to the Charity Commission in Scotland.
An organisation which wishes to hold itself out as a charity in
Scotland must apply to the Inland Revenue for recognition.
Such bodies are called "recognised bodies" and the Inland

**Register** Revenue maintains a register of them. Charities which are
registered in England and Wales are not required to register and
are deemed to be charities in Scotland. The Lord Advocate has
powers similar to those of the Charity Commissioners contained
in section 8 of the Charities Act to investigate and supervise
recognised bodies including English and Welsh charities which
operate in Scotland. The relevant Scottish legislation is the Law
Reform (Miscellaneous Provisions) (Scotland) Act 1990.

All Scottish charities are required to produce annual
**Supervision** accounts and to provide any member of the public who asks
with a copy of their most recent accounts and of their charitable
objects. A reasonable fee may be charged. A charity which fails
to prepare accounts or to supply copies may be prevented by an
order of the Court of Session from carrying out specified
activities. The court may also prevent a body from representing
itself as a charity; it may suspend any person concerned in its
management and appoint a judicial factor; its funds may be
frozen and where misconduct is proven authorise the transfer of
charitable funds to another body. persons who have been
convicted of an offence involving dishonesty; are undischarged
bankrupts; who have been removed from being concerned in the
management of any charitable body under the Act or are
disqualified from being a company director under the Company
Directors Disqualification Act 1986 are disqualified from being
involved in the management or control of a Scottish charity.

Further information can be obtained from the Scottish
Charities Office which has produced a useful guide entitled
"The Supervision of Charities in Scotland". Inquiries about
charitable status should be addressed to the Inland Revenue.
Both addresses are in Appendix E.

The Commissioners are given certain supervisory powers
**Charity** over recognised bodies which are controlled from England or
**Commission** Wales or where a person in England or Wales holds property on
**powers** trust for a recognised body which is controlled from Scotland.

The powers conferred on the Commissioners in respect of such bodies by section 80 of the Charities Act are their powers to institute inquiries and call for documents (sections 8 and 9) and their powers to act for the protection of charities under sections 18 and 19 (other than making a scheme).

## Jurisdiction over fundraisers

The Charity Commissioners have jurisdiction over all funds which are held upon trust for charitable purposes whether or not a charity has been formally established. Where funds are given to any person for a charitable purpose he holds those funds upon charitable trusts. It follows that he is a trustee of the funds and may not take any part for himself by way of remuneration or otherwise unless the gift was made upon those terms. This point was confirmed in the unreported case of *Jones v. Attorney-General* (1976) referred to in the NCVO Report on Malpractice in Fund-raising for Charity referred to in more detail in Chapter 12 and more recently in another unreported case *Reg. v. Wain* (1993).[48] Where the Commission becomes aware of a fundraiser retaining remuneration or other benefits from money raised for charity they may intervene and use their powers under sections 18–20 of the Charities Act to protect charitable funds.

---

[48] *Decisions of the Charity Commissioners*, Vol. 2, pp. 33–35.

# 4 SETTING UP A NEW CHARITY

A charity may be established by the completion of a formal governing instrument (declaration of trust, company memorandum and articles or constitution), under the terms of a will or by publishing an appeal for funds. Fund-raising appeals, which raise special problems of their own, are considered in Chapter 12.[1] This chapter is concerned with the practical and procedural aspects of setting up a charity regulated by a formal governing instrument and arranging for its registration as a charity.

## Preliminary approach to Charity Commission

Where there is any doubt as to whether the intended activities of the proposed charity are likely to be accepted as charitable, time and costs may be saved by making an initial approach to the Charity Commissioners for advice even before preparing draft documentation. The Charity Commissioners will normally be prepared to indicate whether or not they consider the proposed organisation can be brought within one of the heads of charity, and if it cannot they will sometimes be prepared to give guidance to the organisers as to whether charitable status might be granted if certain activities are abandoned or undertaken by a separate non-charitable body. As much detail as possible should be provided as to the current activities of the organisation or, in the case of a proposed charity, the organisers' intentions.

**Advice**

## Validity of gifts to charity

Any adult of sound mind who is not disqualified from acting as a charity trustee by section 72 of the Charities Act[2] may create a charity with himself as a trustee either alone or with others and whether this is done by setting up a trust, forming a company or unincorporated association or launching a public appeal for funds.

Some gifts for charitable purposes, whether to create a new charity or to support an existing one, may be invalid and may, in certain circumstances, be set aside. For example a gift made by a person who becomes bankrupt within five years may be set aside on the application of his trustee in bankruptcy.[3] A gift made by a person suffering from mental disorder which renders him incapable of managing his property and affairs will be void although the Court of Protection may authorise a patient of the court to make a gift to charity if satisfied that it is such that the

**Bankrupts**

---

[1] See below, p. 191.
[2] See below, Chap. 6.
[3] See Insolvency Act 1986, s.341.

**Patients** patient might be expected to make if he ceased to suffer from a mental disorder and was not subject to undue influence.[4]

**Minors** A gift to charity or the establishment of a charitable trust by a minor will be void in so far as it extends to land. As far as other property is concerned the gift or trust will be voidable at the instance of the minor on attaining his majority.

**Companies** A company may make a charitable gift if the memorandum contains an express power or to do so will promote the objects of the company.

**Trustees** Trustees of a private trust may benefit charity in exercise of a power to apply capital for the benefit of a beneficiary where that beneficiary considers himself to be under a moral obligation to give to charity.[5] Section 55 of the Settled Land Act 1925 gave power to tenants for life of settled land to make gifts of property forming part of the settled estate for certain purposes including use as a school site, place of religious worship and other public or charitable purpose in connection with the settled land, or for the benefit of persons residing, or for whom dwellings may be erected, on the settled land.

# Drafting the governing instrument

The first step is to decide upon the type of structure that will be most suitable. The possibilities are as follows:

(a) Trust
(b) Company (normally limited by guarantee)
(c) Unincorporated association
(d) Body incorporated by Royal Charter

## Trusts

A trust is the traditional structure for a charity and the means by which very many, particularly older, charities are established.

**Advantages of trusts** The points in favour of a trust as the vehicle for a charity can be summarised as follows:

(i) The usual arrangement is for new trustees to be appointed by the founder or by the remaining trustees. This means that the trustees may be self-perpetuating, which provides some assurance that persons who are acceptable to those who originally set up the charity will be appointed as trustees in the future and perhaps reduces the danger of disputes arising in the future as to how the charity should be run.

**Self-perpetuating trustees**

**Confidentiality** (ii) The deliberations of the trustees may be private. Charity trustees are answerable for their conduct only to the court and the Charity Commission. They need not give reasons for the way in which they have exercised their discretion on a particular occasion, nor need they disclose to any interested parties (even potential beneficiaries) any documents or details of their deliberations. They can be called to account if

[4] *Re C.M.G.* [1970] Ch. 574.
[5] *Re Clore's Settlement Trusts* [1966] 1 W.L.R. 955.

they have acted capriciously or from an improper motive or outside the terms of the trust but, otherwise, provided that they have considered all the claims they are aware of, their decisions cannot be questioned.

**Cost**     (iii)   A trust need not be expensive to run. There are no official fees payable nor any of the reporting requirements applicable to companies. Although even quite small charitable trusts (having an income of more than £10,000) must now have their accounts independently examined each year only trusts having an annual income in excess of £250,000 are required to have their accounts audited.[6]

**Certainty of law**    (iv)   The nature and scope of a trustee's duties are well established under English law.

          (v)   A charitable trust which may have as few as two (but preferably three) trustees can be very simple to run. Minimal formalities are required and administrative

**Simplicity** complexity can be kept to a minimum. Both companies and unincorporated associations normally require careful attention to the formalities involved in calling general meetings such as ensuring that proper notices are sent to all those entitled to receive them and ensuring that an accurate register of members is maintained if the proceedings of the charity are to be valid. A small body of trustees, on the other hand, may, within the limits imposed by the trust deed, regulate their proceedings as they wish.

**Disadvantages of trusts**    The objections must frequently made to the use of a declaration of trust can be summarised as follows:

**Inflexibility**    (i)   A charitable trust deed may only be altered by an order of the court or of the Charity Commissioners and then only in certain circumstances (see Chapter 11). It is not unusual for the trustees of a charity to be convinced that an alteration in the trust deed is practical and in the interests of the charity but to be informed that the Charity Commissioners do not consider that there are sufficient grounds for altering the trust deed by a scheme or for making the alterations proposed by the trustees.

**Personal liability**    (ii)   Trustees do not have the advantage of limited liability.

**Trustees: removal and appointment**    (iii)   From time to time new trustees must be appointed and the trust assets transferred into the names of the new trustees. Furthermore, it is possible only in certain limited circumstances to remove a trustee.

**Delegation**    (iv)   There are restrictions on the delegation of trustees' powers.

These objections are not all equally valid.

**Powers to vary administrative provisions**    **Inflexibility**   The objection that a trust is inflexible can be met by careful drafting. It is accepted practice to include in a declaration of trust a power to vary the administrative provisions

[6] Charities Act, s.43(2) and (3) and see below, Chap. 10.

of the deed. It is recommended that all charitable declarations of trust should contain such a power in order to avoid the trouble and expense of applying to the Charity Commissioners for a scheme to vary the terms of the trust. This will enable alterations to be made to the trust deed in circumstances where a scheme might, in many cases, be refused, such as where the trustees wish to widen their powers of investment or management in order to meet changing circumstances. Even in cases when the Charity Commissioners agree to a scheme to vary the trusts the terms of the variation will not necessarily be in a form acceptable to the trustees and the procedure for obtaining a scheme will certainly involve considerable correspondence, expense and delay. A charity may after all exist for several generations and provisions appropriate to the 1990s may well be unsuited to the 2090s. The inclusion of a power of variation will guarantee some flexibility for the future.

**Power to vary the objects clause**

As a result of the Commission's present practice of normally only considering applications from established bodies they have had to review their attitude to powers to amend the objects clause. it is now accepted that such a power is acceptable subject to the Commissioners' prior written consent and a suitable clause is included in Information Sheet 2 (Minimum requirements for governing instruments) which is included in the Registration Pack. The clause is reproduced in Appendix C. A power to amend clauses which provide for trustee remuneration, the payment of premiums on trustee indemnity policies and that trustees should not benefit from the charity should all be subject to the same condition that prior consent should first be obtained from the Commission.

A further problem is that a variation of the objects of the charity will not always apply to property held prior to the variation. Whether or not it does so will depend on the intentions of the donor of the property. Did he intend his gift to be used solely for the purposes of the charity as they were at the time of the gift or did he have in mind that the purposes might be altered? This must be ascertained from the particular facts of

**Extent of variation**

each case. For example, a wealthy individual who settles his own property on charitable trusts and instructs his solicitor to include a power of variation in the deed clearly intends the power of variation to apply to the settled property. But it is more difficult to draw this conclusion where a number of individuals are invited to subscribe to a fund for a specific project. In such cases it would be necessary to demonstrate that the power of variation had been drawn to the donors' attention or that they had foreseen the possibility of their gifts being applied for some other purpose before the trustees could direct these funds to the new objects of the charity without the need for a *cy-près* scheme. The practical solution to these problems is that, however limited the

**Wide objects clause**

intended scope of the proposed activities may be, the objects should be drafted in wide terms. For example, a charity set up to promote research into heart disease should have as its main object the relief of sickness generally. The activities of the charity may then be changed without any variation of the trust deed being required if this is found to be desirable provided that the new activities still come within the terms of the original objects clause. This will enable the charity to adapt its activities to changing circumstances without the need to obtain the consent of the Charity Commission.

**Personal liability of trustees**   There is more substance in this objection to the trust structure. The extent to which a trustee may incur personal liability is of particular concern to those involved with charities actively engaged in enterprises involving commercial activity of any kind including property development, the provision of services such as education or the promotion of drama or music or which employ more than a few individuals. Problems can also arise where property (particularly leasehold property) is held. There are occasions when trustees may find themselves personally liable for losses which they would have avoided as directors of a charitable company such as where a claim is made for wrongful dismissal of an employee, breach of contract or occupier's liability. Some problems of liability can be solved by incorporating the trustee as a body corporate under the Charitable Trustees Incorporation Act

**Insurance**   1872.[7] Other potential liabilities can be covered by insurance and the trustees will in most cases be able to reimburse themselves from the funds of the charity but they will be at risk if the funds are insufficient to cover the liability. This topic is dealt with in detail in Chapter 7. The organisers should, therefore, give careful thought to the kind of activities proposed and the likelihood or not of any claims arising. In general, a trust is most suitable for grant-making charities (that is charities whose main activity is raising and distributing funds for the promotion by others of charitable objects) and less so for charities actively involved in commercial or quasi-commercial operations such as schools, colleges or hospitals. For the same reason (as well as for the taxation advantages) trustees of charitable trusts wishing to engage in trading operations in order to raise funds, for example the selling of Christmas cards or other goods, should establish a separate trading company which covenants its income to the charity (see Chapter 12).

**Appointment and removal of trustees**   The need for new trustees to be appointed from time to time to replace vacancies in the body of trustees and for the trust assets to be transferred into the names of the new trustees, which will necessarily involve some trouble and expense, is a further objection to the trust structure. Potential difficulties can be minimised by arranging for any investments and land of the charity to be held in the

**Custodian**   name of a custodian trustee (see page 87) or nominee, avoiding
**trustee**   the need for a transfer of assets on a change of trustees. Alternatively the trustees may be incorporated as a body corporate under the Charitable Trustees Incorporation Act 1872. The provisions of section 83 of the Charities Act (see Chapter 6) may also, if applicable, simplify the procedure in the case of land. However, serious problems can arise if the formalities for the appointment of new trustees are not observed

[7] See Chapter 6.

or if the charity's assets are not vested in new trustees when they are appointed.

Problems can also sometimes arise if a trustee who is for some reason unsuitable or has behaved improperly is not willing to retire voluntarily. In the absence of any specific power to remove a trustee, an application may be made to the court for **Removal of** his removal under section 41 of the Trustee Act 1925 or to the **trustees** Charity Commissioners for his removal under section 18 of the Charities Act but it is unlikely that any remedy will be available unless the administration of the trust has deteriorated to such a degree as to damage the interests of the charity. The converse is, of course, that trustees are independent of the membership of the charity and may act as they consider right in the interests of the charity without fear of being removed because their actions are not approved by others who are involved in the work of the charity.

If greater involvement of the members is desirable the trust deed may provide for this but where the charity is to be effectively controlled by or the trustees are to be answerable to the membership, a company or unincorporated association may be a more suitable structure.

## Companies limited by guarantee

Although a company limited by shares may occasionally be registered as a charity the structure is not generally suitable for a charity and is not discussed in this book.

**Advantages of** The main advantages of incorporating the charity are:—
**companies**

- (i) the power to alter the memorandum and articles;
- (ii) the protection of limited liability;
- (iii) the machinery for involving the members in the running of the charity; and
- (iv) the corporate identity;

The company format is also familiar to many businessmen and accountants which may be an additional point in its favour.

**Flexibility**   The statutory powers to alter the memorandum and articles of a company (the most important of which appear in sections 4 and 9 of the Companies Act 1985) permit the variation of both the principal objects of the company (which appear in the Memorandum of Association) and the regulations which govern administrative matters (the Articles of Association). The prior written consent of the Commissioners is required if any alteration to the objects clause or any other provision in the Memorandum and Articles of Association **Power of** concerned with the manner in which the company's property **variation** may be applied is to be effective.[8] An alteration to the objects which has the effect that the company is no longer established for exclusively charitable purposes will not affect any property which has been given to the charity or represents such property or income from it. Such property will continue to be applicable only for the original purpose. A copy of the Commissioners' consent to the alteration must be submitted to Companies

[8] Charities Act, s.64, and see Chapter 11.

House with the copy of the special resolution authorising the alteration.

It was decided in *Liverpool and District Hospital for Diseases of the Heart v. Att.-Gen.*[9] that property held by a charitable company for its general purposes was not held upon trust (in the strict sense of the word) for the charitable purposes of the company but was held by it beneficially subject to the terms of the memorandum and articles which imposed a legally binding obligation that it should be applied solely for charitable purposes. It would seem, therefore, that where the objects of the company are altered but remain exclusively charitable, all property held by the company for its general purposes whether acquired before or after the variation may thereafter be applied for the new purposes.

**Charitable company property**

There may be occasions when property should not be regarded as being held for the general purposes of the company. Where, for example, funds are raised from the public for the purposes of the charity it is possible, depending upon the intentions of the donors at the time, that the funds raised will be held by the company upon trust for its purposes rather than beneficially. In such a case a subsequent variation of the objects of the company will not affect those funds which will continue to be held for the original purposes. The Commissioners may be prepared to intervene if they consider that a variation of the objects of a charitable company may defeat the intentions of members of the public who have contributed funds to it.

**Limited liability**   The protection of limited liability may be thought desirable if the charity is likely to be involved in any kind of quasi-commercial activity: for example running workshops for disabled people may require the charity to enter into contracts or employ people and this could give rise to liability on the part of the charity. This protection will probably not be required in the case of charities which will seldom be involved in development schemes or trading ventures where limited liability is of prime importance and trustees may protect themselves against many of the hazards inherent in their operations by insurance. But those involved in the administration of the charity may well prefer to minimise the risk of liability. This topic is dealt with in detail in Chapter 7. It should be realised, however, that limited liability does not always provide protection since banks and others lending money to charitable companies may, in some cases, require personal guarantees from the directors and those entering into transactions with the company may insist on the individual directors entering into any contract in their personal capacity. Nor is the protection from liability absolute. The circumstances where directors of charitable companies may be personally liable for losses are set out in Chapter 7.

**Limitations to protection**

**Involvement of members**   Sometimes a degree of involvement on the part of the members is desirable, because they are the main source of funds for the charity or because it is

[9] [1981] Ch. 193.

**Accountability**

felt that the members shall have ultimate control over those managing the company. In such cases a company may have advantages. The directors are answerable to the members for the conduct of the company's affairs and capable of being removed from office by resolution of the company. This distinguishes the company structure sharply from that of a trust. It is possible to admit new members without undue formality and (if necessary) power may be included to expel members.

**Convenience**

**Corporate identity** Since a company is a body corporate with perpetual succession, the need for the property of the charity to be transferred into the names of new trustees from time to time is dispensed with. A company may also be more familiar to businessmen and so facilitate fund-raising and other dealings with the charity. The arrangements for a company to enter into commercial contracts, (for example employment contracts for staff, hiring of premises, advertising, etc.) are likely to be considerably less cumbersome than in the case of a trust.

**Disadvantages of companies**

Generally speaking a company is now no more expensive to run than any other type of charity. The threshold for a compulsory audit is a gross income of £250,000 per annum, the same as for an unincorporated charity. A more substantial objection to a company structure is that people who are unfamiliar with it may find it difficult to understand the structure and the respective roles of the members and the trustees/directors. The need to comply with the requirements of company law to notify Companies House of any changes of directors, and holding general meetings of the members makes the appointment of a company secretary who is familiar with the requirements of the Companies Act essential.

## Unincorporated associations

**Advantages of unincorporated structure**

**Flexibility**

**Cost**

**Variation of constitution**

An unincorporated association has certain advantages over other types of organisation, the chief being its flexibility since it is possible to tailor the constitution to fit the individual case. In particular, this vehicle is well suited to charities where the involvement of many individuals and organisations is desirable. A good example is the village hall where the membership of the association is usually wide and the management is vested in a relatively small committee composed of individuals elected from among the members and representatives of local organisations (see Precedent 3 in Appendix A). Different patterns of constitution can be devised to meet different requirements varying from something close to the structure of a trust where control is in the hands of a committee of management with restricted membership to a democratic structure where the general membership has ultimate control over the way in which the association is administered. An unincorporated association is free of the statutory controls to which companies are subject and can be inexpensive to run.

A well-drafted constitution will include a power to alter its terms, usually subject to the approval of a certain percentage of the membership and, as with a trust, changes to the objects

**Charity Commission Objects clause** clause may be allowed subject to the prior written consent of the Charity Commission (see Information Sheet 2). As with a trust it is advisable for the objects clause to be drafted in wide terms from the outset to provide for the possibility that the charitable objects originally selected will prove to be unsuitable in the course of time and make any application to the Commission for approval of a change unnecessary.

**Disadvantages of unincorporated structure** One drawback of an unincorporated body is that if the charity becomes inactive great difficulties can sometimes be encountered in identifying the persons with the authority to take decisions as to the disposal of the assets or locating a quorum having power to take decisions. This is particularly so when inadequate records have been kept as is often the case when interest in a project has lapsed. These problems can be overcome (see Chapter 6) but not without cost.

**Trustees** A further objection to an unincorporated structure is that provision must be made for individuals to be appointed as trustees to hold the assets, and problems frequently arise in cases where the trust property continues to be vested in persons no longer connected with the running of the charity or where the society has become defunct. In either case it may be difficult or impossible to trace the person in question. A custodian trustee **Custodian trustee** may, once again, prevent this difficulty arising and the Charity Commissioners have power to vest property in suitable persons where the trustee or persons having the power to appoint trustees cannot be identified. However, a certain amount of research is necessary in an attempt to trace the persons having the power to appoint new trustees before the Commissioners will feel able to exercise the powers given to them by section 16 of the Charities Act and this can be a severe burden on the resources of a small charity.

Finally, both members of the management committee and sometimes the members of the association itself may incur personal liability (see Chapter 7).

## Royal Charter

A Royal Charter will normally only be granted to a substantial organisation having a clear public purpose. The grant of a Royal Charter undoubtedly confers upon a charity considerable status and all applications are carefully considered by the Privy **Privy Council Office** Council Office which will scrutinise the proposed Charter with a view to ensuring that it is workable and appropriate to the kind of activity which is to be undertaken. The grant of a Charter does not of itself confer charitable status and separate application must be made to the Charity Commission once the Privy Council approval has been obtained to the draft Charter although it may well be sensible to submit a preliminary draft to the Commissioners in order to ensure the proposals are acceptable in principle.

**Inflexibility** A disadvantage of a Royal Charter is the difficulty of amendment. Any alteration to the Charter is usually effected by a grant of a Supplementary Charter which must be approved by the Privy Council as well as the Charity Commission, both being likely to raise points of principle as well as comments on the drafting though increasingly Charters now allow changes to be made to administrative provisions by resolution of the members subject to approval by the Privy Council. For this reason a Royal Charter is suitable only for national bodies with substantial assets or income such as universities.

# Branches, subsidiary funds and sections

**Determining status**

Many charities have branches, sub-groups and affiliated organisations with differing degrees of independence and it is often difficult to know when these should be registered as separate charities. Practice at the Charity Commission was not consistent in the past but the topic has been clarified recently during the preparation of the Charities Statement of Recommended Practice for Accounting (SORP) (see Chapter 10). The point to be decided in each case is whether or not an organisation is independent of the parent organisation. If it is independent it must be separately registered. If not it may shelter under the umbrella of the main charity. While there are very many ways in which organisations may be linked some pointers which may indicate that an organisation is independent of its parent include:

**Independent charities**

> it has its own constitution or trust deed;
> it uses a different name;
> it is financially independent;
> it is not controlled by the main charity;
> the trustees are not the same as those of the main charity;
> the trustees are not appointed by the main charity.

In such cases the charity will be separately registered and will need to submit its own annual report and accounts to the Commission each year.

## Umbrella funds

**Subsidiary funds**

It is not unusual for a charity to have a number of subsidiary charitable funds established as independent trusts and originating, perhaps, from legacies or gifts and having purposes separate from those of the main charity but connected with its work. Where the main charity or its officers are the trustees of such a fund it may be registered as a subsidiary of the main charity using its registration number. The accounts of the subsidiary may be included in those of the umbrella charity but the accounts must identify the assets belonging to the subsidiary and how the income has been applied.

## Designated or special funds

Many charities have property or cash which may only be used for specified purposes within the overall purposes of the main charity. This may be because of a condition when the gift was made or for some other reason. Some funds will not need to be separately registered if the main charity is the trustee and the fund can be dealt with as a subsidiary or designated fund of the charity but they will be treated as designated funds of the main charity.

## Branches and sections

**Independence *vs.* subsidiary**

Many national charities have a branch network. Where these take the form of separate organisations governed by a model constitution but not answerable to the parent organisation except possibly through paying an affiliation fee, attending an annual meeting or appointing a representative to the parent body's governing body each branch will be a separate charity which should be registered separately.

Charities such as community associations may have groups within their structure which have been formed to carry on specific activities. The relationship between the parent body and the branch or section may change over the years, but it is important to identify whether a section such as a play group or drama association is a separate charity which should be registered as such, an independent voluntary group or part of the overall structure of the community association. It is likely that a section which was established at the same time or in conjunction with the community association will be a section of the association rather than an independent group. Where it was an existing organisation which affiliated to the community association it is probably a separate body which, if charitable, should be registered. The implications of this distinction for the purpose of the accounts and assets of each body is considered in Chapter 10.

**Financial control**

In some cases the parent may exercise some control over the branch's activities through the appointment of representatives to its committee of management or retaining power to remove individual members whose activities are thought to be contrary to the interests of the parent. This will point to the branch being a part of the main charity but whether or not it is fully independent will depend on the facts of each individual case. The references later in this chapter to delegation may be relevant here.

Where the branch is responsible for raising and spending its own funds without reference to the parent it is likely to be a separate charity and will need to be separately registered.

**Duties of parent charity's trustees**

Charity trustees are required to take full responsibility for funds under their control and may only delegate this duty in so far as permitted by the trust deed or constitution. It is therefore most important to ascertain whether a connected organisation is independent or is in reality a part of the main charity. The charity trustees of the parent must ensure that funds held by a branch which is controlled by or is a subsidiary of the main charity are properly administered and may be personally liable if they fail to do so. The accounts of the parent should give details of all branch assets even when the day to day control has been delegated to the branch. The specific reference to this in the Statement of Recommended Practice on Accounting for Charities has made many charities with branches or subsidiaries aware of this fact and that they will need to review their administrative arrangements.[10]

# Registration of the charity

## When registration is required

**Compulsory registration**   Any charity having:

(a) permanent endowment (defined in section 96(3) of the Charities Act) or
(b) the use and occupation of land; or
(c) whose income from all sources is £1,000 or more

is required[11] to be registered unless:

(a) it is an exempt charity by virtue of Schedule 2 to the Charities Act,
(b) it is excepted from the requirement to register by regulations made under section 3(5),
(c) it is a place of worship.

(See Chapter 3, pp. 47–49 for details of exempt and excepted charities.)

## Umbrella charities

The Charities (Amendment) Act 1995 allows charitable funds which have the same trustees to be treated as one for the purposes of registration. The impetus behind this change was the establishment of National Health Service Trusts and the transfer to them of responsibility for several thousand separate charities many of which would be compulsorily registrable. This would have imposed a great burden both on the Charity Commission and the Trusts. The Act allows the main charity to be registered as an umbrella charity and for the funds for which it is responsible to shelter under the same registration.

**Duty to apply**     It is the duty of those responsible for a charity which is compulsorily registrable to apply to the Commissioners for registration. if they do not do so the Charity Commissioners may issue directions requiring them to do so and failure to comply is punishable in the same way as disobedience to a High Court order.[12]

**Voluntary registration**   A charity which is not required to register other than an exempt charity may nonetheless apply voluntarily to be registered and it is often an advantage to a charity that it should be registered since while it is on the register it is conclusively presumed to be a charity. The Commission will consider requests for registration from charities which are not obliged to register when substantial funds are likely to be lost if the charity is not registered. They will also consider cases where the minimum requirements are likely to be met in the first year.

[10] See below, p. 163.
[11] Charities Act, s.3.
[12] Charities Act, s.87.

Charities which intend to raise funds from the public should seek to register voluntarily since registration helps to establish the credentials of the organisation and many institutions will only make grants to charities which are registered. The Commission has tightened up its procedures recently and is not now prepared to register charities which are not currently operating or are unlikely to do so in the near future.

## Application for registration

In 1996 the Commission altered the registration procedure quite radically and introduced a new Registration Pack designed **Registration** to give detailed information to prospective charitable bodies on **Pack** the requirements for charitable status, types of legal structure and the registration procedure. The principal change from the Commission's previous practice is that in general applications will only be considered from organisations which are already established. Draft documents will only be considered in exceptional cases. The reason for this, apparently, was that large numbers of applications were received by the Commission which subsequently did not proceed which wasted a considerable amount of its officers' time. An initial request to the Charity Commission for application forms for registration is now likely to be met with leaflet CC21 "So you want to start a charity?" providing information on the advantages and disadvantages of setting up a charity and the requirements for registration. If the applicant wishes to proceed he will be sent the full application pack which contains three leaflets, CC 21 (a), (b) and (c), which give detailed information on what constitutes a charitable purpose, the different types of governing instrument and the responsibilities of charity trustees, the registration process and what the reporting requirements are for registered charities. The following information sheets are also supplied:

Research Trusts
Minimum requirements for governing document
**Information** Trustees benefitting personally from the charity
**sheets** Guidance on when to use a memorandum & articles of
association
Guidance on when to use a trust deed
Guidance on when to use a constitution or rules
Preparation of governing document check list
Standard governing documents
Fund-raising & trading
Counselling and
Investments.

The information sheets set out the Commission's current practice and views on these topics and detailed guidance which in the past would have had to be obtained from an experienced charity lawyer or consultant.

## Establishing the charity

The next step will be for the governing document (trust deed, constitution or memorandum & articles of association) to be executed.

## Companies

In the case of a company incorporation must take place. A company limited by guarantee the objects of which are the promotion of commerce, art, science, education, religion, charity or any profession and whose memorandum or articles require all its profits to be applied in promoting its objects, prohibit payment of dividends to members and provide that on winding up the assets shall be transferred to another similar body or to charity is exempt from the need to include the word "limited" in its name.[13] A statutory declaration by a solicitor, director or secretary in the prescribed form must be submitted to Companies House with the incorporation papers. A company which comes within the provisions of section 30 may change its name after incorporation by passing the appropriate resolution. Again a statutory declaration must accompany the notice sent to Companies House.

**Omission of "limited" from name**

Once the company has been incorporated a certified copy (signed by a solicitor) should be sent with a copy of the certificate of incorporation to the Commission with the application.

## Unincorporated associations

The constitution or rules of the association should be adopted at a meeting of the management committee. A careful minute should be made of the resolution and a copy of the constitution or rules should be signed by the chairman and attached to the minute. A certified copy of the constitution or rules should be submitted to the Charity Commission with the application.

## Trust deeds

A trust deed will have to be executed as a deed by each of the trustees and any other party to the deed (such as a founder or donor) signing it in the presence of a witness. The deed will have to be sent to the Stamp Duty Office for adjudication but only 50 pence duty is payable. Again a certified copy of the stamped deed should be sent to the Commission.

**Stamp duty**

## The application

The application form (Form APP1) should then be completed. The form asks for detailed information about the activities or proposed activities of the organisation and should be accompanied by any supporting documentation such as publicity material, brochures, articles or prospectuses which may help to clarify its work or intentions. The Commission has

[13] Companies Act 1985, s.30.

power to require such information as they think fit to be supplied to them[14] and time can be saved by anticipating this. The Commission will need to be satisfied that the activities of the organisation will be charitable before agreeing to register. They will be reluctant to register if the governing document is in a charitable form but they suspect that the activities will not be charitable and it is preferable to provide them with all relevant background information in order to avoid giving a misleading impression of the charity's work.

The application form is designed to reveal any potential problems such as benefits to trustees (see below), the possible use of a charity for the purpose of tax avoidance and concealed benefits to donors or members of trustees' families. The Commission will monitor suspect organisations with particular care during their early years.

The first charity trustees are required to sign a declaration consenting to act as trustee and stating that they are not disqualified from acting as a charity trustee.[15]

## Some practical points

**Benefits to individuals**   As was seen in Chapter 2 an organisation directed towards the benefit of individuals rather than the public at large is not charitable. Incidental benefits to individuals are permissible but it is a question of fact in each case whether the balance or poise of the organisation is for public or private benefit. This can be an area of difficulty in many cases and applicants should in such cases address the point from the outset. The difficulty frequently arises where a building is to have a dual purpose, part charitable part social.
**Social benefits**   Where the social element is substantial it may be best to separate the two elements so that, for example, a bar in a village hall is run independently of the charity although its profits may be applied for the benefit of the charity.[16]

Benefits to individuals may also jeopardise charitable status when a substantial part of the work of a professional
**Professional**   organisation is directed to promoting the interests of the
**benefits**   members. The solution in such a case may be to establish two separate organisations. On the one hand a charity to carry out the work of promoting high standards in the profession which should be a charitable purpose and on the other a non-charitable body to undertake the non-charitable work.

Difficult problems can arise when an individual wishes to
**Disposals to**   convert what has been private property such as a private school
**charity**   or an historic house into a charity. If property is to be sold to the new charity steps should be taken to ensure that only a fair market price is paid. If the property is to be leased the rent should be reasonable and the obligations of the charity under the terms of the lease should not be unduly onerous. An independent valuer should be appointed to advise the charity in order to ensure that the terms are fair. While it may not be

[14] Charities Act, s.3(6).
[15] See below, p. 83.
[16] See the Charity Commissioners' leaflet, *Provision of Alcohol on Charity Premises*, CC27.

necessary to demonstrate that the arrangements confer a preferential benefit on the charity at the very least it must be established that they are not unduly advantageous to the individuals concerned at the expense of the charity. In particular any benefits such as rights of occupation reserved to individuals must be carefully scrutinised. These may also give rise to tax problems.[17] Where property is to be given to the charity outright there is a clear benefit to the charity and it may be reasonable for the donor to retain rights of occupation and access but again there may be Inheritance Tax problems. However, the benefits should not outweigh the benefits to the public as might be the case, for example, if public access to an historic building was very restricted and the property continued effectively to be used as a private house. Where property is to be sold or leased to the charity at market rates there will be no such justification for the original owners to derive any benefit.

**Remuneration of trustees**

The Charity Commissioners modified their views on the question of the remuneration of trustees in 1994 and their present approach on this and on the related topic of the employment of trustees is set out in leaflet CC 11 dated August 1994. Previously the Commissioners would raise objections where the governing instrument allowed trustees to be paid for their services as trustees and would only sanction the appointment of an employee as a trustee if they were satisfied that this was necessary in the interests of the charity. The inclusion of a clause allowing the payment of professional trustees such as solicitors and accountants for their professional services has always been permitted.

The current position is that registration will not be refused because the governing instrument includes a power to pay trustees reasonable remuneration for acting as trustee. If the document authorises the payment of a specific sum the Commissioners will need to be satisfied that the amount is reasonable in relation to the work involved. If it appears that the trustee will be receiving a disproportionate benefit from the proposed charity the Commissioners may conclude that the trustee is in effect a beneficiary of the organisation which will therefore not be established for exclusively charitable purposes and registration will be refused. The best course is to include a power to pay only reasonable remuneration and the trustee in question should be required to absent himself from any meeting when his remuneration is being discussed. A provision which is believed to be acceptable to the Commissioners can be found in Appendix C.

Where a charity is to be set up with funds raised from the public the considerations are more complex. Unless it has been made clear to the donors in advance that the trustees are to be paid all donations will be held on trust for the charitable purposes for which they were given and may not be used to remunerate the trustees. This is discussed in more detail in Chapter 12.

In the case of an established charity which has no power to pay trustees in the governing instrument it may not be possible

**Retained benefits by donors of property** *(margin heading)*

---

[17] See the section on Inheritance Tax in Chap. 8.

for the trustees to use a power of variation to add a suitable provision permitting remuneration since this is likely to be a breach of their fiduciary duty. An application to the Charity Commissioners will be necessary and may not be successful. This is discussed in Chapter 11.[18]

**Payment for professional services**   A professional person who is a trustee may be authorised to charge for services performed for the charity in his professional capacity and clause V of Precedent 1 is the Commissioners' preferred wording. It will be seen that this does not authorise non-professional trustees to charge for services provided in the course of their business but the clause may be extended to non-professional trustees. Clause 5 of the memorandum of a charitable company (Precedent 2) prohibits remuneration being paid to members of the managing committee even for professional services but again a suitable clause permitting professional members of the Committee to make a reasonable charge for their services may be added.

A corporate trustee which charges for its services is not acceptable to the Commissioners as a managing trustee of a charity although they will not object to one acting as custodian trustee.

**Trustee insurance**   A specific power for the charity to pay premiums on policies designed to protect trustees against personal liability must be included, if required, since such a payment will be a benefit to the trustees. A suitable clause can be found in Appendix C and the topic is discussed in Chapter 7.

**Trustees as employees**   It is becoming more common for an employee of a charity to be appointed as a charity trustee. But this kind of arrangement does create problems. The employee/trustee will immediately be in a position where his interests as an employee may conflict with his duties as a trustee. Such arrangements are acceptable to the Charity Commissioners but restrictions should be written into the governing instrument to ensure that the charity trustee in question should absent himself from discussions and should not be entitled to vote on the terms of his employment. There should always be a majority of trustees who are not employees. In practice it is seldom necessary for an employee to be a trustee as well. The employee may always be invited to attend trustee meetings and contribute to discussions.

**Delegation**   It is a general principle of trust law that a trustee should not delegate the performance of his duties to others and the Commissioners extend this rule to all types of charity. The Commissioners will not normally object to a power for the

**Delegation to committees**   trustees to delegate to certain of their number if this is shown to be in the interests of the charity. Where there is to be a large number of trustees or meetings are likely to be held infrequently it may be desirable for the conduct of the day-to-day administration to be delegated to committees or individual trustees and a provision authorising this will usually be accepted by the Commissioners provided it requires regular reports from the sub-committee and that it should operate within a prescribed budget.[19]

[18] See p. 185.
[19] See Appendix C.

**Delegation to non-trustees**

The Commissioners are now more ready to permit a power to be included in the trust deed for trustees to delegate their duties to outsiders who may be able to influence the expenditure of trust funds than they used to be. If such an arrangement is considered desirable the power should be in the form set out in Appendix C. This provides that in addition to the normal restrictions mentioned above there should always be at least one charity trustee at a meeting for there to be a quorum.

**Delegation of investment powers**

A provision allowing trustees to delegate investment decisions to an investment manager is a standard provision in private trusts and the court has recently been willing to confer such a power on trustees on an application being made under Trustee Act 1925, s.57.[20] Such provisions are acceptable in charitable governing instruments provided that the charity trustees are required to supervise the manager and receive regular reports from him. Similarly, a power to appoint a nominee to hold the charity's investments should not cause any problems.[21]

## Education and propaganda

Another area which frequently causes problems arises from the distinction between education and propaganda as it is relevant to charities. This was explained in Chapter 2. When seeking to register a charity in the field of education, particularly where the subject-matter has a social or political dimension, it is advisable to provide evidence from the outset to persuade the Charity Commissioners and the Inland Revenue that education in its true sense is intended and that it is not the intention to promote a particular view or theory. Where the subject matter is out of the ordinary expert opinion should be provided in order to satisfy the Commissioners that it is a worthwhile subject for public education. The charity should direct its efforts towards providing the public with information so that individuals may form their own judgment. It should not seek to impose any particular opinion on the public.

## The registration procedure

The application for registration will be dealt with in the first instance by non-legally-qualified staff who have, nonetheless, considerable experience in charity law and are able to refer to a large number of precedents.

**Use of model documents**

An expedited procedure is available in cases where a standard form of governing instrument has been agreed with organisers and with the Inland Revenue. This has been done for a large number of charities having either a number of branches or where many organisations exist having similar aims. These range from organists' associations to Boy Scouts groups and

---

[20] *Steel v. Wellcome Custodian Trustees Ltd.* [1988] 1 W.L.R. 167 and *Anker-Petersen v. Anker-Petersen* (1991) L.S.Gaz. June 1, 1991, discussed in *Trusts & Estates*, Vol. 7, No. 3.

[21] See *Decisions of the Charity Commissioners*, Vol. 2, p. 28–32.

playing fields associations. These governing instruments will be agreed at this stage without further correspondence.

**Commissioners' model documents**

The Commissioners have issued models for a charitable trust, a constitution of an unincorporated association and memorandum and articles of association for a charitable company. Use of these models in straightforward cases may facilitate registration provided that the objects of the organisation will be charitable. They are reproduced in Appendix A. The models for a charitable company and trust will need to be reviewed by a lawyer, as they contain few powers or provisions allowing flexibility in the way the charity will be administered.

The majority of applications will be dealt with by administrative staff in the registration division. They may ask for further information before giving their view on whether the organisation is charitable.

## Processing the application

The staff in registration division are guided by policies established within the Commission. Nevertheless, they are not legally qualified and can sometimes take bad points, misinterpret the way the policy guidelines should be applied in a particular case or gain an erroneous impression of the activities of the organisation. The first response should not therefore be regarded as necessarily final.

Unusual cases or cases which raise legal points will be referred to the legal division for advice, and at this stage the applicant may find himself in correspondence with a lawyer although more often the legal view will be transmitted through the registration staff. Where there seems to be a fundamental disagreement over the charitable status of an organisation it is sometimes helpful to arrange to meet the lawyer dealing with the matter either with, or without the officer dealing with the application. This can sometimes clear up misunderstandings which have arisen in the course of the correspondence and establish the bona fides of the applicants if this seems to be in doubt. The correspondence is likely to proceed at a leisurely pace though efforts are being made to speed up the process. In a genuine case of urgency matters can often be resolved with surprising speed. A time scale of six months for completion of the registration process should be allowed for in a relatively simple case and longer in a more complicated one.

**Time-scale for registration**

## The Inland Revenue

The Inland Revenue, as a person who may be affected by the registration,[22] will be notified if the Commission intends to register an organisation which is unusual or where the decision may set a precedent. The term "a person who is or may be affected by the registration" has been construed restrictively and in practice is confined to the Inland Revenue and rating authorities. A person who has an interest in property which may be transferred to a proposed charity is not affected by

**"a person affected"**

[22] Charities Act, s.4(2).

registration and has no power to object to registration.[23]

## Changing the document

The governing document may not be wholly acceptable to the Charity Commission in its current form. If they consider that the activities of the organisation are charitable and there are no other insuperable problems the registration division staff may suggest that changes should be made to the documentation and will confirm that registration will then be allowed. If the applicant organisation is established as a company or as an unincorporated association with a power of amendment it will be a relatively simple matter for the necessary resolutions to be passed. A certified copy of the amended document should then be submitted to the Commission. If the proposed charity has been set up under a trust deed the position is a little more complicated since a non-charitable purpose trust is likely to be void. Any property held by the trustees on the trusts of the deed will be held on a resulting trust for the donor. If there are a number of donors or some of the donors cannot be traced this will create serious difficulties. All trusts should therefore be set up with a nominal payment to the trustees only so that the arrangements can be unravelled if necessary without undue cost. It is also sensible to delay transferring assets to any proposed charity until the organisation has been registered in order to ensure that the exemption from stamp duty for conveyances or transfers or leases to a body established for charitable persons will be available.[24]

## Acceptance as a charity

If the Charity Commission is satisfied that the organisation is charitable and the Inland Revenue has not objected, the applicant will be notified that the organisation is acceptable for registration. An application form will be sent for completion requiring information which will appear on the Register such as the stated objects, the activities to be carried on and the name and address of the person who will act as correspondent for the charity. Details of the charity's bank and building society accounts will also be requested but these will not be available to the public.

## Charity names

The Charity Commission has power under section 6 of the Charities Act to direct a registered charity to change its name where the current name is the same or too like that of another charity (whether registered or not) or is likely to mislead the public as to its nature or activities. The charity may also be directed to change its name where this includes any of the terms specified in the Charities (Misleading Names) Regulations

---

[23] See Charity Commissioners' Report (1976) paras. 62 to 64.
[24] Finance Act 1982, s.129.

1992[25] or may give the incorrect impression that the charity is connected with the government or any local authority or any body or individual or where the name is in the opinion of the Commission offensive.

The direction must be made within twelve months of registration and the trustees of the charity must give effect to it despite any provision in the governing document and notify the Commission of the new name and the date when it was adopted. The Commission has no power to direct an exempt charity to change its name.

# Reference to the Board of Charity Commissioners

**Appeal against refusal to register**　An appeal against a decision not to register may be made to the Board of Charity Commissioners by any organisation which is fully constituted and which, if it was established for exclusively charitable purposes, would be compulsorily registrable. In cases where draft documentation only has been submitted it will be necessary for the organisation to be established before an appeal can be made and for sufficient assets to be transferred to it to make it eligible for compulsory registration (see Chapter 3). The **Procedure**　appellant will be invited to submit written legal argument for consideration by the Board and the Inland Revenue will also be invited to put forward its views. Only written submissions will be considered and the Board may require additional information before coming to a decision.

A person affected by the registration of an organisation as a charity, in practice only the Inland Revenue and a rating **Appeal against**　authority, see above p. 72, may also appeal to the Board against **registration**　a decision to register. In such a case the appellant will submit a formal memorandum of objection and the proposed charity will be invited to provide legal counter-argument.

The determination of the Board will be communicated to the parties once a decision has been made and they will be informed of their right of appeal to the High Court. The determination of the Board cannot be rescinded unless new information becomes available or a change of circumstances occurs (such as a relevant High Court decision).

# Appeals to the High Court

There is no procedure for appeal against the Charity Commissioners' refusal to register an organisation which is not compulsorily registrable. Many organisations register voluntarily because they would otherwise find it difficult to raise funds and a refusal to register can therefore be a serious set-back, but such organisations are obliged to accept the decision of the officials in the Charity Commission responsible for the registration of charities and may not appeal either to the Board or to the High Court. A person interested who is aggrieved by a

[25] See above, Chapter 3, p. 51.

decision to register such an organisation may appeal in the usual way.

**Procedure**

**Costs**

An appeal to the High Court against a decision of the Charity Commissioners does not constitute "charity proceedings" and there is no need for authorisation by the Charity Commissioners before proceedings are instituted or defended. The great expense of an application to the court deters most organisations from appealing against the Commissioners' refusal to register it as a charity and there have been few such cases since the Charities Act was passed. Aware that in most cases there is effectively no appeal against their decisions the Commissioners consider that they should take a generous approach to the interpretation of the legal principles established by the few reported cases on charitable status and that they should generally favour charity. If they adopted a strict approach this would, they feel, prevent charities from meeting the changing needs of society.[26]

**Role of Attorney-General**

An appeal against a decision of the Board not to register should be commenced by an application in the Chancery Division. The Attorney-General is a necessary party to such an appeal in his role as the protector of charities.[27] Any organisation considering such an appeal should approach the Attorney-General to enlist his support if possible. The Attorney-General may, however, seek to have his costs paid by the proposed charity.

An appeal may also be brought against a decision of the Commissioners to register an organisation as a charity by any person who has objected to registration, such as the Inland Revenue. Again the charity should try to obtain the support of the Attorney-General in the proceedings.

## The effect of registration

An organisation which is registered as a charity is for all purposes conclusively presumed to be a charity (Charities Act, s.4(1)) though mistakes can be rectified.

If an appeal is made to the High Court against a decision of the Charity Commissioners to register or to retain the organisation on the register, the entry is suspended and is deemed not to be on the register until the suspension is lifted.

[26] See Charity Commissioners' Report (1985), paras. 24 to 32.
[27] R.S.C. Ord. 108, r. 5.

# 5 THE WORDING OF THE OBJECTS CLAUSE

**The importance of correct drafting**

The correct drafting of the objects clause is of crucial importance in the registration process. It is on this that the success or failure of many applications for charitable status depends and great care should therefore be taken in framing suitable wording. The inclusion of extraneous material or lack of clarity in stating the objects may lead the Charity Commissioners or the Inland Revenue to ask misconceived questions and even occasionally to the refusal of registration when the proposed activities themselves could, if properly expressed, have been brought within a charitable framework.

This chapter is intended to give some broad guidelines for the drafting of objects clauses and the interpretation of clauses in existing documents. Although most of the principles have been developed in relation to trusts, they are nonetheless relevant to companies and unincorporated associations. For consideration of more technical matters concerning the construction of charitable trusts the standard textbooks on trusts and charities should be referred to.

## Exclusivity of charitable purposes

A charity is defined in section 96 of the Charities Act as "any institution, corporate or not, which is established for charitable purposes ..." and section 97 provides that charitable purposes means "purposes which are exclusively charitable according to the law of England and Wales." It is therefore essential that the stated purposes are worded in such a way as to ensure that only purposes which are clearly charitable may be pursued.

The requirement that the intended purposes must be exclusively charitable is illustrated by the case of *Morice v. Bishop of Durham*[1] in which a bequest to the Bishop for "such objects of benevolence and liberality" as he should most approve was held to be void for uncertainty even though the Bishop was willing to execute the trusts in favour of charity. Other examples

**Examples**

of purposes which have been held not to be exclusively charitable are "pious purposes" "philanthropic purposes" "missionary work" and "the work of the parish." It must be clear that there is an obligation to devote the fund exclusively to charitable purposes. It is insufficient that the whole of the fund could within the terms of the gift be applied to charitable purposes if it could also be applied to purposes which are not charitable. In *Ellis v. I.R.C.*[2] a trust to provide a building for use as a Roman Catholic Church or chapel or for other purposes which were clearly charitable was rendered invalid by the

[1] (1805) 10 Ves. 522.
[2] [1949] 31 T.C. 178.

inclusion of the following additional words: "or generally in such manner for the promotion and aiding of the work of the Roman Catholic church in the district" as the trustees may prescribe. This was held to authorise the use of the building for non-charitable purposes and the trust was held invalid.

Particular care must therefore be taken when drafting to analyse the words used to ensure that they could not be interpreted as including non-charitable purposes.

## Construction of "and" and "or"

**Conjunctive construction of "or"**

A number of cases have turned on the question how the word "or" should be construed where there is a gift to charitable purposes or to purposes which are non-charitable, for example, for "charitable or public purposes." In most cases a gift for such purposes will not be charitable since it could within the terms of the gift be applied for non-charitable purposes, the word "or" being construed in its normal sense as expressing alternatives. This construction has been made in the following cases: "charity or works of public utility" "charitable or benevolent purposes" and "charitable or public purposes."[3]

In some cases, however, the court has been prepared to interpret "or" not as expressing alternatives but as expressing a condition or a series of conditions which must be observed in carrying out the terms of the gift. If one of those conditions is charitable the gift will be a valid charitable gift. In effect "or" is interpreted as meaning "and." Clearly such phrases should be avoided when drafting.

**Disjunctive construction of "and"**

A gift for charitable and non-charitable purposes ("charitable and benevolent"; "charitable and deserving") is normally construed conjunctively, as expressing certain qualifications both or all of which must be met in applying the gift. However, occasionally "and" may be construed disjunctively, as expressing alternatives. This is more probable where the number of qualifications is large, since it is unlikely that the donor would have intended the gift to be subject to a large number of conditions.[4] However each case will turn on its particular wording. A gifts for "religious, charitable and philanthropic projects" has been held not to be charitable as has a gift for "benevolent, charitable and religious purposes." In a recent case[5] a trust for "education and welfare," was held to be invalid. The court decided that since it was difficult to imagine a purpose connected with the education of a child which was not also for the child's welfare the term "welfare" could not be interpreted as qualifying education and must have a wider meaning if it had any meaning at all.

## Statutory validation

**1954 Act**

The Charitable Trusts (Validation) Act 1954 was passed in order to save for charity gifts which suffer from certain limited defects which would otherwise cause them to fail. It is very

---

[3] See *Blair v. Duncan* [1902] A.C. 37.
[4] *Re Eades* [1920] 2 Ch. 353.
[5] *Att.-Gen. of the Bahamas v. Royal Trust Co.*, 1986 1 W.L.R. 1001.

restricted in its scope and has caused considerable difficulties of interpretation.

The Act applies only to instruments taking effect before December 16, 1952, which contain "an imperfect trust provision." This is defined (section 1) as "any provision declaring the objects for which property is to be held or applied, and so describing those objects that, consistently with the terms of the provision, the property could be used exclusively for charitable purposes, but could nevertheless be used for purposes which are not charitable." The effect of the Act is that an imperfect trust provision is deemed to have effect as if during the period to December 16, 1952, the objects were charitable and thereafter the property is to be held or applied for the declared purposes only insofar as they are charitable. The Act also applies to fund-raising appeals.

**Effect of validation**

The scope of the Act has been considered in a number of cases from which the following principles may be drawn:

**Scope of the Act**

(1) While a provision such as "charitable or benevolent purposes" is clearly an imperfect trust provision, difficulties of interpretation have arisen where the objects are expressed in wide terms which could include charitable as well as non-charitable purposes. It seems that the Act will only apply where one of the stated objects is charitable or at least has "a flavour of charity" about it. A trust for "welfare purposes" has been held to be an imperfect trust provision[6] since the term was considered to imply the relief of poverty which is a primary object of welfare trusts. However, it seems that where the stated purposes do not have a clear charitable connotation, for example "philanthropic or benevolent" the trust will not be validated.

(2) Neither a private discretionary trust such as a discretionary trust for the benefit of employees nor a trust which is for some other reason (for example uncertainty) invalid can be validated under the Act.

(3) In *Re Gillingham Bus Disaster Fund*[7] an appeal published in a newspaper was held to be an instrument for the purposes of the Act.

Section 3 of the Act contains some protection for persons who might otherwise have had a claim based on the invalidity of the gift.

## Vagueness

Vagueness of the stated objects is a defect which will render an organisation non-charitable. In *I.R.C. v. Baddeley*[8] it was said by Lord Reid that "it is of course necessary that the purposes should be sufficiently precise to enable a court to determine, if a question should arise, whether a particular activity is authorised

---

[6] *Re Wykes Will Trusts* [1961] Ch. 229.
[7] [1959] Ch. 62.
[8] [1955] A.C. 572 at 598.

by them or not." It must be clear that only charitable purposes
are intended. The employment of vague and indefinite
expressions such as "the promotion of the religious social and
physical well-being" of the residents (the wording in question in
the *Baddeley* case) will make it impossible for the court to
conclude that only charitable purposes are authorised. However
a gift may still be charitable even though the motives or ultimate
aims of the donor are vague and indeterminate, if it is
established that the proposed activities are themselves
charitable. Thus in *Re Koeppler's Will Trust*[9] the aims of the
institution which was to benefit under the will were the
"formation of an informed international public opinion and the
promotion of greater co-operation in Europe and the West in
general," aims which were too comprehensive to be charitable.
However the gift was construed as a gift to the institution itself
and since its work was held to be clearly educational the gift was
upheld. The wide and vague scope of the testator's underlying
purpose in making the gift did not affect the charitable nature of
the work or of the gift to promote that work.

## Ambiguity

Many problems of interpretation have arisen through use of
inaccurate names, ambiguous descriptions and references to
institutions which have ceased to exist or have been
amalgamated with others. The importance of expressing the
purposes of the charity in clear and unambiguous terms and of
checking the correct name of any charity or other institution
which is to benefit can hardly be over-emphasised.

Although a detailed discussion of the principles of
construction in relation to charitable trusts is beyond the scope
of this book a brief indication of the most important
considerations may be helpful.

The court leans in favour of charity. The application of this
general rule to questions of construction means that if a gift is
reasonably capable of two interpretations, one of which would
make it charitable and the other void, the court will adopt the
former.

**Ambiguous expressions**     Extrinsic evidence may be admitted in order to elucidate
the meaning of ambiguous expressions. Evidence may be
admitted to clarify the meaning the donor generally attached to
the words in dispute but it is not permissible to introduce
evidence in order to contradict or alter the clear meaning of
words in the instrument. Thus evidence of the connections of a
settlor with a particular religious sect has been allowed in order
to clarify the meaning of a trust for "godly preachers of Christ's
Holy Gospel."[10] But evidence to show that a testatrix had used
the term "worthy causes" in her will to mean charitable
purposes was not admissible since it only related to that
particular occasion as distinct from her habitual usage.[11] In
construing ancient deeds the court may admit evidence of usage

[9] [1986] Ch. 423.
[10] *Shore v. Wilson* [1842] 9 Cl. & F. 355.
[11] *Re Atkinson's Will Trusts* [1978] 1 W.L.R. 586.

which, where the terms are ambiguous, support one or other interpretation since it is presumed that the charity has been administered in accordance with its trusts. Long usage will not however contradict the clear expression of a trust.[12]

If there is doubt about the identity of the recipient of a gift, extrinsic evidence may be admitted in order to resolve the point. A slight inaccuracy of description such as the substitution of "vicar" for "rector" or the use of a former name is immaterial if **Questions of** the identity of the intended recipient is otherwise clear. Where a **identity** charity changes its name and/or its objects the charity itself still continues in existence and is entitled to receive the gift. In other cases the institution which was intended to benefit may have been amalgamated with another and the court will then order to gift to be made to the new body.

Sometimes the description given of the object of the gift could apply to more than one institution or charity. Where the institution has simply been wrongly named and the gift might have been intended for any one of two or more institutions with similar names or engaged in work in similar fields then evidence of the donor's connections with or interest in one of them may be relevant. Failing evidence of this kind the location of the institution may be a determining factor where a place name forms part of the name of the institution. Thus a gift to the "Westminster Hospital Charing Cross" has been given to the Charing Cross Hospital rather than to the Westminster Hospital.[13] If the intended institution has been divided into two, the fund will also be divided.

Where, despite enquiry, it has not been possible to ascertain which of two institutions was the intended beneficiary the court will order the fund to be divided between them but, this will be by way of a variation of the trusts under the court's powers to make schemes (see Chapter 10).

The accurate use of a name creates a strong presumption that the holder of the name was intended to benefit which will only be overcome in exceptional circumstances.[14]

**Gifts to religious** So many problems arose in the eighteenth and nineteenth **groups** centuries over the interpretation of gifts to non-conformist religious sects that legislation was passed providing that where a place of worship was held upon trusts which did not expressly state the particular doctrines to be practised there, 25 years usage was to be conclusive evidence of the purposes for which the property was held.[15] Similar provisions in relation to catholic charities were contained in the Roman Catholic Charities Act 1860, 20 years usage being conclusive. Many dissenting sects authorise the use of model trust deeds in order to avoid this kind of problem.

**Gifts to office** A gift to the holder of an office, such as a rector or mayor, **holders** does not necessarily imply that he takes in his official capacity rather than for his own individual benefit. The question may be resolved by reference to the terms of the gift but will otherwise fail for uncertainty. A gift to a charitable institution however will

---

[12] *Att.-Gen. v. Smythies* (1833) 2 R. & M. 717.
[13] *Bradshaw v. Thompson* (1843) 2 Y. & C.C.C. 295.
[14] *Re Raven* [1915] 1 Ch. 673 and *N.S.P.C.C. v. N.S.P.C.C.* [1915] A.C. 207.
[15] Non-conformist Chapels Act 1844.

take effect as a gift for its general purposes unless the contrary can be implied from the wording of the gift.

**Need for accuracy**
It is therefore essential, when drafting a gift to charity, to ensure that the recipient is accurately named or described (by reference, in the case of a registered charity, to the Central Register of Charities or to The Law Society's Charity and Appeals Annual Directory) and that the purposes are precisely and accurately stated.

## The Administration of Justice Act 1982

**Rectification**
If the court is satisfied that because of a clerical error or a failure to understand the testator's instructions a will does not carry out the testator's intentions then it may order that the will shall be rectified. An application must be made under section 20 of this Act within six months of the grant of probate or letters of administration. it is now possible therefore, but only in the case of wills, for evidence to be introduced to show that wording which is not ambiguous, nevertheless, does not represent the donor's wishes.

**Ambiguous wording in wills**
Section 21 of the Administration of Justice Act 1982 provides that if any part of a will is meaningless or ambiguous on the face of it (such as where the amount of the bequest is left blank) or proves to be ambiguous in the light of surrounding circumstances then, extrinsic evidence including evidence of the testator's intentions may be admitted in order to establish the correct interpretation.

# Perpetuity

A trust for charitable purposes may continue in perpetuity. This is the one exception to the rule that a trust for an indefinite period is void for perpetuity. However, the rule against perpetuities applies to charitable trusts in the following situations.

**Conditional gifts to charity**
Where there is a gift to charity subject to a prior condition, that condition must be fulfilled within the perpetuity period or the gift over may be void. A gift over to charity which was to take effect when vivisection was abolished by law, an event which might have occurred after the perpetuity period, was void.[16] It is now necessary to wait and see if the gift over will take effect within the perpetuity period (Perpetuities and Accumulations Act 1964, section 3).

**Gift over from charity**
A gift over from a charity to an individual, or for a non-charitable purpose upon the occurrence of a condition will take effect only if the condition is fulfilled within the perpetuity period. An example of such a condition was where property was given to trustees to establish schools with a proviso that if the Government were to establish a general system of education the property should pass to the donor's heirs. This constituted a gift subject to a condition which, since it might occur outside the

---

[16] *Re Wightwicks Will Trusts* [1950] Ch. 260.

perpetuity period, was held to be void and the charity took outright.[17]

If, however, the gift to charity is construed not as an absolute gift subject to a condition, but as a gift for a period determinable on the occurrence of certain events, the perpetuity **Determinable** rule will not apply. Gifts for schools were frequently made **gifts** determinable upon the closure of the school when the property would revert to the donor's family. Such interests are normally expressed as being effective "during" a certain period or "while" certain conditions are fulfilled.

**Gifts between** A gift over from a charity to another charity is valid **charities** whenever it might occur. In *Christ's Hospital v. Grainger*,[18] 200 years after the initial gift the donee failed to observe the directions of the will for one year. The court upheld the condition of the will that the legacy should in these circumstances be transferred to another charity.

## Impossibility and illegality

**Illegal** A gift to a charity subject to an illegal condition will take effect as an absolute gift to the charity. If the gift is subject to a condition **Impossible** which from the outset or, subsequently becomes impossible to comply with, the property given will also vest in the charity free of the condition unless there is a gift over.

---

[17] *Re Bowen, Lloyd Phillips v. Davis* [1893] 2 Ch. 491.
[18] (1849) 1 Mac. & G. 460.

# 6 APPOINTMENT, RETIREMENT AND REMOVAL OF CHARITY TRUSTEES

The term "charity trustees" is defined in section 97 of the Charities Act as meaning the persons having the general control and management of the administration of a charity. The expression is not, therefore, confined to trustees of charitable trusts but includes the directors of charitable companies and members of committees of management of unincorporated charitable associations. This chapter describes the rules contained in the Charities Act for disqualifying certain persons from acting as charity trustees. A brief outline is then given of the formalities for the appointment and retirement of trustees, directors and committee members which applies equally to non-charitable organisations. The powers of the Charity Commissioners in respect of charity trustees are then explained.

## Disqualification of trustees

Although the Commissioners had power under the Charities Act 1960 to remove a trustee from office if he had been guilty of misconduct or mismanagement and in certain other circumstances there were no provisions similar to those in the Company Directors (Disqualification) Act 1987 to prevent such **Sections 72 and** a person from acting as a trustee again. Nor was there anything **73 of the** to stop a person convicted of fraud or theft from becoming a **Charities Act** trustee of a charity. These omissions have now been corrected.

Sections 72 and 73 Charities Act provide that a person is disqualified from acting as a charity trustee or a trustee for a charity (*i.e.* custodian or holding trustee) if:

    (a)  he has been convicted of an offence involving dishonesty or deception;

    (b)  he has been adjudged bankrupt or his estate has been sequestrated and he has not been discharged;

    (c)  he has made a composition or arrangement with his creditors and has not been discharged;

    (d)  he has been removed from office by the Commissioners under the Charities Act on the grounds of misconduct or mismanagement in the administration of a charity for which he was responsible, facilitated or contributed to or to which he was privy or by the High Court;

    (e)  he has been removed from the management or control of any body under the Law Reform (Miscellaneous Provisions) (Scotland) Act 1990;

    (f)  he is disqualified from acting as a director of a company by an order made under the Company Directors

Disqualification Act 1987 or is subject to an order under the Insolvency Act 1986 for failing to pay under a county court administration order.

**Spent convictions**

A conviction which is spent under the Rehabilitation of Offenders Act 1974, does not disqualify a person from acting as a charity trustee.

**Leave to act**

An undischarged bankrupt who has been given leave to act as a director of a charitable company under Company Directors Disqualification Act 1986, s.11 is not disqualified from acting as a charity trustee.

A person who is disqualified from acting does not automatically vacate office unless the governing document so provides, but he may not act as trustee of the charity while disqualified. In the case of a charitable trust he may be replaced by appointing another trustee under section 36(1) of the Trustee Act 1925 which provides that a trustee who is incapable of acting may be replaced.

A person who has been disqualified as a director of a company may act as a director of a charitable company if leave has been given under the terms of the disqualification order or by the court (s.72(3)).

**Waiver**

The Charity Commissioners have power (s.73(4)) to waive a person's disqualification and allow him to act as a charity trustee but this does not override the provisions of the Company Directors Disqualification Act 1986 to allow a person who is prohibited from acting as a director under that Act to be a director of a charitable company. The policy of the Commissioners in considering applications for waiver of disqualification is set out in Volume 1 pp. 26–28 and Volume 2 pp. 11–13 of the Decisions of the Charity Commissioners. Such matters as the gravity of the offence and any potential risk to the trust fund or the reputation of the charity will be relevant. The other trustees must support the application in writing. There is a presumption that an undischarged bankrupt or a person who has made a composition with his creditors is unfit to act as a charity trustee[1] and the applicant must be able to satisfy the Commissioners that a waiver should be granted. It seems that an application is more likely to succeed if the trustee in question will not be chairman or treasurer or a signatory on the charity's bank account. A waiver is unlikely to be granted where the applicant is involved in the charity's financial administration or fund-raising or has a controlling interest in a company in which the charity has an investment or has given property to the charity.

**Register**

The Commissioners keep a public register of persons who have been removed from office by them or the High Court.

**Offences**

A person who acts as a charity trustee while disqualified is guilty of a criminal offence punishable by up to two years in prison or a fine or both. This does not apply in the case of an undischarged bankrupt or person disqualified under the Company Directors Disqualification Act 1986 or the Insolvency Act 1986 who acts as a director of a charitable company while

---

[1] *Re Barker's* Trusts [1875] 1 Ch. 43.

disqualified. Such persons are subject to sanctions under those acts.

# Beneficiaries as Trustees

There is an increasing trend towards including beneficiaries of a charity or potential beneficiaries in the body of trustees. While this may be desirable for many reasons it can also give rise to problems. Conflicts of interest may arise and it may not always be easy for beneficiaries to give full weight to the wider interests of the charity. Provided that safeguards are included in any position in the governing document to minimise the risk of a conflict of interest the Commission generally support the appointment of beneficiaries as charity trustees. The governing document should require the beneficiary trustee to be absent from any meeting at which any donation or benefit to him is discussed.

# Trustees of charitable trusts

## Who may be a trustee

**Office holders**

**Individuals**    Any adult person who is not disqualified from acting as a charity trustee by section 72 of the Charities Act may be a trustee. The appointment of a minor as a trustee is void. A trustee may be appointed by name or by virtue of his office, for example the chairman for the time being of a parish or district council, the headmaster of a school or the rector of a university. However, successive holders of the office will not automatically have the assets of the charity vested in them and care should therefore be taken to ensure that this is done on each occasion. Alternatively, the assets may be vested in a custodian trustee or the official custodian for charities so that the need for property to be transferred into the names of new trustees on each change of trustees is dispensed with.

**Local authorities**

**Corporations**    A corporation may, if its constitution so authorises, hold property on charitable trusts either alone if it is a trust corporation or jointly with individuals subject to the restrictions on the numbers of trustees mentioned below. City livery companies and municipal corporations frequently act as trustees of charitable trusts. Local authorities (county councils, district councils, London borough councils and parish and community councils) may hold property upon charitable trusts for the benefit of the inhabitants of their area or part of it, except property to be held upon trust for the benefit of the poor or upon ecclesiastical trusts.[2] The Charity Commission have encountered cases where a local authority acting as sole trustee of a charity has applied charitable funds for some other local purpose and are also concerned that conflicts of interest may arise. They are not therefore now prepared to appoint a local authority as a sole trustee of a charity unless fully satisfied that this will be in the charity's best interests.[3]

[2] Local Government Act 1972, s.139.
[3] *Decisions of the Charity Commissioners*, Vol. 1, p. 29.

A bank trustee company may act as a charity trustee but their charges are substantial and, as was mentioned in Chapter 4, the Commissioners do not approve of the payment of fees to a trustee and do not consider a corporate trustee which charges for its services to be suitable as the managing trustee of a charity although it may be acceptable as a custodian trustee.

The Public Trustee is precluded from acting as trustee of a charitable trust.[4]

**Incorporation of Trustees**

The advantage for trustees of charitable trustees of arranging for property to be vested in the Official Custodian for Charities is that this makes it unnecessary for the property to be vested in the names of new trustees from time to time when changes occur through deaths and retirements. Now that the Official Custodian will no longer hold property other than land[5] many, particularly smaller, charities will have to take responsibility for ensuring that changes in the body of trustees are properly documented and the charity's property transferred which will add to the expenses and inconvenience of administration. A solution to these problems is for the trustees to seek incorporation. The procedure has recently been simplified.[6] Trustees of a registered, exempt or excepted charity may apply to the Commissioners for a certificate of incorporation and if this is granted the trustees will become a corporate body able to sue and be sued in the name of the trust. The rights and liabilities of the trustees will pass automatically to the successors. The application for incorporation must be in writing signed by the trustees. Incorporation does not affect the responsibilities of the individual trustees or the risk of them incurring personal liability (s.64).

The Commissioners may attach conditions to the certificate of incorporation. They also have power to dissolve the corporate body[7] and the property of the charity will then vest in the individual trustees again.

It is likely that an increasing number of charities will take advantage of the simplified incorporation procedure.

**Perpetual trustee**

**Corporation sole**   A corporation sole is an entity having perpetual succession constituted in a single person by virtue of his office or function. A corporation sole may hold real and personal property in perpetuity even though there may be vacancies in the office from time to time. They were originally mainly ecclesiastical in origin but are now various. For example, the Sovereign is a corporation sole as are some government ministers and officers, such as the Secretary of State for Defence and the Treasury Solicitor. The corporations sole most likely to be encountered in the context of charity are the religious corporations such as a Church of England archbishop and bishop, a vicar, a rector, a dean and an archdeacon. It is now usual for a rector or vicar to be replaced as trustee of a charity with the local diocesan board of finance as custodian trustee and the parochial church council as managing trustee.

---

[4] Public Trustee Act 1906, s.2(5).
[5] See Chap. 3.
[6] Charities Act, Part VII.
[7] Charities Act, s.61.

## Custodian trustees

The role of a custodian trustee is to hold the trust assets. He plays no part in the administration of the charity which is in the hands of managing trust and he must deal with the trust assets in accordance with the directions of the managing trustees unless he is aware that to do so would constitute a breach of trust. He is entitled to be reimbursed for his expenses.

**Advantages** A two tier structure of custodian trustee and managing trustees is particularly useful where a large number of people are involved in the running of the charity and there are frequent changes in the membership of the body of trustees. The appointment of a custodian trustee avoids the need for assets to be transferred to new trustees on every new appointment and for a number of signatures to be obtained each time assets are disposed of.

The appointment of a custodian trustee also prevents problems arising when there has been a failure to transfer trust assets in to the names of the new trustees with the result that difficulties arise in establishing title to the charity property. Failure to vest securities in new trustees can occasionally result in loss of the charity since holdings, if registered in the name of the last surviving trustee, can become confused with his personal holdings. For these reasons where it is possible that the formalities will not be complied with, perhaps particularly where the charity is small or locally run and professional advisers will not be involved, consideration should be given to appointing a corporate custodian trustee to hold the assets of the charity. Banks will provide this service and are permitted to charge at the current rate permitted under the Public Trustee Act 1906. In the case of Church of England charities the Central Board of Finance or, for local charities, the Diocesan Boards of Finance may act as custodian trustees. Other Christian churches such as Methodists and Congregationalists have corporate bodies with similar functions.

**The official custodian** Land belonging to a charity may be held by the Official Custodian for Charities as custodian trustee. No specific provision in the trust deed is required to authorise the appointment of the Official Custodian and the Commissioners will, on the application of the charity, vest property in him by order and without charge.

## Appointment of trustees

**The number of trustees**   There is no upper limit on the number of trustees of a charitable trust. The restrictions imposed by section 34 of the Trustee Act 1925 in the case of trusts of land do not apply but there should always be two trustees or a trust corporation unless only one trustee was originally appointed and no land is held by the charity.[8] A corporation appointed to be a trustee of a charity either by the court or the Commissioners is a trust corporation for the purposes of the Act. Since trustees of a charity may act by

[8] Trustee Act 1925, ss. 14 and 37 and Charities Act, s.35.

majority it is desirable in practice for there to be at least three trustees.

**The initial appointment**    The first trustees are normally appointed by the donor in the trust deed. However, if none are appointed or those appointed are incapable of acting, are dead or refuse to act the trust does not fail for want of trustees. Once a trust has been created the donor or other person who holds the trust property will be the trustee and may appoint new trustees to carry out the terms of the trust. If inadequate machinery for the appointment and retirement of trustees is provided in the trust deed then an application may be made to the Charity Commissioners for a scheme under section 16 of the Charities Act (see Chapter 11).

*Absence of trustees*

**Appointment under the Trustee Act 1925**    In the absence of specific provisions in the trust deed sections 36 to 40 of the Trustee Act 1925 will apply to a charitable trust in the same way as to a private trust. These provide that a new trustee may be appointed in place of a trustee who:

(a) is dead;

*Grounds for replacement*

(b) remains outside the United Kingdom for more than 12 months;

(c) desires to be discharged;

(d) refuses or is unfit to act;

(e) is incapable of acting; or

(f) is an infant.

Absence abroad must be for a continuous period of twelve months in order to bring the power into operation. As to what constitutes unfitness there is little authority. It seems that since bankruptcy or conviction of a crime are grounds for the removal of a trustee by the court[9] they would also be grounds for his replacement under section 36. Presumably, misconduct in relation to the administration of the charity and disqualification under Charities Act, s.72 would also enable a trustee to be replaced under the section.

**Express powers of appointment**    The power of appointing new trustees may be conferred upon any individual by name or upon the holder of an office. The powers may be set out in detail in which case they will be interpreted strictly or the appointor may simply have the statutory powers conferred upon him. The appointor may appoint himself (if not specifically precluded from doing so) but where he is exercising the statutory power he may only appoint himself as a replacement trustee not as an additional trustee.[10]

*Self appointment*

The trust deed may also impose restrictions upon the exercise of the power of appointing new trustees, for example by requiring that the trustees should possess certain residential, educational or other qualifications. Such limitations may be imposed for good reasons but, in the case of a new charity should generally be avoided because of the possibility of

*Qualifications of trustees*

[9] *Ibid.*, s.41.
[10] Trustee Act 1925, s.36(6).

changing circumstances resulting in their becoming inappropriate in which case the trusts of the charity will require alteration. Sufficient safeguards can probably be achieved by conferring the power of appointing new trustees on the holder of an office connected with the area in which the charity is to operate or with the kind of work it is to undertake.

Even when no express restrictions appear in the trust deed the trustees of charities for religious purposes or for the benefit of persons of a particular religion or denomination should be persons professing those beliefs. It has been held[11] to be improper to appoint as trustees of such a charity persons who do not do so and the Charity Commissioners have refused to appoint trustees of a religious charity who are unconnected with that religion.

**Devolution of trusteeship**   In the absence of any person having the power of appointing new trustees the power is vested in the surviving or continuing trustees unless the trust deed provides otherwise.

**Death of sole trustee**   On the death of a sole or the last surviving trustee and if the power of appointing new trustees is not under the terms of the trust deed vested in any particular individual then the power of appointing new trustees passes to his personal representatives (*i.e.* his executors or, if he died intestate, those to whom Letters of Administration have been granted). Until new trustees are appointed they may exercise all the powers of a properly appointed trustee of the trust.

## Supplementary provisions for the appointment and retirement of trustees

**Additional trustees**   Section 37 of the Trustee Act 1925 permits the appointment of additional trustees and of a separate set of trustees for property held on distinct trusts.

**Retirement of trustees**   A trustee may retire from his trusteeship without another being appointed in his place subject to the consent of his co-trustees and any person having the power of appointing trustees but, only if on his retirement there will remain a trust corporation or at least two individual trustees.[12]

**Removal of a trustee under a special power**   Although such a power, often conferred upon a settlor, is not unusual in the case of private trusts it is seldom found in a charitable trust. A power to remove trustees should not affect the charitable status of a trust and could operate to ensure the charity continues to be administered in accordance with the settlor's

**Not a veto**   intentions but the Charity Commission may object to a provision which would effectively impose a veto on the trustees' exercise of their powers.

[11] *Re Norwich Charities* (1837) 2 Myl. and Cr. 275.
[12] Trustee Act 1925, s.39.

**Memorandum of appointment of discharge**

**Vesting of property** Where a trust deed provides that trustees may be appointed and discharged by a resolution of the trustees, a memorandum of the appointment or discharge which is executed as a deed by the person presiding at the meeting (or as directed in the trust deed) and attested by two persons present at the meeting will operate to vest any property subject to the trust (except shares stock or other property which can only be transferred by an alteration in the books of a company or other body, leasehold property requiring a licence or consent to assign and mortgages) in the new or continuing trustees.[13] For a memorandum see Appendix A, Precedent 5 (p. 224).

In other cases section 40 of the Trustee Act 1925 provides that a deed of appointment or discharge which contains a declaration that the property subject to the trust shall vest in the new trustees that will have the same effect.

**Stocks and shares**

Government stock and other securities may only be transferred into the names of the new or continuing trustees by transfers signed by the persons in whose name they are registered.

# Directors of charitable companies

## Who may be a director

Directors of a charitable company are usually described in the Articles as trustees or members of a management committee but in order to differentiate them from trustees they will be referred to in this section as directors. An adult person or corporation may be appointed a director of a charitable company except:

(a) an undischarged bankrupt who may only be appointed with the leave of the court[14];

(b) a person prohibited by the Articles. These may, for example, bar persons of unsound mind or who are over a certain age;

(c) a person who had been disqualified by the court from acting as a director (see below).

## Appointment of directors

The first directors will be appointed by the subscribers to the company. There need only be one director although a larger number is preferable.

**Charitable company precedent**

Thereafter, the appointment and retirement of directors will be governed by the Articles of Association. The precedent for a charitable company (Appendix A, Precedent 2) requires new directors (members of the managing committee) to be either recommended by the directors or proposed for election by a member. The Articles may require the directors' approval before a person can be proposed for election. This gives the incumbent directors a degree of control over the future administration of the charity. It is normal for the continuing

[13] Charities Act, s.83.
[14] Companies Act 1985, s.302.

directors to appoint persons to fill casual vacancies on the board. The precedent also provides for members of the committee to retire in rotation but these arrangements may be adapted to meet specific requirements. The precedent follows that given in Table C of the Companies Act 1985 in providing for directors to be appointed for a three year term but again this may be varied as required. Where no set term of office is specified in the Articles directors hold office at will subject to the members' power to remove them (see below). This is an undesirable state of affairs which is best avoided by inserting a suitable provision in the Articles.

## Disqualification

There are a number of different situations in which a person may be disqualified by law from acting as a director of a company.

**Disqualification for misconduct**
Sections 2 to 5 of the Company Directors Disqualification Act 1986 authorise the court to make an order disqualifying a person from acting as a director of a company or from acting as a liquidator or from being concerned with the promotion, formation or management of a company in the following circumstances:

**Criminal conviction**
(a) where a person is convicted of an indictable offence in connection with the promotion, formation, management or liquidation of a company;

**Default in filing returns, etc.**
(b) where a person appears to have been persistently in default in relation to the requirements of companies legislation for the filing and delivery of any returns, accounts or documents or for the giving of any notices;

**Fraud**
(c) where in the course of winding up a company it appears that a person has been guilty of fraudulent trading or fraud;

**Offences under companies legislation**
(d) where a person is convicted for contravention of any provision of the companies legislation requiring a return account or document to be filed or notice given and has in the preceding five years been convicted of not less than three such offences.

Sections 6 to 8 of the Act have also extended the powers of the court to disqualify a person from acting as a director. The court will make a disqualification order against a person if

**Disqualification for unfitness**
satisfied that he is or has been a director of a company which has gone into insolvent liquidation or in respect of which an administration order is made or a receiver appointed and that his conduct as director makes him unfit to be concerned in the management of a company.

A disqualification order may also be made under section 6 of the Act on the application of the Secretary of State if after an enquiry into the affairs of the company under section 437 of the Companies Act 1985 it seems to him to be expedient. A person who acts as a director while disqualified or an undischarged bankrupt is guilty of an offence punishable by fine or imprisonment.

## Removal of directors

**Members' power to remove**

Section 303 of the Companies Act 1985 gives the members power by ordinary resolution to remove a director and to replace him at the same meeting. The power of removal exists despite any provision in the articles or any financial or other arrangements with the director concerned although he may still be entitled to compensation. "Special notice" (as defined in section 379 Companies Act) must be given to the company of the resolution, and there are other formalities required including the giving of notice to the director concerned who is permitted to make a statement in his defence to the members.

The standard form of Articles for a company limited by guarantee set in Table C to the Companies Act 1985 specifies certain other circumstances which will result in a director automatically vacating office. The office of director will be vacated if:

(a) he becomes bankrupt or makes any arrangement with his creditors;

(b) he is or may be suffering from mental disorder and is either admitted to hospital for treatment or an order is made for his detent or for the appointment of a receiver;

(c) he resigns by giving notice to the company;

(d) he is absent from meetings of directors for more than six months and the directors resolve that he shall vacate office.

These provisions are optional but are included in most Articles of charitable companies. Where they are included the director will vacate office automatically in the specified circumstances without the need for any further action on the part of the directors. Additional provisions may be included if appropriate. Where directors are elected from among the members of the company the Articles may provide that loss of membership shall result in automatic vacation of office. Disqualification under the Charities Act may also be included as causing a director to vacate office. Individuals who are 70 years old or more may only be appointed as directors with the approval of the members in general meeting unless the Articles provide otherwise (Companies Act, s.293).

Normally the Articles of a charitable company will provide for directors to hold office for a prescribed period of two or three years and that they should then resign and, if they wish to continue as directors, put themselves forward for re-election at the Annual General Meeting. The particular arrangements can be tailored to suit the individual requirements of those concerned.

**Expiry of term of office**

# Administrators of unincorporated associations

## Persons holding property

In considering the appointment, retirement and removal of charity trustees in the context of an unincorporated association a distinction must be made between the persons in whose name any property of the association is held and those who are concerned with the general administration of the charity. Any property of the association (whether land, stock exchange securities, cash or other assets) must be held in the names of one or more individuals (not necessarily members of the association) **Contractual or** who will hold it either as trustees or subject to the contractual **trustee** relationship of the members as set out in the constitution or **relationship** rules of the association.

Land will in most cases be held by the nominated individuals as trustees for the charitable purposes of the association or, in some cases, for a more limited purpose within the general objects of the charity, for example a plot of land may be acquired by a school support fund to provide a playground and may be held on trust for this specific purpose. Stocks and shares may also be registered in the names of individuals as trustees. The terms of the trusts upon which the property is held will be ascertained from the documents of title, the terms of any gift of the property and the wording of the constitution.[15] A well-drafted constitution will provide that on dissolution the assets will be applied for charitable purposes and provide for the **Trustees of land** property of the association to be held by trustees. Any conveyance or transfer of property to the association should direct that it should be held upon trust for the charitable purposes of the association.

The arrangements for the appointment, retirement and removal of the trustees will be as set out in the section of this chapter which dealt with charitable trusts.

Other assets of a charitable association such as cash at the **Bank accounts** bank, motor vehicles, shares and moveable items including furniture and equipment are more likely to be held subject to the contractual relationship which binds the members of the association and is set out in the rules or constitution. Two or more members will usually be authorised by the committee of management to operate the charity's bank account. Changes in the bank mandate will be made by the committee in accordance with the constitution. Similarly the nominal ownership of other assets may be altered on the direction of the managing committee under the constitution and the nominated owners will be obliged to take whatever steps are required to transfer the property in question to their successors. The nominated individuals hold the property not for themselves but according to the terms of the constitution which will in the case of a charity provide that the assets may only be applied for charitable purposes.[16]

---

[15] *Neville Estates v. Madden* [1962] 1 Ch. 832.
[16] See *Re Recher's Will Trust* [1972] Ch. 526 and *Re Lipinski's Will Trust* [1976] Ch. 235.

## The committee of management

The position of the officers of the association and the committee of management to whom the management of the association's affairs are delegated will be governed exclusively by the constitution, the contract regulating the relationship of the members of the association.

The committee of management may consist of elected members or persons appointed by outside organisations or a combination of the two. For example the provisions included in the Charity Commission's standard constitution for village halls **Elected and** provide for a mix of elected and nominated members, the latter **representative** being appointed to represent local organisations likely to be **members** using the hall such as the Women's Institute, Boy Scouts, parish council and local sports clubs. Additionally, *ex-officio* members may be included such as the rector or vicar of the parish and the chairman of the parish council and a limited number of members may also be co-opted by the committee itself thus enabling individuals with special talents or expertise to contribute to the association. Precedent 3 in Appendix A provides for elected and nominated members. More elaborate provisions can be incorporated to suit particular cases. It is **Appointment for** desirable for the members of a committee of management to be **limited term** appointed for a limited term (two or three years) the first members being appointed for shorter periods so that some members retire each year thus ensuring continuity. This makes it less likely that the administration will remain too long in the hands of the same people with the danger that a clique may form or enthusiasm will wane.

There are no limits on the numbers of committee members although it will be impractical to have too large a body. Restrictions upon who may be appointed may, if desired, be imposed by the constitution.

The arrangements for the appointment and retirement of the chairman, secretary, treasurer and other officers of the association will also be governed by the constitution. They may, as in Precedent 3 (p. 238), be elected by the members of the association each year or they may be appointed by the committee.

Precedent 3 sets out various circumstances in which a committee member will vacate office including failure to attend **Removal from** meetings. These may be adapted for particular cases. A power to **office** expel members whose conduct is considered to be injurious to the association is frequently seen in the constitutions of private members clubs and may also be included in the constitution of a charitable association and the exercise of such a power may (where committee members are required to be members of the association) indirectly lead to removal from the committee. Where there is such a power its terms must be strictly observed. For example, if the rules require that a decision should be taken at a special meeting it is not sufficient for the matter to be **Expulsion of** considered at an ordinary meeting. The expulsion of a member **members** should be effected in accordance with the principles of natural justice which require that the association should give the **Natural justice** member concerned reasonable notice of the allegations made against him and provide him with an opportunity to defend himself.[1] Natural justice may be excluded by the constitution but it would not be appropriate to do so in the case of a charity which is established for public purposes. The power of expulsion should also be exercised in good faith. The decision may be invalid if it is shown to have been motivated by malice or some improper reason, as was held to be the case where a member was expelled in order to prevent him from bringing proceedings for a previous invalid expulsion.[2]

It is advisable for the constitution of the association to include provisions reflecting the principles of natural justice where there is to be a power to expel members in order to avoid the expense and adverse publicity of a claim against the association if a dispute should arise.

If the claim of a member that he has been wrongfully expelled is upheld by the court, he will be entitled to a declaration that he is still a member of the association and may be awarded damages although this last is perhaps unlikely in the case of a charitable association which may not confer benefits on members.

# Concurrent powers of the High Court and Charity Commissioners

Section 16(1)(b) of the Charities Act gives the Charity Commissioners the same powers by order to appoint new charity trustees and to vest the property of the charity in them and to discharge and remove charity trustees and officers and employees of a charity as are exerciseable by the High Court in charity proceedings.

**Appointment of trustees**  These powers are most frequently used to appoint a new trustee where it is otherwise inexpedient, difficult, or impractical to do so, for example if the last remaining trustee cannot be traced. Reasonable steps should be taken by the charity to identify the persons having the power of appointing new trustees before an application is made to the Commissioners, although there is nothing to prevent the exercise of these powers even where a valid power of appointment (express or statutory) is capable of being exercised by an individual who has been identified.

A new trustee may also be appointed in a place of one who is convicted of a serious criminal offence, is bankrupt, incapable by reason of mental disorder or is a corporation in liquidation.

**Removal of trustees**  A trustee may also be replaced if he has been guilty of a wilful breach of trust or where there is friction between the trustees, so that if a trustee continued to act the administration of the trust would be impeded.[3] It is unlikely that the Commissioners would use these powers except where a section 6 inquiry has revealed misconduct or maladministration.

---

[1] *John v Rees* [1970] 1 Ch. 345.
[2] *Tantussi v. Molli* (1886) 2 T.L.R. 731.
[3] Trustee Act 1925, s.36.

These powers are normally exercised by the Commissioners rather than the court for reasons of economy. An application to the court would require the authority of the Commissioners under section 33 of the Charities Act which will not be given if the matter can be dealt with by them.

The Charity Commissioners may not exercise their jurisdiction under section 16 in any case which they consider more suitable to be decided by the court because of its contentious nature or because it gives rise to questions of law or fact. This seems to preclude the Charity Commissioners from acting where there is a dispute between trustees or between trustees and a beneficiary.

**Application for order under s.16**

The Charity Commissioners may only exercise the powers given to them by section 16 on the application of the charity or under an order of the High Court that a matter should be referred to them for the making of a scheme or the Attorney General. An application to the Commissioners for an order under section 16 should be made by a majority of the trustees. In the case of a charity with an income of £500 or less a year an application may be made by one or more of the trustees, any person interested in the charity or in the case of a local charity two inhabitants of the locality. This does not apply to exempt charities.

**Notice**

Before exercising their power to remove a trustee under section 16 the Commissioners are required to give notice by post addressed to their last known address to each of the trustees of the charity unless they cannot be found or have no address in the United Kingdom or are party to the application. Where the trustee, employee or agent of a charity is to be removed by the Charity Commissioners without his consent one month's notice must be given to him before the order is made.[20]

**Appeals**

An appeal may be made to the High Court against any order of the Charity Commissioners within three months, by the charity, any of the trustees of the charity, or any person who has been removed as a trustee unless his removal is made by the concurrence of the other trustees. A certificate must, however, be obtained from the Charity Commissioners or the court that it is a proper case for appeal. (Section 16(12) and (13)).

# Powers of Charity Commissioners

Section 18(5) of the Charities Act confers upon the Charity Commissioners further powers to act for the protection of charities which are exerciseable without the need for an application from the charity.

**Appointment of new trustees**

They may[21] appoint a new charity trustee:

(a) to replace a trustee they have removed
(b) where there are no trustees or the remaining trustees are unable to apply for the appointment of new trustees
(c) where there is a simple trustee and they consider it necessary to increase the number

---

[20] Charities Act, s.20(3)
[21] *Ibid.*, s.18(4).

(d) where they consider an additional trustee should be appointed because a trustee refuses to act or cannot be found or is outside England and Wales.

These powers are of use where there is no person who may apply for an order under section 16 or where there is no quorum or where the trustees or other persons who could apply refuse or neglect to do so. For example an application to the court or the Charity Commission may be made where no trustees are appointed, where no grant of probate is made or letters of administration taken out in respect of the estate of the last surviving trustee or where the person having the power of appointing new trustees is a minor, or where for some other reason the arrangements for appointing trustees have broken down.

**Suspension of trustees and others**
Section 18(1) of the Charities Act gives the Commissioners power to suspend from office for 12 months a charity trustee, officer, agent or employee of a charity. This power may be exercised of their own motion but only after an inquiry under section 8 has been instituted and they are satisfied that there has either been misconduct or mismanagement in the administration of the charity or the suspension is necessary or desirable to protect the charity's property or ensure it is properly applied.

**Removal of trustees and others for misconduct**
Suspension of a charity trustee officer agent or employee may be a prelude to his removal under section 18(2). Where after a section 8 inquiry has been instituted the Commissioners are satisfied both that there has been misconduct or mismanagement and that it is necessary or desirable to protect the charity's property or ensure its proper application they may of their own motion remove a charity trustee, officer, agent or employee from office who has been responsible for or privy to or facilitated the misconduct or mismanagement.

The Commissioners maintain a register of persons who have been removed under section 18 and such persons are disqualified from acting as charity trustees.[22]

**Removal of trustees further powers**
Enhanced powers were conferred on the Commissioners by the Charities Act 1992 to remove charity trustees from office which now appear in section 18(4) of the Charities Act. They may remove a charity trustee by order of their own motion who in the last five years has been declared bankrupt or had his estate sequestrated or made an arrangement with his creditors despite the fact that he has since been discharged and will not be automatically disqualified from acting.

They are also empowered to remove a trustee:

(a) which is a corporation in liquidation;
(b) who is incapable of acting through mental disorder;
(c) who has not acted and will not declare himself willing to act or otherwise;
(d) where he is outside England and Wales or cannot be found or does not act and this impedes the administration of the charity.

---

[22] See above p. 83.

Again one month's notice must be given to any person removed from his position as trustee employee or agent without his consent before the order removing him is made. Before removing a charity trustee, officer, agent or employee under section 18, or appointing a trustee of their own motion the Commissioners are required[23] to notify each of the charity trustees of their intention.

**Prosecution**

The Commissioners were very cautious in the exercise of their more limited powers under the 1960 Act and it is likely that they will be reluctant to remove a trustee unless there is clear evidence of misconduct. In 1995 only 9 trustees were removed from only 2 charities.[24] If the individual is to be prosecuted no steps will be taken to remove him until after a guilty verdict has been returned.

**Appeals**

Similar provisions for appeals against an order of the Charity Commissioners apply to orders made under section 18 as are set out in respect of orders made under section 16.

The reference in sections 16 and 18 to officers and employees of a charity include company secretaries, wardens of almshouses, treasurers of unincorporated associations and the holders of such offices as fellows of university and chaplains of educational foundations.

**Appointment of receiver and manager**

The Charities Act 1992 gave a new power to the Commissioners to appoint a receiver and manager for a charity. They are empowered to do so[25] when, having instituted an inquiry under section 8 they are satisfied either that there has been mismanagement or misconduct or it is necessary or desirable to protect the property of the charity or ensure it is applied properly.

Section 19 of the Charities Act contains detailed provisions relating to the appointment and role of a receiver and manager. He may be given as much of the powers of the charity trustees as the Commissioners by order direct and he may exercise any of those powers to the exclusion of the trustees. He may seek advice from the Commissioners under section 29 of the Charities Act 1960 and obtain protection in the same way as charity trustees. A receiver and manager may not be an officer or employee of the Commissioners, and most often is an accountant.

The appointment of a receiver and manager will enable the administration of a charity to be placed upon a proper footing and the charity to continue to function while a section 8 inquiry is proceeding and the management of the charity may be in disarray.

---

[23] Charities Act 1960, s.18(12).
[24] Report of Charity Commission for 1995. p. 14.
[25] Charities Act, s.18(1)(vii).

# 7 PERSONAL LIABILITY

The risk of incurring personal liability is a matter of growing concern to people who are or are thinking of becoming charity trustees. Some well publicised financial failures of established charities have increased the level of anxiety and many prospective charity trustees will want advice on the likelihood and degree of personal risk involved.

In the last edition of this book it was stated that it was unusual for a charity trustee who has behaved honestly to suffer financial loss. This is still the case but the collapse of the property market and the recession have made many charities vulnerable. An increasing number are wholly or largely dependent on funds from other charities, local authorities or central funds which can be cut off or substantially reduced at short notice perhaps leaving the charity trustees with long term commitments which cannot be escaped. The importance of cautious financial management cannot be overemphasised.

It is not a straightforward matter to give comprehensive and comprehensible advice on the extent and degree of risk of personal liability. Not only do the chances and circumstances of incurring liability vary from one kind of charitable activity to another but the type of charitable structure is also highly relevant. The position of trustees of charitable trusts, directors of charitable companies and members of management committees of unincorporated associations will be considered in turn.

The likelihood and degree of risk for an individual depends on whether he is a trustee of a charitable trust, a director of a company or a person involved in administering an unincorporated association. Each case will be considered in turn.

## Trustees of charitable trusts

### The trustees' expenses

The general rule is that a trustee is not expected to do any work at his own expense. A trustee should, in the interests of the trust, use his judgment not to incur unnecessary expense but he is entitled to be indemnified against all reasonable costs and expenses which he may incur in the course of his duties provided that those costs and expenses are incurred properly.[1] A trustee is for example entitled to be paid reasonable travelling expenses and where it is necessary to employ an agent such as a surveyor or a valuer his fees may be charged to the trust fund. The cost of taking legal advice or proceedings in order to protect the assets of the charity may be discharged from the trust fund.

**Right to reimbursement**

[1] See s.30(2) of the Trustee Act 1925 and *Re Grimthorpe's (Baron) Will Trusts* [1958] 1 All E.R. 765.

## Liability for loss to the trust fund

**Losses where no breach of duty**

Occasionally losses can be suffered in the course of administering the charity. A poor investment may be made or a business run by the charity may make a loss. A trustee will not be personally liable if he has acted reasonably and there has been no breach of duty on his part.[2]

If loss is caused to the trust fund through the default of an agent employed by a trustee in good faith the trustee will not himself be liable unless in employing the agent or continuing to employ him the trustee failed to take the care which an ordinary prudent business man would in managing his own affairs.[3]

## Breach of trust

A trustee may be made personally liable if he commits a breach of trust and as a result the charity suffers loss.

**Unauthorised acts**

**Negligence**

**Personal profit**

**Standard of care**

**What constitutes a breach of trust?**   A trustee commits a breach of trust where he acts in a way which is not authorised by the terms of the trust deed or neglects to fulfil his duties as a trustee. Breaches of trust therefore cover a wide variety of misconduct and include actions which can be regarded as purely technical breaches such as investing in an unauthorised manner (which may even be to the advantage of the trust) as well as negligence and acts of dishonesty or fraudulent conversion of the fund to the trustee's own use. A breach of trust will, for example be committed if payments are made to beneficiaries who do not fulfil the qualifications laid down by the terms of the trust or in furtherance of purposes which are outside the objects for which the trust was established. A trustee will also be in breach of trust if he falls short of the standard of care required of him in administering the trust fund such as where he fails to invest the fund or puts it at risk through making speculative investments. A grave breach of trust will occur if a trustee, instead of acting only in the interests of the trust, deals with the trust assets in such a way as to derive some personal benefit, perhaps by arranging for money to be lent to a company with which he is connected at less than the market rate or for property to be acquired by him at less than the proper value.

The standard of care required of a trustee generally in his dealings with the trust assets in that of an ordinary prudent man of business in relation to his own affairs.[4] A more exacting standard is demanded in investment matters namely that which a prudent business man would observe in making an investment for people for whom he felt morally obliged to provide. A higher standard of care is required where the trustee is a professional who is paid for his services. If such a trustee fails to provide the skill and care he professes to have he will be liable for any loss which results.[5]

---

[2] Trustee Act 1925, s.23 and see *Re Lucking's Will Trust* [1968] 1 W.L.R. 866.
[3] *Re Vickery* [1931] 1 Ch. 572.
[4] *Re Luckings Will Trust* [1968] 1 W.L.R. 866.
[5] *Bartlett v Barclays Trust Co.* [1980] 1 Ch. 515.

For a fuller discussion of this subject the standard works on trusts and trustees should be referred to.

**Extent of liability for breach of trust**   The principle upon which the courts act is that trustees who have committed a breach of trust which has resulted in a loss to the trust fund must make good that loss. Any profits which may be made as a result of the breach are however due to the trust. Consequently if the trustees have failed to invest they are liable to reimburse to the trust the income which has been lost to it. Where an investment has been sold and the proceeds invested in an investment which is not authorised either under the terms of the trust or under the general law the trustees may be required to re-purchase the original holding, any additional cost in excess of the proceeds of sale of the unauthorised investment being borne by the trustees themselves. If trustees have paid out trust assets to a non-qualified beneficiary or if through their fault property is lost to the trust they may be required to restore the loss to the trust fund with interest.

**Reinstatement of trust fund**

Where a trustee has traded on his own behalf with trust assets or has been guilty of fraud or other misconduct the courts seek to ensure that he retains no profit for himself. In such cases the defaulting trustee may be required to repay the principal to the trust together with any profits he may actually have made. Alternatively he may be assumed to have received compound interest at 1 per cent over the clearing banks' base rate and will be required to pay this amount.[6]

**Private profit**

In cases where the breach has been committed as a result of ignorance or mistake rather than dishonesty the court has considerable discretion and will often take a lenient view so as to limit the liability of the trustees to the period after they became aware that they were acting in breach of trust or even from the date when proceedings were commenced.[7]

**Court's discretion**

It sometimes happens that trustees commit more than one breach of trust and that both losses and gains result to the trust fund. The trustees may only set off the gains against the losses where they result from the same transaction or the same course of transactions.

**Who is liable for breach of trust?**   A trustee is only liable for his own acts and defaults and not for those of his co-trustees (Trustee Act 1925, s.30). Each of the trustees actually involved in a breach of trust is personally liable for the whole of the resulting loss regardless of the degree of blame attaching to him. This can operate harshly in practice. For instance where one trustee has allowed trust funds to be controlled by a co-trustee who misapplies them both will be equally liable even though the involvement of the first trustee has been passive only.[8] Both are concerned in the breach of trust however since the one could not have made the improper investment had the other not failed in his duty to exercise proper care over the trust assets or improperly delegated investment decisions to his co-trustee.

**Joint and several liability**

[6] *Wallersteiner v. Moir (No. 2)* [1975] Q.B. 373.
[7] See *Re Freeston's Charity* [1978] 1 W.L.R. 741.
[8] *Wilkins v. Hogg* (1861) 31 L.J. Ch. 41.

If only one of the trustees concerned in the breach of trust is sued he will be entitled to contribution from his co-trustees except where he has been found guilty of fraud.

**Right to contribution**

The Civil Liability (Contribution) Act 1978 now gives a statutory right of contribution by which any person who is liable in respect of damage suffered by any person or body may recover contributions from another person who is also liable. The extent of the contribution is at the discretion of the court and would in theory permit unequal contributions by trustees. The right expires two years after judgment is given against the trustee or a compromise is reached by which the amount payable by him is agreed (s.10).

**Civil Liability Contribution Act 1978**

Occasionally a trustee may be held solely liable for the loss. Where a breach of trust has been committed in reliance upon the advice of a solicitor trustee the latter may be required to indemnify his co-trustee.[9] A trustee who has himself benefited from the breach of trust may also be liable to indemnify his co-trustees.[10]

**Right to indemnity**

A trustee who retires in order to facilitate a breach of trust or with the knowledge that a breach of trust is likely to take place will be equally liable with the trustees who actually commit the breach.[11] A new trustee will not be liable for breaches of trust committed before his appointment but he cannot entirely ignore what has occurred before. If he becomes aware that a breach of trust has been committed by the former trustees he has a duty to have the matter rectified if possible[12] and may render himself liable with those who were actually responsible if he fails to do so.

## Protection for trustees

In many cases trustees of a private trust who are uncertain whether any particular course of action is permitted under the terms of the trust or consider such a course of action to be in the interests of the trust although it would strictly speaking constitute a breach of trust may protect themselves by obtaining an indemnity from the beneficiaries. This is not possible in the case of a charitable trust. In such a situation the trustees may (with the consent of the Charity Commissioners) apply to the court for directions or, (and this procedure is almost always preferable for reasons of speed and economy) to the Charity Commissioners for advice under section 29 of the Charities Act. If they act in accordance with this advice they will be protected against any claim for breach of trust. They may also, if they think it appropriate, apply for a scheme to give them additional powers. There is therefore no reason for trustees of a charity to run the risk of committing a deliberate breach of trust.

**Protection under s.29 of the Charities Act**

Where a breach of trust has been committed the trustees may in certain limited circumstances be absolved from their personal responsibility to make good any resulting loss to the charity. A trustee who has acted honestly, reasonably and ought

[9] *Re Linsley* [1904] 2 Ch. 785.
[10] *Bahin v. Hughes* (1886) 31 Ch.D. 390.
[11] *Head v. Gould* [1898] 2 Ch. 250.
[12] *Harvey v. Olliver* (1887) 57 L.T. 239.

**Relief from liability**

fairly to be excused for the breach and for failing to obtain the directions of the court before committing a breach of trust may be relieved of liability by the court at its discretion (Trustee Act 1925, s.61). What is considered reasonable will depend upon the particular circumstances of each case. Where the breach of trust has arisen through an error of fact or law protection is more likely to be granted if the trustees conscientiously sought to carry out the terms of the trust in accordance with the generally held view of the law, (see *Re Wightwick's Will Trust*,[13] a case where the trustees acted in the belief, which as it turned out was incorrect, that the Anti-Vivisection Society was charitable). In cases where there is doubt as to the correct course to be adopted the trustees should obtain legal advice.[14]

**Professional advice**

Expert advice should always be obtained from some suitably qualified person before important decisions are taken. A stockbroker or investment adviser should be asked to recommend any changes of investment in writing. Decisions concerning land or property should not be taken without first seeking advice from an estate or land agent. Trustees are not expected to be experts in all fields which the charity may be involved in but they are expected to avail themselves of those who are. Failure to do so may amount to a breach of trust. If trustees have acted in accordance with suitable advice they are unlikely to be made liable for any resulting loss.

Section 30 of the Trustee Act 1925 gives protection to a trustee where the loss has been caused solely by the fraud or default of a co-trustee but this protection is not available where he himself has contributed to the loss, for example by allowing his co-trustee to receive or hold the trust property or failing to obtain restitution when he becomes aware of what has occurred. Section 23 of the Trustee Act 1925 gives trustees general protection from liability for the default of an agent employed in good faith to undertake any transaction on behalf of the trust and entitles them to reimbursement of all charges and expenses. However, the trustee may still be liable if he himself is at fault in, for example failing to exercise proper supervision over the agent's activities.[15]

## Liability to third parties

**Contractual liability**

Since a trust has no independent existence apart from the individuals who make up the body of trustees, trustees who enter into a contract with a third party do so in their personal capacity and are personally liable. This is the case even where those dealing with the trustees are aware that they are acting in their capacity as trustees. A trustee is therefore personally responsible for all liabilities arising under the terms of the contract but he will be entitled to be indemnified from the trust assets provided that the liability has been properly incurred. A

**Liability in tort**

trustee may also be personally liable in tort for damages in respect of any breach of duty on the part of the trustees as occupiers of land, as employers or for negligence of employees

[13] [1950] Ch. 260.
[14] *Re Allsop* [1914] 1 Ch. 1.
[15] *Re Lucking's Will Trust* [1968] 1 W.L.R. 866.

or agents for whom they are vicariously liable. A claim for wrongful dismissal may also be made against the individual trustees. Again a trustee who has acted reasonably and with due care will be entitled to reimbursement from the trust fund. It is usual to cover such risk by insurance but trustees may incur personal liability for any uninsured losses.

**Trust fund insufficient to cover liability**

It is possible that the trust fund will be insufficient to cover the liabilities incurred by the trustees. In such a case they may find themselves personally liable even when they have acted perfectly properly and since there is no limitation of liability a trustee could be made bankrupt as a result of liabilities incurred by him in his capacity as a trustee. This situation is not likely to arise where the principal activity of the charity is the investment of funds and the distribution of income or capital, but covenants under leases can cause problems particularly where the lease is a long one. The circumstances may have changed radically by the time any liability arises and the charity's funds may be inadequate to cover it. If possible trustees should limit the extent of their liability to the assets of the charity.

**Higher risk activities**

The risk will be increased if the trustees engage in speculative ventures such as property development or carry on trading activities. Trustees should therefore involve themselves in such activities only with great caution after they have satisfied themselves that the assets of the charity are adequate to cover the potential liability. If possible personal liability should be expressly excluded in any contract with a third party and steps should be taken to insure against foreseeable risks. Where the trading activity is likely to be long-term and substantial, the trustees should consider setting up a separate company with limited liability for this purpose (see Chapter 8). Speculative investments are generally speaking unsuitable for any but the largest trusts (see the section on investment in Chapter 10).

**Liability after retirement**

A trustee does not, on retirement, cease to be personally liable under a contract he has entered into while a trustee. His personal liability continues and on his death his personal representatives assume his responsibilities. Normally this will not be significant since the majority of liabilities entered into by trustees in the course of administering a trust are of a short term nature such as when trustees authorise the sale or purchase of stock exchange investments or contract to purchase a property. In such situations they will, if they are prudent, have ensured that funds are available to cover the liability.

**Long term liabilities**

Long term liabilities are sometimes incurred by trustees where, for example, they take a long lease of property which imposes onerous covenants on them as tenants or enter into undertakings under a mortgage agreement. In such cases liabilities may arise many years later when the parties to the agreement have long since retired as trustees but they, rather than the present trustees, will be liable under the terms of the agreement. Having parted with the trust assets the former trustees will be obliged to join the present trustees in the action brought against them and to obtain reimbursement from the trust fund. Any trustee who is considering undertaking long-term obligations in the course of administering the trust fund should give the matter careful consideration and should take professional advice before committing himself.

This particular problem may be avoided by incorporating the body of trustees under Part VII of the Charities Act. Incorporation has the effect that the trustees for the time being will be a continuing body which can sue or be sued in the name of the charity. All rights and liabilities of the individual trustees before incorporation will become rights and liabilities of the corporate body and in future individual trustees will not incur personal liability under contracts entered into on behalf of the charity.

**Incorporation of trustees**

This will be a considerable advantage where trustees intend to enter into long term liabilities such as covenants under a lease since the liabilities of the trustees will become the liabilities of the corporate body (subs. (3)). The problem mentioned above that trustees who have retired may still remain liable under covenants will not arise since the liabilities will fall on the body corporate rather than the individuals.

Incorporation does not affect the potential personal liability of trustees for breach of their duty (s.54).

## The trustees' lien

Where trustees are entitled to an indemnity from the trust fund for liabilities incurred by them as trustees they have a lien over the trust assets to the extent of their claim. This means that they have a first charge on the trust assets and may sell or mortgage them in order to reimburse themselves.

**First charge over trust assets**

The position is not so simple in cases where the trustees' lien is on land owned by the charity. Section 38 of the Charities Act provides that no land held in trust for a charity may be mortgaged or charged without an order of the Commissioners or the court unless certain formalities are observed. These include the obtaining and consideration of advice on such matters as the terms of the charge and the ability of the charity to repay the sum borrowed (see Chapter 10). Failure to comply does not invalidate the charge in so far as a person who in good faith acquires an interest in the land for money or money's worth. In many cases this may protect the trustees particularly where their liability arises through no fault or action on their part. But it is more doubtful if they will be protected when they deliberately incur debts on behalf of the charity (a bank overdraft for example) which if they were to be repaid would require the disposal of land belonging to the charity thus effectively giving the trustees a charge over the land.

# Directors of charitable companies

One of the principal reasons for establishing a charity as a company is that this is considered to give protection from personal liability to those responsible for running the charity.

**Protection from personal liability**

Directors of companies with limited liability are not as a rule personally liable for any trading losses incurred by the company or for any liabilities of the company incurred in the

**Exceptions** course of promoting its objects. There are a number of exceptions to this general rule which are set out below and furthermore, persons contracting with a company such as banks or other organisations providing credit facilities often require personal guarantees from one or more directors. The benefits of limited liability are therefore not as comprehensive as is sometimes thought.

A director of a charitable company may be personally liable in any of the following situations:

(a) when he is in breach of his fiduciary duty;

(b) where, having no authority to do so, he purports to commit the company and the company suffers loss;

(c) where there is a failure on behalf of the company to comply with the statutory obligations laid down by the Companies Acts;

(d) where he acts negligently;

(e) where there have been some wrongful acts on the part of directors prior to liquidation of the company or the company has continued to trade when there was no prospect of avoiding an insolvent liquidation;

(f) where a person who has been disqualified acts as a director.

These will be considered in turn.

## Breach of fiduciary duty

Just as trustees of a charitable trust are under a duty to act in the interests of the beneficiaries of the trust and not to place themselves in a position where a conflict of interest may arise, so directors of a company are under a duty to act in the interests of **Duties of** the company. The directors must, in principle, consider first the **directors** interests of the company's creditors (although only to the extent of the company's indebtedness to them—they need not consider the creditor's more general interests), second the continued business of the company for the benefit of the members and third the interests of employees. In the case of a charitable company it would seem that the furtherance of the charitable objects of the company should be the predominant consideration under the second head but there is no authority that the director's obligations are any different than in the case of a trading company.

Section 35(3) of the Companies Act 1985 as amended by the Companies Act 1989 requires directors of companies to observe the limitations on their powers flowing from the **Ultra vires** company's memorandum. Where directors act outside the terms **actions** of the memorandum or carry out an unauthorised transaction and the company incurs a loss as a result the individual directors may be liable to the company. A non-charitable company may, by special resolution after the event, ratify the invalid action on the part of the directors and by a separate special resolution relieve them of liability. In the case of a charitable company the prior written consent of the Charity Commissioners is required (Charities Act s.65(4)).

**Liability for losses**

A director who acts in breach of his fiduciary duty, for example by using the company's assets to procure a benefit to himself, will be personally liable for any losses to the company which may result.

**Statutory duties**

Part X of the Companies Act 1985 imposes a number of statutory duties on directors of companies. Broadly speaking these apply in circumstances where the interests of the directors are at variance with the interests of the company. Some transactions are forbidden (*e.g.* a company may not make a loan to a director); others require the consent of the members in general meeting to be effective, for example when a director acquires something of value from the company. The relevant provisions are widely drawn so as to cover dealings not only with directors personally but also with their spouses and associates. Since the memorandum of a charitable company will invariably forbid any benefits to members, transactions even in the second category, which confer a benefit on a director who is a member

**Liability for breach**

of the company, will normally not be permitted. Directors may incur personal liability as a result of a breach of any of these rules. The Companies Act 1985 permits certain such transactions to be approved either before or after the event by the company in general meeting or, in the case of voidable transactions, affirmed but section 66 of the Charities Act now provides that in certain cases the prior written consent of the Charity Commissioners is required if such approval or affirmation is to be valid. The transactions affected are:

(a) payments for loss of office or retirement;
(b) payments on loss of office or retirement in connexion with the transfer of the company's undertakings or property;
(c) inclusion in an employment contract of a term allowing employment for more than five years;
(d) arrangements whereby assets are acquired from a director;
(e) payments to meet expenses incurred by directors.

The Companies Acts contain detailed provisions relating to such transactions and in any case of potential conflict of interest a director should take legal advice.

## Acting outside the scope of his authority

A director who acts within the scope of his authority (as determined by the board) and with reasonable diligence will not be personally responsible for any losses which may occur. Directors have a duty to act within the scope of the powers conferred on them by the memorandum of association[16] but a transaction which is *ultra vires* is nevertheless valid as far as third parties are concerned. The members of the company may bring proceedings to prevent a director acting outside the company's powers and a director may be made liable to compensate the

[16] Companies Act 1985, s.35.

**Ratification by company**
company for any loss resulting from an *ultra vires* act. The company may ratify an unauthorised act of a director by special resolution and release him from personal liability but in the case of a charitable company the board should first obtain sanction from the Charity Commission under section 26 of the Charities Act.

## Acting negligently

The standard of care required of a director of a company is lower than that expected of a trustee. Broadly speaking the standard is that which would be expected of an individual acting on his own behalf. Provided that he has acted honestly he will not be made liable unless he has been grossly negligent. The standard required of part-time unpaid directors is lower than where they are full time employees of the company which will only occasionally be the case for a charity. Nevertheless directors have been held liable when they have failed to exercise proper control and supervision over the running of the company and have allowed it to be effectively run by one of their number or have allowed payments to be made without due inquiry.[17]

## Failure to comply with statutory obligations

**Obligations concerning records, meetings, etc.**
The Companies Acts impose a large number of statutory obligations on companies including obligations to keep proper accounting records, file promptly at the Companies Registry annual audited accounts and returns in connection with their activities, keep records of the appointment of directors and secretaries and notify the Companies Registry and register any charges over company assets. They are also required to hold periodic meetings and to make certain information available to members. Failure to comply with these requirements may render the directors personally liable to be fined. Failure to

**Disqualification**
comply on a number of occasions may result in the disqualification of the individual from acting as a director (see Chapter 6). Directors would be well advised to ensure that they received continuing professional assistance from their auditors or company secretary to ensure that these matters are properly dealt with.

## Offences and liability connected with insolvency

The circumstances in which a director may incur personal liability now include situations where the director has not in any way acted dishonestly.

**Wrongful trading (section 214 of the Insolvency Act 1986)**   Although unusual it is by no means impossible that a charitable company should get into financial difficulties and that the directors should be tempted to continue the company's activities in the hope that additional funds will be raised. In such

---

[17] *Re City Equitable Fire Insurance Co.* [1925[ Ch. 407.

**Trading while insolvent** situations they should act with extreme caution. Where a director realises that his company is insolvent and there is no reasonable prospect of avoiding a liquidation he should immediately take steps to minimise the potential loss to the company's creditors. If he fails to do so and allows the company to continue trading he may be required by the liquidator of the company to contribute personally to the assets of the company.

In assessing whether or not the director should have realised that there was no reasonable prospect of avoiding a liquidation he will be assumed to have the particular knowledge skill and experience which might reasonably be expected of a person carrying out the same functions as are carried out by that director in relation to the company and the general knowledge skill and experience that the director actually possesses. A **Standard required of directors** director is therefore expected to conform to an objective standard of ability and in addition he is required to use his individual skills to inform himself of the current position of the company. It will not be a sufficient excuse to say that he was unaware that the company was in difficulties in taking account of his training and the standard expected of a director of such a company he should have been aware of the situation.

An honest and conscientious director could therefore in certain circumstances find himself personally liable if he permits the company to continue trading when it is effectively insolvent and the company subsequently goes into insolvent liquidation though it is most unlikely in practice. These provisions should **Cautious approach** encourage directors to adopt a cautious approach when their company is in difficulties and to take steps sooner rather than later to protect their creditors.

If the directors find themselves in a situation where the company is in danger of wrongful trading their first duty is to the creditors. Their interests are not likely to be safeguarded by the director resigning, which may be his first impulse, although resignation may be desirable if the director finds himself in a minority where he feels that the majority are acting improperly. Furthermore, while the best, or only proper course of action may be to stop the company's activities and place it in liquidation that in itself is likely to lead to the creditors receiving less than their full entitlement and the directors should consider **Emergency funding** all the alternatives. In the case of a charity emergency funding may be available.

**Fraudulent trading (section 213 of the Insolvency Act 1986)** If a company which is wound up appears to have carried on its business with the intention of defrauding its creditors or for any fraudulent purpose any persons knowingly concerned may be required to contribute personally to the company's assets.

**Delinquent directors (section 212 of the Insolvency Act 1986)** A director or other officer of a company who has misapplied company assets or has been guilty of misfeasance or breach of duty in relation to the company may be required to repay or restore the property with interest or to compensate the company.

## Disqualification (Company Directors Disqualification Act 1986, s.15)

A person who is involved in the management of a company while he is disqualified may be made liable for all the debts of the company incurred during that time. The circumstances in which a person may be disqualified from acting as a director were considered in Chapter 6.

# Members of unincorporated associations

**Liability of trustees**

**Custodian trustee**

Property of a charitable unincorporated association is usually held by two or three trustees appointed by the managing committee but not necessarily members of it. They will hold the property upon trust for the purposes of the association. Their position will be similar to that of a custodian trustee since their functions will be limited by the rules of the association and they will normally be obliged to act in accordance with the decisions of the committee of management in dealing with the trust property. Like custodian trustees they must ensure that the trust property is dealt with in accordance with the terms of the trust and they should refuse to comply with the directions of the members of the association if to do so would be a breach of trust. Like trustees of charitable trusts the trustees will be personally liable under any covenants contained in the lease or conveyance but because they are not identical to the managing committee who control the administration of the charity they will not be entitled to an automatic indemnity from the funds of the association in respect of these liabilities (which can of course be very onerous) unless this is provided by the rules or by agreement with the members of the committee.[18] Where the documentation includes a statement that the trustees are acting as trustees for the association it is arguable that they are entitled to an indemnity but it is not safe to rely on this. Even if the association is required by its rules to indemnify the trustees this protection will be worthless if the charity's assets are inadequate to cover the expenses. Prospective trustees should enter into long term commitments of this kind only after taking legal advice and where they are satisfied that the charity's finances are adequate to cover any potential liabilities.

### Breach of rules

**Liability of members**

The rules of an unincorporated association constitute the contract between the members. If a member or officer of the association breaches the rules by applying the funds of the association for purposes which are not authorised he may be liable to reimburse the association.[19] This applies both where there has been some fault or wrongdoing on the part of the member or officer concerned and where the breach was of a more technical nature such as where funds are applied to provide facilities which are outside the scope of the charity's

---

[18] *Wise v. Perpetual Trust Co.* [1903] A.C. 139.
[19] *Baker v. Jones* [1954] 1 W.L.R. 1005.

objects. It is possible that in the latter type of case the court would not consider it to be in the interests of the charity to order reimbursement particularly if the breach was committed in good faith.

## Liability in contract and tort

**Liability of individual members**
An unincorporated association, having no legal existence apart from its members cannot be liable under a contract or for damage to third parties or for breach or in respect of any duty imposed by statute. Liability falls upon the individual members, upon particular individuals or office holders or upon the members of the management committee (depending upon the circumstances) according to the general law of agency.

**Right to reimbursement**
Generally speaking and subject to the terms of the constitution a member who incurs personal liability in the course of his work for a charity which is an unincorporated association is entitled to reimbursement from its funds provided that he has acted properly, within the terms of the constitution and the authority conferred upon him and he has not been negligent. It should be noted that the Charity Commissioners would object to a provision in the constitution which provided for any person to be indemnified from the property of the charity in respect of negligence or breach of the terms of the constitution and the individual concerned will be responsible for any loss.

Members will not normally be obliged to contribute more than their subscriptions and consequently, if the charity's funds are insufficient the member concerned may have to bear any shortfall personally.

**Precautions**
It is clearly most important that all those concerned with an unincorporated charitable association and in particular the members of the committee of management, who are most likely to incur personal liability, should ensure that the terms of the constitution are strictly complied with, reasonable care is taken in dealing with the charity's affairs, commitments are only entered into if sufficient funds are available and competent agents and employees are appointed and properly supervised. Proper insurance should be taken out to cover any foreseeable risks and in particular in respect of liability in respect of the occupation of land. Special care should be taken where personal guarantees are demanded from members. These should not be given without first obtaining legal advice. The National Council for Voluntary Organisations has prepared a guidance note for those concerned with running unincorporated voluntary organisations which is available on application to the Council. The address is given in Appendix E.

All those who are liable are equally so and one who has contributed more than his share is entitled to a contribution from his fellows (Civil Liability (Contribution) Act 1978).

**Identity of principals**
**Contract** An individual who enters into a contract on behalf of an association is acting as its agent and if he is acting within the terms of his authority those authorising him will be liable as principals. The identity of the persons authorising him will

depend upon the rules of the association and the particular circumstances. Where the committee has been entrusted by the membership with running the association and carrying out this role have authorised the transaction in question all the committee members will be individually liable under the contract. This is likely to be the normal situation.[20] Occasionally however an officer may be specifically authorised by the rules to enter into contracts and in such a case the members as a whole may be individually liable.

**Contract without authority**　　Where an officer or individual member enters into a contract without authority or in excess of his authority then he may be personally liable unless his actions are subsequently ratified by the management committee or the membership in which case the members of the committee or the individual members, as the case may be, will assume responsibility for the obligations under the terms of the contract.

**Limits to authority**　　Even where an individual enters into a contract with the authority of the membership he is not entitled to commit the members to make any payment in excess of the funds of the association unless specifically authorised to do so. He has no authority to pledge the credit of the members and will not be entitled to an indemnity from them for the excess unless the rules authorise or the members authorise the transaction. Any person entering into a contract on behalf of the association should, therefore, ensure for his own protection that he will be acting within the terms of the authority given to him by the committee or the members and that the association has sufficient funds available to cover the liability or, if funds are not available, that he has authority to pledge the credit of the members. Members should ensure before authorising a particular contract that adequate funds are available or they may be liable for any shortfall.

**Property**　　Where individual trustees are to hold land for a charitable unincorporated association they should ensure that the constitution provides for them to be indemnified against liabilities they may incur in connection with the property (see clause M in Precedent 3, Appendix A).

**Liability in tort**　　Individual members may also find themselves personally liable in tort, for example in cases of **Duty of care**　negligence or nuisance where it can be shown that they had a duty of care (see *Prole v. Allen and Others*)[21] which concerned a member who was appointed a steward of the club). The individual members of a management committee responsible for appointing an agent or employee who is negligent or commits the act complained of will each be vicariously liable or, if the agent is responsible to or employed by the members then all the members, will be liable.

**Occupiers' liability**　　Individual members may also be personally responsible for a failure to comply with the duties imposed by statute on the occupiers of property and employers. Once again the question of who is liable will depend on the particular facts of each case. In the case of land held by trustees the individual trustees are most

---

[20] *Bradley Egg Farms v. Clifford* [1943] 2 All E.R. 378.
[21] [1950] 1 All E.R. 476.

likely to be liable as occupiers but in some cases, particularly where the property is used for the purposes of the association, liability may fall on the membership as a whole or on the management committee. Substantial responsibilities are imposed upon employers in respect of their employees ranging from the protection of employees from danger to obligations connected with unfair dismissal, redundancy and other employees rights. These obligations will fall upon the persons who are the employers in each particular case. In most cases this will be the members of the committee of management but an individual member may occasionally find himself in this position.

**Indemnity** Individual members of the committee of management or of the charity who find themselves personally liable as a result of a claim in tort will be entitled to reimbursement from the charity's assets provided that their liability was incurred as a result of actions undertaken by or on behalf of the charity. This will not be the case where the tortious act was one for which the individual was responsible personally rather than on behalf of the charity. A libellous statement by an individual committee member is an example of an act for which there would not be any right of reimbursement. Although there does not appear to be any authority on the point it seems arguable that where the committee are jointly responsible for a tort, perhaps for failing to ensure that the activities of the charity are carried on safely, they should not be able to look to the charity's funds to pay any damages which may be awarded against any of their number but that all should be personally liable.[22]

Where the funds of the charity are insufficient to cover the individual's liability he will be personally responsible for the balance due.

# Protection for charity trustees

**Insurance** Many of the obvious risks can be covered by suitable insurance and it is in the interests of charity trustees to obtain adequate cover against occupiers liability in particular. Where particular hazards are likely to arise in the course of a charity's activities appropriate policies can often provide protection. Fund-raising events like horse shows can be spoilt by accidents or result in financial loss through bad weather but it is usually possible to obtain insurance cover for the likely risks. Professional indemnity insurance may be appropriate in some cases. Suitably drafted exclusion clauses on tickets or notices can avoid some types of claim.

Charity trustees are increasingly aware of the dangers of incurring personal liability and many seek to protect themselves **Trustee** by taking out insurance. Trustee insurance is now provided by **Insurance** many insurance companies at reasonable cost and will cover charity trustees against any breach of duty, dishonesty or fraud on the part of any of their co-trustees or their employees and libel or slander committed on behalf of the charity (for example

---

[22] See *Bolton v. Stone* [1951] A.C. 850.

in a newsletter). Where the charity is a company Directors and Officers insurance will protect in addition against breaches of company law and potential liability for wrongful trading under the Insolvency Act 1986. Such policies may also provide protection for the funds of the charity against loss caused by the default of the charity trustees.

Where potential trustees are deterred from acting because of the risk of personal liability the payment of premiums from charitable funds may be in the best interests of the charity but because such a payment will confer a benefit on the trustees specific power is required in the governing instrument. Wording for such a power which has been approved[23] by the Commission can be found in Appendix C. The Commission has stated[24] that insurance may cover the cost of a successful defence against criminal prosecution. In such cases the Charity Commissioners do not object to premiums for such policies being paid from the funds of the charity provided the policy does not cover individual trustees for their own negligence, dishonesty or recklessness. Where the trustees' powers do not permit the payment of premiums for such a policy, the Commissioners will authorise this by order if satisfied that there are special circumstances which justify the provision by the charity of insurance. A simpler solution may be for individual trustees to pay a small proportion of the total premium which is calculated to represent the cost of the cover for personal liability.

**Incorporation**

In some cases where there is a substantial risk of individual members incurring personal liability, the best course may be for a new charitable company to be formed to carry on the work of the trust or unincorporated association. Although the protection of limited liability is not total (see above) there are some advantages including, in particular, the corporate identity which makes it less likely that individual charity trustees will be sued personally. A company is recommended wherever the charity will be carrying on any kind of business activity such as a hospital, nursing home or school.

## Penalties under the Charities Act

Recent legislation has ushered in a stricter regime which imposes criminal sanctions on charity trustees who breach certain of its provisions. These apply to those who have the general management and control of a charity, whatever form the charity takes, and in some cases to employees and volunteers as well. The obligations, infringement of which can lead to criminal proceedings, are more fully described in Chapter 10 but are summarised below.

**Status of charity to appear on documents section 15**

A charity which has an annual income of more than £5,000 must ensure that certain documents issued by it state the fact that it is a registered charity. A person who issues or authorises a document which does not bear such a statement is guilty of an

---

[23] *Decisions of the Charity Commissioners*, Vol. 2, p. 26.
[24] *Decisions of the Charity Commissioners*, Vol. 4, pp. 28–29, and see also the Scottish case *The Governors of the Dollar Academy Trust v. H.M. Advocate* [1994].

offence punishable by a fine. This applies not only to charity trustees but also to employees or even it seems voluntary helpers. The offence is one of strict liability.

**Audit of accounts section 43**

Where charity trustees have failed to prepare accounts the Commissioners may require an audit to be carried out and the cost may be recovered from the trustees.

**Failure to submit annual reports etc. section 49**

Persistent failure without excuse to comply with the requirements to provide an annual report and attached accounts, an annual return or to provide copies of accounts to members of the public on request under sections 45, 47 and 48 renders the person responsible open to a fine. Presumably all the charity trustees concerned will be equally liable unless one of their number has been made responsible for compliance.

**Acting as trustees while disqualified section 73**

The 1992 Act introduced for the first time provisions similar to those in the Companies Acts prohibiting certain persons from acting as charity trustees (see Chapter 6). A person who acts while disqualified is liable to receive a term of imprisonment or a fine or both.

**Providing false or misleading information section 11**

A person who knowingly or recklessly provides the Commissioners with false or misleading information or suppresses, alters, conceals or destroys any document he should produce to the Commissioners will be guilty of an offence punishable by imprisonment or a fine or both. This offence is not confined to charity trustees.

Proceedings under these sections of the Charities Act require the prior consent of the Director of Public Prosecutions (section 94).

# Protection for charity trustees under sections 26 and 29 of the Charities Act

A measure of protection may be obtained by those persons responsible for administering a charity against charges of breach of trust or misapplication of charity funds by applying in writing to the Charity Commissioners for advice under section 29 on any matter affecting their duties. The protection extends to directors of charitable companies and those concerned with the running of charitable unincorporated associations as well as

**Advice under s.29**

trustees of charitable trusts. If they act in accordance with such advice they will be protected against any allegation that they have not acted properly or have not complied with the terms of the governing instrument. This provision of the Charities Act gives assistance in cases where it is unclear whether or not a certain course of action is in accordance with the terms of the governing instrument or is otherwise proper and will protect those responsible for administering the charity from any personal liability which they might otherwise incur if the action contemplated proves to be wrongful. It is unnecessary for all the persons who administer the charity to apply. A minority who are in doubt as to the propriety of a certain course of action may do so. The protection is not available however if the applicant knows or suspects the advice is given in ignorance of the material facts or if the court has, prior to the application, given a decision on the matter.

**Authority under section 26**

The Charity Commissioners also have power by order made under section 26 of the Charities Act to authorise any transaction, whether or not it is within the powers of the charity trustees, if they consider it to be expedient in the interests of the charity. If the charity trustees act in accordance with such an order they will be deemed to have acted properly and within the scope of their powers and will therefore be protected from any allegations that they have acted wrongfully. Before taking any action which may not be authorised by their governing instrument charity trustees should, in their own interests, apply to the Charity Commissioners for an order under section 26.

## Injunction

Where it is feared that those administering a charity intend to apply funds for purposes outside the scope of its objects an injunction to prevent this may be sought.[25] The usual procedure would be for the Attorney General to make the application in the High Court. The Charity Commissioners should be approached for advice on how to proceed.

## Limitation of actions

**Limitation Act 1980**

No special rules apply to charities and charity trustees against whom an action is brought are therefore entitled to the protection of the Limitation Act 1980. A claim against a charity trustee in contract or tort or in respect of a breach of trust will be barred by statute six years after the cause of action has accrued. However a claim against a trustee of a charitable trust in respect of any fraud or fraudulent breach of trust or to recover trust property which has been converted by the trustee to his own use may be brought at any time.[26] There are a number of claims not covered by the statute such as a claim to set aside a purchase by a trustee of trust property or claims for equitable remedies such as specific performance. Even in such cases the court may refuse to enforce a claim against the charity trustees where there has been substantial delay and the circumstances are such that it would be inequitable to do so.

---

[25] *Baldry v. Feintuck* [1972] 1 W.L.R. 552.
[26] Limitation Act 1980, s.21.

# 8 TAXATION

Charities have been granted some relief from taxation since income tax was introduced in 1799. Despite important qualifications on the application of tax relief the Revenue considered that there was still scope for abuse and consequently further restrictions were imposed by the Finance Act 1986 and consolidated in the Income and Corporation Taxes Act 1988.

**Charities established in U.K.**

The definition of "charity" contained in sections 505 and 506 of the Income and Corporation Taxes Act 1988 applies not only to income tax but also to Inheritance Tax and Capital Gains Tax. A charity is defined as "any body of persons or trust established for charitable purposes only." It was decided in *Camille and Henry Dreyfus Foundation, Inc. v. I.R.C.*[1] that "established" in the similarly worded Income Tax Act 1918 meant established in the United Kingdom since only bodies and trusts established in the United Kingdom are subject to the jurisdiction of the Courts of the United Kingdom. Foreign trusts or companies will not therefore be eligible for relief. It should be noted however that the activities of a charity established in the United Kingdom need not be confined to this country.

## Inheritance tax

### Gifts to charity

**Exemption from tax**

Section 23 of the Inheritance Tax Act 1984 (all references in this section are to this Act unless specifically stated otherwise) exempts from inheritance tax dispositions (including both lifetime gifts and gifts by will) by which property is given to a charity or is held for charitable purposes. Since March 14, 1983, there has been no restriction on the amount which may be given free of tax.

**Calculation of relief**

Inheritance tax is charged on the loss to the donor's estate rather than on the value received by the recipient. It might be thought, therefore that in a case where the loss to the donor's estate is greater than the value of the property actually received by the charity, the donor would be taxed on the difference. For example, a gift of a small number of shares in a company might deprive the donor of control with the result that his estate would suffer a reduction in value considerably in excess of the value of the shares received by the charity. However, it is the practice of the Inland Revenue in such a case to allow relief in respect of the whole of the loss to the donor's estate.[2] If the owner of a controlling interest in a company gives his shares in part to a charity and in part to an individual the exemption will cover an appropriate proportion of the total value of both gifts.

For the purposes of valuing property in an individual's estate account must be taken of any property which has, within the preceding five years been the property of a charity or held for charitable purposes as a result of a transfer by that individual or

[1] [1956] A.C. 39.
[2] Inland Revenue Statement of Practice, E.13.

his spouse. Where the value of any such property taken with the property retained by the donor would be greater than if they were valued separately (as may be the case if a set of antique chairs is split, farmland fragmented or a controlling shareholding divided) then the property held by the charity falls

**Related property** within the definition of related property (section 161). The value of the retained property is the appropriate proportion of the retained and related property valued as a whole. The effect of this is that where a person having a controlling interest in a company gives sufficient shares to a charity to deprive himself of control, the shareholding retained by him is valued as if he still has control while it is held by the charity and for a further five years thereafter. Consequently it is not possible for a donor who has transferred two shares to a charity (perhaps later to be purchased by his son) to transfer the remainder of his shareholding to his son at the lower rates of tax applicable to a minority interest for at least five years after the property has left the charity.

## Restrictions on relief

The reservation of benefit rules do not apply to exempt gifts to charities (section 102(5)(d) of the Finance Act 1986) but section 23 contains a number of other important restrictions which must be complied with if a transfer to a charity is to qualify as an exempt transfer. These apply to both testamentary and *inter vivos* dispositions.

**Gift to take effect immediately**

(1.) The gift to charity must take effect immediately. No relief is available if the gift takes effect only after a prior interest or lapse of time. For example, a gift to A for life and on the death of A to charity will be subject to inheritance tax on the gift to A but on A's death there will be no charge since the gift to charity takes effect immediately. If A is the donor's spouse no charge will arise either when the gift is made or on the termination of the life interest.

**Conditions to be satisfied within 12 months**

(2.) If the gift is subject to a condition, tax relief will only be available if the condition is satisfied within 12 months. Examples of conditions which might have the effect of losing the tax relief on the gift would be a provision that the gift should be used to provide books for a library if suitable premises can be found or a gift for a specific charitable purpose which is made conditional upon a certain amount being raised from the public. Such conditions should in general be avoided. When the fulfilment of the condition is important to the donor it is preferable for the gift to be for general charitable purposes at the discretion of the trustees and for a letter of wishes to guide the trustees in applying the fund. This will not assist however if the donor wishes to benefit charity only if the condition is fulfilled. It should be noted that a gift to charity conditional upon the charity making a payment to another person will be treated for tax purposes as a gift of the net sum retained by the charity.

**Defeasible gift**

(3.) A defeasible gift is not eligible for relief. A gift to charity which is either subject to an overriding power of appointment or can be revoked will not therefore qualify for tax relief. However if the gift is not actually defeated within 12 months and thereafter cannot be defeated it will be treated for tax purposes as being indefeasible. The exemption will therefore apply if the power of appointment or revocation is execisable only for a period of 12 months from the time the gift takes effect and is not actually exercised.

**Interest less than the donor's interest**

(4.) A gift to charity of an interest less than the donor's interest in the property is not eligible for relief from tax. A gift of a leasehold interest to charity by the freeholder will therefore be subject to tax (even if, apparently, the lease is valuable) as will a gift subject to a condition that another person should have certain rights (*e.g.* of occupation) over it. The question whether the interest given to the charity is less than the donor's interest is determined in the circumstances prevailing 12 months after the gift.

**Gift for a limited period**

(5.) A gift to charity for a limited period is not eligible for relief. This prevents a donor channelling gifts to third parties through a charity and thus avoiding tax.

**Where donor retains an interest**

(6.) Finally tax relief is not available in cases where the donor retains an interest in the gifted property for himself or his spouse or a connected person. A connected person is defined in section 270 and includes a donor's relatives and their spouses, the trustees of a settlement of which he or a person connected with him is a settlor and a company controlled by him or by a person connected with him. No exemption is available where land or buildings are given to charity subject to a right for the donor or his spouse or a connected person to occupy the property rent free or at less than a commercial rent. In the case of property other than land and buildings over which an interest is retained relief will be granted only if the donor pays full consideration for the retained interest or the interest is such that it does not substantially affect the enjoyment of the property by the charity. Thus a gift of an historic house to charity will be subject to tax if the donor reserves the right for himself and his family to continue to occupy it at less than the full market rent and it will be necessary for the terms of the gift to require the charity to grant a lease to the donor at commercial rates if he is to be permitted to occupy the property. Alternatively the donor might exclude a part of the property from the gift and retain this for his own use.

## Burden of inheritance tax on death

The principle that exempt gifts are free from inheritance tax has important effects when a testator's estate is partly exempt and partly subject to tax as where a legacy or a share of residue is given to charity.

In a straightforward case where a testator leaves a legacy to charity and the remainder of his estate to his children the gift to charity is simply deducted from the estate in calculating the amount on which tax must be paid. For example a testator having an estate of £500,000 leaves £50,000 to charity and the balance to his children. The estate will be divided as follows:

| | |
|---|---:|
| Tax on £450,000 | £120,000 |
| Gift to charity | 50,000 |
| Residue to children | 330,000 |
| | £500,000 |

Had he left the whole estate to his children their net inheritance would have been £360,000. The cost to his heirs of the £50,000 gift to charity is therefore only £30,000.

Where by his will a testator leaves the residue of his estate in equal shares to a charity and to his children this will have the unexpected effect that the charity will receive more than the children. The reason for this is that the children's share will have to bear the tax attributable to it whereas the charity's share of residue will be free of tax. This is the effect of section 41(*b*) which provides that none of the tax attributable to residue shall fall on an exempt gift.[3] For example a testator with an estate of £500,000 leaves his residuary estate equally between his children on the one hand and charity on the other.

| | | |
|---|---:|---:|
| ½ residue to charity | | £250,000 |
| ½ residue to children | £250,000 | |
| less tax | 20,000 | |
| Net residue to children | | £230,000 |

Where the testator wishes the charity and the children to receive equal amounts after all Inheritance Tax has been paid he should make this clear in the terms of the gift by using wording such as "such shares as after deduction of all inheritance tax attributable to them respectively are of equal value".[4]

## Taxation of charitable trusts

Property held upon trust for charitable purposes only is not relevant property for the purposes of the regime applicable to settlements without an interest in possession. It is therefore **Exemption from** wholly exempt from the 10-yearly charge to tax imposed on **charges** trusts in which there is no interest in possession (section 58) nor does any charge to tax arise when property leaves the trust on being applied for the charitable purposes of the trust (which includes expenditure on the administration of the charity).

[3] *Re Benhams Will Trusts* [1995] S.T.C. 210 Ch.D discussed in *Charities Law and Practice Review*, Vol. 3.1.
[4] See Butterworth's Wills Probate and Administration Service Form 1A 221.

**Temporary charitable trust**

Special rules apply in the case of trusts under which property is held for charity for a limited period only since these could otherwise be used for tax avoidance (section 70). Such trusts are still exempt from the 10-yearly charge and from the exit charge so long as the property leaving the trust is applied for charitable purposes. A charge is imposed when property ceases to be held for charitable purposes thus giving rise to a tax liability when the temporary charitable trust comes to an end. A charge will also arise when a disposition by the trustees results in a reduction in value of the property in the temporary charitable trust such as where the trustees omit to exercise a right. No charge is imposed however if the trustees simply make a bad investment or have granted an agricultural tenancy as a result of which the value of the property in the trust has fallen.

The rate of tax payable depends upon the length of time the property has been in the trust excluding the period prior to the introduction of capital transfer tax (March 13, 1975). The rate increases from 0.25 per cent for the first quarter, to 30 per cent when the property has been in the trust for 50 years. The tax charged is the aggregate of the following.

(a)  0.25 per cent for each of the first 40 complete successive quarters in the relevant period;
(b)  0.20 per cent for each of the next 40;
(c)  0.15 per cent for each of the next 40;
(d)  0.10 per cent for each of the next 40;
(e)  0.05 per cent for each of the next 40.

The amount on which the tax is charged is the amount by which the value of the property subject to charitable trusts is reduced and, if the tax is to be paid out of the trust, the amount of the tax.

# Capital gains tax

## Taxation of charities

**Taxation of Capital Gains Act 1992**

Charities are entirely exempt from capital gains tax (section 256) of the Taxation of Capital Gains Act 1992 (all references in this section are to this Act unless specifically stated otherwise) insofar as property is applicable and applied for charitable purposes. Any gains arising in the course of the administration of the charity are therefore exempt and no tax liability arises when assets are applied by a charity in furtherance of its charitable objects. it was held in *I.R.C. v. Slater (Helen)*

**Property applied for charity**

*Charitable Trust*[5] that property is applied for charitable purposes when it is transferred outright by one charitable institution to another unless the transferor knows or ought to know that the property will be misapplied by the transferee. The fact that the two charities are closely connected is immaterial. In that case the property transferred was added to the recipient charity's general funds and not distributed but, despite this, relief was allowed. However the Finance Act 1986 has now imposed an obligation upon charity trustees to take reasonable steps to

[5] [1982] Ch. 49.

ensure that property transferred to a non-U.K. body will be applied for charitable purposes if relief from capital gains tax is to be allowed.[6]

**Property leaving charity**

A charge to tax will arise under section 256(2) where property ceases to be held upon charitable trusts, for example, on the termination of a limited time charity.

**Executors**

A charity which is entitled to the residue of a deceased person's estate has no interest in the underlying assets until the completion of the administration but only a right to have the estate properly administered. The executors are therefore liable to pay tax on any gains arising during the course of administration.[7] Once the administration is completed and the charity is absolutely entitled as against the executors or trustees the exemption will be available.

**Companies**

The exemptions from capital gains tax allowed to charitable trusts extend also to corporation tax on chargeable gains accruing to companies established for exclusively charitable purposes (I.C.T.A. 1988, s.345(2)).

## Gifts to charity

**Individuals**

A gift or transfer at an undervalue by an individual or a corporation to a charity is wholly exempt from tax being treated for the purposes of the capital gains tax legislation as a disposal giving rise to neither gain nor loss (section 257). Any gain arising on a sale to a charity will be taxable even if the price was less than the market value, but no charge to tax will arise if the consideration does not exceed the amount which would be allowable in calculating the gain (that is the aggregate of the acquisition costs, expenses and indexation allowance).

**Settlement**

Where property is transferred from a settlement to a charity no tax liability arises on the deemed disposal if the charity becomes absolutely entitled to the settled property provided that no consideration is received by any person (section 257(3)).

**Tax effective gifts**

A donor who intends to make a gift to charity should always give assets which have increased in value to the charity direct so that they can be sold free of tax by the charity. If he sells the assets himself and gives the proceeds to charity he will be liable for tax on the gains regardless of his intention to benefit the charity.

## Income tax

### Income of charities

**Sections 505 and 506**

The principal exemption from income tax is contained in sections 505 and 506 of the Income and Corporation Taxes Act 1988 (all references in this section are to this Act unless stated otherwise) which provides that exemption from income tax may be claimed in respect of income which forms part of the income of a charity or which is applicable to charitable purposes only in so far as it is applied to charitable purposes only. Section 9(4)

---

[6] See pp. 126–129 for a full discussion of the restrictions imposed by the Finance Act 1986.
[7] *Prest v. Bettinson* (1982) T.C. 437.

provides that a similar exemption applies to the income of a charitable corporation.

**Income which may be exempt**   The exemption extends only to income from the following sources:

**Rents and profits**

(a) the rents and profits of land and interests in land taxable under Schedules A or D. The exemption covers rent payable under a lease and income from leasehold as well as freehold property. It does not apply to profits derived from transactions such as the sale of land which constitute capital rather than income payments;

**Interest and annual payments**

(b) interest, annuities and dividends on stocks and shares taxable under Schedules C, D or F; any yearly interest or other annual payment including covenanted payments, interest on a bank or building society deposit account and money out on loan; and income representing a distribution from a company. By concession interest which is not yearly such as interest on a current account) and profits on discounting transactions, are granted exemption from tax (Extra-Statutory Concession B9) if such income forms part of the income of a charity or is applicable to charitable purposes only;

**Maintenance of places of worship**
**Profits of a trade**

(c) interest, annuities and dividends taxable under Schedule C which are applicable solely to the repairs of a cathedral, college, church or chapel or building used solely for divine worship;

(d) profits of a trade carried on by a charity in the course of carrying out a primary purpose or by the beneficiaries.

All income from a source outside the section will be subject to tax and in order to qualify for relief the income must be actually applied to charitable purposes only.

**Income applied to charitable purposes only**   The courts have considered what constitutes an application for "charitable purposes only" on a number of occasions and the following principles can be inferred from these decisions and the practice of the Inland Revenue:

**Application for non-charitable purposes**

(a) The fact that an organisation is established for exclusively charitable purposes is not conclusive in deciding whether it is eligible for relief from income tax. If income of the charity has actually be applied for a non-charitable purpose, such as the benefit of private individuals, tax relief will not be available. In *I.R.C. v. Educational Grants Association*[8] income of the association (which was conceded to be a charity) was applied in the provision of scholarships almost exclusively for the children of employees of the Metal Box Company. This was held to be a private purpose and consequently tax relief was refused.

**Administration costs**

(b) The relief is available in respect of income applied to meet the cost of the administrative expenses of the charity. Difficulties may be encountered where the cost

[8] [1967] Ch. 993.

of administration appears to take up an undue proportion of the charity's income and relief may be disallowed. Relief may also be refused where expenses have been incurred improperly.

(c) The charity is not required to spend all its income in the year in which it is received. Part may be retained as a reserve for the future and if desired it may be reinvested without losing tax relief. However, a charity

**Accumulations**

which accumulated all its income over a substantial period of time would risk losing its entitlement to relief and could be removed from the register of charities under section 3(4) of the Charities Act. If substantial amounts are to be added to reserves it is advisable to explain the reason why this is necessary when applying for repayment of tax. Accumulating income may also bring the provisions of section 505(2) to (8) into operation.[9]

(d) Payments under a covenant will not qualify as annual

**Payments under covenant**

income payments forming part of the income of the charity if the covenantor receives substantial benefits from the charity. On the contrary they will constitute only one element in calculating the total income of the charity, the cost of providing the benefits being another. In such cases the covenantor is not entitled to deduct tax before making the payments nor may the charity reclaim the tax paid.[10] Insignificant benefits may be ignored and many charities confer some minor amenities or benefits on those who contribute to their funds. The question of what constitutes a substantial benefit was considered in *Taw and Torridge Festival Society v. I.R.C.*.[11] The Society in that case allowed members certain privileges including seats for performances at reduced rates. If full advantage was taken of the concession in the year this would have been worth approximately a quarter of each member's annual subscription. This constituted a benefit which was too substantial to be ignored. In practice the Revenue will ignore benefits worth less than 25 per cent of the covenanted payments (see the Inland Revenue guidance note for charities on Deeds of Covenant).

Section 59 of the Finance Act 1989 provided that the restriction on benefits to covenantors should not apply in the case of a payment to a charity whose sole or main purpose is either:

(a) the preservation of property or

(b) the conservation of wildlife

and the benefit received by the covenantor is the right of admission to view the property or wildlife which is being preserved or conserved for public benefit.

Why these particular types of charity should receive privileged treatment is not at all clear.

---

[9] See below, p. 128.
[10] *I.R.C. v. National Book League* [1957] Ch. 488.
[11] [1959] T.R. 291.

**Motive**

(e) The motives of those administering the charity are immaterial so long as the income is actually applied for a charitable purpose. Nor does it matter than an outsider derives some incidental benefit from the application.[12]

**Foreign charities**

(f) A charity which is established abroad is not entitled to relief in respect of its U.K. source income.[13]

## Profits of a trade

The exemptions from income tax set out in section 505 and described above do not extend to trading profits taxable under Schedule D except in two situations (section 505(1)(*e*)):

**Tax relief allowed**

(a) when the trade is undertaken in the course of carrying out a primary purpose of the charity such as where a theatre trust charges the public for tickets in order to cover the cost of the performances or a trust to preserve an historic house charges an entrance fee in order to meet the expense of maintenance—see, for example *I.R.C. v. Falkirk Temperance Cafe Trust*,[14] and

(b) when the trade is mainly carried out by the beneficiaries of the charity (*e.g.* workshops for the disabled).

**Bazaars and jumble sales**

By concession[15] the trading profits of voluntary organisations, derived from bazaars, jumble sales, gymkhanas, carnivals, firework displays and similar activities arranged by voluntary organisations or charities for the purposes of raising funds for charity will not be taxed if the organisation does not trade regularly, the trading is not in competition with other traders, the activities are supported by the public substantially because they are aware that the profits will be devoted to charity and the profits are actually transferred to charities or applied for charitable purposes.

The sale of goods which have been given to a charity is not considered by the Revenue to be trading but all other trading activities will be subject to income tax unless they fall within the exceptions mentioned above or are covered by the extra statutory concession.

**Permanent trading**

A charity which intends to carry on large scale or permanent trading operations should set up a separate non-charitable company to undertake this work.[16]

## Property development

**Development profits**

Generally speaking speculative undertakings such as property development are not suitable activities for a charity and are best left to professionals. However where a charity owns land which is suitable for development the trustees may be tempted to try and obtain at least a share of the development profits for the

[12] *Campbell v. I.R.C.* [1970] A.C. 77.
[13] *Camille and Henry Dreyfus Foundation Inc. v. I.R.C.* [1956] A.C. 39.
[14] [1927] 11 T.C. 395.
[15] Inland Revenue Concession C.4 (1985).
[16] See below, p. 129 and Inland Revenue booklet CS2 "Trading by Charities".

benefit of the charity rather than sell to a developer and allow him to take all the profits for himself.

The profits of the development will be subject to tax under Schedule D and will not be covered by the exemption given by section 505(1)(*a*) in respect of the rents and profits of land. If an arrangement is made with a developer for the charity to sell at an enhanced price reflecting the potential profits to be obtained from the development or for the charity to share the eventual profits this is likely to come within the terms of section 488 (artificial transactions in land) and the additional benefit accruing to the charity will be subject to income tax.

If it is considered appropriate for the charity to develop land itself (and this will depend largely upon the size of the charity, and whether it has access to expert advice and people who are familiar with the problems which are likely to arise—property development is not a suitable undertaking for amateurs) this can best be done by forming a subsidiary non-charitable trading company specifically for the purpose. The advantages of this arrangement are that those involved in the enterprise will have the protection of limited liability and, if the profits are paid to the charity, tax paid by the company can be recovered.[17]

# The restrictions imposed by sections 505 and 506

## The purpose of the legislation

It has been estimated that the tax benefits conferred on charities are worth over £500 million a year. There was some concern in the mid-eighties that these substantial fiscal benefits were conferred on charities with in some cases little or no benefit to the public. In particular it was thought to be unsatisfactory that charities whose income, through the idleness or lack of imagination of those who run them, is accumulated rather than being applied for charitable purposes should still be eligible for tax relief and that the use of charities for tax avoidance appeared

**Tax avoidance** to be increasing. Two particular methods of tax avoidance which took advantage of the tax concessions for charities were identified. One involved a United Kingdom trading company establishing two charities, one in the United Kingdom and one in a foreign tax haven. The trading company would covenant its income to the United Kingdom charity which would recover tax on the covenanted payments. These funds would then be transferred to the offshore charity and would eventually be used not for charitable purposes but for the benefit of the trading company or its owners. Another misuse of charities involved the

**"Captive"**
**charity** creation of a "captive" charity which would make interest free loans to its parent company or would benefit private individuals in other ways.

A stricter regime for both income tax and capital gains tax was introduced in 1986 in order to combat these abuses which applies to the larger endowed charities. The relevant provisions

[17] See below, pp. 128–130

appear in sections 505 and 506 and Schedule 20 to the I.C.T.A. 1988.

## Relevant income and gains

**Restrictions**

The restrictions do not apply to smaller charities having "relevant income and gains" of less than £10,000 in any period of assessment or, in the case of a company, accounting period. For the purposes of the section "relevant income and gains" includes only income and gains which would be taxable were it not for the concessions allowed by section 505(1) and the Capital Gains Tax Act 1979, s.145. It does not include donations, legacies, and street collections which would not in any event be taxable although donations from companies which are treated as a charge on the income of the company under section 338 of the Income and Corporation Taxes Act 1988 and payments from another charity are relevant income. The restrictions do not therefore apply to the many charities which derive most of their income from gifts and donations from individuals. If the Revenue consider that two charities are acting in concert with the purpose of avoiding tax the Board may by notice (which may be appealed against by the charities) direct that the restrictions shall apply notwithstanding they do not have income and gains of £10,000. (s.505(7)).

## Qualifying and non-qualifying expenditure

**Expenditure for charitable purposes**

**Distributions to non-U.K. bodies**

**Qualifying expenditure**    The section makes a distinction between qualifying and non-qualifying expenditure. Qualifying expenditure is defined in section 506 and Schedule 20 as expenditure for charitable purposes (which it will be remembered includes the cost of administering the charity). A payment to a non-U.K. body will, however, be treated as qualifying expenditure only if the charity has taken reasonable steps to ensure that the payment will actually be applied for charitable purposes only. There is no guidance as to what steps will be considered reasonable and this will no doubt vary from case to case. The Revenue is not prepared to give general advice on this point but it is possible to obtain their views on particular cases and to ascertain whether the steps taken so far will be adequate or not. It seems that a charity which intends to transfer funds to a non-U.K. resident body would normally be expected to have obtained documentary evidence of its purposes and activities and the intended use of the funds. If large sums are involved it would be usual to monitor the use of the funds to ensure they are applied for the proper purpose. This may not be necessary where the sums involved are small. The size, status and reputation of the recipient may also be relevant in determining the steps which should be taken.

**Non-qualifying expenditure**    The concept of non-qualifying expenditure includes not only expenditure for non-charitable purposes (which would in any event be in breach of trust or *ultra vires* in the case of a company) but extends to expenditure on investments and loans which are not "qualifying" investments or loans as defined in section 506 and Schedule 20.

**Qualifying investments**     Investments (other than mortgages) which are authorised investments under the Trustee Investments Act 1961, investments in companies which are quoted on a recognised Stock Exchange or dealt with on the Unlisted Securities Market, units in a unit trust or in a common investment fund established exclusively for charities, any interest in land which is not held as security for a debt, and deposits with banks and institutions licensed under the Banking Act 1979 at a commercial rate unless part of an arrangement by which a loan is made to another person are qualifying investments. All other investments (including, in particular, shares in private companies) are non-qualifying and expenditure on such investments is non-qualifying expenditure.

**Qualifying loans**     Expenditure on loans to other charities and to beneficiaries of the charity, deposits on current account with a recognised bank or institution licensed under the Banking Act 1979 (unless part of an arrangement whereby a loan is made by the bank to some other person) and other loans which on a claim being made by the charity the Revenue accepts as being for the benefit of the charity and not for the avoidance of tax will be qualifying loans. All other loans will be non-qualifying loans.

## Withdrawal of tax relief

If in any 12 month chargeable period the total income and gains of the charity exceed its qualifying expenditure then tax relief will be disallowed on an amount equal to any non-qualifying expenditure which may have been incurred by the charity during the period. Where a charity accumulates all or part of its income during the year its relevant income and gains will exceed its qualifying expenditure but this will not result in the withdrawal of tax relief unless there has been non-qualifying expenditure. A charity may therefore accumulate some of its income and gains during the course of the year as a reserve for future projects but if any income or gains has been applied on non-qualifying expenditure then relief will be disallowed to that extent.

**Excess of income over qualifying expenditure**

**Payment of tax**     A charity which is liable to tax under these provisions may select those items of income or gains which are to be subject to tax (all covenanted payments being treated as one item) and if it fails to do so within 30 days of being required to, the Inland Revenue will make the selection on its behalf. Qualifying expenditure will be treated as coming first from any income and gains of the charity which are taxable in any event.

Where in any year the total expenditure has exceeded the relevant income and gains of the charity and non-qualifying expenditure for the year has not been accounted for under the rules described above the non-qualifying expenditure will be related back to previous years and tax relief withdrawn accordingly.

**Practical difficulties**     The provisions contained in sections 505 and 506 give rise to considerable practical difficulties particularly in relation to payments to non-U.K. bodies. A charity may not know for some time whether or not tax relief will be allowed in full and therefore what income is available for its charitable purposes. Individuals who covenant more than £1,000 to charity will be unable to recover high rate tax relief in respect of payments which, as a result of sections 505 and 506, are subject to tax and even where relief is allowed there are likely to be delays in many cases (I.C.T.A., s.683(4)).

**Effect on covenants**

## Subsidiary trading companies

As mentioned above a charity's trading profits are not eligible for tax relief (unless they come within s.505(1)(*e*)). Of equal concern is the fact that a charity which engages in permanent or substantial trading activities will be in danger of losing its charitable status.[18] Very many charities now wish to trade in order to raise funds and arrangements whereby a charity wishing to engage in trading activities forms a non-charitable company to undertake the trade are common. The trading company may then either covenant its profits to the charity or give them under s.338 I.C.T.A. 1988,[19] which is then able to obtain tax relief on the profits. Although the Charity Commissioners encourage charities to establish a trading company which will transfer its profits to the charity as explained above a number of problems must be surmounted before a suitable structure can be put in place. These are set out briefly in the Commission's booklet "Fund-raising and Charities" and more comprehensively in Inland Revenue guidelines on Trading by Charities.

**Establishing a Trading company**

The Commission is of the opinion that the formation of a trading company is a speculative undertaking and is therefore unsuitable for a charity. It will not accept a specific power to form trading companies. It is a matter of construction of the governing instrument whether or not the investment powers are wide enough to cover the formation of companies. Again it is likely that such an investment would be regarded as a breach of trust for the trustees of a charitable trust or association. The standard Articles of a charitable company do not usually authorise the formation of a trading, as opposed to a charitable, subsidiary.

**Power to establish a trading company**

The solution which is usually suggested is for the cost of formation to be met by well-wishers rather than from the funds of the charity. The shares can then be transferred to the charity or retained as a completely separate enterprise.

The establishment of a trading company is only a beginning. It will need capital if it is to start trading. Again there are difficulties in the way of capital being provided by the charity. The charity trustees will need to decide if it is a proper investment, not only permitted by the terms of the governing instrument but a reasonable use of the charity's funds. The market rate of interest must be charged or if some other scheme is entered into to finance the company proper financial advice must be obtained to ensure that the terms are reasonable and in the interests of the charity. Presumably the fact that the

**Funding a trading company**

---

[18] See above, p. 25.
[19] See below, p. 131.

company's profits will be paid to the charity should be an important consideration.

A loan to or investment in a private company is not a qualifying investment for the purposes of I.C.T.A. 1988, s.506 unless the Board of Inland Revenue are satisfied that it is for the benefit of the charity and not made to avoid tax.[20] The Revenue are usually willing in straightforward cases to give approval even though the underlying intention is clearly to save tax.

**Qualifying investment**

**Covenant of profits**

Once established the company may covenant all its profits to the charity for a period which may exceed three years. The covenanting company is required to deduct income tax before making payments under the covenant and the charity will then reclaim the tax which has been paid. This arrangement now applies even when the charity is itself a company (sections 505 and 506) whereas previously a subsidiary trading company was permitted to pay its profits gross to the parent company. In order to minimise cash-flow problems for charities the Inland Revenue have stated that they will be prepared to make a provisional repayment of tax deducted by a subsidiary trading company without first verifying the correctness of the claim in cases where the arrangements are known to the Revenue in advance and they are satisfied that the affairs of the charity are in order. The Inland Revenue require strict compliance with Schedule 16, which requires the company to account to the Revenue for the tax within 14 days from the end of the relevant quarter, if the payment is to be allowed as a charge on the income of the company. A company which has covenanted its profits to a charity will therefore almost certainly have to pay over its profits before these can be ascertained. Companies will usually pay over more than the likely amount of the profits on the basis that the charity will reimburse any excess and will have to account to the Revenue for tax accordingly. Where this occurs and the tax reclaimed by the charity exceeds its entitlement the Revenue will usually make an adjustment in later repayment claims rather than seeking repayment from the charity. Excess tax paid by the company will be repaid to it or set against other liabilities.[21]

**Deduction of tax**

A further practical difficulty arises from the fact that the covenant applies only to profits actually paid during the course of the trading and therefore tax relief is available only in respect of payments made during the company's accounting period. The profits for the year will probably not be finally calculated until after the end of the year but nonetheless payment should not be delayed until after the year end or relief will be lost. The trading company should therefore pay before the end of its financial year an estimated amount which is likely to exceed the actual profits, the excess to be repaid by the charity in due course. If income tax has already been paid by the trading company on the total amount paid over to the charity it will be necessary for the company to obtain repayment of the excess from the Revenue.

**Timing of payment to charity**

[20] Sched. 20, para. 9, and see Inland Revenue booklet CS2, "Trading by Charities".

[21] Revenue Statement of Practice S.P. 3/87.

**Gift Aid** An alternative which may be preferable for the company since it confers greater flexibility is for payments to be made under the Gift Aid arrangements. A donation of a sum of cash to a charity is deductible from the profits of the company as a charge on income (I.C.T.A., s.339) but relief is only available where the company is controlled by different individuals from the charity. Tax relief is not available in respect of payments from a company where a connected person will receive a benefit in consequence of the payments.[22] A connected person is defined in section 839 of the I.C.T.A. 1988 to include a company or unincorporated association which is controlled by the same person as the paying company and a person or persons (which would include trustees) who control the paying company either alone or together with persons with whom they are connected. Close companies must give £250 or more to qualify for relief.

Payments to the charity must be made under deduction of tax and again the tax must be accounted for within fourteen days of the end of the relevant quarter.

There is no simple method of avoiding the problem of calculating the amount of the year's profits within the permitted time as tax relief is available only in respect of payments of cash. It may be preferable for the company to retain part of its profits even if it has to pay some tax rather than to experience a cash shortage.

## Covenants to charities

**Four year covenant** A covenant is a legally binding agreement made by deed by which the covenantor undertakes to pay a certain amount each year from his income to a charity. In order to be effective for tax purposes a covenant must be for a period which is capable of exceeding three years—hence the four year covenant.

### Covenants by individuals

**Basic and higher rate relief** A covenant is an efficient method of giving to a charity which assures the charity of a continuing income for the period of the covenant. Not only can the charity recover the basic rate tax paid by the covenantor but the covenantor may also obtain repayment of the higher rates of tax paid by him which are attributable to the covenanted sum. A person paying tax in the 1996/7 tax year at a marginal rate of 40 per cent was able to give £1,000 to charity at a cost to himself of only £600. There is now no limit on the amounts on which tax relief is given. The following table shows the cost to the taxpayer of a covenanted payment of £100 after deduction of basic rate tax in the tax year 1996–7

---

[22] I.C.T.A. 1988, s.339(3B) and see p. 134 below.

| Marginal rate of tax % | Payment net of basic rate tax | Received by charity | Cost to taxpayer |
|---|---|---|---|
| 24 | £100 | £131.50 | £100.00 |
| 40 | £100 | £131.50 | £75.01 |

It is necessary that at the outset the covenant is capable of continuing for more than three years but the fact that payments are discontinued before the expiry of the stated period or indeed before three years have elapsed will not affect the tax relief which may already have been allowed. A covenant is, however, a legally **Legally binding** binding agreement and the charity could in these circumstances enforce payment under it. The covenant need not specify a particular period. It may, for example continue for the lifetime of the covenantor or for some other indeterminate period or for a fixed number of years provided that the period is capable of continuing for longer than three years. A covenant which can be terminated by the covenantor voluntarily is not effective for tax purposes. A provision enabling payments to cease in the event of unemployment for example must be carefully drafted. A covenant containing a power to bring the covenant to an end may still be effective for tax purposes until such time as the power is actually exercised provided that it cannot be exercised within the three year period.[23]

**Time limit** The tax relief may be lost to the charity if a claim for repayment is not made within six years of the time when the payments were due under the terms of the covenant. In a recent case payments under a covenant were made late and the claim for repayment of tax which was made within six years of the date when the payments were in fact made was disallowed since more than six years had elapsed from the time the payments were due to the charity.[24]

**Deed** A covenant must be made by deed signed by the covenantor in the presence of a witness. Forms of covenant acceptable to the Revenue are provided in a Guidance note for Charities on Deeds of Covenant[25] and reproduced in Appendix C.

**Drafting** Care should be taken in the case of a four year covenant that a period which cannot exceed three years is not inadvertently specified. This can occur if four annual payments are required by the deed the first payment being due on the date of the deed in which case the last payment will be due exactly three years later and the covenant may not be capable of exceeding three years. A payment made before the date of the deed will not be eligible for tax relief since it will have been made voluntarily. However, in practice the Revenue may be prepared to concede relief if the payment was made in the same tax year.

**Fixed sum** A fixed sum should be specified in the deed or an amount which is ascertained by reference to a set formula (*e.g.* a percentage of profits or fees) since if payments are variable tax relief may only be obtained on the lowest payment made during the continuance of the covenant, this being treated as the annual payment which has been covenanted.

[23] I.C.T.A. 1988, s.671(2) as amended by Finance (No. 2) Act 1992, s.27.
[24] *I.R.C. v. Crawley and Others* [1987] S.T.C. 147.
[25] Charities Series No. 1.

The covenant may be for a sum net of basic rate tax or for a gross sum. The former is the most convenient for the covenantor as the amount he pays each year will not change with the rate of tax although the amount which can be reclaimed by the charity will vary. A covenant to pay a gross sum imposes on the covenantor the duty to calculate the amount that must be paid each year in order to leave the covenanted sum in the hands of the charity once tax has been repaid by the Revenue.

### Restrictions on higher rate relief

**Restrictions**

Section 683(4) of the Income and Corporation Taxes Act 1988 provides that where an individual makes annual covenanted payments to charity of £1,000 or more and because of the restrictions imposed by section 505 (the charity having incurred unqualified expenditure—see above), tax relief is not available to the charity on those payments, then the donor is not entitled to higher rate relief in respect of the covenanted payments. An element of uncertainty has therefore been introduced. Repayment of tax may be delayed until the affairs of the charity have been agreed with the Revenue. It will be recalled that where a liability to tax arises under section 505(3) the charity may select which items of income shall be treated as taxable. Higher rate tax relief will be unavailable only if the tax payable is attributable to the covenanted payments.

## Inland Revenue tax pack

The Revenue have produced a helpful information pack which is available free of charge from tax offices to help charities ensure that covenants in their favour are valid and effective for tax purposes and that the proper procedures for reclaiming tax are followed. It contains a guidance note on drafting covenants, precedents and sample forms for use by charities.

## Gift Aid

The introduction of Gift Aid in 1990 and the steps taken since then to simplify it and extend its scope have been of great benefit to charities.

**Relief for single cash payments**

The rules on Gift Aid appear in section 25 of the Finance Act 1990. The relief is given in respect of payments of £250 or more in cash by U.K. residents to charities and certain other institutions specified in sections 507 and 508 such as the British Museum and scientific research organisations. The gift may be paid by credit card, bank transfer or cheque as well as in cash but payments in kind will not qualify. Tax relief under the Gift Aid scheme cannot be claimed for money paid under a covenant. There is no upper limit on the amount of payments.

**Deduction of tax**
Tax must be deducted by the donor who must account to the Revenue for the tax within the usual time limits.

**Certificate**
A certificate in form R190(SD) which can be obtained from Inland Revenue FICO should accompany the payment.

**Minimum amount**
A single cash payment of at least £250 must be made in order to qualify for relief from tax. The payment may be made in instalments but each instalment must be at least £250. The payment must be an outright gift. A loan or gift subject to repayment terms will not qualify.

**Benefits to donors**
Neither the donor nor any person connected with the donor may receive any benefit in consequence of the gift (connected persons are defined in section 839) unless the benefit is worth no more than 2.5 per cent of the payment or £250. This allows the donor to receive literature about the charity or possibly some minor reduction on entry fees or tickets but would seemingly preclude unlimited free entry to their properties by conservation charities for example.

**Inland Revenue guidance**
The Revenue has produced a guidance note on Gift Aid which can be obtained from FICO.[26]

## Gifts by companies

Tax relief is also available on gifts by U.K. resident companies to charities. The rules appear in sections 338 and 339 of the **Sections 338, 339 I.C.T.A. 1988.** A payment to charity of a sum of money which is paid from the company's profits but is not deductible in computing its profits nor is it paid under a covenant is allowed as a charge on the income of the company for the purpose of calculating corporation tax. A charitable company is not entitled to claim relief under these provisions. The relief is available for donations to the bodies mentioned in sections 507 and 508.

**Tax deduction**
The company must deduct tax on the donation and account for it to the Revenue (s.339(3)).

**Close companies**
Some additional conditions are imposed by section 339 (3A) to (3E) before tax relief is available on donations by close companies (defined in section 414 of the I.C.T.A. 1988 as a company controlled by five or less participants). These are similar to those for individuals. Relief is restricted to payments of £250 or more after tax is deducted.

The payment must be an outright gift and neither the close company nor any connected person (defined in s.839) may receive any benefit in consequence of making it which is worth more than 2[1/2] per cent of the net value of the gift after deducting tax or £250.

**Certificate**
A certificate in form R240(SD) must be completed confirming that tax has been deducted.

[26] I.R. 113, "Gift Aid—A Guide for Donors and Charities".

# Payroll deduction schemes (I.C.T.A. 1988, s.202)

**Up to £1,200** An employer may, if so requested, deduct up to £1,200 per annum (1996/7) from an employee's pay and transfer it direct to an approval agency which will pass the payments on to the charity or charities selected by the employee. The payment will be deducted from the employee's total income in calculating his liability to tax. The approved agencies are charities, such as the Charities Aid Foundation, which the Revenue are satisfied will be prepared and able to give effect to the detailed arrangements for collecting and distributing payments stipulated in regulations made by the Treasury. The schemes must be approved by the Board of Inland Revenue. The agencies may levy a charge for their services and a maximum of 5 per cent has been approved. The cost to the employer of running the scheme may be deducted from his profits in calculating his tax liability.

**Agencies** A list of the agencies which have been approved to administer payroll deduction schemes will be found in Appendix G.

# Council tax and rates

Under sections 1 and 2 of the Local Government Finance Act 1992 Council Tax is payable in respect of all dwellings which are not included in the non-domestic rating list or exempt from it **Council tax** under Local Government Finance Act 1988, Part III. Fifty per cent of the tax is calculated by reference to the value of the property and the balance according to the number and circumstances of the residents. There are no specific reliefs from the tax for charities.

The reliefs given under the former rating system for many charities providing accommodation for beneficiaries have not **Care homes** been carried forward to the new tax. Almshouses, homes for the elderly and communities providing care for the mentally ill are now subject to the Council Tax. Accommodation provided for an employee of a charity in order for him to carry out his duties (for example a boarding school master) is fully taxable. Resident staff of a home providing care will be liable to pay the tax.

The owner, tenant, resident and any person occupying under a license of any residential property are jointly and **Liability** severally liable for payment. Where a property is divided into separate parts to provide smaller family units each will be regarded as a separate dwelling and valued individually for the purpose of calculating that part of the tax attributable to the property.

**Reliefs** Reductions are available for some residents, for example a single person occupying a property is eligible for 50 per cent reduction on the individual element in the charge (a reduction of 25 per cent of the total bill). Further reductions are available for people who receive pensions or disability allowances.

Individuals on low income may be eligible for rebates. Permanent residents of homes providing care (for example the elderly and sick) may be left out of account altogether in calculating the individual element in the tax where the property is effectively their sole residence. This means that although the tax will apply to many charities which were previously exempt the amounts actually paid will in many cases be relatively small.

Property occupied by a person who is disabled and which has been adapted to his needs will be put in one lower rate band than would otherwise apply.

**Non-domestic rates**
Properties other than residential properties are subject to non-domestic rates under Local Government Finance Act 1988, Part III. Where a property is wholly or mainly used for charitable purposes (including administration) either by the charity which owns it or by another charity 80 per cent relief is automatically available and the rating authority may allow 100 per cent relief (section 47).

**Charity Shops**
As under the rating system it seems that property which is occupied for ancillary purposes such as fund-raising or managing the charity's assets will not be eligible for relief but property which is used wholly or mainly for the sale of goods donated to the charity is treated as being occupied for charitable purposes if the proceeds (less expenses) are paid to the charity (section 64).

**Exemption**
Specific exemption from rates is given (section 51 and Schedule 5) to properties used for:

> public religious worship
> training or keeping occupied people who are disabled or
>       suffering from illness
> the welfare or the disabled and
> workshops for the disabled.

# Taxation of individuals receiving charity payments

## Income support

Regular payments from a charity of up to £20 per week are disregarded in assessing entitlement to Income Support. Occasional payments (for example at Christmas) will also be ignored as will gifts in kind unless they become regular.

## Scholarships

Income received by way of a scholarship by an individual who is receiving full time instruction at an educational establishment is free from income tax. "Scholarship" includes bursaries, exhibitions or other educational endowment. The value of a scholarship which is provided by an employer or any person connected with an employer for a member of the employee's family is, however, treated as provided by reason of his employment and if he is a director or higher paid employee is therefore subject to income tax (section 165 of the Income and

Corporation Taxes Act 1988). However the scholarship will avoid tax if in the relevant year only 25 per cent of payments from the fund are paid to members of employees' families.

## Income tax

**Voluntary payments**

Payments by a charity to individuals (or indeed institutions) which are made in furtherance of its charitable purposes should not be subject to income tax in the hands of the beneficiary provided that they are voluntary and give rise to no legal entitlement. Even if made on a regular basis (perhaps to provide nursing care for the sick or to supplement the income of the poor) charitable donations made at the discretion of the charity trustees which can be discontinued at any time are not taxable receipts. The position could be different if the beneficiary was given a legal right to the payments (*e.g.* by a covenant or annuity) or if the payments could be said to constitute a pension to a former employee under section 133 of the Income and Corporation Taxes Act 1988. Care should be taken therefore to structure regular payments in such a way that no legal entitlement is conferred upon the beneficiary. A payment which is received by virtue of an office or employment (*e.g.* a payment to a minister of religion to augment his stipend or for the benefit of a master at a school) will be taxable in the hands of the recipient. Such payments are not regarded as being truly voluntary.[27]

**Payments to office holders**

---

[27] *Benyon v. Thorpe* 14 T.C. 1; *Stedeford v. Beloe* 16 T.C. 505.

# 9 VALUE ADDED TAX

There was an outcry when VAT was introduced in 1973 because in contrast to the long standing reliefs from direct tax there were no special concessions for charities. Despite this, charities have only managed to obtain some relatively minor concessions and VAT continues to provide charities with serious problems.

The legislation is contained in the Value Added Tax Act 1994 and regulations made under it and all references to sections in this Chapter are references to this Act. H.M. Customs & Excise publish *The VAT Guide* (H.M. Customs & Excise Notice 700) and several much needed explanatory leaflets on specific topics. The following are particularly relevant:

| | |
|---|---|
| 701/1 | Charities |
| 701/41 | Sponsorship |
| 701/5 | Clubs and Associations |
| VAT Notice 706 | Partial Exemption |
| VAT Notice 742B | Property Ownership |
| VAT Notice 701/47 | Culture |

What follows is a brief outline of the relevant rules as they affect charities but the topic is complex and where large sums are involved a charity should always seek specialist advice.

**VAT on supplies to charities**

Charities are not exempt from VAT on goods and services they purchase. They have to pay VAT just like any other individual or business on all but zero-rated goods and services such as food, books and children's clothes and certain equipment for use by the handicapped (see section 30 and Schedule 8, and exempt goods and services such as insurance and postal services (see section 31 and Schedule 9). These are discussed in more detail below.

**Input tax**

A charity which carries on a business for VAT purposes and is registered for VAT may reclaim VAT paid on supplies to it which relate to taxable (including zero-rated) supplies made by it in the course of the business (input tax). For example a charity selling Christmas cards may claim the VAT on supplies attributable to the production and sale of the cards such as the cost of printing and packaging. Otherwise charities are unable to recover VAT on purchase of goods and services which relate to exempt or non-business activities. This is a heavy burden on many charities.

**Output tax**

Charities whose taxable turnover exceeds the threshold for registration (at present £47,600) are obliged to register for VAT and to charge and account for output tax on their taxable supplies. Most charities, however, do not carry on a business or are exempt and do not have to charge VAT. The meaning of "business" for VAT purposes is described below.

**Registration for VAT**

Where a charity incurs substantial VAT on inputs it may wish to consider the possibility of registering for VAT in order to recover some or all of the tax. A charity may only register for VAT if it is supplying goods or services (other than exempt supplies) in the United Kingdom in the course of a business carried on by the charity (section 4).

Although it is unusual for a charity to carry on a business for VAT purposes it is not impossible and some charities are able to claim that part of their activities constitutes a business. An example might be services provided to a local authority in return for payment under a contractual agreement. In addition many charities sell goods such as Christmas cards on a small scale though for income tax purposes these activities are usually best carried on by a separate trading subsidiary (see Chapter 8).

# What is a business?

The question of whether or not a charity is carrying on a business is crucial in determining its ability to reclaim VAT it has paid on goods and services supplied to it.

The definition of a business for the purposes of VAT is much wider than simply trading for profit and many charities may in the course of their activities carry on some business activities which will bring them within the scope of the VAT legislation.

A business includes any activity which involves the supply of goods or services to others for some consideration even where this is only equal to or less than the cost of providing them. The frequency of the activity will be relevant in deciding whether or not there is business activity and a single isolated event will not normally constitute a business. But a regular annual event such as a theatrical performance or horse show will be a business activity.

## Consideration

The payment of consideration is a vital element in business activity. The provision of services such as free legal advice and counselling at law centres, rescue services, free access to exhibitions or museums and holding religious services will not constitute business activity. Such activity is outside the scope of VAT.

**Donations and grants**
Raising money from the public by means of donations and legacies is non-business activity provided that the donors do not receive any consideration other than a flag, sticker or emblem of minimal value. Grants by a charity to beneficiaries who do not contribute any service to the charity in return is non-business.

**Welfare**
Welfare services and related goods supplied to distressed people for the relief of distress at a price consistently 15 per cent below cost and the provision of meals on wheels are treated as non-business activity (Leaflet 701/1 para. 10(*b*)).

## Business activities

**Subscriptions**
The provision of facilities or other advantages to members of a society or association on payment of a subscription is always business activity (section 94(2)(*a*)). Many charities give some benefits to members on payment of a subscription. These may

range from the right to priority in booking tickets to the receipt of educational material connected with the work of the charity. The right only to participate in the management of the charity does not bring the charity within the scope of paragraph (*a*) (section 94(3)). The members of an unincorporated association or charitable company may be required to pay a subscription and have the right to vote at the AGM but it does not mean that the charity is carrying on a business where this is the only advantage of membership. Where part of the subscription can be attributed to the provision of a newsletter which qualifies for zero-rating as printed matter, Customs will allow that part of the subscription to be zero-rated with the apportionment usually done on the basis of cost.

**Admission to premises**

The admission of persons to premises on payment of consideration is always business activity (section 94(2)(*b*)). Charities such as zoos, historic buildings and art galleries which charge an entrance fee are therefore always engaged in business activity, but admission charges may in some cases be exempt (see below).

**Advertisements**

Charities which include advertisements in their own publications such as brochures, programmes or annual reports may benefit from a concession whereby the payments they receive for the advertisements may, if they wish, be treated as outside the scope of VAT. The concession applies only where 50 per cent of the advertisements are from private individuals. Where the proportion of private advertisements is lower than 50 per cent the selling of advertising space will be treated as business activity and the payments will be subject to VAT. (See below for zero-rating of fund-raising advertisements by charities.)

## Exempt supplies by charities

Certain activities of charities which would otherwise be regarded as business activities and subject to VAT are exempt. These are set out in Schedule 9. The effect of exemption is that the supply of the goods or services in question by the charity is not taxable (section 4(2)) and the charity is not obliged to charge VAT on the goods or services supplied. The result for the charity is that the activity is treated as not giving the right to input tax deduction and consequently even where the charity is registered for VAT regard cannot be had to this activity in calculating the charity's entitlement to credit against input tax which has been paid. (See below.)

**Education— Schedule 9 Group 6**

Primary or secondary education at a school within the meaning of the Education Acts, education and research at a university are exempt from VAT as is research or vocational training provided by other establishments which are precluded from distributing any profits and apply any profits which are made towards continuing or improving the services provided. The exemption includes recognised courses teaching English as a foreign language, youth clubs and examination services.

**Welfare services**

**Schedule 9
Group 7**

Care and medical treatment in any registered hospital or nursing home is exempt and the provision of welfare services by a charity otherwise than for profit. "Welfare services" are defined as services directly connected with the care, treatment or instruction designed to promote the physical or mental welfare of the elderly, sick, distressed or disabled, the protection of children or young persons and the provision of goods associated with this work

Spiritual instruction by religious institutions is also exempt provided it is not primarily a recreational or holiday activity. The supply of accommodation or catering is not exempt unless it is ancillary to the care, treatment or instruction.

**Schedule 9
Group 13**

Charges made by public bodies (local authorities, government departments and other public bodies) or by voluntary organisations (bodies which may not distribute profits, apply all profits towards continuing or improving the facilities in question and which are managed and administered by volunteers) for admission to certain places and events are exempt. The exemption applies to admission charges to museums, art galleries and zoos and to cultural events of theatre, music or dance. The exemption is not available if it would disadvantage a commercial enterprise. VAT which has been paid on such admission charges from January 1, 1990 may be reclaimed.

**Reclaim**

## Fund-raising events

**Schedule 9
Group 12**

In principle and subject to the threshold for registration, VAT would apply to any fund-raising event which constitutes a business such as events attended by people on payment of a fee and the sale of goods and services such as commemorative items and advertising space in connection with the event. However there is an important exemption for charities, companies which are wholly owned by a charity and whose profits are payable to the charity. The exemption also applies to certain other bodies specified in section 94(3) or Schedule 9 Group 9 Item 1 and Group 13 Item 2. These are non-profit making bodies with political, philanthropic, philosophical or patriotic purposes, trades unions and professional bodies, learned associations and campaigning or pressure groups. Also included are the non-profit-making bodies providing facilities for sport or physical recreation or cultural activities mentioned. The exemption applies to the supply of goods and services in connection with a fund-raising event organised by one or more charities for charitable purposes or by a qualifying body for its own benefit. The exemption applies to admission charges, the sale at the event of items such as brochures, T-shirts and other merchandise, advertising space in programmes and sponsorship payments.

**Exempt events**

The fund-raising events covered by the exemption are fetes, balls, bazaars, gala shows, performances and similar events which are organised by a charity or more than one charity or by a company owned by a charity which covenants its profits to charity. Included are banquets, film premieres, first nights and concerts. Events which take place over several days fall within the exemption only if a single admission charge allows entry on every day.

The exemption applies only where the event is not a regular event or one of a series of similar events. Regular annual events such as an annual fund-raising ball will be exempt but a programme of events for which a season ticket or reduced charge is available or consecutive performances of a play or opera **One-off events** will not. Similar events held in different places may qualify for exemption as may different types of event held in the same place.

The VAT charged to people attending a fund-raising event which does not fall within the exemption may be limited by making a basic charge for admission and asking those attending to make a voluntary donation. The basic charge must be high enough to cover costs and the fact that an additional payment is **Reducing VAT** voluntary must be clearly stated on all publicity material. No **charge** special benefits may be allowed to those making a voluntary donation. In these circumstances VAT will be payable only on the basic charge. The additional donation will be outside the scope of the tax.

## Sponsorship

A form of fund-raising which can cause an unexpected VAT liability is a sponsorship arrangement under which the sponsor provides financial support for activity which is not covered by the exemption for fund-raising events in return for some benefit such as publicity. Where the sponsor receives something in addition to or simple acknowledgement of his support (for example, publicity or free entry) this is likely to be regarded as a commercial arrangement and the charity may have to account to H.M. Customs & Excise for VAT on payments received. The benefits to the sponsor may be very small as was illustrated in the case of *C&E Commissioners v. Tron Theatre Ltd.*[1] In this case a donation of £150 entitled sponsors to benefits worth approximately £15 with the result that VAT was chargeable on the full donation. The payments must be taken into account in calculating whether the charity's business turnover exceeds the threshold for registration. If it does the charity must charge VAT on all payments and other benefits received under the sponsorship agreement. See VAT leaflet 701/41.

# Reclaiming VAT

As mentioned above it is only charities which are registered for VAT (*i.e.* those charities which are carrying on a business) which can recover the VAT paid on their inputs. A charity which is registered for VAT may claim credit for VAT paid on its inputs against its liability to account for VAT charged on supplies it makes in the course of its business. If the value of VAT it has paid on inputs exceeds the VAT it has charged on supplies during any quarter it will be entitled to repayment of the balance.

**Partial** But where a charity which is registered for VAT makes **exemption** exempt supplies such as the provision of welfare services or the

[1] [1994] S.T.C. 177.

sale of tickets at a fund-raising event included in Schedule 9 Group 12 its ability to reclaim VAT will be limited.

**De minimis**
Where the VAT on inputs attributable to exempt supplies is £625 per month or less on average during the relevant quarter year and the exempt input tax is 50 per cent or less of its total input tax the charity may be treated as fully taxable and will be able to claim all VAT on supplies to it. The proportion which can be so attributed to exempt supplies must be calculated for each VAT return. The method of calculation is set out in VAT Notice 706.

**Claimable proportion**
In other cases it will be necessary to calculate how much input tax can be claimed. All tax paid on goods and services used only for the purpose of making taxable supplies may be claimed but none which is attributable only to exempt supplies can be. Some items may be readily attributable only to particular supplies but there will always be some goods and services (administration costs for example) which will be used partly for exempt supplies and partly for taxable supplies. The proportion attributable to exempt and taxable supplies respectively must be calculated. Only the latter proportion of input tax paid can be claimed.

**Non-business activities**
Where a charity which is registered for VAT also engages in non-business activities (as will almost always be the case) the proportion of input tax which can be claimed must be calculated. Where supplies can be attributed wholly to business or non-business use the tax paid on them can be claimed or not as the case may be. But where goods and services are used partly for business and partly for non-business purposes then it will be necessary to work out the proportion of use which can be attributed to business purposes and only this proportion of input tax can be claimed. Usually discussions will be held with Customs and Excise and a compromise agreed.

# Zero-rating—Schedule 8

**Zero-rated inputs Talking books, etc.**
The VAT burden on charities has been mitigated to some extent by charging a zero rate of tax on certain supplies to them. The concessions are contained in Schedule 8.

The supply to a charity for the blind of talking books, radios and cassette recorders and other equipment for loan to the blind or those suffering from serious visual impairment is zero-rated (Group 4). The tapes themselves are standard-rated.

**Buildings**
Services provided to a charity in the course of constructing a new building or self-contained annexe which will be used for administrative purposes or to provide charitable non-business (*i.e.* voluntary) services or as a community centre or village hall are zero-rated (Schedule 8 Group 5). The fees of architects, surveyors and other persons providing supervision of the work are not included in this category. The grant of a freehold interest or a lease of more than 21 years of property to be used for such purposes will also be zero-rated. Subsequent assignments of the lease or payments made under the lease are standard-rated. If, within ten years, there is a change of use or a disposal of the

property so that it will not be used for a qualifying purpose some of the VAT saved may be reclaimed by HM Customs & Excise. The VAT treatment of new buildings is a complex topic and specialist advice should always be obtained.

**Lifeboats** The supply, repair and maintenance of boats and equipment used for sea rescue are zero-rated (Group 8 Item 3).

Certain goods and equipment bought by or for donation to a charity for use for the personal use or care of sick or disabled people are zero-rated. Examples are ambulances, wheelchairs **Medical supplies** and other special equipment for the handicapped (Group 12). The cost of adapting premises for use by handicapped or disabled people is also zero-rated (Group 12 Items 7–9, 11–13). The supply of medicinal products for use by a charity for medical or veterinary diagnosis, treatment or research is zero-rated (Group 15 Items 9, 10).

The donation of goods for sale or export by a charity is **Charity Shops** zero-rated as is the sale of donated goods in a charity shop and the sale of such goods by a non-charity when a profit-shedding covenant is in operation. (Group 15 Item 1.)

Zero-rating applies to advertising on television, radio, cinema and newspapers by charities in order to raise funds or as **Advertising** a means of informing the public of their activities (Group 15 Item 8). The concession applies to publicity given to fund-raising events as well as direct appeals for funds. Advertisements in programmes, collecting boxes, stickers and tickets are covered but not clothing such as tee-shirts, calendars or commemorative items.

The cost of artwork and typesetting of printed material is zero-rated but not the cost of making a television, radio or cinema advertisement.

In order to qualify the advertisement should contain a direct appeal for funds such as "please support X" or "please give generously". Advertisements for staff or for pupils of a charitable school do not qualify.

A charity wishing to claim zero-rating on goods and services **Declarations** supplied to it must provide the supplier with a suitable certificate confirming the use to which the relevant item or property will be put. Examples will be found in VAT leaflet 701/1.

**Donated goods** The supply of donated goods by a charity or by a company or trader who has covenanted all his profits to a charity is also zero-rated (Group 15 Items 1–3) and VAT need not be charged on such goods.

**Advantage of** Zero-rating benefits charities in that suppliers of goods **zero-rating** within the various concessions outlined above are not required to charge VAT. Charities which are not registered for VAT and would otherwise have had to pay the tax without being able to pass it on in the course of a taxable business are in effect treated a if they were able to reclaim the tax.

Charities which acquire goods or services from other EU countries will be able to account for the VAT at the zero rate when they are brought into the country only if they are registered for VAT. Charities which are not registered will not be able to do this and will have to pay VAT on them at the rate which applies in the country of purchase.

# 10 THE ADMINISTRATION OF A CHARITY

## General principles

**Duties of charity trustees**

Charity trustees are defined in Charities Act, s.97 as "the persons having the general control and management of the administration of a charity" and the term therefore includes directors of charitable companies, members of committees of management of unincorporated associations and trustees of charitable trusts. In the broadest terms the duty of a charity trustee is to promote the interests of the charity and to ensure that its assets are applied only for its charitable purposes. The restrictions imposed upon charity trustees by statute and the practice of the Charity Commissioners are designed to these ends. Many of the principles which are applied have their origins in the law of trusts but now extend to all charities regardless of how they are constituted. For example, the rule that trustees of charitable trusts should act gratuitously applies equally to directors of companies and members of the committees of management of unincorporated associations.

Most of the principles explained below apply to all charity trustees but specific points which apply only to trustees of charitable trusts or directors of charitable companies will be mentioned as the chapter progresses.

## General powers and duties of charity trustees

### Duty on appointment

**Control of assets**

The first duty of a charity trustee on his appointment is to understand the terms of the governing instrument and to ensure that all the assets of the charity are under the control of the charity trustees and all sums due to them are recovered. He should take reasonable steps to satisfy himself that the funds of the charity have been properly administered in the past and if he finds they have not he should take steps to rectify the position or he may render himself liable for the faults or omissions of his predecessors in office. (See Chapter 7.)

### Compliance with the terms of the governing instrument

**Qualifications of the beneficiaries**

The terms of the governing instrument must be strictly complied with and in particular the qualifications of the beneficiaries, the area in which the charity is required to operate and the manner in which benefits are to be distributed must be observed. If any of the requirements of the governing instrument create difficulties the trustees should consider applying to the Charity Commissioners for advice under section 29 of the Charities Act or for a scheme to vary the purposes of the charity rather than acting outside the scope of their powers and putting themselves at risk of being made personally liable to restore the charity funds which have been misapplied.

**Authority under section 26**

In cases where the charity trustees' powers do not permit a particular administrative action which appears to be in the interests of the charity the Commissioners may authorise it under section 26 of the Charities Act. For example they will often be prepared to allow capital representing permanent endowment to be spent on renovating property on condition that it is recouped over a period.

**Ex gratia payments**

From time to time charity trustees may conclude it is in the interests of the charity to apply funds for purposes which, strictly speaking are outside the terms of the governing instrument. They may perhaps wish to add to the pension of a long-term employee on his retirement. Difficult cases can also arise where charity trustees feel there is a moral claim on them either to make a payment where there is no legal obligation to do so or to waive wholly or in part their entitlement to receive property. This kind of situation arises quite often where gifts to charity are made by will and the charity receives more than the testator intended or the testator omitted to provide satisfactorily for someone with a claim upon him. This can put the charity trustees in an invidious position. They have no power to apply the funds of the charity for purposes outside the objects of the charity but they may reasonably feel that if they were acting as individuals they would wish to relinquish all or part of the gift.

Previously a charity needed the authority of the Attorney General to make an *ex gratia* payment. Now the Commissioners have powers under section 27 of the Charities Act to authorise charity trustees to apply charity property or waive a right to receive property in pursuit of a moral obligation. The Commissioners must act under the Attorney General's supervision. Applications should be made to the Commissioners setting out the circumstances and why the trustees feel they are under a moral obligation. If the Commissioners refuse to give the necessary authority an application may be made to the Attorney General.[1] This procedure is only available in cases where the charity has no legal obligation to make the payment. For example payments to employees who are made redundant or dismissed may be made under the power to compromise claims (see below). The Commission has issued a leaflet "*Ex Gratia* Payments by Charities" CC7, which explains the Commission's practice.

**Charitable companies**

Section 35(3) Companies Act 1985 requires the directors of a company to observe the limitations imposed by the memorandum on their powers. The Act (as amended by the Companies Act 1989) nonetheless provides that acts or transactions which are not connected with the company's objects or authorised by the memorandum are valid and binding

---

[1] See *Re Snowden* [1970] Ch. 700

on the company and any third party and that as far as a third party acting in good faith is concerned the powers of the directors to bind the company or to authorise others to do so are unlimited.

**Ratification**

Where a director of the company has acted outside the scope of the memorandum or beyond his powers he may be liable for any losses which result. The members may, if they wish, by special resolution after the event ratify an act or transaction which is *ultra vires* and release the director from liability. An act which is within the objects of the company but is outside the powers conferred by the memorandum may be sanctioned by the members by an ordinary resolution either before or after the event. These provisions of the Companies Act 1985 apply to charitable companies but are subject to some further limitations.

**Charities Act, section 65**

**Third parties**

Where the company is established for charitable purposes a third party may only enforce an act or transaction which was *ultra vires* or outside the directors' powers if he was unaware that the company was a charity or he has given full consideration in money or money's worth and was unaware that the act or transaction was outside the terms of the memorandum or beyond the powers of the directors (section 65 of the Charities Act). A person who has subsequently acquired for full consideration property which was transferred by a company outside its powers acquires a good title provided that he did not have notice that the transaction may have been invalid. The burden of proving that a third person did not know the company was a charity or that the transaction was outside the objects or beyond the directors' powers is placed on the party making that claim.

**Protection of directors**

The members are not able to ratify a transaction or exonerate a director from liability under section 35 of the Companies Act 1985 without the prior written consent of the Charity Commissioners (section 65(4)).

## Protection of the trust fund

The preservation of the assets of the charity should be an important consideration for charity trustees. In making investment decisions professional advice should always be obtained and steps taken to ensure that the best possible price is obtained when assets are sold. Charity trustees, unlike individuals, should not be influenced in their dealings by personal feelings or moral obligation. Their sole consideration should be the interests of the charity. Difficult problems can arise when a claim is made against the charity such as when

**Compromising claims**

there is a dispute over the correct interpretation of a will or a claim is made under the Inheritance (Provision for Family and Dependants) Act 1975 where the charity is the residuary beneficiary under a will. The charity trustees must not allow personal feelings of sympathy for the claimant to affect their decisions since their overriding duty is to act in the best interests of the charity and if, having taken appropriate advice, they consider that they have a strong case they should pursue it. If on the other hand they believe that there would be some advantage to the charity if the claim was compromised (perhaps because their case is weak or to proceed might bring the charity into disrepute) they may properly compromise the claim. Normally they will act on the advice of counsel. Trustees of charitable trusts have power under Trustee Act 1925, s.15 to compromise claims. The powers of most charitable companies will be wide enough to permit the directors to agree to a compromise. If there is any doubt as to whether the charity trustees have adequate powers the Commissioners should be approached for authority to do so.

**Rejecting a gift**  Charity trustees may sometimes wish to reject outright a gift or legacy. Again they should bear in mind that their personal feelings are irrelevant. The interests of the charity should be the only consideration and there are seldom likely to be occasions where these would be served by renouncing a gift. The effect of such renunciation would be that funds due to the charity would be applied for non-charitable purposes and consequently charity trustees should only refuse gifts in the most exceptional circumstances an then only with the prior approval of the Charity Commissioners. An exceptional case concerned the

**Alcoholics Anonymous** charitable arm of Alcoholics Anonymous. The charity apparently satisfied the Commissioners that to accept substantial gifts would be harmful to the charity being contrary to the principle of self-help upon which it is based. The Commissioners authorised the charity to promote a private Act of Parliament which would authorise it to disclaim gifts of more than £1,000. These rejected gifts would then be applied for the purposes of another charity concerned with alcohol abuse.[2]

**Preventing dishonesty** Charity trustees should take reasonable precautions against dishonesty on the part of their employees and agents and, indeed, their fellow-trustees. The following points may seem obvious but are frequently overlooked and in at least one well-publicised case substantial losses have been incurred as a result. The signatures of at least two trustees should be required to operate bank accounts. Where a large number of cheques for small amounts is needed a separate account may be opened upon which cheques up to a limited amount may be drawn by a sole signatory. All assets should be registered in the names of all the trustees or a Custodian Trustee. The conduct of the charity's finances should not be left in the hands of a single person, whether an officer, employee or a trustee. Charities having an income of more than £100,000 are, from March 1, 1996, required[3] to have their accounts audited and trustees of many smaller charities will think it desirable to obtain a formal audit. The cost of a full audit may be excessive for small charities which may opt to have their accounts examined by an independent person (see below pp. 160–163). Where officers and employees habitually handle large sums of cash fidelity insurance should be taken out against the possibility of dishonesty on the part of any person. Proper procedures should be instituted to ensure that at least two persons are present when cash or cheques are processed.

[2] Charity Commissioners Report 1986.
[3] Charities Act, s.43.

# Dispositions of land sections 36 to 40 of the Charities Act

The Woodfield Report recommended that the need for the Commissioners to give consent to land transactions should be abolished and a system instituted whereby certain guidelines had to be observed. This proposal has been adopted. The relevant provisions appear in Part V (sections 36–40) of the Charities Act. Safeguards are established which are designed to ensure that a proper market price is obtained when land is disposed of and that the scope for abuse is limited. The Charity Commission leaflet "Disposing of Charity Land" summarises the regime (CC28).

## Sales leases and other dispositions (section 36)

Land held by or in trust for a charity may now be sold or leased or otherwise disposed of without the consent of the Commissioners provided that certain requirements are fulfilled and the disposition is not to a person who is a connected person (defined in Schedule 5) or a trustee for or nominee of a connected person. Connected persons include the charity trustees their relatives and spouses and companies controlled by them. The Commissioners' consent is still required for dispositions to connected persons and where the statutory requirements are not observed.

**Exempt and excepted charities**
Exempt charities are not subject to the restrictions imposed by section 36 but charities excepted from the need to register are now required to comply.

**Dispositions not covered (subsection (9))**
The restrictions on transactions which are contained in section 36 do not apply to dispositions authorised by statute or a scheme of the Commissioners. Nor do they affect dispositions at less than the full market price to another charity or to leases in favour of a beneficiary of the charity at less than the market rent.

**Section 36 requirements (subsection (3))**
The restrictions imposed on land transactions are similar in many respects to those which used to be imposed by the Commissioners before they would give their consent under section 29 of the Charities Act 1960 (now repealed).

**Surveyor's report**
The charity trustees must obtain and consider a written report by a qualified surveyor.

**Advertisements**
The sale or other disposal must be advertised in the manner recommended by the surveyor unless he advises that it would not be in the best interests of the charity to advertise. The Commissioners' past experience was that a higher price was obtained in 50 per cent of cases as a result of advertising for higher offers and it is likely that there will be a few cases where the surveyor will advise against advertising.

**Best terms**
The charity trustees must then decide on the basis of the report and the results of the advertisements that the term of the disposition are the best that can be reasonably obtained.

**Short leases subsection (5))**
The requirements of section 36 are more relaxed when the disposition in question is the grant of a lease by a charity for a term of seven years or less. Before such a grant is made the charity trustees must obtain advice from someone they believe to be able to provide them with competent advice and having

considered the advice they must be satisfied that the terms are
the best that can reasonably be obtained. There is no need to
advertise. As mentioned above this does not apply to leases to
beneficiaries of the charity at less than the market rent.

Section 37 requires any contract for sale or lease (including
a short lease) of land held by or in trust for a charity and the
transfer, lease or conveyance by which the disposition is effected
to contain statements:

**Contracts,
transfers and
conveyances**

(i)   that the land is held by or in trust for the charity
(ii)  that the charity is or is not an exempt charity and
whether or not the disposition is subject to the
restrictions imposed by section 36 or is excluded under
subsection (9) and
(iii) (if that is the case) that the restrictions apply to the
land.

**Land
Registration
Rules**

Rule 62 of the Land Registration Rules 1925 prescribes the
wording for dispositions of registered land.

**Land used by the
charity
(section 36(6))**

Where charity trustees wish to dispose of land which is held
on trusts which require it to be used for the purposes of the
charity they must in addition to complying with the
requirements outlined above give at least one month's prior
public notice of their proposals and invite representations. Only
after considering any representations may they proceed.

**Protection of
purchasers
(section 37(4))**

A disposition of land subject to section 36 which has not
been carried out in compliance with its requirements is
nonetheless valid in favour of a person who in good faith
acquires an interest in the land for money or money's worth.

**Land transferred
to charity**

Section 37(5) requires that all contracts for sale, lease or
other disposition and all conveyances, leases and other
instruments as a result of which land will be held by or in trust
for a charity must state that the land will be held by or in trust
for a charity, whether the charity is an exempt charity and if it is
not exempt that the restrictions on disposals contained in s.36
will apply. Rule 122 of the Land Registration Rules 1925
specifies the wording for dispositions of registered land.

## Mortgages (section 38 of the Charities Act)

Land held by or in trust for a charity may not be mortgaged or
charged without an order of the Charity Commissioners or the
court unless the following restrictions are complied with.

**Proper advice**

Where the land is to be mortgaged or charged as security for
a loan the trustees must obtain and consider written advice on:

(a)  whether the loan is necessary to enable the charity
trustees to carry out a particular project;
(b)  whether the terms are reasonable and
(c)  the ability of the charity to repay the loan on the
proposed terms.

The advice must be given by someone considered by the trustees
to be a person who has ability and practical experience in

**Exempt charities**

**General authority for mortgage**

**Mortgage documents (section 39)**

**Protection for third parties**

financial matters and who has no financial interest in the loan. An officer or employee of the charity may be asked to advise.

The restrictions do not apply to exempt charities but excepted charities are affected.

Section 38 does not apply where general authority is given by statute or scheme of the Commissioners or the court.

The documentation for the mortgage or charge must contain statements that the land is held by or in trust for a charity; whether or not the charity is exempt or there is general authority for a mortgage. Where the restrictions imposed by section 38 apply the trustees must give a certificate either that the Commissioners consent has been given or, if not, that the trustees have obtained and considered the required advice (s.39(2)).

A mortgage to which section 38 applies is valid in favour of a person who in good faith acquires an interest in the land in question for money or money's worth whether or not the restrictions imposed by the section have been observed (s.39(4)).

## Rentcharges

**Release**

**Costs**

Rent charges are almost never created nowadays but in the past it was a very common method of giving to charity. Because the amount was invariably of a fixed amount inflation has eroded the value and it will be in the best interests of a charity entitled to a rentcharge for it to be released in return for the payment by the land owner of a capital sum. The procedure has been simplified (Charities Act, s.40) by dispensing with the need for the Commissioners' consent where the consideration paid by the land owner is 10 times the annual payment or more. If the total amount received by the charity in consideration for the release of the rentcharge is £500 or less the costs of the charity in proving its title to the charge may be recovered from the landowner.

## Insurance

**Normal risks**

**Full value**

Charity trustees should insure buildings and their contents and any valuables owned by the charity to their full value against all normal risks. Trustees of charitable trusts and the trust deed, constitution or memorandum of association should specifically authorise this. Trustees of land have all the powers of an absolute owner (s.6(1), Trusts of Land and Appointment of Trustees Act 1996 — in force from January 1, 1997) which will include full insurance. In the absence of a specific power trustees of other charitable trusts only have power to insure property up to three quarters of its value (Trustee Act, s.19) but should apply to the Commission for authority to insure to the full value.

## Benefits to charity trustees

It is a general principle of trust law that a trustee should carry out his duties as a trustee gratuitously. As was pointed out by Fox L.J. in *Re Duke of Norfolk's Settlement Trusts*[4] this may on occasion conflict with the need to obtain the highest possible

[4] [1982] 1 Ch. 61.

standard of administration of the trust. The conclusion was reached in this case that the court has jurisdiction to authorise

**Remuneration of trustees**

the remuneration of trustees or an increase in their remuneration where, having regard to the nature of the trust, the experience and skill of the trustee and the likely amount of his charges, this appears to be in the interests of the trust. The Charity Commissioners have said, in consequence of this decision, that they will be prepared to register as a charity an institution the governing instrument of which authorises the remuneration of trustees and to authorise increased remuneration but only in exceptional circumstances where they are satisfied that the provisions are reasonable and necessary.[5] Where in the case of a substantial charity the trustees of which may be required to spend considerable time and effort on trust matters and where difficulties are encountered in finding trustees of high calibre, an application should be made to the Charity Commissioners for a variation of the governing instrument to allow trustees to be paid for their services. But if the application is to be successful a good case will have to be made out. Normally approval will be refused.[6]

Similar considerations apply when professional persons or businessmen, such as solicitors, stockbrokers or accountants,

**Payment for services**

are appointed as trustees of a charitable trust and wish to charge for services to the charity performed in their professional capacity. The general rule of equity is that a trustee should not profit from his trust nor should be place himself in a position where his interests may conflict with his duties as trustee but the advantages of appointing professional persons as trustees is well appreciated and most modern deeds establishing private trusts contain a power for trustees to charge for their professional services to the trust. The Charity Commissioners accept that the services of professional persons as trustees may be advantageous to a charity and that they should be permitted to charge for their professional services. They will request the inclusion of a standard clause which has been discussed in Chapter 4 and which appears in each of the model documents in Appendix A.

**Trustees as employees**

The employment of a trustee in a salaried position will also conflict with the principle that trustees should not benefit from the trust and specific provision in the governing instrument will be required to authorise this. The Charity Commissioners will not object to the inclusion of such a provision in the case of a charity applying for registration as a charity but will not authorise a change to the governing instrument of an established charity unless satisfied that the services of that particular individual in both capacities are, in the particular circumstances, necessary in the interests of the charity. This is discussed in more detail in Chapter 11. In most cases it will be sufficient for the employee to attend meetings and give his opinion and advice without the need for him to be a charity trustee and this will be the preferred option. In the few cases where it is accepted that an employed person should be a trustee the Commissioners will seek to have written into the governing instrument provisions

---

[5] Charity Commission leaflet CC9 and see Chapters 4 and 11.
[6] The court refused to authorise remuneration of trustees in the unreported case of *Smallpiece v. A.G.* 1992.

designed to eliminate the potential conflict of interest (see Chapters 4 and 11).

These principles are also applied to charitable companies and unincorporated associations.

Since the charity trustees' overriding concern must be to act in the interests of the charity it follows that, unless authorised by specific powers in the governing instrument, they should not

**Other benefits** apply the charity's assets or funds so as to benefit themselves. it is therefore improper for a charity trustee to occupy charity property at less than the market rent or to benefit from facilities or services provided by the charity. Nor should they direct business to themselves or their connections (unless the charity is to benefit from lower charges or advantageous terms). This does not mean that they need be out of pocket. They are entitled to

**Reasonable** be reimbursed any reasonable expenses they may incur in the
**expenses** course of their duties. Such items as postage, stationery used for the business of the charity and the cost of telephoning on its behalf may also be paid by the charity. Travelling expenses to attend meetings or otherwise deal with the charity's affairs are permissible. A dinner or other entertainment for the trustees may be provided at the charity's expense if this will promote the purposes of the charity by encouraging suitable people to act as trustees or stimulating interest in its work.[7] The scale of entertainment should, however, be appropriate to the size of the charity and should take up only a small proportion of the annual income.

Not infrequently charity trustees wish to engage one of their number to provide goods or services to the charity. These can range from the provision of legal advice to the supply of building material. While there is nothing to prevent the trustee providing goods or services free of charge or at cost it would be improper

**Profits at** for him to make a profit at the expense of the charity. Not only
**charity's expense** would this infringe the rule that a charity trustee should not profit from his office but it would also run counter to the principle that a trustee should not put himself into a position of a potential conflict of interest. As mentioned above it is usual for professional trustees such as solicitors and accountants to be permitted to charge for professional services. A reasonable market rent may also be paid to a trustee for the use of his property and a modest rate of interest on money loaned to the charity which does not exceed the rate which would be obtained if the cash was placed on deposit at a clearing bank. The loan agreement should be properly documented at the outset. Only where they are satisfied that it is in the interests of the charity will the Commissioners agree to a provision in the governing instrument authorising trustees who are businessmen to charge for goods or services. In the absence of such a provision authority should be obtained from the Charity Commissioners. This will only be granted in exceptional cases where they are convinced that the arrangements are beneficial to the charity. They will also wish the charity to ensure that the charge is reasonable and that the trustee concerned is not involved in the decision whether or not to employ him.

---

[7] *Re Coxen* [1948] Ch. 747.

**Purchase of land by trust**    Special rules apply to the purchase by a trustee of land owned by a trust. Such a purchase is voidable at the instance of the Attorney-General even though the transaction may be at full market value. A trustee of a charitable trust who wishes to purchase trust property should first retire and even then the transaction may be voidable if he is shown to have taken advantage of information obtained by him during his trusteeship. If, however, a trustee is willing to pay a higher price than anyone else and the transaction is in every other respect in the interests of the charity the Charity Commissioners may be prepared to authorise it under section 23 of the Charities Act and an application to the Charity Commissioners should be made in writing with full details of what is proposed. A sale, lease or other disposition of land owned by a charity to a charity trustee or other connected person (defined in Schedule 5 of the Charities Act) requires the consent of the Charity Commissioners.[8]

Quite apart from the general rule that charity trustees should not themselves benefit at the expense of the charity the memorandum of a charitable company will forbid the company **Company** to confer benefits on directors. Directors of companies are also **directors** subject to restrictions under company law (see Chapter 7). In particular property transactions between a director and the company require the approval of the members. A director must disclose any interest, whether direct or indirect which he may have in a proposed contract with the company and loans and guarantees in connection with loans to directors are prohibited.[9] The Companies Act 1985 allows the members of the company in general meeting to approve certain payments and other benefits to directors and confirm voidable transactions such as **Charity** where a director acquires property from the company. Such **Commission** approval or confirmation will be ineffective without the proper **approval** written consent of the Charity Commissioners (section 66 of the Charities Act).

The Commissioners have no power to authorise an action which is prohibited by the Companies Acts.

## Investment

Trustees of charitable trusts may only invest in securities which are authorised either by the trust deed or by the Trustee Investments Act 1961. Trustees who hold property on behalf of an unincorporated association are in a similar position. They may have wider powers of investment conferred on them by the constitution but failing this they will have only the statutory powers. Unless specifically excluded the statutory powers are additional to any specific powers of investment contained in the trust deed or constitution.

**Statutory powers**    Many charities, particularly older ones, have only the statutory powers of investment. The Act divides **Trustee** permissible investments into two categories, narrower range and **Investments Act** wider range. If the trustees wish to invest in wider range investments, mainly equities, they are required to divide the

[8] Charities Act 1992, s.36(2) (see p. 49 above).
[9] Companies Act 1985, Pt. X.

fund into two equal parts only one of which may be invested in wider range investments. The investments which fall within the narrower range and wider range respectively are set out in the First Schedule to the Act which is reproduced at the end of this book. Section 70 of the Charities Act gives power to the Secretary of State to order that trust funds should be divided between narrower and wide range investments in different proportions to those specified in the 1961 Act. An order was made in 1995 to increase the proportion of the trust fund which may be invested in wider range investments to 75 per cent.[10] Regulations may also be made to authorise charity trustees to invest in investments not included in the Schedule to the Trustee Investments Act (section 71). Again no regulations have yet been made. Trustees are required to obtain proper advice before investing in any investment other than those specified in Part I of the Schedule (bank deposits and Savings Certificates).

The Trustee Investments Act was introduced in order to allow trustees to take advantage of the potential capital growth which can be achieved through investment in equities. However it is generally acknowledged that the provisions of the Act are now outdated. Few investment managers would recommend that half a portfolio should be invested in gilt edged stock or similar securities as the Act requires. Modern trust deeds invariably contain a wide power of investment and should continue to do so until amending regulations are made.

**Express powers**   Express powers of investment contained in a declaration of trust or the constitution of an unincorporated association must be carefully adhered to and will be strictly construed. Even where they are phrased in very wide terms such as where a deed gives trustees the powers of investment of a beneficial owner this will not authorise trustees to engage in speculative investment. The court has on one occasion sanctioned investment by a charity in traded options (*Trustees of* **Speculative** *the British Museum v. Att.-Gen.*)[11] but this was an exceptional **investments** case. The court was influenced by the size of the fund and the availability of top-class specialist advisers and it is thought that few other charities will be comparable. The Charity Commissioners do not consider traded options to be a proper investment for a charity and have stated (in their 1985 and 1986 Reports) that they consider the underwriting of new share issues to be speculative and therefore unsuitable for charities other than in the wholly exceptional case where the charity is a substantial institutional investor participating in a new issue.

Care must also be taken to ensure that an investment in a **Qualifying** non-qualifying investment as defined in Schedule 20 to the **investments** Income and Corporation Taxes Act 1988 does not affect the tax exempt status of the charity.[12]

The Commissioners' view (see leaflet CC20 "Fund-raising **Subsidiary** and Charities") is that investment in a subsidiary or connected **trading** trading company is speculative and therefore not appropriate for **companies** a charity.

[10] The Charities Trustee Investments Act 1961, Order 1995.
[11] [1984] 1 W.L.R. 418.
[12] See Ch. 9.

**Duties of trustees**

**Investment generally**　Subject to the specific provisions of the trust deed trustees of charitable trusts should balance the interests of both present and potential beneficiaries. This means that their investment policy should maintain a reasonable balance between capital and income and that they should not select investments which are hazardous or which may endanger the capital of the trust fund in the interests of short term gain or increased income. This is not to say that they must avoid all risk since some degree of risk is inherent in almost any investment. A trustee will not be penalised for an error of judgment so long as he has acted with reasonable care, prudence and circumspection.

**Ethical investment**

Charity trustees may not allow their own personal opinions or moral judgments to affect their investment decisions. Their duty is to promote the interests of the charity and this is best done by seeking to maximise the return on capital of funds they hold as investments. They should not be influenced by non-financial considerations if this might endanger the funds for which they are responsible. It is only proper for the trustees to take non-financial considerations into account where this will still allow an adequate spread of investments.[13] If the trustees consider that the charitable purposes for which funds are held requires that certain types of investment should be avoided or that such a policy is in the interests of the charity they may adopt an ethical investment policy but only in so far as this is compatible with obtaining the best possible financial return on capital.

**Safeguarding the trust fund**

Trustees must take reasonable steps to safeguard the trust fund. The standard of care required of a trustee of a charitable trust is that of an ordinary prudent man of business investing for people for whom he feels morally obliged to provide. In practice this means that where the fund is invested in stocks and shares they should obtain written advice regularly from a stockbroker and it will normally be in order for them to act in accordance with that advice. Land and buildings should be kept in good repair and not allowed to deteriorate. Again the trustees will normally be protected if they follow the advice of a qualified agent or surveyor in dealing with properties they own.

If the trustees own a controlling interest in a company it is not sufficient for them to rely upon the expertise of the directors. A prudent man of business in such a position would ensure that he was provided with full information about the affairs of the company and if he became aware of mismanagement he would call the directors to account and if necessary take steps to have them removed. (See *Bartlett v. Barclays Bank Trust Co.*)[14] This may be particularly relevant when a charity owns a subsidiary trading company.

These rules apply also to unincorporated associations except in so far as the constitution provides specifically for investment.

**Directors' duties**

Directors of charitable companies are not subject to the restrictions on investment imposed on trustees. The directors are under an obligation to ensure that the company's assets are

---

[13] *Harries and Others v. Church of England Commissioners for England and Another, The Times*, October 30, 1991.
[14] [1980] 1 Ch. 515.

properly invested or to delegate their duties to competent agents. They are entitled to purchase any investment so long as they consider the transaction to be for the benefit of the company subject to the control of the members (*Burland v. Earle*).[15] Directors of a non-charitable company are not required to avoid speculative investments so long as they act with ordinary care and prudence (*Sheffield and South Yorkshire Permanent Building Society v. Aizlewood*).[16] But a charitable company is not established for profit and in this and other **Speculative** respects is similar to a trust. It can therefore perhaps be **investments** reasonably argued that the trust rule should also apply to charitable companies. The Charity Commissioners appear to accept this since they consider speculative investment to be unsuitable for any charity however constituted.

The Commission's opinion on the suitability of such investments as derivatives and foreign currencies are set out in *Decisions of the Charity Commissioners*, Vol. 3, pp. 18–28. Although this statement of their view is made in the context of requests for wider investment powers by established charities they emphasise the general point that speculative investments of this nature should only be made where there is some specific practical advantage to the charity from the transaction. This may be the case if the charity requires foreign currency in order to carry out its work abroad and the purchase of an option may protect the charity from fluctuations in the rate of exchange.

**Common investment funds**   Many charities are very small and obtaining proper investment advice and good rates of return on capital may be difficult or uneconomic for them in consequence. The trustees are nevertheless under a duty to obtain proper advice on their investments and to manage them properly. Sections 24 and 25 of the Charities Act provide a solution to this problem in authorising the establishment of **Advantages** common investment funds and common deposit funds enabling charities, which are otherwise unrelated, to pool their investments and take advantage of the economies of scale which will result. A wider spread of investments than would otherwise be available to a small charity and the benefits of professional management at a reasonable cost are further advantages of common investment funds. Such funds are themselves charities and are established by a scheme of the court or of the Commissioners. They are managed by trustees and each charity which participates is entitled to a share of the capital and income of the fund in proportion to its contribution. Any two or more charities may apply to the Charity Commissioners for the establishment of a common investment fund. All charities are authorised to participate in common investment funds by section 24(7) of the Charities Act unless the governing instrument specifically prevents this. See the Commission's leaflet "Common Investment Funds and Common Deposit Funds", CC15.

---

[15] [1902] A.C. 83.
[16] (1890) 44 Ch.D. 412.

**Income reserves**    Adverse comments on the practice of some charities of continuing to solicit funds from the public while retaining substantial reserves led the Charity Commission to issue guidance setting out their views on when this is permissible. The guidance (Charities and the Retention of Income Reserves) confirms that it may be in the interests of the charity to build up a reserve of income which is justified in relation to its identified needs. They give a number of examples such as where it is necessary to build a fund to pay for a particular project or repair a building or to protect against fluctuations of income. In these and similar circumstances the trustees may be justified in deciding to accumulate funds provided they have power to do so. The reasons for the decision should be set out in a note to the accounts. They also recommend that if the trustees wish to continue to appeal to the public for funds they should explain their policy in the appeal literature in order to avoid alienating their supporters.

# Delegation

Trustees of charitable trusts are required to act personally and should not delegate the performance of any of their powers or discretions to others unless specifically authorised by the trust **Trustees** deed. They may however appoint agents (Trustee Act 1925, **appointing an** s.23) such as solicitors, bankers and stockbrokers to transact **agent** business on their behalf including the receipt and payment of money and will not be liable for any loss arising from the default of the agent provided that the agent was employed in good faith, that the trustees acted with common prudence in appointing him and that he was employed only to do acts within the scope of his normal business (*Re Vickery*).[17] Even if the appointment was proper the trustees are still required to supervise the activities of the agent with common prudence or they may not be entitled to an indemnity (section 30(1)). The statutory power to appoint agents permits the employment of a stockbroker to sell and purchase investments on behalf of the trustees and they may ask for his advice on investment matters but normally the investment decisions will be taken by the trustees themselves in **Delegation to** the light of his advice. This rule is subject to any specific **outsiders** provision in the trust deed. Where the trustees wish to add a power of delegation to the governing document the Commission will in suitable cases be willing to make a scheme to allow this. (See Chapter 11.) In particular they will readily agree to the inclusion of a power to delegate investment decisions to an investment manager.

Unlike trustees of private trusts trustees of charitable trusts **Trustees act by** need not act unanimously. They may therefore delegate the **majority** exercise of their duties to committees of their number provided that decisions are taken by a majority of the whole body of trustees.

[17] [1931] 1 Ch. 572.

**Directors powers to delegate**

The articles of association of a charitable company will normally include a power for directors to delegate the execution of decisions to sub-committees, managing directors or agents. However they are still required to exercise proper control and supervision over the delegates.

**Unincorporated charities**

The power of members of a committee of management of an unincorporated charity to employ agents and delegate their authority will depend upon the wording of the governing instrument. Again a power to delegate decisions to outsiders is not normally acceptable to the Charity Commissioners. Similar considerations apply as outlined above in connection with trusts.

## Powers of attorney

**Trustees**

Section 25 of the Trustees Act 1925 authorises a trustee to delegate all his powers to another person by power of attorney signed in the presence of a witness for a period not exceeding 12 months. The donee may not be the sole other trustee. Notice must be given by the donor before or within seven days of giving the power to his co-trustees and to any person having the power of appointing new trustees. This provision is particularly useful if a trustee is going abroad or is in hospital and trust business must be attended to during his absence.

An enduring power of attorney extends to powers and discretions under a charitable trust.[18]

# Statutory duties of charity trustees

The Charities Act imposes certain duties on all persons having the general control and management of the administration of a charity.

## Registration

**Duty to register**

Section 3(7) imposes a duty on all charity trustees of a charity which is required to register (see Chapter 3) to apply to the Charity Commissioners for registration and to supply such information as may be required. Where a charity ceases to exist or there is any change in the trusts or in the registration particulars the Charity Commission should also be notified.

**Changes in registration particulars**

## Annual returns

Charity Trustees of registered charities are required by Charities Act, s.48 to prepare and submit to the Charity Commission an annual return in a prescribed form. This is designed to provide the necessary information to enable the Register to be kept up to date. Persistent failure to comply is a criminal offence punishable by a fine. Matters such as a change of correspondent of the charity and up to date information on the income of the charity must be reported.

[18] Enduring Powers of Attorney Act 1985, s.3(3).

## Official publications

Section 5 of the Charities Act requires that any charity which had a gross income of more than £10,000 in its last financial year must state the fact that it is a registered charity legibly and in English on the following documents:

(a)  all notices, advertisements and other documents in which donations are solicited for the charity;

(b)  all bills of exchange, promissory notes, endorsements, cheques and orders for money or goods which purport to be signed on behalf of the charity;

(c)  all bills rendered by the charity, invoices, receipts and letters of credit.

A person who signs or issues or authorises the issue of any such document which does not contain the required statement is guilty of an offence and may be fined. The offence may be committed by employees or agents as well as charity trustees but the latter should ensure that their staff are aware of the law.

## Schemes

*Cy-près* **schemes**

Charity trustees have a duty under section 13(5) of the Charities Act to take the necessary steps to enable a *cy-près* scheme to be made where the existing trusts prevent the effective use of the trust assets for charity (see Chapter 11). The Charity Commissioners have power under section 16(6) of the Charities Act, where charity trustees of a charity which has been established for at least 40 years have unreasonably refused or neglected to apply for a scheme for the administration of a charity, to apply to the Secretary of State for him to refer the matter to them with a view to making a scheme. Despite this, every review of or enquiry into local charities reveals considerable numbers which are dormant or have substantial accumulations of income, the trusts of which are out of date or which are too small to be effective and which should be put in order by amalgamation, modernisation of purposes or disposal of the capital under the provisions of ss.74–75 Charities Act.

**Reviews of local charities**

The benefit of a thorough review of local charities is generally accepted as one method of overcoming the apparent reluctance of many charity trustees to take the steps needed to put to good use the funds for which they are responsible. But such reviews have generally had only a temporary effect and the Woodfield Report recommended[19] that this might be overcome to some extent if local voluntary organisations like Rural Community Councils were more closely involved in the review procedure.

# Accounts

**Accounting requirements**

A major point of concern expressed in the Woodfield Report[20] was the failure of very many charities to submit accounts to the Charity Commissioners and the lack of enforcement. Steps have been taken since then to improve the ability of the

[19] *Paras.* 86–91.
[20] *Paras.* 51–63.

Commissioners to ensure compliance with the requirements of the Charities Acts and to regulate more closely the manner in which charities keep accounts.

**Contents of accounts**

Charitable funds are held for public purposes. It is therefore essential that adequate information is available to the public and the Commissioners so that they can be satisfied that charitable funds are being properly applied for those purposes and to help the charity trustees to ensure that the best possible use is being made of them. The new accounting requirements are designed to achieve this and to facilitate comparisons between charities. The statutory framework is contained in sections 41 to 49 of the Charities Act and The Charities (Accounts and Reports) Regulations 1995[21] which came into force on March 1, 1996. The accounts of all charities affected for accounting periods commencing on or after that date must be prepared in accordance with the new regulations. The accounting rules apply only to a limited extent to exempt and excepted charities (see below).

**Duty to keep accounting records**

Charity trustees of all charities regardless of size (other than exempt charities which are specifically dealt with in section 46) are obliged by Charities Act, s.41(1) to keep accounting records which:

(a) disclose at any time the financial position of the charity and

(b) enable them to prepare annual accounts in the required form (see below)

and these records must be kept for six years. In particular trustees must ensure that the records contain day to day entries showing all receipts and payments and the nature of the receipts and payments and particulars of the assets and liabilities of the charity. It is no longer sufficient for records to be brought up to date at the end of the financial year when the accounts are prepared. Proper books must be maintained throughout the year.

## Form of accounts (section 42)

**Duty to prepare annual accounts**

The charity trustees of every charity which is not an exempt charity have a duty to prepare annual accounts. New recommendations on the manner in which charities should prepare their accounts were formulated by a working party set up by the Charity Commission. These have now been approved by the Accounting Standards Board and have been issued as a new Statement of Recommended Practice (SORP) with effect from 1st March 1996. The recommendations apply to all charities. They are not legally binding but set out the best practice. Much of the SORP will not be relevant to smaller charities and where a charity has an income in any financial year of £100,000 or less the trustees may elect to prepare a simple

**Annual accounts of smaller charities**

form of accounts consisting of a receipts and payments account and a statement of assets and liabilities. The Commission has produced a guide "Accounting for the Smaller Charity", which sets out the best practice on the preparation of accounts of

---

[21] S.I. No. 2724.

smaller charities which have decided to produce accounts on this basis. There is no legal requirement as to the contents of accounts prepared in this way but trustees are recommended to follow those parts of the charities SORP which are relevant. The guide includes a standard form for accounts prepared on a receipts and payments basis which can be obtained free of charge from the Commission. The form of accounts shows a simple statement of receipts during the year broken down into receipts from donations, trading activities and income-producing assets and payments analysed to show direct expenditure including administration expenses. A second Commission guide "Accruals Accounting for the Smaller Charity" gives similar guidance to charities with an income of £100,000 or less, which choose to prepare their accounts on an accruals basis.

**Annual accounts of larger charities**

The accounts of all charities which have an income in the year in excess of £100,000 must be in the form prescribed in the Regulations. Regulation 3 requires the statement of accounts to include a statement of financial activities and a balance sheet prepared in accordance with the methods and principles specified in Part III of Schedule 1 to the Regulations.

The intention behind the Regulations is to prescribe a form of charity accounts which reflects the special nature of charities generally and will enable individual charities to provide an adequate and intelligible statement of their finances. Many charities will have to make substantial changes in the way in which they prepare and present their accounts in order to comply. The form and contents of the accounts is specified in Schedule 1 to the Regulations.

**Statement of financial activities**

In place of the traditional division of the charity's assets into capital and income there must now be a single statement of financial activities which will give details of both capital and revenue and a comprehensive analysis of the movements of the charity's resources. The distinction between capital and income, it is suggested, is not relevant to most charities and the income and expenditure account is often actually misleading. The new approach will provide a more informative and comprehensible statement of the charity's affairs and will show all the charity's receipts for the accounting period and how they have been used. Any restrictions on the expenditure of capital will be shown by analysing income resources, the application of resources or movements of resources by reference to the type of fund to which it relates. Much more detail will be required in the statement of financial activities than formerly would have appeared in most charities' accounts. The matters which are now required to be included are specified in Part I Schedule 1 to the Regulations.

Incoming resources must now be analysed to show donations, investment income and income from trading activities. Expenditure must be divided into expenditure on administration, fund-raising and publicity and direct promotion of the charity's objects. Other items which are required to be included are transfers between funds, gains or losses on disposals of fixed assets, funds brought forward from previous years and carried forward to the next financial year.

**The Balance Sheet**     The contents of the balance sheet are specified in Part II of Schedule 1. The balance sheet showing the state of the charity's financial affairs at the end of the year in question must include fixed assets divided into intangible assets (copyrights and other intellectual property), tangible assets used by the charity (offices, etc.) and investments. Current assets such as debtors, cash and investments must be shown separately and any restrictions on how funds may be used should be identified.

**Value of assets**     Fixed assets must be shown at market value if they are investments. This will require an annual revaluation where this is practicable (*e.g.* for stock exchange securities). Paragraphs 175–179 of the Charities SORP suggests that for other assets such as land a "reasonable approach" is adopted such as a five-yearly revaluation. The basis of the value given should be disclosed in the notes to the accounts.

**Methods and principles**     The statement of financial activities and balance sheet must be prepared in accordance with the methods and principles set out in Part III of Schedule 1. These are that the statement of financial activities should give a true and fair view of the incoming resources throughout the period covered and the balance sheet should give a true and fair view of the state of affairs of the charity at the end of the financial year. Corresponding figures for the previous year should be shown. The values of assets and liabilities should be determined in accordance with the Charities SORP.

**Notes to the accounts**     Certain information must be given (if not in the accounts themselves) by way of notes to the accounts. These are set out in Part IV of Schedule 1 and include the accounting policies adopted in preparing the accounts; the nature and purpose of all significant funds of the charity; details of remuneration paid to trustees; the cost of any trustee indemnity insurance policy; details of any transaction in which a trustee has an interest; any loan or guarantee secured on the charity's assets; auditor's remuneration; grants to another charitable institution (as specified in paragraphs 137–139 of the Charities SORP); detailed description of the different categories of fixed assets, debtors and creditors and any other relevant financial commitments of the charity. Details of the turnover and net profit must be given of any body which is connected with the charity and information on its relationship with the charity (see below).

## Accounting for branches or sections

The trustees of a charity are responsible for the financial affairs of its "branches" or "sections". Paragraphs 45 to 49 of the Charities SORP states that branches should be accounted for in the accounts of the main charity. Although the legal position has not changed the clear statement in the Charities SORP has caused many charities to review the position of its subsidiaries and connected organisations. A branch is defined in paragraph 2 of Appendix 1 to the Charities SORP as either:

> "(a)  simply part of the administrative machinery of the main charity; or

(b)  a separate legal entity which is administered by or on behalf of the main charity and whose funds are held for specific purposes which are within the general purposes of the main charity. "Legal entity" includes a trust or unincorporated association formed for a charitable purpose. The words "on behalf of" should be taken to mean that, under the constitution of the separate entity, a substantial degree of influence can be exerted by the main charity over the administration of its affairs; or

(c)  in England and Wales, a separate legal entity not falling within (b) which the Charity Commission has directed under section 96(5), Charities Act 1993 should be treated as part of the main charity for accounting purposes."

**A part of the administrative machinery**   Many charities have a regional organisation with offices, branches or groups carrying on their charitable purposes in different parts of the country or abroad. The degree of autonomy of these may vary considerably. They may have separate bank accounts and raise funds for their own activities yet still be within the overall structure of the parent charity and subject to its control. The terms of the constitution or trust deed of the main charity may contain indications as to the status of the regional groups. Where on the other hand a regional group is established as a distinct body having its own constitution and is not under the control of the main charity it is likely to be a separate charity rather than a branch and will have to be separately registered (if eligible) and be responsible for the preparation of its own accounts.

**A separate legal entity**   Some charities, in particular community centres, village halls and sports and recreation associations will have local groups and clubs as members of the charity and entitled to nominate members of the management committee and to priority use of facilities. These may be part of the structure of the main charity and will not exist

**Sections**   independently of it. They should be contrasted with separately constituted clubs or associations which are not part of the structure of the community association but pay an affiliation fee and may be entitled to reduced fees for hiring the hall. These latter groups will not be controlled by the management committee of the centre and will not be branches. Any funds they hold will belong to the group rather than the community centre and the community centre will not be responsible for accounting for them.

Subsidiary trusts established for purposes within the overall charitable purposes of the main charity may constitute branches
**Subsidiary**   where the main charity or its officers are the trustees of the
**trusts**   subsidiary or exercise control over it. Examples might be scholarship funds administered by a learned society.

Associations established to support a charity, such as "Friends" of a museum or hospital may also fall within this category.

Branches or sections of a charity may operate separate bank accounts and these may constitute separate funds of the main charity, dedicated to the specific activities carried on by the group. They should be accounted for as designated funds applicable only for the specific purposes of the branch. It is important that the individuals who run the branch are made aware that the funds they hold belong to the main charity though their use will be restricted to branch purposes.

**Separate charities treated as part of main charity**   The Commissioners have power under section 96(5) of the Charities Act to direct that a separate charity may nonetheless be treated as forming part of another charity for any of the purposes of the Act including the preparation of accounts. The most important category of these are the large number of health service charities which would otherwise have had to prepare and submit separate accounts. These are now dealt with under the "umbrella" of the relevant National Health Service Trust. The Trust will still need to maintain financial records for each subsidiary charity.

**Trading companies**   Where a charity conducts non-charitable activity (trading or fund-raising) through a non-charitable subsidiary consolidated accounts are recommended by the Charities SORP (paras. 54–68) in order to give a true and fair view of the charity's activities.

## Benefits

The new accounting rules will confer considerable benefits on all those involved with charities. More information will be available to the responsible authorities making it easier for them to review charitable activities; the public will find it easier to understand how charitable funds are being applied and to compare different charities; the charities themselves will have to adopt a more rigorous approach in preparing their financial records which will enable the trustees to obtain a better appreciation of the financial position of their charity.

## Audit or Independent Examination

Section 43 contains new requirements for the accounts of charities (depending on their annual income or expenditure) to be audited or independently examined. The Regulations contain detailed provisions as to the conduct of audits and examinations. These provisions do not apply to exempt charities or to excepted charities which are not registered voluntarily (see below).

The accounts of charities which have a gross income or the annual expenditure of which exceeds £250,000 in the year to which the accounts relate or in either of the two preceding years must (section 43(2)) be audited by a person who can be appointed a company auditor under section 25 of the **Income over** Companies Act 1989. Members of the Institute of Chartered **£250,000** Accountants, the Association of Certified Accountants, the Institute of Chartered Accountants in Ireland and the Institute of Chartered Accountants in Scotland are eligible. The Regulations (para. 6) set out the duties of an auditor.

**Income £250,000 or less**

Charities whose income or expenditure is less than £250,000 in the relevant year and the two preceding years are not required to have their accounts audited (though they may if the charity trustees wish) but must nonetheless have them examined by an independent examiner (section 43(3)). The examiner need not be an accountant but should have, in the opinion of the charity trustees, the ability and experience to carry out the examination properly. There is no definition of independence but someone other than the charity trustees, their spouses, relatives and business associates and employees of the charity should be selected. A person who supplies goods or services to the charity will also probably not be regarded as independent. The Regulations (para. 7) specify the form and content of the report. In particular, the examiner is required to state whether anything has come to his attention which gives him cause to believe that records have not been kept or the accounts do not accord with the records.

**Income £10,000 or less**

Small charities whose income or expenditure is £10,000 or less are not required to have their accounts audited or independently examined (section 43).

**The annual report**

All registered charities must (section 45(1)) prepare a report for each financial year giving details of the activities of the charity and such other matters as are prescribed in the Regulations. Paragraph 10 of the Regulations specifies the contents of the annual report. Every annual report must state the name of the charity, if a company, its company registration number, the principal address of the charity and its registered office if it is a company and the names of the trustees. Where the gross income of the charity is £100,000 or less for the year a brief summary of its main activities and achievements in relation to its objects is sufficient. Larger charities are required to provide a review of all activities including material transactions, significant achievements and achievements in relation to its objects, important events and any likely future developments. The report must also contain a description of the organisational structure. Special provisions apply to common investment funds.

**Submission of report and accounts (section 45(3))**

Charity trustees must submit the annual report and, attached to it, the accounts for the year to the Commissioners within ten months of the end of the financial year to which they relate. Charities which have neither gross income or expenditure over £10,000 in a year need only submit the annual report and accounts to the Commission if requested (s.45(3A)). Persistent failure to comply without reasonable excuse is a criminal offence punishable by a fine.

**Accounts available to the public**

The accounts of registered charities which are submitted to the Charity Commissioners in accordance with section 45 will be available for public inspection at the Commissioners' offices.

The 1992 Act introduced a new element of public accountability in the requirement (now section 47 of the Charities Act) that every charity must provide a copy of its latest accounts to a person who requests them in writing. They must do so within two months of the request but may charge a reasonable fee for so doing. This provision applies to exempt and excepted charities as well as to registered charities and consequently many charities whose accounts have hitherto been concealed from public scrutiny will be obliged to reveal this financial information.

## Accounts of exempt and excepted charities

**Exempt charities**

Exempt charities (see Chapter 3 for which charities are exempt charities) are required by section 46 of the Act to keep proper books of accounts and statements of account covering consecutive periods of not more than 15 months which include an income and expenditure account and a balance sheet. These must be kept for six years. They are not subject to the provisions for accounts contained in sections 41–45 of the Act. Exempt charities are not required to submit accounts to the Charity Commissioners but as mentioned above they are obliged by section 47 of the Act to provide a copy of the most recent accounts to any person who requests them to do so in writing. The charity may charge a reasonable fee to cover the costs involved.

**Charities excepted by regulation**

Charities which are excepted from the obligation to register by regulations made under the Act (see Chapter 3) and which have not registered voluntarily are not obliged to submit accounts to the Commissioners or to prepare and submit an annual report. In all other respects such charities are subject to the provisions of the Act in relation to accounts. Such charities must therefore have their accounts prepared in the required form and have them examined or audited, depending upon the size of their annual income.

The Charity Commissioners may require a charity which is excepted from registration to submit an annual report in accordance with section 45.

**Small charities**

Charities which are not required to register because they fall within Charities Act, s.3(5)(c) (charities having no permanent endowment, nor the use or occupation of land nor an annual income of more than £1,000) and have not registered voluntarily are not obliged to have their accounts examined or to prepare and submit an annual report to the Commissioners or to submit their accounts but they are otherwise subject to the provisions for accounts.

**Charitable companies**  The requirements of the Charities Act with regard to the form, audit or examination of accounts do not apply to charitable companies which are regulated by the Companies Acts. These have recently been relaxed and charitable companies having a turnover during the year of up to £90,000 are not required to have their accounts audited though unaudited accounts must still be submitted to Companies House. Charities with an income of £250,000 or less may choose to obtain an independant accountant's report that the accounts comply with the Companies Act. All charitable companies' accounts should comply with the Charities SORP. Where section 45 Charities Act applies the accounts of a charitable company must also be submitted to the Commissioners with the annual report.

# Litigation

**Protection of assets**

Charities are in no different position to other organisations as far as taking legal proceedings to enforce their rights and protect their assets are concerned. As was explained earlier charity trustees have a duty to act in the interests of the charity and where this involves taking legal action themselves or defending the charity in proceedings brought against it they may do so and the cost of taking legal advice will be a proper charge on the charity's funds. The consent of the Charity Commissioners is not required to bring or defend proceedings.

If they consider it to be in the interests of the charity to do so they may agree to compromise a claim made by or against them. Section 15 of the Trustee Act 1925 specifically authorises trustees of trusts to do so.

**Charity proceedings**

Charities differ from other organisations however in that there are restrictions placed upon certain types of legal proceedings known as "charity proceedings". Charity proceedings are defined in section 33(8) of the Charities Act as proceedings brought in any court of England and Wales under the court's jurisdiction with respect to charities or brought under the court's jurisdiction with respect to trusts in relation to the administration of a charitable trust.

**What are charity proceedings**

Any court proceedings on a question of charitable status, such as an appeal against a refusal to register, are clearly charity proceedings. Similarly any proceedings brought to challenge an order of the Charity Commissioners will be charity proceedings. An application to the court by charity trustees for a declaration in relation to the exercise of their powers or the construction of the trust deed or constitution[22] are charity proceedings as is a claim that charity trustees have committed a breach of trust or acted unconstitutionally.

**Who may bring charity proceedings**

Charity proceedings may be instituted by the charity itself or by any of the charity trustees. In the case of a local charity proceedings may be brought by any two inhabitants of the locality which is the area of benefit of the charity.

It is not open to any member of the public to bring charity proceedings however well intentioned he may be. In order to have the necessary standing he must be a "person interested in the charity". It is not enough for a person to have a close concern for the charity. The founder of a charity was held not to be a person interested in *Bradshaw v. University College of Wales*.[23] The interest needs to be substantially greater than the interest of an ordinary member of the public. In the case of *Re Hampton Fuel Allotment Charity*[24] the Borough Council in whose area the charity owned land was held to be a person interested and entitled to bring proceedings against the trustees.

**A person interested**

Charity proceedings may not be taken without the

---

[22] *Brooks v. Richardson & Others*, *The Times*, January 28, 1990.
[23] [1987] 3 All E.R. 200.
[24] In *Re Hampton Fuel Allotment Charity* [1988] 2 All E.R. 761 and see *Haslemere Estates Ltd. v. Baker* [1982] 1 W.L.R. 1109.

**Commissioners'
consent**

Commissioner's authority. If the matter can be dealt with by the Commissioners under their statutory powers they may not consent to the proceedings. The need for the Commissioners consent to charity proceedings was intended to prevent charities being troubled by frivolous or ill-founded claims. In practice however the Commissioners will not wish to prejudge any issue raised and will usually give consent. The Commissioners' authority is not required where the charity concerned is an exempt charity. If the Commissioners refuse their consent to proceedings an application may be made to a judge of the Chancery Division for leave to take proceedings.

**The Attorney-
General**

The Attorney-General is the protector of charities and is a necessary party to any charity proceedings. In some cases where an application for leave to take proceedings is made the Commissioners may refer the matter to the Attorney for him to take over the action (section 33(7)). This will only be done where the applicant appears to have a good case which it is in the interests of the charity to pursue. It is not necessary for an application for leave to take proceedings to be made before the Commissioners refer a matter to the Attorney. They will do so where they consider it desirable for legal proceedings to be taken. However the Attorney will only take proceedings himself in exceptional cases and in particular where payment of his costs are assured. Normally proceedings will be taken in the name of an individual who will act as relator and will be responsible for providing the evidence and for the Attorney's costs.

Where it has been found impossible to resolve a dispute it is always worthwhile speaking to the Treasury Solicitor's office to ascertain if the Attorney might be willing to take on the case.

# Data protection

The Data Protection Act 1984 was introduced to meet concern about misuse of private information held on computer. The Act gives certain rights to individuals and imposes certain obligations and standards on individuals and organisations which hold personal information about living individuals.

**Membership lists**

Charities which keep lists of the names and addresses of their members or supporters for the payment of subscriptions, to send them educational material or information about the charity or in order to seek donations or financial support from them may find that they are affected by the Act.

**Automatic
processing
Personal
information**

The Act only applies where information is kept on computer. Information which is kept manually, on a card index system for example, is outside the scope of the legislation.

Any information about living, identifiable individuals, even where this is restricted to the names and addresses, is data covered by the Act.

**Registration**

A charity which keeps personal data on computer is obliged to register with the Data Protection Registrar unless one of the exemptions applies. A fee (£75 at present) is payable for registration for three years. Failure to register may lead to prosecution and a fine.

The application for registration must give details of the purposes for which the data is held, their type, the sources from which they are obtained and to whom they will be disclosed. This information is entered on the Register and restricts the use to which the information may be put.

The charity may only disclose data it holds to persons or bodies described in the register entry. It may only pass on its membership lists to others if this is provided for in its application for registration.

**The exemptions**    The exemptions from the requirement to register are limited in scope. They are:

(1) personal data held by an individual for personal, family, household or recreational purposes;

(2) data which the user is required by law to make available to the public (*e.g.*, a company's register of members);

(3) data required to safeguard national security;

(4) data held only for calculating or paying wages or pensions or for dealing with sales and purchases or preparing accounts;

(5) data held by members' clubs relating to the members;

(6) personal data held for the purpose of distributing articles or information to individuals.

Where an exemption applies there is no requirement to register under the Act and individuals do not have the right of access to data held about them but the scope of the exemptions is very limited. Many charities will be obliged to register.

The exemption for data used for payrolls and accounts will apply only to simple organisations and will not be available if the **Payrolls and** data is also used to distribute articles or information **accounts** unconnected with the accounts or payroll.

Many charities hold personal information on computer **Mailing lists** mailing lists. They will be exempt from the need to register only if the data is used solely for the distribution of articles or information and provided that only names and addresses are held and the individuals are asked if they object to the information being held. The data may only be used for these limited purposes and not, for example for fund-raising appeals.

Advice as to whether a charity should register can be obtained from the Office of the Data Protection Registrar (see Appendix E) which issues a number of explanatory leaflets. If an application is made to register, the purposes for which the data is held must be specified.

When a charity is registered under the Act it is required to observe the Data Protection Principles contained in Schedule 1 of the Act and failure to do so may be a criminal offence. Even where registration is not necessary the Principles set out a good standard of practice.

**Data protection** The Principles are that all personal data will be:
**principles**

(1) collected fairly and lawfully

(2) held only for the purposes described in the registration entry

(3) used only for those purposes and disclosed only to the people described in the entry

(4) adequate, relevant and not excessive for the purpose for which they are held

(5) accurate and kept up to date

(6) held no longer than necessary

(7) protected by proper security

(8) accessible to the individuals concerned who may have them corrected or deleted.

**Rights of individuals**

An individual whose personal data is held by a charity is entitled to be provided with a copy of the entry and to check the charity's entry on the register. This will show to whom the data may be disclosed.

# 11 VARIATION

## Introduction

The powers of the court to make schemes for the administration of charities are exercisable concurrently by the Charity Commissioners.[1] It is important to appreciate that the purposes of a charity (*i.e.* the objects for which it is established) may only be altered in the limited circumstances set out in section 13 of the Charities Act and then only to the extent necessary (*cy-près*) to give effect to the donor's intentions. The meaning of the term "*cy-près*" is discussed below. Subsidiary conditions or administration provisions on the other hand may be varied under the inherent jurisdiction of the court as seems expedient in the interests of the charity. It is sometimes not easy to

**Administrative provisions v. purposes**
distinguish between administrative provisions and purposes which may only be altered in the circumstances set out in section 13. In *Re J. W. Laing Trust*[2] the donor gave property for general charitable purposes with a direction that the fund should be wholly distributed within ten years of his death. Because of the very great increase in the value of the fund it was accepted that the donor's wishes as to the organisations which should benefit could not be carried out if this condition was retained. The Charity Commissioners had refused to make a scheme dispensing with the directions on the basis that it was fundamental to the terms of the gift and could therefore only be dispensed with if the requirements laid down by section 13 were met. The court held that the direction was of an administrative nature and could be dispensed with by the court in exercise of its inherent jurisdiction. This should be contrasted with the case of *Re Lysaght*[3] where a restriction on potential beneficiaries was treated as part of the fundamental purpose of the gift.

## Variation of charitable purposes

The willingness of the courts to give effect to the charitable intentions of the donor by varying the original terms of the gift where these subsequently proved incapable of being put into effect is another example of the favour shown to charities.

**Favourable treatment of charity**
Provided that certain conditions were fulfilled the courts of chancery were prepared to give effect to the donor's assumed intention to benefit charity by substituting new purposes for those which had failed, thus saving for charity gifts which on general trust principles would have reverted to the donor or his estate.

[1] Charities Act, s.16.
[2] [1984] Ch. 143
[3] [1966] 1 Ch. 191.

The circumstances in which the court and the Charity Commissioners may alter the purposes of a charitable gift by schemes are limited to those now set out in section 13 of the Charities Act.

## Jurisdiction

Jurisdiction to vary the purposes of a charity exists only where the terms of the gift are otherwise legal and not contrary to public policy and the donor intended to benefit charity generally. The original justification for the court's assumption of jurisdiction appears to have been that effect was being given to the donor's intention to benefit charity generally, although he had chosen a particular method which has proved to be ineffective. It must be clear therefore that such an intention does indeed exist. If the failure of the original charitable purposes **Subsequent** occurs after the charity has been in existence (subsequent **failure** failure) a general charitable intention will be presumed. If on the other hand the trusts fail from the outset (initial failure) then the court must be satisfied that the donor indeed intended to benefit charity generally and not solely the particular purpose set out in the governing instrument.

**Initial failure** The question to be decided in cases of initial failure is whether the substance of the donor's intention was to benefit charity. Where this can be established but the method prescribed by the donor could not be carried out for practical or other reasons the court will give effect to the underlying intention by prescribing a suitable method of giving effect to the donor's wishes. In contrast, where the court concludes that the donor wished only to benefit charity in a specific way which cannot be carried out, the gift will fail. Buckley J. put the distinction between a general and specific charitable intention in the following way in *Re Lysaght*[4]:

**General** "A general charitable intention, then, may be said to be a **charitable** paramount intention on the part of a donor to effect some **intention** charitable purpose which the court can find a method of putting into operation, notwithstanding that it is impracticable to give effect to some direction by the donor which is not an essential part of his true intention—not, that is to say, part of his paramount intention. In contrast, a particular charitable intention exists where the donor means his charitable disposition to take effect if, but only if, it can be carried into effect in a particular specified way."

The distinction between a general and a particular **Practical** charitable intention is not always easy to discern in practice but **difficulties** a particular intention is more likely to be inferred if the details given by the donor as to how the gift is to be applied are very detailed or if conditions are attached which appear to have particular significance in the donor's mind. A general charitable **Examples** intention has been found where a testator gave property to found music scholarships which were to be confined to children

4 [1966] 1 Ch. 191 at 202.

from particular orphanages. The gift was refused because of these restrictions and the court held that they could be dispensed with since they were not essential to the donor's primary intention.[5]

A case where no general charitable intention was found was *Re Wilson*[6] where the testator gave the property upon trust to pay the salary of a schoolmaster who was to teach in a school which had not been built but which he expected would be built with funds raised from the public. Detailed directions were given for the running of the school. The court found that the testator had intended only to benefit charity in the particular way set out in the will and that consequently there was no evidence of a general charitable intention.

**Gifts to NHS hospitals**　The Charity Commission published their views on gifts to NHS hospital trusts where the hospital has subsequently closed in *Decisions of the Charity Commissioners*, Vol. 3. This contains a useful summary of the various possibilities.

## Schemes where there is initial failure

**Failure of charitable gifts**　There are many reasons why a charitable purpose may fail at the outset. For example, the fund may be insufficient for the stated purpose; a gift may be made to an institution which does not exist either because no such institution can be found which matched the description given or because the institution closed down before the gift was effected; the gift may be for a purpose which is impractical or impossible, perhaps because the consent of some person or body is required which is not forthcoming or conditions imposed by the donor make the gift impracticable. In such cases where a general charitable intention on the part of the donor is established a scheme will be made to alter the purposes and give effect to the underlying wishes of the donor.

**Examples of failure**

A gift to a charity which has been amalgamated with another charity before the gift takes effect or has been reorganised or renamed does not fail if it is for the charity's general purposes. This is so whether the reorganisation was effected by a scheme of the Charity Commissioners or under powers contained in the trust instrument or informally. In each case the original charity continues in existence[7] and the gift is valid and takes effect as a gift to the reorganised charity being treated as an addition to the assets of the original charity and therefore applicable for the revised purposes. Nor does a gift which is for a specific purpose fail if the charity to which it has been made has been reorganised provided that the specific purpose can be carried out by the new charity. However, the position is different if the gift is to a charity which has been dissolved and its assets distributed. In such a case the gift will fail and a scheme will be required to carry the donor's intentions into effect.

**Situations where gifts do not fail**

**Dissolution**

[5] *Re Woodhams* [1981] 1 W.L.R. 493.
[6] [1913] 1 Ch. 314.
[7] *Re Faraker* [1912] 2 Ch. 488; *Re Bagshaw* [1954] 1 W.L.R. 238.

**General rule**  **Unidentified donors—Charities Act, s.14**  The general rule is that property given for a specific charitable purpose which has failed at the outset cannot be applied for some different purpose if no general charitable intention can be imputed to the donor **Exception** but is held on a resulting trust for the donor. An exception has been made by section 14 of the Charities Act. This provides that if property has been given by a donor who cannot be identified or found after statutory advertisements and inquiries have been made or who disclaims his right to the property in a prescribed **Reasonable** form the purposes for which it is held may be varied *cy-près*. The **inquiries** form of the statutory advertisements is specified in the Charities (*Cy-près* advertisements, Inquiries and Disclaimer) Regulations 1993 which also require them to be published in a newspaper or periodical distributed throughout the area in which the appeal was made. Where property has originated from cash collections or in such a way that individual donors are not distinguished or from lotteries, sales, competitions or other money-raising activities it is conclusively presumed that the donors cannot be identified without the need for advertisements and inquiries.[8] **Power of court** Moreover the court (but not the Charity Commissioners) may order that property may be treated as belonging to unidentified donors even though the conditions mentioned above are not fulfilled if the amounts are so small that it would be unreasonable to incur the expense of returning them to the donors or it would otherwise be unreasonable to do so (perhaps because of lapse of time since the gift was made).

In practice it is preferable, where possible, for property given to charity by donors who cannot be identified to be treated as a gift which has failed subsequently thus enabling a scheme to alter the purposes to be made without the need to make inquiries for donors which can be expensive and time consuming. Therefore if the purpose for which the property was given was capable of fulfilment at any time this may be treated as subsequent failure. For example a plan to build a village hall might be abandoned because of escalating costs. If there were sufficient funds at any stage of the appeal to build a hall of any kind however inadequate the Commissioner may be prepared to treat the appeal as having failed subsequently and will authorise the application of the funds for alternative purposes by scheme without the need for advertisements and inquiries.

## Schemes where there is subsequent failure

The Charities Act 1960 widened the powers of the court and the Charity Commissioners to make schemes to alter the purposes of a charitable gift. Before 1960 a variation could only take place if the original purposes failed or became impractical to carry out or were illegal. If the trusts were capable of being put into effect then there was no jurisdiction to vary them even though a variation might enable the fund to be put to better use. The donor's wishes had to be followed if this was at all practicable.

---

[8] s.14(3).

The circumstances in which the purposes of a charity may now be varied are set out in section 13(1) of the Charities Act as follows:

**Charities Act, s.13**

(*a*)  where the original purposes, in whole or in part
    i(i)  have been as far as may be fulfilled; or
    (ii)  cannot be carried out, or not according to the directions given and to the spirit of the gift

**Purposes fulfilled or impossible**

Paragraph (*a*) describes circumstances in which jurisdiction to alter the purposes of a charity would have existed even before the passing of the Charities Act 1960.

Sub-paragraph (i) would permit a variation of the original purposes where, for example, funds given for research into a particular disease remain after a cure has been found.

Sub-paragraph (ii) covers situations where the donor has made the gift subject to conditions which make it impracticable or impossible. Such a case was *Re Lysaght*.[9] The testatrix left property to the Royal College of Surgeons to found a medical studentship but directed that Jews and Catholics should be excluded. The College refused to accept the gift on these terms as being contrary to its principles and the court was prepared to dispense with the conditions to enable effect to be given to the intentions of the testatrix. Apprenticing charities provide a modern example. Charities to assist poor apprentices to buy the tools of their trade were common in earlier centuries but little use for such funds can be found now. The Charity Commissioners accept that these purposes can no longer be carried out and will vary the trusts of such charities to the education and training of young persons in the original area of benefit.

**Re Lysaght**

A case decided before the Charities Act 1960 was passed where a restriction of the class of beneficiaries was held to render the purposes of the charity impossible to carry out was *Re Dominion Students Hall Trust v. Att.-Gen.*[10] The charity ran a students' hall which under the terms of the trust was restricted to male students of European origin. It was held that it was unnecessary for the purposes to be absolutely impracticable for the court to have jurisdiction to vary them *cy-près*. In this case the colour bar was considered liable to defeat the object of the charity and therefore to render the purposes of the charity impossible to carry out in a broad sense and a *cy-près* scheme was ordered to delete the objectionable condition.

**A pre-1960 decision**

Another case where impossibility was given an extended meaning was *Re Campden Charities*[11] where a very considerable increase in the funds available for the relief of poverty coupled with substantial changes in the area of benefit and the practices of the community since the gift was made were held to be grounds for a scheme to vary the purposes of the charity.

**Another early case**

The concept of "the spirit of the gift" which appears several times in section 13 has been defined as "the basic intention underlying the gift, that intention being ascertainable from the

**"The spirit of the gift"**

[9] [1966] 1 Ch. 191.
[10] [1947] Ch. 183.
[11] (1881) 18 Ch.D. 310.

terms of the relevant instrument read in the light of admissible evidence" (Pennycuick V.-C. in *Re Lepton's Will Trusts*).[12]

**Provision for surplus funds**

(b) where the original purposes provide a use for part only of the property available by virtue of the gift

Under this paragraph a scheme may be made to provide for surplus funds arising because the original purpose did not exhaust the amount available such as where an appeal for funds is too successful and a balance remains after the original purposes have been carried out. (Chapter 12 describes how this situation can be avoided.) Another situation in which this paragraph might apply is where the value of the original gift or the income derived from it have substantially increased in value. This frequently causes problems in the case of ancient gifts of land for charitable purposes. If the land is sold and fetches a substantial sum the income from the invested proceeds may well greatly exceed the amount contemplated by the donor and which it is practical to apply in furtherance of the original purposes. A scheme may be made to widen the objects so that the surplus may be put to good use. Schemes could also have been made in these circumstances before 1960.

**Amalgamation to promote effective use**

(c) where the property available by virtue of the gift and other property applicable for similar purposes can be more effectively used in conjunction, and to that end can suitably, regard being has to the spirit of the gift, be made applicable to common purposes.

This provision specifically widened the existing powers of the court and the Charity Commissioners to make schemes to vary the purposes of a charity since there is no requirement for failure or impracticality. It has enabled a number of small local charities for the relief of poverty to be amalgamated in order to form larger funds. The very small size of a great number of ancient charities for the relief of poverty, some having an income of only a few pounds a year, which are thought to serve little useful purpose in modern conditions, were the subject of considerable concern for some time and are still thought to be a problem today. A simplified procedure for amalgamating small charities now exists (see the discussion on modernising small charities below). Many small, ancient charities were also subject

**Outdated qualifications**

to stringent conditions as to the way in which help should be given (*e.g.* clothing, bread or coal) or the qualifications of beneficiaries (*e.g.* windows, spinsters, orphans or persons attending a particular church) which made them largely irrelevant in modern conditions. After the passing of the Charities Act 1960, reviews of local charities for the relief of poverty were instituted in a number of counties under the powers given by the Act with a view to amalgamating small charities into larger groups having more substantial funds

**Dispensing with the donor's restrictions**

available for more general purposes. Such groupings frequently involved dispensing with the donor's restrictions on the way in which funds might be applied and, so that all the charities in the

---

[12] [1972] Ch. 276.

group covered the same district, it was often necessary to enlarge areas in which benefits might be distributed.

**Modernisation of areas of benefit and qualifications of beneficiaries**

(*d*)  where the original purposes were laid down by reference to an area which then was but has since ceased to be a unit for some other purpose, or by reference to a class of persons or to an area which has for any reason since ceased to be suitable, regard being had to the spirit of the gift, or to be practical in administering the gift.

This paragraph also extended the powers of the court and the Commissioners and it gives them considerable flexibility in adjusting the original purposes, particularly of ancient charities, to modern conditions and circumstances. The areas of benefit can be enlarged and, presumably, (although this is seldom if ever done) reduced to make them coincide with modern administrative areas. There are many instances, particularly with ancient charities, of classes of beneficiaries being varied on the basis that they have ceased to be suitable. For example it is usually considered invidious for widows or spinsters to be the sole objects of a charity for the relief of poverty and the scope of such charities may usually be widened to include all poor persons in the relevant area although the Commissioners may insist on the trustees giving preference to the members of the original class.

**Modernisation of purposes**

(*e*)  where the original purposes, in whole or in part, have, since they were laid down
    (i)  been adequately provided for by other means; or
    (ii)  ceased, as being useless or harmful to the community or for other reasons, to be in law charitable; or
    (iii)  ceased in any other way to provide a suitable and effective method of using the property available by virtue of the gift, regard being had to the spirit of the gift

**Provision by the state**

Many purposes coming under the fourth head are now provided for by central or local government, and trusts for the repair of roads and bridges and the provision of other public utilities to be varied under sub-paragraph (i). Trustees of charities for the relief of poverty sometimes request a variation of the purposes of their charity since, they claim, the state now provides the assistance which formerly was provided only by charity. This argument is not accepted by the Charity Commissioners. There may not now be the degree of poverty that existed in the eighteenth and nineteenth centuries but poverty is a relative term and they consider that it is always possible to find people whose standard of living is below the accepted norm particularly among the unemployed and families with several children. The Commissioners will not therefore permit funds for the relief of need to be directed to other purposes though they are normally prepared to make the trusts more flexible by widening the area of benefit eliminating restrictive conditions under paragraphs (*c*) and (*d*).

Sub-paragraph (ii) needs no comment.

Sub-paragraph (iii) seems to give the Commissioners scope to adjust the purposes of a charity to enable better use to be made of the property subject to the trusts. In practice they have been reluctant to do so, except in the poverty cases mentioned above, unless satisfied that the original purposes have failed. It is difficult to persuade them that the original purposes should be varied because they are outdated except in such clear cases as where the donor directed the distribution of clothing, bread or coal to the poor where standard relief of need purposes will be readily substituted. Normally where the original purposes are capable of being carried out the Commissioners will not agree to make a scheme to vary them.

**More effective use of trust property**

## The extent of variation

**The *cy-près* principle**   Since the original justification for the court's assuming jurisdiction to vary the trusts of a charity which had failed or was impracticable or illegal was that effect was thereby given to the donor's general charitable intentions it therefore follows that the new purposes should be close to those originally specified. The expression "*cy-près*" appears to originate from the Normal French meaning "near this" which has evolved over the centuries to mean "as near as possible."[13] In recent times courts have required the substituted purposes to be varied only as much as is necessary to give effect to the original intentions of the donor and this principle still applies even in cases where the purposes are varied under the extended powers in section 13.

**Origins**

**Modern application**

**Preserving the donor's intentions**   The need to balance as far as possible adherence to the donor's original intentions with making the gift effective can give rise to differences of approach between the Charity Commissioners and the charity trustees. A solution to the difficulties encountered by the charity trustees which seems to them to be practicable may be rejected by the Charity Commissioners as departing too far from the original terms of the gift. In consequence restrictions may be retained or imposed which the charity trustees would prefer to be dispensed with. The Charity Commissioners argue that people will be deterred from giving to charity if they think that their wishes will be ignored and their gift diverted to purposes which they had not intended and there is certainly merit in this argument. However it is also arguable that in adopting a somewhat cautious approach the Commissioners have not used their powers as imaginatively as it was thought they might when the Charities Act was passed.

**The Commissioners' approach**

This problem was commented on in the Woodfield Report.[14] The Report recommended that the possibility of relaxing the strict application of the doctrine should be considered. In their Annual Report for 1989 (paras. 73–76) the Charity Commissioners responded to this criticism by saying

[13] See Sheridan and Delancey, *The Cy-près Doctrine* (1959).
[14] Paras. 83–85.

that in future their staff would be expected to be more flexible in their approach to these problems and stating that in certain respects the strict rules which had been applied in the past would be relaxed.

**Applications for cy-près schemes**

**Cy-près schemes**    When applying to the Commissioners for a cy-près scheme to vary the original purposes of a charity the charity trustees should be able to satisfy them that the conditions of section 13 are complied with so that they have jurisdiction to make a cy-près scheme and they should be able to suggest what in their view is the most suitable use for the property of the charity. They should therefore be aware of what type of substituted purposes are likely to be acceptable. Some broad principles are set out below. These do not represent strict rules and exceptions may be made in particular cases. They are however guidelines which may help the trustees of a charity in framing an application for a cy-près scheme.

**Guidelines to cy-près application**

**Diversion from one head of charity to another**

**The head of charity**    A scheme will not normally be made which might divert property devoted to one head of charity to another. In the case of a charity for the relief of poverty in a particular parish the cy-près application will be the relief of poverty in that and neighbouring parishes rather than for wider purposes within the same parish. The underlying intention of the donor is taken to be the relief of poverty rather than the benefit of the inhabitants of the parish. The Commissioners now accept that there is no legal prohibition on purposes coming within one head of charity being widened to include purposes coming within another but this will only be allowed in particular circumstances. Perhaps a case can be made for such an approach where there is no suitable wider area which could usefully absorb the charity's funds or where the donor founded other charities for the benefit of the same area, so demonstrating his wish to help the inhabitants of the area generally. It will be necessary to make a good case why the general rule should not apply.

**Original area of benefit retained**

**Areas of benefit**    The Commission will not normally make a scheme under which any part of the original area of benefit is excluded even if this means a considerably larger area is taken in. Where a scheme to amalgamate local charities into a group is proposed the size of population in the areas served by the charities in question will influence their decision. They will be reluctant to substantially widen the area of benefit of one charity if the inhabitants of that area will not benefit in return from another charity or charities of similar size in the proposed group. But where this would prevent the reorganisation or rationalisation of a charity or group of charities the principle may give way to more practical approach.

The cy-près application for a charity established for the benefit of a local school or hospital or other charitable institution will be for the benefit of the school or hospital which now serves the original area even though it may also serve a much larger area. For example, when a school has been closed inquiries will be made as to which school is now attended by children who would formerly have attended it and funds originally for the benefit of the closed school will be diverted to that school.

**Restricted class of beneficiaries**   If restrictions on the class of beneficiaries are making it difficult for the charity to spend all its income the Commissioners will normally be prepared to

**Dispensing with restrictions**

make a scheme to dispense with them. An example might be where the beneficiaries are the widows of persons killed in the Second World War or where there are no longer a large number of members of the beneficial class such as orphans. However, in order to preserve the donor's intentions the substituted class will be as close as possible to that originally specified. In the examples given above the substituted beneficiaries would probably be the widows of servicemen killed on active service and young people under 18 respectively. Alternatively the new purposes may require a preference to be given to the members of the original class.

The best way of ensuring that good use is made of a small charity's funds is to amalgamate it with one or more other

**Amalgamating small charities**

charities so that a worthwhile fund is created. Although they have stated that charities with similar but not identical purposes may be amalgamated the Commissioners can sometimes raise difficulties where it is hoped to group together various small charities having differing purposes.

**Restrictions on the methods of benefit**   As was mentioned above, many ancient charities, particularly those for the benefit of the poor, were established in terms which are no longer practicable. There are still many examples of charities to provide fuel and clothing for the poor, to equip apprentices, to endow the preaching of an annual sermon and for other purposes which are no longer suited to modern conditions. The Commissioners will need little persuasion to conclude that such purposes have "ceased" ... to provide a suitable and effective method of using

**Substitution of wider purposes**

the property" and will substitute wider purposes such as the relief of the poor, the education of young people or the advancement of religion in the original locality. In cases where the restrictions imposed by the original purposes are not so obviously inappropriate the Charity Commissioners will often require small but less stringent restrictions to be imposed in order to preserve as far as possible the donor's intentions. A

**Priorities**

solution to the problem of finding a suitable *cy-près* application is now more often found by giving the original class of beneficiaries priority. The trustees are then obliged to consider if suitable beneficiaries can be found whom the donor would have wished to benefit before making distributions to a wider class.

**Power of amendment**

It is now the Commission's practice to include a power to amend the administrative provisions in any *cy-près* scheme so that in future it will not be necessary for a scheme to be made.[15]

Finally three special cases should be mentioned.

**Schools**   The Education Act 1973 confers upon the Secretary of State for Education wide powers to modify trust deeds or

[15] *Decisions of the Charity Commissioners*, Vol. 3, pp. 29–31 and below pp. 183–187.

other instruments relating to schools as may be required as a result of any changes affecting a school or the establishment of a school and also to provide for the endowment of any voluntary school which is held for the purpose of providing religious education. In other cases a scheme of the Charity Commissioners may be required.

**Site held on charitable trusts**  When a voluntary aided school is closed the site itself will often be found to be held upon charitable trusts under the School Sites Acts 1841 to 1852. These acts facilitated the grant of land for the purposes of building school and residences for teachers and the trusts include a reverter to the donor's heirs if it ceases to be used for this purpose. Where a school is transferred to another site rather than being closed it may be possible for the Commissioners by scheme to direct that the proceeds of the property should be held upon trust for similar educational purposes in connection with the new school attended by those children who would formerly have attended the school which has closed.

**Reverter of Sites Act 1987**  Difficulties could arise where a school was closed and the site should have reverted to the donor's heirs. After many decades it was often impossible to find heirs but the proceeds of sale of the property could not be applied for educational purposes but had to be retained in case a claim was ever made. The Reverter of Sites Act 1987 provides a mechanism allowing the Commissioners to make a scheme to enable the proceeds to be used in these circumstances for educational purposes. The Revenue announced an extra statutory concession in 1994 in respect of any capital gains tax or income tax charges which would otherwise arise when a school site reverts to a settlor who, or whose estate, cannot be identified. Charitable status will be lost temporarily until an Order is made under the Act.

**Service charities**  It was noted in Chapter 1 that the promotion of the *esprit de corps* of the armed forces is a good charitable purpose. A large number of such charities exist including drill halls and funds to support the battalion or regimental messes in various ways some owning silver and other **Reorganisation of regiments or battalions** property of great historical interest. When reorganisations take place whereby battalions or regiments are amalgamated or disbanded these funds (known as Service (Non-Public) Funds) are not automatically provided for by the relevant Order in Council and a scheme of the Commissioners may be required. Such scheme will be made without question substituting the new regiment or battalion for the old. In some cases a number of subsidiary funds may be grouped together in a single fund to promote the efficiency of the regiment or battalion. Funds for the benefit of dependants of members of regiments or battalions which no longer exist will be dealt with in similar fashion though preferences may be retained for dependants of former members of the original unit.

**Church of England charities**  The Pastoral Measure 1983 **Alterations to benefices and parishes** contains special provisions which apply when alterations are made to benefices and parishes. Where property is held for ecclesiastical purposes of the Church of England by an incumbent (either alone or with others) whose benefice is united with another or by the churchwardens or parochial church council of a parish which is united with another that property automatically vests in the incumbent churchwardens or parochial church council of the new benefice or parish and will be applicable by reference to the new benefice or parish. In other cases where a benefice or parish is dissolved an order of the Charity Commissioners may be required.

# Variation of administrative provisions

**Powers of court and Commissioners**

It is a general principle of trust law that the court will not allow a trust to fail for want of the machinery to carry it into effect and the Commissioners have powers to establish schemes for the administration of a charity which are exercisable concurrently with the court (Charities Act, s.16). The powers of the court and the Commissioners to make schemes for the administration of a charity are not limited to the situations set out in section 13 where a *cy-près* variation of the purposes of the charity is permissible. Section 16 contains no limitation on the exercise of the powers although they must be exercised in furtherance of the general duty of the court and the Commissioners to act in the interests of charities. Section 1(3) of the Charities Act imposes

**Promotion of good administration**

on the Charity Commissioners the "general function of promoting the effective use of charitable resources by encouraging the development of better methods of administration. . . ." Generally speaking the Commissioners will readily make schemes to modernise the administration of a charity or to alter provisions in the governing instrument which have been found inconvenient. In particular, they will modernise the arrangements for appointing trustees and will give charities such as almshouses, village halls and recreation grounds "model" administrative provisions which have been evolved over the years and have been found to be practical.

## Delegation

The Commission's approach to allowing established charities wider powers to delegate their investment decisions has been clarified recently.[16] Charity trustees may not delegate investment decisions unless there is clear power in the governing instrument to permit this. A specific power to place the charity's investments in the names of nominees is also necessary. Without such clear authority they will be committing a breach of trust if they appoint an investment manager and allow the investments to be put in the name of their broker's nominee company even though it may be the most economical arrangement. Where there is no such power and the trustees consider that it will be in the charity's interests to enter into a discretionary management agreement with their broker and use his nominee company the Commission will be prepared to make an order under section 26 of the Charities Act where they consider that the circumstances warrant it. Generally speaking an order will be made if the value

[16] *Decisions of the Charity Commissioners*, Vol. 2, pp. 28–32.

of the investment portfolio is over £100,000, there is a large number of transactions and safeguards are included in the agreement with the broker to ensure that the terms of his authority are clear and adhered to, the trustees are kept informed and the arrangement is reviewed at least every two years.

**Investment powers**

One area which can give rise to difficulties concerns the modernisation of investment powers. Most advisers consider the powers of investment contained in the Trustee Investments Act 1961 to be unduly restrictive in modern conditions and well drafted modern deeds invariably widen the trustee's powers. However a large number of charities are still restricted to the statutory powers.

**Determining factors**

Following the court's decision in the case of *Trustees of the British Museum v. Att.-Gen.*[17] the Commissioners said[18] that they would be prepared to widen a charity's investment powers in suitable cases. In coming to a decision the court was influenced by the size of the fund, the width of the proposed powers, the availability of proper advice and the purposes of the charity. The willingness of the court to confer wider powers of investment and the power to delegate investment management was confirmed in *Steel v. Wellcome Custodian Trustees Ltd.*[19] which again concerned a very substantial fund. There the judge indicated that the Trustee Investment Act was out of date and that courts should no longer require there to be special circumstances before granting wider powers to trustees. The case of *Anker-Petersen v. Anker-Petersen* where the trustees of a private trust applied to the court under section 57 of the Trustees Act 1925[20] indicates that the court will very readily widen trustees' powers of investment and borrowing and permit them to delegate investment decisions and use nominees to hold investments subject to reasonable safeguards.

**Commission practice**

Wide powers of investment are now routinely included in well drafted trust deeds and powers of delegation and the use of nominees are also frequently included. Despite modern practice and the cases cited above the Charity Commissioners appear to be reluctant to confer wide powers of investment on charity trustees except where the funds are very substantial indeed as in the *British Museum* and *Wellcome* cases. Such cases are few. Furthermore even where wider powers are granted the Commissioners will usually require that 15% of the fund is confined to "relatively safe" investments. The Commission's approach to requests for wider powers are set out in *Decisions of the Charity Commissioners*, Vol. 3, pp. 18–28.

In the case of smaller charities they seem to consider that adequate flexibility can be obtained through investing in common investment funds. Wider powers will normally only be conferred where the trustees have sufficient financial expertise and the investment advisers are reputable and experienced. The benefit to the charity must be clearly established. Authority to invest in commodities or works of art will not be given and

---

[17] [1984] 1 W.L.R. 418.
[18] Annual Report (1984).
[19] [1988] 1 W.L.R. 167.
[20] L.S.Gaz., May 1, 1991 and see *Trusts & Estates*, Vol. 7, No. 3.

foreign currency should only be bought where necessary for the charity's activities. The Commissioners regard derivatives as speculative investments and therefore unsuitable for a charity unless for a specific financial purpose.

## Trustee remuneration

**Commission authority required**

**Interest of charity**

Specific power to remunerate trustees is required and it is not possible to add such a power where none exists by use of a power of amendment even in the case of a charitable company (*Re French Protestant Hospital*[21] since the trustees would be in breach of their fiduciary duty to use their powers to confer a benefit on themselves. It is necessary to obtain the authority of the Charity Commissioners either by way of a scheme under section 16 where there is no power of amendment or by an order under s 26 to authorise the trustees to exercise a power of amendment to give themselves remuneration. In the case of a charitable company authority must be obtained under section 64 since the change will affect a provision which directs the manner in which the property of the company may be applied (s.64(2)). Although provisions allowing trustees to be paid for their services as trustees or permitting professional trustees to charge for their professional services or the appointment of an employee as a trustee are generally acceptable in a newly established charity (see Chapter 4) the Commissioners are not so ready to authorise similar provisions to be added to the governing instrument of an established charity. The principles which apply were established in *Re Duke of Norfolk's Settlement*[22] and *Smallpiece v. Att.-Gen.*[23] In the former case the court confirmed that the principal consideration was the proper administration of the trust. In the Smallpiece case which concerned a charitable trust the court decided that power to remunerate trustees may be added if it is both "necessary and reasonable in the interests of the charity". The Commissioners have outlined the considerations which may affect their decision if they are asked to authorise the remuneration of trustees in their leaflet on "Remuneration of Charity Trustees" (CC11 dated August 1994). It seems that they will be more inclined to authorise remuneration where the charity is substantial; the trustees are required to provide continual oversight to the charity's affairs rather than simply distributing grants occasionally; where the trustees are substantially involved in the day to day running of the charity which is not delegated to employees or where specialist skills are required which cannot be more economically obtained from outside professionals.

## Trustees as employees

The Charity Commissioners' view is that only in very exceptional cases is it necessary for an employee to be a trustee of a charity. The main objection is that conflicts of interest are likely to arise. A trustee who is employed by his charity can be

[21] [1981] 3 A.E.R. 220.
[22] [1982] Ch. 61
[23] 1991 Unreported.

required to be absent when his terms of employment are discussed but there may be other situations when he is placed in a position where his own interests are in conflict with those of the charity. While a suitable provision allowing a trustee to be employed may be included in a charity's governing instrument from the outset the Commissioners will only authorise a change to a governing instrument to allow this where it is shown to be necessary in the interests of the charity. This is likely to be difficult. Employees may always be present at trustee meetings and the charity can have the benefit of their advice without the need for them to have a vote.

## Procedure

The required procedure for the establishment of a scheme for the administration of a charity is set out in sections 16 and 20 of the Charities Act.

**Application by charity**    An application must be made by the charity (which means in practice a majority of the trustees or members of the management committee) or the Attorney-General. The Commissioners may also settle a scheme if the court directs them to do so. In the case of a charity (which is not an exempt charity) having an income from property of no more than £500 per annum the Charity Commissioners may also act on the application of one of more trustees, any person interested in the charity (presumably this would include a beneficiary) or two or more inhabitants of the area of benefit of a local charity.

If the Charity Commissioners consider the charity trustees have unreasonably neglected or failed to apply for a scheme when it would be in the interests of the charity for them to do so they may, after giving the charity trustees an opportunity to make representations to them, proceed as if an application for a scheme has been made. This procedure is only available in the case of a charity which has been established for at least 40 years and is not an exempt charity (section 16(6)). The Commissioners may also make a scheme where the charity trustees are unable to make an application because of the vacancy in their number or incapacity provided that an application is received from an appropriate number of the trustees (section 16(7)).

**Formalities**    In most cases the need for a scheme will have been discussed at some length with the trustees before any decision as to its contents is taken. They will be asked to complete a formal application for a scheme and a draft scheme will then be prepared by the officer concerned at the Charity Commission and sent to the trustees for approval. As has been indicated, the contents of the scheme may not always be acceptable to the trustees and representations should be made at this stage. It should be remembered however that the Commissioners are exercising quasi-judicial powers and the form and content are ultimately matters for them alone. The arrangements for appeals will be considered below.

**Publicity**    Once the form of the scheme has been agreed it must be publicised. Section 20 requires public notice to be given of the proposed scheme for at least one month. The form the publicity should take will depend upon the nature of the charity. National charities will be required to insert notices in national newspapers. A local charity may satisfy the requirements for publicity by placing a notice in the parish magazine or on the church notice board. Any person who wishes to object to a proposed scheme should make representations to the Charity Commissioners which will be considered by them before they make the necessary order to establish the scheme. A copy of the order, when it has been made, must be available for inspection at the office of the Commissioners and locally in the case of a local charity for one month.

**Power of amendment**

The Commission will now include a power of amendment in a scheme of administration so that in future any necessary changes may be made by the charity trustees.[24] The power will not extend to the objects clause and the consent of the Commissioners will be needed to widen the investment powers or allow trustees to be remunerated.

## Appeals

**Who may appeal**

An appeal may be brought against an order of the Charity Commissioners establishing a scheme by the Attorney-General or by the charity or any of the charity trustees or by any person interested. Two inhabitants of the locality may appeal against an order made in respect of a local charity (section 18(10)).

The court will not interfere with the exercise of the Commissioners' powers unless it is apparent that they have acted unlawfully or that there has been some serious error which requires the court to intervene. It will not substitute some other arrangements which it considers preferable.[25]

In cases where the Commissioners have refused to make a scheme the charity may apply to the High Court for a scheme but the proceedings will be "charity proceedings" and the authority of the Commissioners is necessary before such an application can be heard (section 33(2)).

## Small charities

### Charities Act 1985

The Charities Act 1985 was designed to encourage the trustees of small charities for the relief of poverty to modernise their trusts and improve their effectiveness. The Woodfield Report noted that few charities had made use of the new procedure and recommended that its application should be extended and the formalities simplified.

---

[24] *Decisions of the Charity Commissioners*, Vol. 3, pp. 29–31.
[25] *Re Campden Charities* (1881) 18 Ch.D. 310.

## Charities Act 1993

These recommendations have been put into effect and sections 74 and 75 of the Charities Act now provide a streamlined mechanism to enable many small charities to pay over capital to other charities and modify their objects. The provisions do not apply to exempt charities or to charitable companies. The sections apply to any charity and not, as under the 1985 Act, only to charities for the relief of poverty.

**Income not more than £5,000**

Section 74 applies where a charity's gross income in the previous financial year is no more than £5,000 and no land is held upon trust to be used for the purpose of the charity.

**Transfer of property**

If the charity trustees are satisfied that the present purposes of the charity do not allow its resources to be put to suitable and effective use they may resolve to transfer all the property of the charity to another charity or divide it between two or more charities the purposes of which they consider to be similar to those of their charity as is reasonably practicable.

**Modernising the trusts**

Alternatively the trustees may in these circumstances resolve that some or all of the purposes of the charity should be replaced by other charitable purposes which they are satisfied are as similar to the original purposes as is practical in the circumstances.

**Modernising powers and procedure**

Charity trustees also have power under section 74 to modify any of their powers or the procedure they are required to follow under the terms of the governing instrument.

**Procedure to be followed**

The resolution must be passed by a two thirds majority of those charity trustees who vote and public notice of the resolution must be given. The wording of the resolution and the manner in which notice is given are for the charity trustees to decide. They must send a copy of the resolution to the Charity Commissioners with a statement of their reasons for passing it.

The Commissioners may ask for additional information and are obliged to consider any representations sent to them within six weeks of receiving notice of the resolution. If the resolution appears to have been made in compliance with section 74 the Commissioners will within three months notify the charity trustees that they concur with it. The trustees will then be free to transfer property to the other charities or, as the case may be, the changes made to the trusts of the charity will take effect from the date specified in the notification.

**Power to spend capital**

Section 75 of the Charities Act applies to charities which have permanent endowment not consisting of land and a gross income in the last financial year of no more than £1,000.

Where the charity trustees believe that the expenditure of income alone will not achieve any useful purpose they may resolve that they should be permitted to spend capital. Before doing so they must consider whether it might be possible to transfer the capital to another charity or charities under section 74.

**Procedure**

The charity trustees must follow the same procedure as for resolutions made under section 74.

# Variation under powers contained in the governing instrument

## Variation of administrative provisions

**Power to vary terms of the trust**

It has been suggested in Chapter 4 that a well-drafted declaration of trust or constitution should contain a power to vary the terms of the instrument other than the main objects clause. Any such amendments should be submitted to the Charity Commissioners in draft before they are adopted in order to ensure that they will not prejudice the charitable status of the organisation.

## Variation of the purposes of the charity

**Power to vary purposes**

A declaration of trust or constitution may contain a power to vary the main objects clause although this should be subject to the prior written approval of the Charity Commission.[26] Even if no objections are made to the proposed new objects the Commissioners may require any assets acquired before the variation to continue to be held for the original purposes so that the variation will apply only to assets acquired subsequently. Whether or not this is insisted on will depend upon the particular facts of each case but it seems that the Commissioners consider that the essential point to be established is one of

**Donor's intention**

intentions of the donors of the charity's assets. If donors gave property to a charity for the purposes prevailing at the time without having the possibility of a future variation of the objects drawn to their attention then it is considered that the property in question is held for the original purposes regardless of the power of variation contained in the governing instrument. If on the other hand the assets of the charity were provided by individuals who were aware of the possibility of a variation, who were perhaps concerned in the preparation of the governing instrument, then the revised purpose may apply to those assets.

The Charities Act (section 64) contains restrictions on the power of charitable companies to alter the objects clause of their memorandum of association[27] and any other provisions directing or restricting the way in which property of the company can be applied. Any such alteration is ineffective

**Charitable companies**

without the prior written consent of the Charity Commissioners. A copy of the Commissioners consent should be forwarded to Companies House with the copy of the resolution. This will apply to provisions in the memorandum and articles governing the remuneration of the directors as well as alterations to the objects themselves. It is not yet clear how the Charity Commissioners intend to exercise their powers. It is possible that they will refuse consent where the effect of the

[26] See p. 57 and suggested clauses in Appendix C. pp. 248–249.
[27] Companies Act 1985, ss.4 and 9.

alteration will be that the company's assets will be applied for a substantially different purpose.

An alteration which has the effect of rendering a charitable company non-charitable will be invalid in so far as the existing property of the company is concerned and the income arising from it. Such a change in the memorandum or articles will therefore only affect property acquired by the company after the alterations. (Section 64(1).)

# 12 APPEALS AND FUND-RAISING

## Appeals

**General considerations**

It is seldom appreciated that a person who solicits funds from members of the public for a particular purpose is a trustee of the funds he collects and holds them upon trust for those purposes. If he applies those funds for another purpose he may be guilty of obtaining money by a deception. The purposes for which the funds may be applied will depend on the terms of the appeal and can therefore be established by advertisements, posters, announcements on television or radio or even by the oral statements of collectors or sponsors. It is therefore most important that the terms of the appeal are carefully prepared or considerable difficulties may arise. The case of *Re Gillingham Bus Disaster Fund*[1] illustrates this. The terms of the appeal were established by a letter to a newspaper. Unfortunately the trusts declared in the letter were held to be void for uncertainty and it was necessary to try to identify all the individual donors in order to return the funds to them.

## The terms of the appeal

**Careful drafting essential**

The importance of identifying the precise scope of the purposes for which funds are to be raised before the appeal is launched will be apparent from what has been said above. Problems are unlikely to arise where funds are collected for the general purposes of a registered charity which has a well-drafted governing instrument but in cases where the appeal will establish a new charity it may be necessary for fund-raising to begin before the formal governing instrument has been finalised but in these circumstances it is particularly important that all publicity material is carefully drafted and proper instructions given to all those involved in the campaign to ensure that there is no discrepancy between the aims of the appeal and the terms upon which donations are made. Failure to do this can result in serious problems later on.

When launching an appeal for a particular charitable purpose some thought must be given at the outset to the possibility that the appeal will fail because insufficient funds are collected or for some other reason. The terms of the appeal should state how the funds which have been collected will be disposed of if this situation arises. Perhaps the best arrangement is for the trustees to be authorised to transfer the funds to

**Provision for possible failure**

another charity of their choice. If provision is not made in the appeal literature for the possibility that the appeal will be unsuccessful in achieving its intended goal the funds which have been raised will be held on a resulting trust for the donors.[2] The

---

[1] [1959] Ch. 62.

[2] *Re Ulverston and District New Hospital Building Trusts* [1956] Ch. 622 and see pp. 173–175 above.

**Various of purposes**

court and the Charity Commissioners may have jurisdiction under section 13 of the Charities Act to direct a *cy-près* application of the funds but it may first be necessary to attempt to identify or find the donors of the funds. The procedure was described in detail in the last chapter. If the appeal organisers have the foresight to anticipate this problem laborious enquiries for donors and the need to obtain the Charity Commissioners' agreement to a scheme will be avoided.

**Surplus funds**

Surplus funds can also create problems if an appeal is made for a specific purpose and no provision is made in the terms of the appeal for the possibility that it will be too successful since a scheme of the Charity Commissioners will then be required to authorise their use for some similar purpose.[3] It is a simple matter for the terms of the appeal to include a direction for the disposal of any surplus either for a purpose connected with the appeal or for such charitable purposes as the appeal committee think fit which would permit them to apply the funds to some other worthwhile cause.

These points are relevant whenever an appeal is made for funds for a particular project but it is particularly important when an appeal is launched in the wake of a disaster since it is in such cases that problems often arise.

**Early donations**

Occasionally donations are received before the terms of the appeal have been published and questions may arise as to the purposes for which the funds are held. The Attorney-General has suggested in his guidelines for those making disaster appeals (which are reproduced at the end of this section) that the published appeal should indicate that gifts already made will be added to the fund unless the donors notify the organisers to the contrary within a specified time.

**Power to declare trusts**

Where donations have been made for unspecified charitable purposes before publication of the appeal the persons entrusted with them may, depending on the terms of the gifts, be entitled to declare the trusts upon which they hold them as was the case in *Att.-Gen. v. Mathieson*.[4] The declared trusts must, of course, accord with the intentions of the donors or the Attorney-General may intervene to have them set aside. The case is authority for the proposition that the organisers of an appeal may, even after gifts have been received, declare comprehensive trusts to specify the charitable purposes and to provide, *inter alia*, for the trusteeship and administration of the funds subscribed.

## Disaster appeals

**Problems**

Because disaster appeals are often launched hastily and in a highly emotional atmosphere they are particularly liable to be structured wrongly at the outset with the result that problems may be encountered later which often give rise to great ill feeling. The appeals launched after the Aberfan and Penlee Lifeboat disasters are prominent examples. In order to prevent problems occurring in the future the Attorney-General

[3] *Re Wokingham Fire Brigade Trusts* [1951] Ch. 373.
[4] [1907] 2 Ch. 383.

published guidelines in 1981 for those concerned in such appeals (see below).

**Charitable or non-charitable?**

The first and most important point to be decided is whether or not the fund is to be held on charitable trusts. A gift for the benefit of a particular person or persons or for the benefit of the victims of the disaster without reference to their needs will not be charitable since it will be for the benefit of individuals rather than for a public purpose. If therefore the intention is to make benefits available to the victims or relatives of those affected by the disaster in order to compensate them for their involvement regardless of need, which was apparently the case with the fund raised after the Penlee Lifeboat disaster, the fund should be established on a non-charitable basis. This will have the result that the income of the fund will be subject to tax but as is pointed out in the guidelines the donations to the fund should not give rise to an inheritance tax liability since they are likely to be within the donors' annual exempt amount or below the current threshold.

If the fund is to be established as a charity it must come within one of the four heads of charity, most probably the first.

**Good charitable purposes**

The relief of those involved in the disaster or their relatives and dependants who are in financial need, the relief of those who are sick or injured as a result of the incident or the relief of hardship or suffering caused by or resulting from the disaster will be good charitable purposes. (See *North Devon and West Somerset Relief Fund Trusts*).[5]

**Red Cross Disaster Appeal Scheme**

The British Red Cross has established a scheme to help those who may be involved in launching an appeal in the wake of a disaster. The scheme is directed particularly to local and civic authorities who are most likely to need to launch the appeal. A comprehensive manual has been produced which can be obtained from their headquarters (see Appendix E). This contains detailed guidance on such matters as the choice of charitable and non-charitable funds, taxation, the drafting of press statements and methods of administering the appeal once funds begin to come in. Suitable trust deeds have been prepared and the Red Cross can provide stop-gap trustees until suitable local people can be appointed. Mechanisms have been set in place with the clearing banks and the Post Office for the collection of funds.

## General considerations

**Administration**

The persons who are to be responsible for administering the fund should be identified. Normally a small management committee will be established to conduct the appeal until more permanent arrangements can be made. It is important that proper arrangements should be made for any funds which are raised. A bank account should be opened in the names of at least two of the organisers and clearly identified by reference to the appeal. The members of the committee will be trustees of the funds they receive and should observe the guidelines given in Chapter 10 for the conduct of the finances of the appeal. There

[5] [1953] 1 W.L.R. 1260.

should, for example, be at least two signatories to operate the bank account and proper records should be kept. Proper supervision of all fund-raising activities should be maintained (see below). The committee members will also be responsible for ensuring that all published appeals are in accordance with the agreed purposes and for establishing a formal governing instrument for the future administration of the funds raised. As mentioned above, consideration should be given to the **Provision for** possibility that the appeal will be too successful and provision **surplus** should be made both in the published appeal and in the governing instrument for the destination of any surplus funds. Practical guidance can also be found in a book written by lawyers involved in the appeal after the Bradford disaster. (*Bradford Disaster Appeal—the administration of an appeal fund*, by Roger W. Suddards with Leolin Price Q.C. and Hubert Picarda, 1986).

# The Attorney-General's Guidelines

### "1. The making of the appeal

1.  Those who use these guidelines must remember that no two appeals can ever be quite the same, and should do all that they can to ensure that their own appeal is appropriate to the particular circumstances of their case, and runs into no unforeseen difficulties, whether personal, administrative, or fiscal. Amongst the most important and urgent decisions which must be made will be whether or not a charitable appeal is called for, and it may well be desirable to take advice of such questions before the appeal is issued. Generally speaking, the terms of the appeal will be all-important in deciding the status and ultimate application of the fund.
2.  Once the terms are agreed, it will generally be desirable to publish the appeal as soon as possible, and as widely as appropriate in the circumstances.
3.  Sometimes gifts may be sent before publication of the appeal. If there are more than can be acknowledged individually, the published appeal should indicate that gifts already made will be added to the appeal fund unless the donors notify the organisers (say within 10 days) that this is not their wish.

### 2. Pros and cons of the types of appeal

1.  Charitable funds attract generous tax reliefs; donation to them may do so (and in particular will for the most part be exempt from capital transfer tax). But charitable funds, being essentially public in their nature, cannot be used to give individuals benefits over and above those appropriate to their needs; and the operation of a charitable trust will be subject to the scrutiny of the Charity Commissioners.
2.  Non-charitable funds attract no particular tax reliefs and donations to them are subject to no special tax treatment

(and will have to be taken into account for capital transfer tax purposes unless, as is likely to be the case for the bulk of donations, they are within the normal reliefs). But under a non-charitable trust there is no limit on the amount which can be paid to individual beneficiaries if none has been imposed by the appeal; and only the Court acting on behalf of the beneficiaries will have control over the trust, which will not be subject to scrutiny by the Charity Commissioners.

3. The terms of the non-charitable appeal must be prepared with particular care to ensure that there is no doubt who is to benefit, whether or not their benefit is to be at the discretion of the trustees, and whether or not the entire benefit is to go to the beneficiaries, and if not, for example because specific purposes are laid down and the funds may be more than is required for those purposes, or because the beneficiaries are only to take as much as the trustees think appropriate, what is to happen to any surplus. If specific purposes are laid down, and after they have been fulfilled a surplus remains for which no use has been specified, the surplus will belong to the donors, which may lead to expensive and wasteful problems of administration.

### 3. Forms of appeal

1. If a charitable fund is intended then the appeal could take the following form:—
   "This appeal is to set up a charitable fund to relieve distress caused by the accident/
   disaster          at          on          . The aim is to use the funds to relieve those who may be in need of help (whether now or in the future) as a result of this tragedy in accordance with charity law. Any surplus after their needs have been met will be used for charitable purposes designed:—
   
   (i)  To help those who suffer in similar tragedies.
   (ii) To benefit charities with related purposes.
   (iii) To help the locality."

2. If a non-charitable fund is intended and those affected are to take the entirely of the fund in such shares as the trustees think fit the appeal could take the following form:—
   "This appeal is to set up a fund, the entire benefit of which will be used for those injured or bereaved in the accident/disaster at          on          or their families and dependants as the trustees think fit. This fund will not be a charity."

3. A non-charitable fund in which the trustee would have a discretion to give as much as they think fit to those who have suffered with any surplus going to charity could be set up on the basis of the following form:—
   "This appeal is to set up a fund for those injured or bereaved in the accident/disaster          at

on        and their families and dependants. The trustee will have a discretion how and to what extent to benefit individual claimants: the fund will not itself be a charity but any surplus will be applied for such charitable purposes as the trustees think most appropriate to commemorate those who died."

### 4. Appeals for individuals

It sometimes happens that publicity given to individual suffering moves people to give. In such a case it is particularly desirable for those who make appeals to indicate whether or not the appeal is for a charitable fund. It is also desirable for those who give to say whether their gift is meant for the benefit of the individual, or for charitable purposes including helping the individual so far as that is charitable; if no such intention is stated, then the donation should be acknowledged with an indication how it will be used if the donor does not dissent. Those who make appeals should bear in mind the possibility that generous response may produce more than is appropriate for the needs of the individual, and should be sure to ask themselves what should be done with any surplus.

Thus, if a child suffers from a disease, there are two alternatives, to appeal for the benefit of the child, or to appeal for charitable purposes relating to the suffering of the child, such may help him and others in the same misfortune, for example, by helping to find a cure. It may be that the child will not live long, and so may not be able to enjoy the generosity to him as an individual; alternatively, he may be intended to receive as much as possible, because he faces a lifetime's suffering. Once again, the pros and cons of setting up a charitable fund or a non-charitable fund should be considered before the appeal is made and the appeal should indicate which alternative is intended; once again, even if a non-charitable appeal is made, it may be thought right to make it on terms that any surplus can be used for charity.

### 5. Generally

The suggestions made in this memorandum are only examples of forms which can be used; and before making an appeal it is always wise to seek advice on what form to use. The Charity Commissioners will always be ready as a matter of urgency to advise on the terms of any intended charitable appeal, or to consider whether a proposed appeal is likely to be charitable and if so to advise on the likely consequence.

In conclusion, the Attorney-General would like to emphasise that those organising an appeal should do all they can to make sure that the purpose of the appeal is clear and that donors know how their gifts will be used. This will do much to reduce the risk of confusion and distress. It is considered undesirable to make a general appeal-postponing until the size of the fund is known decisions whether the fund ought to be charitable and whether those affected should take the entire benefit; this can all too easily lead both donors and beneficiaries to form the view that the ultimate result is not what was intended, as well as giving rise to legal problems."

# Fund-raising

**Malpractice**

**Charity fraud unit**

Most charities will seek to raise funds from the public from time to time, and for many this is their only source of finance. There is however considerable opportunity for unscrupulous people to trade on this and upon the generosity of the public and consequently there has been and still is extensive malpractice which is of great concern to those involved in charities. Despite legal restrictions on fund-raising activities, malpractice in fund-raising for charity is still prevalent and this tends to bring all charities into disrepute. The increasing level of fraud and abuse in relation to charity administration and fund-raising led the Metropolitan Police to establish a charity fraud unit within their company fraud department. Concern at the incidence of malpractice in charity fund-raising and the lack of any effective preventive measures had been expressed over many years culminating in the Woodfield Report.[6] Many of the recommendations were based on a report of the N.C.V.O. working party on Malpractice in Fund-raising for charity published in 1986. These recommendations were adopted in the Charities Act 1992. The controls on professional fund-raisers came into force in March 1995. For the first time persons who raise funds for charity in order to make a profit for themselves are subject to statutory controls. The rules on public and house to house collections were revised in the 1992 Act but the new regime has not yet been brought into force. During the course of consultation on the new proposals substantial problems emerged. A working party has been set up with a view to finalising the legislative framework sometimes during 1998. The existing law therefore remains in effect. It is summarised below and the new regime is then briefly outlined.

# Public charitable collections

There has been a licensing system for public collections for many years. The need for it is undoubted. The readiness with which members of the public will give to an apparently good cause is a temptation to the unscrupulous. The regulatory system has developed over a long period of time and is complex.

## Statutory controls prior to implementation of Charities Act 1992

There are a number of statutory restrictions on raising funds from the public which are designed to prevent advantage of being taken of the people's generosity.

### Street collections

Regulations may be made for the control of collections or the sale of articles for the benefit of charitable or other purposes by the Common Council of the City of London, the Commissioner for the Metropolitan Police and, outside London, the

---

[6] Paras. 123–125.

**Organisers' permit**

appropriate district council. The regulations cover the places where and conditions under which the collections may take place. The organisations of any flag day, carnival, rag day or street festival at which funds are to be raised for charity should obtain a permit from the relevant authority for the area before making any arrangements.[7]

## House to house collections

**Scope of the 1939 Act**

Strict controls on house to house collections are imposed by the House to House Collections Act 1939 and regulations made under it. These apply to all appeals to the public made by way of visits from house to house (including business premises such as public houses) to collect funds for any charitable, benevolent or philanthropic purpose. A collection for the purposes of the Act includes not only requests for outright gifts to charity but also occasions where people are induced to buy goods by the belief that part of the proceeds will go to charity.[8] Any person who wishes to arrange such a collection (a "promoter") must apply for a licence to the licensing authority for the area where the collection will take place. The licensing authority is the Common Council in respect of the City of London, the Commission of Police in respect of the Metropolitan Police District and the district council in respect of any other area. A licence may be refused for a number of reasons including where it appears that an inadequate proportion of the funds raised will be received by charity, excessive remuneration will be retained; the applicant is not a fit and proper person, having been convicted of certain offences including fraud or has in the past failed to exercise due diligence to ensure compliance with the regulations by collectors authorised by him. Exemption may be granted by the Home Secretary for collections over wide areas. Applications for licences should be made the first day of the month before the month in which the collection will take place.

**Licences**

**Refusal of licence**

**Time for application**

**Regulation of conduct**

If a licence is granted strict rules will apply to the conduct of the collection, which are set out in regulations made under the Act. The promoter is responsible for ensuring that each collector has a badge or certificate of authority and, if money is to be collected, a collecting box or receipt book. All money collected must be placed in a sealed collecting box or a receipt given for it. No-one under 16 years of age may collect money. Special provisions apply to "envelope collections," *i.e.* where visits are made to houses leaving envelopes for money which will be collected later. The promoter of a house to house collection is required to provide accounts in a form specified in the House to House Collection Regulations 1947 to the licensing authority within a month of the licence expiring. The accounts must be accompanied by vouchers for all expenses and applications for the proceedings and by receipt books.

Where a collection is to be made over a short period for local purposes only the chief officer of police for the area may

---

[7] Police, Factories, etc. (Miscellaneous Provisions) Act 1916, s.5 as amended by Local Government Act 1972, s.251.
[8] *Cooper v. Coles* [1987] 1 All E.R. 91.

**Certificate for local collections** issue a certificate to the promoters who will then be exempt from the requirement to obtain a licence under the Act. They must however comply with the requirement that each collector should have a badge or certificate of authority.

## Collections for war charities and disabled persons

**Statutory prohibition** The War Charities Act 1940 and regulations made under the Act, the provisions of which have been extended to charities for the disabled by section 41 of the National Assistance Act 1948 prohibits any kind of public appeal for funds for the relief of suffering and distress caused by the wars of 1914–18 and 1939–45 or any subsequent war or act of aggression to which the Act is extended by Order in Council. The Act also applies to funds established for the relief of the blind, deaf, dumb or handicapped. Any fund-raising bazaar, sale, entertainment or **Charity must be registered** exhibition on behalf of such a charity is prohibited unless the charity is registered by the appropriate authority in which the charity's administrative centre is situated. The appropriate authorities are the Council of the City of London, the councils of London boroughs, non-metropolitan county councils and metropolitan district councils.

Restrictions are imposed on the management of charities registered under the Act including requirements for the keeping of accounts, the number of persons to administer the charity and for separate bank accounts to be maintained. The War Charities Regulations 1940 contain detailed arrangements for the keeping of the Register and lists of charities refused registration.

The Charity Commissioners are given wide powers over war charities and charities for the disabled including power to direct the removal of the charity from the register of the appropriate authority and, where this has been done, to provide for any funds held by the charity.

**Blind and disabled persons** It is also an offence under the Trading Representations (Disabled Persons) Act 1972 for anyone selling goods by house to house visit, on the telephone or by post to represent that blind or disabled persons have been employed in making or packaging the goods and will benefit from the sale unless the organisation is registered under the War Charities Act (as extended to charities for the disabled).

## The New Regime Charities Act 1992 Part III

When the new legislation is in force (this is not now expected to be before mid-1998) the system for regulating public collections will be considerably simplified. Draft regulations are not yet available and it is only possible here to outline the new regime.

**Permits** It is an offence punishable by a fine for anyone (whether paid or a volunteer) to organise or control the conduct of a charitable collection without either a permit from the local authority in whose area the collection takes place or an order of the Charity Commissioners (section 66). Such a person is called "a promoter".

A public charitable collection includes any appeal to the public for funds for charity which takes place in a public place or by means of visits from house to house where it is represented that all or part of the proceeds will be applied for charitable

**Public collections**  benevolent or philanthropic purposes.

A public charitable collection also includes any offer to sell goods or supply services to the public which is accompanied by a representation that all or part of the proceeds will be applied for charitable benevolent or philanthropic purposes.

The legislation also applies to collections for benevolent or philanthropic but non-charitable purposes such as appeals for the benefit of private individuals.

The definition does not include appeals made at public meetings or in a churchyard, burial ground or other land adjacent to a place of public worship or by means of unattended collecting boxes (section 65(2)).

A house is defined to include separate dwellings such as flats.

**Public places**  The expression "public place" means for the purpose of the legislation any highway or any other place to which the public have access which is not in a building and any public area inside a station, airport or shopping precinct or similar public area within a building.

A public place does not include places to which the public has access only by purchasing a ticket (*e.g.* a seaside pier) nor places to which they have access only for the purposes of the appeal.

It seems that a public place does not include shops, public houses or other business premises which were covered by the previous legislation. Nor does it include churches or other places of worship.

Anyone who intends to promote a public collection must first apply to the local authority for the area in which it is to take

**Applications for permits (section 67)**  place for a permit. The application must specify the time during which the collection will take place, which cannot be longer than twelve months, and specify such other information as will be prescribed in the regulations.

**Time for application**  The application must be made at least one month before the start of the collection.

Before deciding whether or not to grant a permit the local authority is required to consult the police and make such other inquiries as are thought fit.

The local authority may refuse an application for a permit

**Grounds for refusal**  on any of the following grounds:

(a) inconvenience to the public because of the day of the week, the date, the time, the frequency of the locality;

(b) where the collection would be on the same day as another collection already authorised by the local authority or on the day before or the day after unless it is to be on private land and the owner has consented to the collection taking place;

(c) where it appears that the amount likely to be applied to charity would be an inadequate proportion of the likely proceeds of the collection;

(d) where the applicant has been convicted under previous legislation governing public collections[9] or under the present legislation for any offence involving dishonesty which may be facilitated by the grant of a permit;

(e) where they are not satisfied that the applicant is authorised to collect on behalf of the charity for which he claims the collection will be held;

(f) where on a previous occasion the applicant has failed to exercise due diligence to ensure that the collectors were fit and proper persons or that they complied with the conditions of the permit or that badges or certificates of authority did not fall into the hands of unauthorised persons.

Written notice of the decision to refuse a permit and the reason for the refusal must be served on the applicant.

The local authority has, therefore, considerable discretion to refuse permits where there is suspicion that they may be abused. These matters should be considered before submitting the application to the local authority so as to ensure that the application is successful.

**Conditions**
A permit may be issued subject to conditions as to the time or frequency of the collection and the localities and manner in which it may be conducted. Written notice of the decision and the reasons for it must be served on the applicant.

**Withdrawal of permits**
The local authority may (section 70) withdraw a permit or attach conditions to a permit which has been granted or alter the conditions attaching to a permit where they have reason to believe that it was granted on the basis of false information provided by the applicant or that circumstances have changed since it was granted and they would not have granted the permit in the new circumstances.

**Breach**
The local authority may also withdraw a permit where they have reason to believe that there has been or is likely to be a breach of any of its conditions.

Written notice of the withdrawal of a permit and the reasons must be served on the promoter.

**Appeals (section 71)**
An applicant may appeal to a magistrates' court against the refusal of a local authority to grant a permit or a decision to withdraw a permit or attach conditions to a permit or to vary any conditions. The appeal must be brought within 14 days of service of the notice from the local authority. A further appeal lies to the Crown Court against the magistrates' decision.

One of the problems which emerged in the course of the consultation was that in order to obtain permission for a public collection to take place throughout London a separate permit would need to be obtained from each London Borough – a substantial burden.

**National Collections**
The power to authorise public collections over a wider area than that of one local authority has been transferred from the Home Office to the Charity Commissioners. The Charity Commissioners may by order authorise a charity or persons authorised by that charity to conduct public

[9] Police, Factories (Miscellaneous Provisions) Act 1916; House to House Collections Act 1939; Civic Government (Scotland) Act 1982.

collections throughout the whole or a substantial part of England and Wales. It should be noted that such an order may only authorise collections promoted by a charity or persons authorised by it for the benefit of that charity. Conditions may be attached to the authority which may be unlimited in time or for a specific period. Home Office practice was to allow such collections only when a charity had conducted collections in a number of different areas for at least two years without complaint. It seems likely that the Charity Commissioners will adopt a similar practice.

**Revocation**    An order for a collection may be revoked or varied at any time but notice must be served on the charity giving the Commissioners' reasons.

It is an offence punishable by a fine for any person to display a badge or certificate of authority which does not relate to that particular appeal or to display or use anything which resembles a badge or certificate of authority which is likely to

**Offences**    deceive the public.

A person who knowingly or recklessly provides false information in connexion with an application for a permit commits an offence and is liable to be fined.

## Competitions and lotteries

Tombolas and raffles are so much a part of every charity fund-raising event that it is sometimes forgotten that all schemes for distributing prizes by chance ("lotteries") are strictly regulated by law. All lotteries which do not constitute gaming (which in general may only be conducted in premises licensed under the Gaming Act 1968) are unlawful unless authorised by the

**Lotteries and**    Lotteries and Amusements Act 1976 as amended by the
**Amusements Act**    National Lottery etc Act 1993. This Act permits the promotion
**1976**    of games of chance and competitions on a small scale which involve chance but subject to stringent conditions. These rules are unaffected by the Charities Act 1992.

(a)   Small lotteries where the prizes cost not more than £250 and are not given in cash are permitted at exempt

**Exempt**    entertainments such as fetes and dances and other
**entertainments**    social or athletic events. This covers tombolas, raffles and such like. The whole of the proceeds of the entertainment after deducting expenses including the proceeds of the lottery must be devoted to purposes other than private gain and the sale of tickets and the announcement of the winners must take place at the entertainment. The lottery should not be the only or main inducement to people to attend the entertainment.[10]

(b)   Private lotteries are permitted where the sale of tickets
**Private lotteries**    is confined to the members of a society or persons working or living in the same premises. The event may only be advertised in writing at the society's premises or at the relevant place of work as the case may be and the

[10] Lotteries and Amusements Act 1976, s.3.

proceeds must be spent for the purposes of the society or on the provision of prizes. The price of the tickets and the names and addresses of the promoters must be printed on the tickets and tickets may not be sent by post.[11]

**"Society's lottery"**

(c) Section 5 of the same Act authorises a charity to conduct a public lottery (a "society's lottery") selling tickets to the public if the total value of the tickets sold does not exceed £1 million and the society is registered either with the appropriate authority in whose area the headquarters of the charity is situated or with the Governing Board depending upon the total value of the tickets to be sold. Where the value of tickets is more than £20,000 or when added to tickets sold in earlier lotteries held by the society in the same year is more than £250,000 the society must register with the Gaming Board. Where the value of tickets is less than this the society should register with the appropriate authority, namely, the Common Council of the City of London, the appropriate borough council in London or the appropriate district council. Detailed rules for societies' lotteries are set out in section 11 of the Lotteries and Amusements Act 1976 and Schedules 1 and 1A which include requirements that the price of tickets shall not exceed £1, no prize shall be worth more than £25,000 and that the value of the prizes may not exceed half the total value of tickets sold. There are also restrictions on the amount of expenses which may be deducted.

**Gaming Board guide**

The Gaming Board has published a guide "Lotteries and the Law" which summarises the rules and is obtainable free of charge from the Board.

**Offences**

It should be noted that a promoter of a lottery who contravenes the rules relating to lotteries and any person who is a party to the contravention commits an offence which may be punishable by a fine or imprisonment. However, it is a good defence for a promoter if he can prove that the offence occurred without his consent or connivance and that he exercised due diligence to prevent it occurring. It is most important that the relevant rules are studied before a lottery is promoted.

## The abuse of fund-raising methods

From time to time, often as a result of a particular instance of fraud or dishonesty, concern is expressed in the media and in Parliament about the prevalence of malpractice in charity fund-raising. In their 1985 Annual Report the Charity Commissioners referred to a number of problem areas and in 1986 the National Council for Voluntary Organisations produced a comprehensive report on the subject entitled "Malpractice in Fund-raising for Charity" which gave details of the most serious types of abuse and put forward recommendations for steps which might be taken to prevent

**N.C.V.O. report**

[11] *Ibid.*, s.4.

them occurring in the future. The majority of their suggestions involved charities themselves reviewing their methods and procedures. The concern expressed in this report was echoed in the Woodfield Report referred to above which supported a number of the suggestions for reform put forward in the N.C.V.O. report. The government responded to these concerns by including in the Charities Act 1992 controls on the activities of individuals and organisations which engage in fund-raising activities for profit. These are considered in detail below (see pages 205–207). The restrictions were brought into force in March 1995.

    The principal areas for concern were the excessive fees charged by some professional fundraisers, the use of joint enterprises as a method of fund-raising, aggressive or excessively emotional appeals and lack of control over collecting boxes.

**Adverse publicity** Adverse publicity arising from such activities is seriously detrimental to the interests of all charities, not only those directly involved, making the task of raising money by reputable organisations all the more difficult. It is therefore in the interests of every charity to prevent such abuses occurring whenever it is within their power to do so.

## The use of professional fundraisers

For many, particularly smaller, charities, faced with the need to raise substantial sums of money from the public, the services of a professional fundraiser can be invaluable in providing the

**Professionalism and experience** professionalism and experience which they lack. While many professional fundraisers are highly reputable and give much needed help to charities there are others who, because of the methods they employ or the excessive fees they demand, bring the profession as a whole into disrepute. This problem was addressed in the Charities Act 1992 and it is now an offence for any professional fundraiser to solicit funds for a charity unless he has entered into a prior formal agreement in a form prescribed by Regulations.

    As was mentioned above, a donor to charity is making a gift which is held on trust by the fundraiser for the purposes of the charity. The fundraiser is under a duty to pay over the funds he has collected to the charity, subject only to his right to be repaid his reasonable expenses. The fundraiser is not entitled to retain

**Retention of commission or other benefit improper** any commission or other benefit for himself except where the donor has been informed that this is intended.[12] The donor is also entitled to expect that his gift will be applied for the purposes of the charity and the charity trustees are under a duty to ensure that this is what occurs. They will be in breach of this duty if they confer benefits upon individuals which will be the case if excessive fees are paid to fundraisers. It is therefore the duty of charity trustees who intend to employ a professional fundraiser to negotiate reasonable terms and to ensure that he accounts fully to the charity for all the funds raised. It is thought that the following matters should be considered.

[12] *Jones v. Att.-Gen.*, *The Times*, November 10, 1976 and *Reg. v. Wain* (1993) referred to in *Decisions of the Charity Commissioners*, Vol. 2, pp. 33–35.

**Basis of remuneration** Some fundraisers prefer to receive a percentage of the funds raised rather than a set fee. While arrangements such as this certainly provide an incentive for the fundraiser it can also have the result, when an appeal is more successful than was expected, that excessive benefits are received. On the other hand, if the appeal fails the fundraiser may receive very little and this may lead to ill feeling. The Charity Commissioners have stated, in their 1983 Annual **Payment for time** Report, that charities should agree to remunerate fundraisers **and services** only for the time spent and services actually rendered. It is not illegal or necessarily improper for a charity to pay a commission but where this is to be the basis of remuneration it is the duty of the charity trustees to satisfy themselves that this is in the charity's interests.

**Control of funds** A reputable fundraiser will readily agree that all funds raised should be remitted direct to the charity which will then be responsible for paying him his fees and expenses. This is preferable to an arrangement whereby the fundraiser deducts what is due to him before forwarding the balance to the charity since the charity then has no control over the funds raised and has no method of checking that it receives its proper entitlement. It also gives rise to the danger that if the **Danger of** fundraiser becomes insolvent, funds due to the charity but not **insolvency** yet forwarded to it will be seized by his creditors. It is unwise for a charity to agree to funds being paid into a joint bank account with the fundraiser because of the risk of a dispute arising.

**Selection of fundraiser** The Institute of Charity Fund-raising Managers was established in 1983 with the purpose of improving the ethical standards and ability of fund-raising managers and providing training facilities. Members are **Code of practice** required to adhere to a code of practice and checks are made on applicants for membership to ensure that they are reputable and competent. Training courses and workshops are run in order to improve standards. Membership of the Institute therefore provides some assurance to a professional fundraiser's ability and honesty and a charity intending to employ a professional fundraiser is recommended to consult the institute before doing so. The address of the Institute is given in Appendix E. It is also sensible to speak to one or two other charities who have used the particular fundraiser's services recently before making a final choice.

# Restrictions on professional fundraisers

The regime introduced by Part II of the Charities Act 1992 (sections 58 to 64) imposed for the first time restrictions on the activities of individuals and organisations who, for gain, raise funds for charitable and other philanthropic or benevolent institutions.

The new restrictions apply to two types of fundraisers: professional fundraisers and commercial participators. These will be considered in turn. It should be noted that the manner in which charities conduct their own fund-raising activities are not affected. The rules apply only to individuals and organisations who seek to derive a profit by raising funds for charitable and other purposes.

**Professional fundraisers**

A professional fundraiser is defined in section 58 as a person who for gain solicits or procures money or property for charitable benevolent or philanthropic purposes. The definition does not include the charities themselves, their trustees, employees, volunteers or persons who receive only a nominal payment of up to £5 per day or £500 per annum or up to £500 for any particular fund-raising venture. Nor does it include a trading company which is wholly owned by or on behalf of the charity for which funds are being raised. Persons who solicit funds on behalf of a charity on television or radio are also specifically excluded.

**"Soliciting"**

The term "solicit" is explained in section 58(6) and (7). It includes direct personal appeals, requests for funds made on the telephone or on a film or video. Funds can be solicited by letter, by means of a static collecting box or an advertisement. The term also includes organisations which receive funds on behalf of a charity if they charge for this service.

**Commercial participators**

A commercial participator is defined in s.58(1) as a person or organisation carrying on a business other than fund-raising who represents that contributions are to be made to a charity in the course of a promotional venture. Banks and building societies which run affinity card schemes will, for example, be included in this definition as will companies promoting sales campaigns which promise that a payment to charity will be made for every purchase. A "representation" can be made in any way whatsoever, expressly or by implication.

**Prescribed agreement**

Both professional fundraisers and commercial participators are required to enter into an agreement in the form prescribed by the Charitable Institutions (Fund-Raising) Regulations 1994 with a charity before they can solicit funds for the charity or make any representation that contributions will be made to the charity (section 59). The Regulations require the agreement to state the names and addresses of the parties, the date of signing the agreement, the period of the agreement, arrangements for early termination, terms for varying the agreement. The objectives, the methods to be employed and the amount of the remuneration of the professional fundraiser or reward of the commercial participator and how these are to be calculated.

Where a professional fundraiser or commercial participator has solicited funds or made representations that contributions will be made to a charity without first entering into such an agreement with it, the charity may obtain an injunction against him in order to prevent a recurrence.

**Sanctions for breach**

An agreement which is not in the prescribed form will not be enforceable against the charity and a professional fundraiser or commercial participator may not receive any remuneration or expenses which are not authorised by an agreement in the prescribed form. Where there has been a breach of these provisions the charity will therefore in theory be able to claim from the professional fundraiser or commercial participator all the funds raised though there may well be problems in enforcement. In practice agreements of this kind are very often made not by the charity itself but with a subsidiary trading company. It will be necessary therefore, in order to comply with s.59 in this situation for the agreement to be a tripartite one, between the commercial participator, the trading company and the charity.

**Disclosure**       Professional fundraisers and commercial participators are required to inform all those from whom they solicit funds or to whom they make representations that contributions will be made to charity:

(a)  the name of the charity;
(b)  where more than one charity will benefit the proportions in which they will do so and;
(c)  in general terms the method by which the professional fundraiser's remuneration will be calculated or, in the case of a commercial participator, the proportion of the donor's payment or the amount which will be paid to the charity.

Where the fund-raising or commercial venture is undertaken for charitable purposes rather than for the benefit of a particular charity or charities the fundraiser or commercial participator must also inform prospective donors that this is the case and the method by which the money raised will be distributed between different charities. This should be regarded as a minimum standard. Where possible exact figures should be given.

**Radio &**       Special rules apply where funds are solicited for a charity or
**television**     representations are made that money or property will be given to
**appeals (section** charity in radio or television programmes. If as a result of such
**60(4))**         an appeal a donor makes a payment of £50 or more by credit or debit card or agrees to pay £50 or more he may cancel the payment or the agreement to pay by giving notice in writing within seven days. He will then be entitled to a refund if he has paid more than £50. The fundraiser or commercial participator is entitled to deduct from the refund the expense involved in making it and where the payment was made for goods the refund is conditional upon those goods being returned. There is no right to a refund where the payment was made for services which had been supplied when the notice was given. The donor's right to a refund must be stated in the course of the broadcast.

**Fund-raising by**   Where appeals for funds are made or promotional ventures
**telephone**      are communicated over the telephone and a donor makes a
**(section 60(5))** payment by any means including a credit or debit card of £50 or more as a result the donor must within seven days be informed in writing of his right to a refund. The sub-clause is drafted widely enough to cover all solicitations and representations which are made orally but not face to face with the prospective donor nor in the course of a television or radio programme. An example might be a video appeal for funds.

**Home Office**      The Home Office has issued a booklet entitled *Charitable*
**guidance**       *Fund-Raising: Professional and Commercial Involvement*, which can be obtained from HMSO and contains useful guidance on how the new regime applies in practice.

# Unauthorised fund-raising

The difficulty of preventing fund-raising in the name of a charity without its permission was mentioned in the N.C.V.O. report on Malpractice in Fund-Raising for Charity published in 1986. **Passing off** A passing off action has occasionally been successfully brought against an unauthorised fundraiser[13] enabling the charity concerned to obtain an injunction. Recently the British Diabetic Association obtained an injunction against another charity to prevent it using the name "British Diabetic Society" on the grounds that this was likely to damage the Association's goodwill and reputation.[14]

A person who obtains money or property from third parties for a charity or for charitable purposes holds those funds upon trust for the charity or those purposes. A charity may require **Account** such a person to account for the funds or property he has received though he may deduct his reasonable expenses. The practical difficulties of obtaining payment may be insuperable. If the fundraiser does not remit the funds to the charity or apply them to charitable purposes he may be guilty of obtaining money by deception.

Section 62 of the Charities Act 1992 gives a statutory right **Injunction** to a charity to obtain an injunction in certain circumstances against any person who has solicited money or property for the charity or has represented that contributions are to be made to the charity where it is likely that he will continue to do so if not prevented. The provisions apply to volunteers as well as professional fundraisers and commercial participators as defined in section 58. The circumstances in which an injunction can be obtained are:

(a)  where the charity objects to the fund-raising methods used or;
(b)  where the person in question is not a fit and proper person to raise funds for the charity or;
(c)  where the charity does not wish to be associated with a promotional or fund-raising venture in the course of which representations are made that contributions will be given to the charity.

Before an injunction can be granted to the charity must **28 days notice** have given 28 days notice to the fundraiser requesting him to cease his activities and informing him that if he does not an injunction will be sought.

## False claims

It will be an offence for which an individual can be fined to solicit funds or property for an institution claiming that it is a registered charity when it is not (s.63, Charities Act 1992).

---

[13] *British Legion v. British Legion (Street) Ltd.* (1931) 48 Patent Cases 555; *Dr. Barnardo's Homes: National Incorporated Association v. Barnardo Amalgamated Industries Ltd.* (1949) 66 Patent Cases 193; *Guide Dogs for the Blind Association v. New Foundation Trust (Guide Dogs)* 1986 (unreported).
[14] *British Diabetic Association v. Diabetic Society Ltd.* [[1995] 4 A.E.R. 812.

## Collecting boxes

**No statutory controls**

The restrictions in the Charities Act 1992 do not apply to collecting boxes which are left in pubs or shops and there are no statutory controls to ensure that the contents of such boxes are safeguarded. Funds put into a charity collecting box are funds held on trust for charity and it is therefore the duty of the charity concerned to ensure that the boxes are kept safely and the contents remitted to the charity. Furthermore it is a disincentive to prospective donors to find boxes unattended and not emptied regularly. In the case of *Jones v. Att.-Gen.* referred to above in note 12, the judge said that it should not be possible for a collecting box to be opened without detection and that the charity was under a duty to empty the boxes regularly however small the amounts involved. One way of safeguarding the contents of boxes is for numbered seals to be placed on them and for careful records to be maintained and charities using collecting boxes should ensure that they are regularly emptied and the contents safeguarded.

The Institute of Charity Fund-Raising Managers has issued guidelines for the management of static collecting boxes designed to minimise malpractice.

## Dubious fund-raising methods

**Moral blackmail**

The Charity Commissioners have drawn attention to complaints made from time to time about emotional appeals for funds which, it is said, can in serious cases constitute moral blackmail. Of course many fund-raising campaigns depend upon appeals to the public conscience but occasionally this may go too far and provoke distaste and annoyance which are in the long run counterproductive for the charity.

**Telephone appeals**

Criticism has also been made of the use of the telephone to make appeals for funds and in particular the employment of telephone sales staff who are paid on a commission basis because they may be tempted to use exaggerated language in order to ensure a successful appeal and increase their reward. Telephone appeals, even on a commission basis, are not illegal provided that the rules for professional fundraisers are adhered to but a charity which uses such intrusive methods runs the risk of bringing its name into disrepute particularly since such methods have in the past been used by the more dubious fundraisers. The Institute of Charity Fund-Raising Managers has drafted a Code of Practice for its members.

**Network marketing**

Network marketing is sometimes used as a method of fund-raising and it can undoubtedly be highly effective. The system gives every member of the network a direct financial incentive to add to the numbers of donors involved. Each member of the network receives a payment for every donor introduced by him directly or by a person previously introduced by him and so on down the line. Substantial sums can be raised in this way and a member of a network who is successful in creating an active network himself can reap considerable rewards.

The main objection to the system is that although the charity may receive some funds from the enterprise the real beneficiary will be the network marketing company. The fees and rewards to the company and to the members of the network are likely to be considerably higher than the payments to the charity.

It seems likely that every person recruited to the network will be within the definition of a professional fundraiser for the purposes of section 58 of the Act. If so each individual will need to enter into an agreement with the charity in the prescribed form before recruiting any members himself.

Some of the pitfalls of multi-level selling schemes, as network marketing is also known, are spelt out in a D.T.I. leaflet ("Multi-level Selling Schemes—a guide to the Pyramid Selling Legislation") which can be obtained from the Department in London.

## Advertising

The Independent Television Commission (I.T.C.) Code of Advertising Standards and Practice include specific reference to charities. Rule 12 provides that advertisements soliciting donations or promoting the needs or objects of bodies financed by donations may only be accepted on satisfactory proof of registration as a charity and the organisation must be willing to provide details of their constitution, activities and accounts. The charity will also be required to give assurances that trustees and staff do not have a financial interest in any transactions undertaken by the charity; the proceeds of the appeal will be applied for the stated purposes and that the names of the contributors will not be disclosed without permission.

Religious advertising was not permitted until 1993. Religious organisations which do not practice or advocate illegal behaviour and whose observances are normally accessible to the public may now advertise under the Code for the following purposes:

(a) to publicise such events as services meetings or festivals
(b) to describe the organisation's activities
(c) to offer publications or other merchandise.

Religious advertisements may not expound religious doctrines, play on fear or seek to exploit vulnerable groups.

# 13 DISSOLUTION OF A CHARITY

A charity may be dissolved in the following circumstances:—

1. on the distribution of all its assets for charitable purposes:
2. on the transfer of all its assets to another charity;
3. at the expiration of the permitted time in the case of a "time" charity; or on the occurrence of an event giving rise to a gift over to non-charitable purposes.

## Distributions for purposes of charity

**Prohibition against spending capital**

Where the governing instrument permits the distribution of both capital and income the charity may be brought to an end by the charity trustees applying all of the assets for the permitted charitable purposes. Where there is a prohibition against spending capital, as is the case with many, particularly old-established, charitable trusts, this course will not be open to the charity trustees unless the Charity Commissioners are prepared to vary the terms of the trust. It is doubtful if the Commissioners have power to authorise a variation which would enable the charity to be brought to an end and their normal approach would be to suggest that the charity would be amalgamated with other charities having similar purposes.

**Small charities**

As explained in Chapter 11 new provisions were introduced in 1992 (now appearing in sections 43 and 44 of the Charities Act) to permit trustees of very small charities having an income of £1,000 or less and permanent endowment which does not consist of land to confer power on themselves to spend capital.

**Charitable companies**

These difficulties will not affect charitable companies which are free to spend both capital and income and to dissolve the company if this is thought appropriate by the members. Whether or not a charity which is an unincorporated association is able to spend capital will depend upon the terms of its constitution.

## Transfer of assets to another charity

**Unlawful delegation of trustees' powers**

The memorandum of a charitable company invariably provides that any surplus assets on dissolution should be transferred to another charity but in the case of a charitable trust or unincorporated association this is not necessarily so and will only be permissible if authorised specifically by the governing instrument. Even if there is no restriction on applying capital a charity regulated by a declaration of trust or constitution may still be prevented from transferring assets to another charity as opposed to applying its funds in direct promotion of its objects (in the absence of a specific power to do so) since this may constitute an unlawful delegation of the trustees' powers.

Modern deeds and constitutions will normally include a power to pay funds to another charity but advice should be taken before any transfer is made. Where the governing instrument specifically authorises the transfer of assets to another charity this may be a proper application of the charity's funds provided that the purposes of the recipient charity are identical to or include the purposes of the donor charity and the trustees consider that the transfer is the best way of promoting the purposes of the charity. But if the proposed transfer is not authorised by the governing instrument it will be permissible only if sanctioned by the Charity Commissioners and this is likely only if the provisions of section 13 of the Charities Act (the circumstances in which a *cy-près* scheme may be made) are satisfied. Even then, the Commissioners will be more likely to suggest that the charity should be amalgamated with another having similar purposes.

The Commissioners will normally be sympathetic if the trustees consider that the trust deed or constitution by which the charity is governed is outmoded or no longer suitable for the needs of the charity and that the best way of promoting the purposes of the charity will be for a new charity to be formed and the assets of the first charity to be transferred to it. This is often done where the trustees are concerned about personal liability and wish to form a charitable company to carry on the work of the charity.

**Small charities**

A simple mechanism exists for small charities with an income of no more than £5,000 to resolve that the assets of the charity shall be transferred to another charity or divided between two or more charities. Details were given in Chapter 11 (pages 187–188).

## Charities limited in time

A charity which, under the terms of its governing instrument, continues only for a specified period after which the assets pass to some non-charitable object, come to an end at the expiration of the specified time as does a charity which is subject to a gift over to non-charitable purposes in certain specified conditions. The adverse tax treatment of such charities, which was discussed in Chapter 8, has made them of less significance than formerly.[1]

## Procedure

**Removal from the register**

When a charity comes to an end notice should be given to the Charity Commissioners so that the charity may be removed from the register. Before any transfer of assets takes place the charity trustees should ensure that all their liabilities are met, since once they have parted with the property of the charity they will have no funds available to meet liabilities and may find

[1] See above, pp. 109 and 121.

themselves personally liable and recovery from the transferees difficult.

## Cases where no dissolution occurs

A charity is not dissolved because it is reorganised, renamed or amalgamated with another charity whether this is done by a scheme of the Charity Commissioners,[2] or the court, under the terms of the governing instrument,[3] or informally.

[2] *Re Faraker* [1912] 2 Ch. 488.
[3] *Re Bagshaw* [1954] 1 W.L.R. 238.

# APPENDIX A

## Charity Commissioners' Model Documents

*Note*: These should be read in conjunction with the Commission's Information Sheet 2 (included in the Registration Pack)

PRECEDENT 1

MODEL DECLARATION OF TRUST FOR A CHARITABLE TRUST

THIS DECLARATION OF TRUST IS MADE

the .......... day of ...................................... 19..... by

(a) ............................................................................

............................................................................

............................................................................

............................................................................

("the first trustees" who together with the future trustees or trustee of this deed are referred to as "the trustees")

**WHEREAS** the first trustees hold

(b) ............................................................................

............................................................................

on the trusts declared in this deed and it is contemplated that further money or assets may be paid or transferred to the trustees upon the same trusts.

NOW THIS DEED WITNESSES AS FOLLOWS:

## A Administration

**Clause A** The charitable trust constituted by this deed ("the Charity") and its property ("the trust fund") shall be administered and managed by the trustees under the name of

............................................................................

or by such other name as the trustees from time to time decide with the approval of the Charity Commissioners for England and Wales ("the Commissioners").

## B   Objects

**Clause B**   The trustees shall hold the trust fund and its income upon trust to apply them for the following objects ("the objects")

[in .........................................................................................

("the area of benefit")]: ...........................................................

.........................................................................................

.........................................................................................

.........................................................................................

.........................................................................................

.........................................................................................

.........................................................................................

.........................................................................................

.........................................................................................

.........................................................................................

## C   Powers

**Clause C**   In furtherance of the objects but not otherwise the trustees may exercise any of the following powers:[1]

(i) to raise funds and invite and receive contributions: Provided that in raising funds the trustees shall not undertake any substantial permanent trading activity and shall conform to any relevant statutory regulations;

(ii) to buy, take on lease or in exchange, hire or otherwise acquire any property necessary for the achievement of the objects and to maintain and equip it for use;

(iii) subject to any consents required by law to sell, lease or otherwise dispose of all or any party of the property comprised in the trust fund;

(iv) subject to any consents required by law, to borrow money and to charge the whole or any part of the trust fund with repayment of the money so borrowed;

(v) to co-operate with other charities, voluntary bodies and statutory authorities operating in furtherance of the objects or of similar charitable purposes and to exchange information and advice with them;

(vi) to establish or support any charitable trusts, associations or institutions formed for the objects or any of them;

(vii) to appoint and constitute such advisory committees as the trustees may think fit;

(viii) to employ such staff (who shall not be trustees) as are necessary for the proper pursuit of the objects and to

---

[1] Additional powers may be included to authorise accumulation of income, payment of premiums for trustees insurance and remuneration and to allow the trustees to carry on the proposed activities of the trust.

make all reasonable and necessary provision for the payment of pensions and superannuation to staff and their dependants;

(ix) to permit any investments comprised in the trust fund to be held in the name of any clearing bank, any trust corporation or any stockbroking company which is a member of the Stock Exchange (or any subsidiary of such a stockbroking company) as nominee for the trustees and to pay any such nominee reasonable and proper remuneration for acting as such;

(x) to delegate to any one or more of the trustees the transaction of any business or the performance of any act required to be transacted or performed in the execution of the trusts of the Charity and which is within the professional or business competence of such trustee or trustees: Provided that the trustee shall exercise reasonable supervision over any trustee or trustees acting on their behalf under this provision and shall ensure that all their acts and proceedings are fully and promptly reported to them;

(xi) to do all such other lawful things as are necessary for the achievement of the objects.

## D   Appointment of trustees (Option 1)

**Clause D**

(1) Subject to the provisions of clause . . . . . . the first trustees shall hold office for the following periods respectively:

. . . . . . . . . . . . . . . . . . . . . . . . . . . . . . . . . . . . . . . . . . . . . . . . . . . . . . . . . . . . . . . . .

. . . . . . . . . . . . . . . . . . . . . . . . . . . . . . . . . . . . . . . . . . . . . . . . . . . . . . . . . . . . . . . . .

. . . . . . . . . . . . . . . . . . . . . . . . . . . . . . . . . . . . . . . . . . . . . . . . . . . . . . . . . . . . . . . . .

. . . . . . . . . . . . . . . . . . . . . . . . . . . . . . . . . . . . . . . . . . . . . . . . . . . . . . . . . . . . . . . . .

. . . . . . . . . . . . . . . . . . . . . . . . . . . . . . . . . . . . . . . . . . . . . . . . . . . . . . . . . . . . . . . . .

(2) There shall be at least three trustees. Every future trustee shall be appointed for a term of . . . . . . years by a resolution of the trustees passed at a special meeting called under clause . . . . . . . If a trustee is to be appointed to replace a trustee who is leaving office he or she may be appointed not more than three months before the other trustee leaves office but shall not take office until the other trustee has left office. In such a case the retiring trustee shall not be entitled to vote in favour of his or her own appointment.

(3) In selecting persons to be appointed as trustees, the trustees shall take into account the benefits of appointing a person [who through residence, occupation, employment or otherwise has special knowledge of the area of benefit or] who is [otherwise] able by virtue of his or her personal or professional qualifications to make a contribution to the pursuit of the objects or the management of the Charity.

(4) When any new trustee is appointed the trustees shall ensure that any land belonging to the Charity which is not vested or about to be vested in the Official Custodian for Charities or in a

custodian trustee and all other property of the Charity which is not vested or about to be vested in the Official Custodian for Charities, a custodian trustee or a nominee is effectively vested in the persons who are the trustees following such appointment.

(5) If for any reason trustees cannot be appointed in accordance with the foregoing provisions, the statutory power of appointing new or additional trustees shall be exercisable.

## E   Appointment of trustees (Option 2)

**Clause E**   (1) There shall be at least three trustees. Every future trustee shall be appointed by a resolution of the trustees passed at a special meeting called under clause . . . . . . .

(2) In selecting persons to be appointed as trustees, the trustees shall take into account the benefits of appointing a person [who through residence, occupation, employment or otherwise has special knowledge of the area of benefit or] who is [otherwise] able by virtue of his or her personal or professional qualifications to make a contribution to the pursuit of the objects or the management of the Charity.

(3) When any new trustee is appointed the trustees shall ensure that any land belonging to the Charity which is not vested or about to be vested in the Official Custodian for Charities or in a custodian trustee and all other property of the Charity which is not vested or about to be vested in the Official Custodian for Charities, a custodian trustee or a nominee is effectively vested in the persons who are the trustees following such appointment.

(4) If for any reason trustees cannot be appointed in accordance with the foregoing provisions the statutory power of appointing new or additional trustees shall be exercisable.

## F   Appointment of trustees (Option 3)

**Clause F**        (1) The body of trustees shall consist when complete of . . . . . . persons being:
. . . . . . ex-officio trustee(s);
. . . . . . nominated trustee(s); and
. . . . . . co-opted trustee(s).

(2) The ex-officio trustee(s) shall be . . . . . . . . . . . . . . . . . . . . . . . . . . .

. . . . . . . . . . . . . . . . . . . . . . . . . . . . . . . . . . . . . . . . . . . . . . . . . . . . . . . . . . . . . . . . .

(3) The nominated trustee(s) shall be appointed by . . . . . . . . .

. . . . . . . . . . . . . . . . . . . . . . . . . . . . . . . . . . . . . . . . . . . . . . . . . . . . . . . . . . . . . . . . .

. . . . . . . . . . . . . . . . . . . . . . . . . . . . . . . . . . . . . . . . . . . . . . . . . . . . . . . . . . . . . . . . .

. . . . . . . . . . . . . . . . . . . . . . . . . . . . . . . . . . . . . . . . . . . . . . . . . . . . . . . . . . . . . . . . .

Each appointment shall be made for a term of four years at a meeting convened and held according to the ordinary practice of the appointing body. The chairman of the meeting shall cause the name of each person appointed to be notified forthwith to the trustees. The person appointed may be, but need not be, a member of the appointing body.

(4) The first trustees shall be the first co-opted trustees and shall hold office for the following periods respectively

..............................................................................

..............................................................................

..............................................................................

..............................................................................

..............................................................................

(5) Future co-opted trustees shall be persons [who through residence, occupation, employment or otherwise have special knowledge of the area of benefit or] who are [otherwise] able by virtue of their personal or professional qualifications to make a contribution to the pursuit of the objects or the management of the charity. They shall be appointed for a term of five years by a resolution of the trustees passed at a special meeting of which not less than 21 days' notice has been given.

(6) If for any reason trustees cannot be appointed in accordance with the foregoing provisions, the statutory power of appointing new or additional trustees shall be exercisable.

## G   Eligibility for trusteeship

**Clause G**   (1) No person shall be appointed as a trustee:
(a)  unless he or she has attained the age of 18 years; or
(b)  in circumstances such that, had he or she already been a trustee, he or she would have been disqualified from office under the provisions of the following clause.

(2) No person shall be entitled to act as a trustee whether on a first or on any subsequent entry into office until after signing in the minute book of the trustees a declaration of acceptance and willingness to act in the trusts of the Charity.

## H   Determination of trusteeship

**Clause H**   A trustee shall cease to hold office if he or she:
(1) is disqualified from acting as a trustee by virtue of section 72 of the Charities Act 1993 (or any statutory re-enactment or modification of that provision);
(2) becomes incapable by reason of mental disorder, illness or injury of managing and administering his or her own affairs;
(3) is absent without the permission of the trustees from all their meetings held within a period of six months and the trustees resolve that his or her office be vacated; or
(4) notifies to the trustees a wish to resign (but only if at least two trustees will remain in office when the notice of resignation is to take effect).

## I   Vacancies

**Clause I**   If a vacancy occurs the trustees shall note the fact in their minute book at their next meeting. Any eligible trustee may be re-appointed. So long as there shall be fewer than two trustees none of the powers or discretions hereby or by law vested in the trustees shall be exercisable except for the purpose of appointing a new trustee or trustees.

## J   Ordinary meetings

**Clause J**   The trustees shall hold at least two ordinary meetings in each year.

## K   Calling meetings

**Clause K**   The first meeting of the trustees shall be called by

...................................................................................................

or if no meeting has been called within three months after the date of this deed by any two of the trustees. Subsequent meetings shall be arranged by the trustees at their meetings or may be called at any time by the chairman or any two trustees upon not less than ten days' notice being given to the other trustees.

## L   Chairman

**Clause L**   The trustees at their first ordinary meeting in each year shall elect one of their number to be chairman of their meetings until the commencement of the first ordinary meeting in the following year. The chairman shall always be eligible for re-election. if the chairman is not present within ten minutes after the time appointed for holding a meeting or there is no chairman the trustees present shall choose one of their number to be chairman of the meeting.

## M   Special meetings

**Clause M**   A special meeting may be called at any time by the chairman or any two trustees upon not less than four days' notice being given to the other trustees of the matters to be discussed, but if the matters include an appointment of a trustee [or a proposal to amend any of the trusts of this deed] then upon not less than 21 days' notice being so given. A special meeting may be called to take place immediately after or before an ordinary meeting.

## N   Quorum

**Clause N**   There shall be a quorum when at least one third of the number of trustees for the time being or two trustees, whichever is the greater, are present at a meeting.

## O   Voting

**Clause O**   Every matter shall be determined by a majority of votes of the trustees present and voting on the question. The chairman of the meeting shall have a casting vote whether he or she has or has not voted previously on the same question but no trustee in any other circumstances shall give more than one vote.

## P    Minutes

**Clause P**    The trustees shall keep minutes, in books kept for the purpose, of the proceedings at their meetings.

## Q    Accounts

**Clause Q**    The trustees shall comply with their obligations under the Charities Act 1993 (or any statutory re-enactment or modification of that Act) with regard to:

  (1)  the keeping of accounting records for the Charity;
  (2)  the preparation of annual statements of account for the Charity;
  (3)  the auditing or independent examination of the statements of account of the Charity; and
  (4)  the transmission of the statements of account of the Charity to the Commissioners.

## R    Annual Report

**Clause R**    The trustees shall comply with their obligations under the Charities Act 1993 (or any statutory re-enactment or modification of that Act) with regard to the preparation of an annual report and its transmission to the Commissioners.

## S    Annual Return

**Clause S**    The trustees shall comply with their obligations under the Charities Act 1993 (or any statutory re-enactment or modification of that Act) with regard to the preparation of an annual return and its transmission to the Commissioners.

## T    General power to make regulations

**Clause T**    Within the limits of this deed the trustees shall have full power from time to time to make regulations for the management of the Charity and for the conduct of their business, including the calling of meetings, the deposit of money at a bank and the custody of documents.

## U    Bank account

**Clause U**    Any bank account in which any part of the trust fund is deposited shall be operated by the trustees and shall be held in the name of the Charity. All cheques and orders for the payment of money from such account shall be signed by at least two trustees.

## V    Trustees not to be personally interested

**Clause V**    [(1) Subject to the provisions of sub-clause (2) of this clause]. No trustee shall acquire any interest in property belonging to the Charity (otherwise than as a trustee for the Charity or receive remuneration or be interested (otherwise than as a trustee) in any contract entered into by the trustees).

[(2) Any trustee who is a solicitor, accountant or other person engaged in any profession may charge and be paid all the usual professional charges for business done by him or her or his or her firm when instructed by the other trustees to act in a professional capacity on behalf of the Charity: Provided that at no time shall a majority of the trustees benefit under this provision and that a trustee shall withdraw from any meeting of the trustees at which his or her own instruction or remuneration, or that of his or her firm, is under discussion.]

## W  Management of land

**Clause W**  Subject to any consents which may be required by law, the trustees shall either sell or let any land belonging to the Charity which is not required to be retained or occupied in furtherance of the objects.

## X  Leases

**Clause X**  The trustees shall ensure that on the grant by them of any lease the tenant shall execute a counterpart lease. Every lease shall contain a covenant on the part of the tenant for the payment of rent and a proviso for re-entry on non-payment of the rent or non-performance of the covenants contained in the lease.

## Y  Repair and insurance

**Clause Y**  The trustees shall keep in repair and insure to their full value against fire and other usual risks all the buildings of the Charity which are not required to be kept in repair and insured by the tenant and shall also insure suitably in respect of public liability and employer's liability.

## Z  Amendment of Trust Deed[2]

**Clause Z**  (1) The trustees may amend the provisions of this deed, provided that:

- (a) no amendment may be made to clause ... (the objects clause) [unless it appears to the trustees that the objects can no longer provide a suitable and effective method of using the trust fund];
- (b) no amendment may be made to [clause ... (the objects clause),] clause ... (trustees not to be personally interested clause) or this clause without the prior consent in writing of the Commissioners; and
- (c) no amendment may be made which has the effect of the charity ceasing to be a charity at law.

(2) Any amendment shall be made by deed under the authority of a resolution passed at a special meeting of the trustees.

[2] The clause should be amended to allow alterations to the objects subject to the Commissioners' consent. A suitable clause is given in Appendix C.

(3) The trustees should promptly send to the Commissioners a copy of any amendment made under this clause.

**IN WITNESS whereof the parties hereto have hereunto set their respective hands the day and year first before written**

Signed as a deed by the said:

..............................................................................

in the presence of:

..............................................................................

Witness's name:

..............................................................................

Witness's address:

..............................................................................

..............................................................................

..............................................................................

..............................................................................

**Repeat these words for each party to the deed.**

PRECEDENT 2

# Model memorandum and articles of association for a charitable company

### The Companies Acts 1985 and 1989

**Company Limited by Guarantee and not having a Share Capital**

Memorandum of Association of

..............................................................................

1. The Company's name is .............................................

..............................................................................

(and in this document it is called "the Charity").

2. The Charity's registered office is to be situated in England and Wales.

3. The Charity's objects ("the Objects") are ..........................

..............................................................................

..............................................................................

..............................................................................

........................................................................

4. In furtherance of the Objects but not otherwise the Charity may exercise the following powers:

( ) to draw, make, accept, endorse, discount, execute and issue promissory notes, bills, cheques and other instruments, and to operate bank accounts in the name of the Charity;

(   to raise funds and to invite and receive contributions: provided that in raising funds the Charity shall not undertake any substantial permanent trading activities and shall conform to any relevant statutory regulations;

( ) to acquire, alter, improve and (subject to such consents as may be required by law) to charge or otherwise dispose of property;

( ) subject to clause 5 below to employ such staff, who shall not be directors of the Charity (hereinafter referred to as "the trustees"), as are necessary for the proper pursuit of the Objects and to make all reasonable and necessary provision for the payment of pensions and superannuation to staff and their dependants;

( ) to establish or support any charitable trusts, associations or institutions formed for all or any of the Objects;[3]

( ) to co-operate with other charities, voluntary bodies and statutory authorities operating in furtherance of the Objects or similar charitable purposes and to exchange information and advice with them;

( ) to pay out of the funds of the Charity the costs, charges and expenses of and incidental to the formation and registration of the Charity;

( ) to do all such other lawful things as are necessary for the achievement of the Objects.[4]

5. The income and property of the Charity shall be applied solely towards the promotion of the Objects and no part shall be paid or transferred, directly or indirectly, by way of dividend, bonus or otherwise by way of profit, to members of the Charity, and no trustee shall be appointed to any office of the Charity paid by salary or fees or receive any remuneration or other benefit in money or money's worth from the Charity: Provided that nothing in this document shall prevent any payment in good faith by the Charity:

(1) of the usual professional charges for business done by any trustee who is a solicitor, accountant or other person engaged in a profession, or by any partner of his or hers, when instructed by the Charity to act in a professional capacity on its behalf: Provided that at no time shall a majority of the trustees benefit under this provision and that a trustee shall withdraw from any meeting at which his or her appointment or remuneration, or that of his or her partner, is under discussion;

[3] The models for a charitable trust, company and unincorporated association have been drafted and approved by the Charity Commissioners.

[4] A power to borrow should be added. Additional powers should be included so that the charity is enabled to carry out its intended objects. A power to pay premiums on insurance policies to protect trustees should also be included (see Chapter 7) and a power to remunerate trustees.

(2) of reasonable and proper remuneration for any services rendered to the Charity by any member, officer or servant of the Charity who is not a trustee;

(3) of interest on money lent by any member of the Charity or trustee at a reasonable and proper rate per annum not exceeding 2 per cent less than the published base lending rate of a clearing bank to be selected by the trustees;

(4) of fees, remuneration or other benefit in money or money's worth to any company of which a trustee may also be a member holding not more than 1/100th part of the issued capital of that company;

(5) of reasonable and proper rent for premises demised or let by any member of the Company or a trustee;

(6) to any trustee of reasonable out-of-pocket expenses.

6. The liability of the members is limited.

7. Every member of the Charity undertakes to contribute such amount as may be required (not exceeding ú10) to the Charity's assets if it should be wound up while he or she is a member or within one year after he or she ceases to be a member, for payment of the Charity's debts and liabilities contracted before he or she ceases to be a member, and of the costs, charges and expenses of winding up, and for the adjustment of the rights of the contributories among themselves.

8. If the Charity is wound up or dissolved and after all its debts and liabilities have been satisfied there remains any property it shall not be paid to or distributed among the members of the Charity, but shall be given or transferred to some other charity or charities having objects similar to the Objects which prohibits the distribution of its or their income and property to an extent at least as great as is imposed on the Charity by Clause 5 above, chosen by the members of the Charity at or before the time of dissolution and if that cannot be done then to some other charitable object.

**We, the persons whose names and addresses are written below, wish to be formed into a company under this memorandum of association.**

---

Signatures, Names and Addresses of Subscribers

---

Dated:

Witness to the above Signatures:

Name:

Address:


Occupation:

**The Companies Acts 1985 and 1989**

**Company Limited by Guarantee and not having a Share Capital**

Articles of Association of

.................................................................................

## Interpretation

1. In these articles:

"the Charity" means the company intended to be regulated by these articles;

"the Act" means the Companies Act 1985 including any statutory modification or re-enactment thereof for the time being in force;

"the articles" means these Articles of Association of the Charity;

"clear days" in relation to the period of a notice means the period excluding the day when the notice is given or deemed to be given and the day for which it is given or on which it is to take effect;

"executed" includes any mode of execution;

"the memorandum" means the memorandum of association of the Charity;

"office" means the registered office of the Charity;

"the seal" means the common seal of the Charity if it has one;

"secretary" means the secretary of the Charity or any other person appointed to perform the duties of the secretary of the Charity, including a joint, assistant or deputy secretary;

"the trustees" means the directors of the Charity (and "trustee" has a corresponding meaning);

"the United Kingdom" means Great Britain and Northern Ireland; and

words importing the masculine gender only shall include the feminine gender.

Subject as aforesaid, words or expressions contained in these Articles shall, unless the context requires otherwise, bear the same meaning as in the Act.

## Members

2. (1) The subscribers to the memorandum and such other persons or organisations as are admitted to membership in

accordance with the rules made under Article 61 shall be members of the Charity. No person shall be admitted a member of the Charity unless his application for membership is approved by the trustees.

(2) Unless the trustees or the Charity in general meeting shall make other provision under Article 61, the trustees may in their absolute discretion permit any member of the Charity to retire, provided that after such retirement the number of members is not less than two.

## General meetings

3. The Charity shall hold an annual general meeting each year in addition to any other meetings in that year, and shall specify the meeting as such in the notices calling it; and not more than fifteen months shall elapse between the date of one annual general meeting of the Charity and that of the next: Provided that so long as the Charity holds its first annual general meeting within eighteen months of its incorporation, it need not hold it in the year of its incorporation or in the following year. The annual general meeting shall be held at such times and places as the trustees shall appoint. All general meetings other than annual general meetings shall be called extraordinary general meetings.

4. The trustees may call general meetings and, on the requisition of members pursuant to the provisions of the Act, shall forthwith proceed to convene an extraordinary general meeting for a date not later than eight weeks after receipt of the requisition. If there are not within the United Kingdom sufficient trustees to call a general meeting, any trustee or any member of the Charity may fall a general meeting.

## Notice of general meetings

5. An annual general meeting and an extraordinary general meeting called for the passing of a special resolution appointing a person as a trustee shall be called by at least twenty-one clear days' notice. All other extraordinary general meetings shall be called by at least fourteen clear days' notice but a general meeting may be called by shorter notice if it is so agreed:

- (1) in the case of an annual general meeting, by all the members entitled to attend and vote; and
- (2) in the case of any other meeting by a majority in number of members having a right to attend and vote, being a majority together holding not less than 95 per cent of the total voting rights at the meeting of all the members.

The notice shall specify the time and place of the meeting and the general nature of the business to be transacted and, in the case of an annual general meeting, shall specify the meeting as such.

The notice shall be given to all the members and to the trustees and auditors.

6. The accidental omission to give notice of a meeting to, or the non-receipt of notice of a meeting by, any person entitled to

receive notice shall not invalidate the proceedings at that meeting.

## Proceedings at general meetings

7. No business shall be transacted at any meeting unless a quorum is present. Ten persons entitled to vote upon the business to be transacted, each being a member or a duly authorised representative of a member organisation, or one tenth of the total number of such persons for the time being, whichever is the greater, shall constitute a quorum.

8. If a quorum is not present within half an hour from the time appointed for the meeting, or if during a meeting a quorum ceases to be present, the meeting shall stand adjourned to the same day in the next week at the same time and place or to such time and place as the trustees may determine.

9. The chairman, if any, of the trustees or in his absence some other trustee nominated by the trustees shall preside as chairman of the meeting, but if neither the chairman nor such other trustee (if any) be present within fifteen minutes after the time appointed for holding the meeting and willing to act, the trustees present shall elect one of their number to be chairman and, if there is only one trustee present and willing to act, he shall be chairman.

10. If no trustee is willing to act as chairman, or if no trustee is present within fifteen minutes after the time appointed for holding the meeting, the members present and entitled to vote shall choose one of their number to be chairman.

11. A trustee shall, notwithstanding that he is not a member, be entitled to attend and speak at any general meeting.

12. The chairman may, with the consent of a meeting at which a quorum is present (and shall if so directed by the meeting), adjourn the meeting from time to time and from place to place, but no business shall be transacted at an adjourned meeting other than business which might properly have been transacted at the meeting had adjournment not taken place. When a meeting is adjourned for fourteen days or more, at least seven clear days' notice shall be given specifying the time and place of the adjourned meeting and the general nature of the business to be transacted. Otherwise it shall not be necessary to give any such notice.

13. A resolution put to the vote of a meeting shall be decided on a show of hands unless before, or on the declaration of the result of, the show of hands a poll is duly demanded. Subject to the provisions of the Act, a poll may be demanded:

(1) by the chairman; or
(2) by at least two members having the right to vote at the meeting; or
(3) by a member or members representing not less than one-tenth of the total voting rights of all the members having the right to vote at the meeting.

14. Unless a poll is duly demanded a declaration by the chairman that a resolution has been carried or carried unanimously, or by a particular majority, or lost, or not carried by a particular majority and an entry to that effect in the minutes of the meeting shall be conclusive evidence of the fact without proof of the number or proportion of the votes recorded in favour of or against the resolution.

15. The demand for a poll may be withdrawn, before the poll is taken, but only with the consent of the chairman. The withdrawal of a demand for a poll shall not invalidate the result of a show of hands declared before the demand for the poll was made.

16. A poll shall be taken as the chairman directs and he may appoint scrutineers (who need not be members) and fix a time and place for declaring the results of the poll. The result of the poll shall be deemed to be the resolution of the meeting at which the poll is demanded.

17. In the case of an equality of votes, whether on a show of hands or on a poll, the chairman shall be entitled to a casting vote in addition to any other vote he may have.

18. A poll demanded on the election of a chairman or on a question of adjournment shall be taken immediately. A poll demanded on any other question shall be taken either immediately or at such time and place as the chairman directs not being more than thirty days after the poll is demanded. The demand for a poll shall not prevent continuance of a meeting for the transaction of any business other than the question on which the poll is demanded. If a poll is demanded before the declaration of the result of a show of hands and the demand is duly withdrawn, the meeting shall continue as if the demand had not been made.

19. No notice need be given of a poll not taken immediately if the time and place at which it is to be taken are announced at the meeting at which it is demanded. In other cases at least seven clear days' notice shall be given specifying the time and place at which the poll is to be taken.

## Votes of members

20. Subject to Article 17, every member shall have one vote.

21. No member shall be entitled to vote at any general meeting unless all moneys then payable by him to the Charity have been paid.

22. No objection shall be raised to the qualification of any voter except at the meeting or adjourned meeting at which the vote objected to is tendered, and every vote not disallowed at the meeting shall be valid. Any objection made in due time shall be referred to the chairman whose decision shall be final and conclusive.

23. A vote given or poll demanded by the duly authorised representative of a member organisation shall be valid notwithstanding the previous determination of the authority of the

person voting or demanding a poll unless notice of the determination was received by the Charity at the office before the commencement of the meeting or adjourned meeting at which the vote is given or the poll demanded or (in the case of a poll taken otherwise than on the same day as the meeting or adjourned meeting) the time appointed for taking the poll.

24. Any organisation which is a member of the Charity may by resolution of its Council or other governing body authorise such person as it thinks fit to act as its representative at any meeting of the Charity, and the person so authorised shall be entitled to exercise the same powers on behalf of the organisation which he represents as the organisation could exercise if it were an individual member of the Charity.

## Trustees

25. The number of trustees shall not be less than three but (unless otherwise determined by ordinary resolution) shall not be subject to any maximum.

26. The first trustees shall be those persons named in the statement delivered pursuant to section 10(2) of the Act, who shall be deemed to have been appointed under the articles. Future trustees shall be appointed as provided subsequently in the articles.

## Powers of trustees

27. Subject to the provisions of the Act, the memorandum and the articles and to any directions given by special resolution, the business of the Charity shall be managed by the trustees who may exercise all the powers of the Charity. No alteration of the memorandum or the articles and no such direction shall invalidate any prior act of the trustees which would have been valid if that alteration had not been made or that direction had not been given. The powers given by this article shall not be limited by any special power given to the trustees by the articles and a meeting of trustees at which a quorum is present may exercise all the powers exercisable by the trustees.

28. In addition to all powers hereby expressly conferred upon them and without detracting from the generality of their powers under the articles the trustees shall have the following powers, namely:

(1) to expend the funds of the Charity in such manner as they shall consider most beneficial for the achievement of the objects and to invest in the name of the Charity such part of the funds as they may see fit and to direct the sale of transposition of any such investments and to expend the proceeds of any such sale in furtherance of the objects of the charity;

(2) to enter into contracts on behalf of the Charity.

## Appointment and retirement of trustees

29. At the first annual general meeting all the trustees shall retire from office, and at every subsequent annual general meeting one-third of the trustees who are subject to retirement by rotation or, if their number is not three or a multiple of three, the number nearest to one third shall retire from office; but, if there is only one trustee who is subject to retirement by rotation, he shall retire.

30. Subject to the provisions of the Act, the trustees to retire by rotation shall be those who have been longest in office since their last appointment or reappointment, but as between persons who became or were last reappointed trustees on the same day those to retire shall (unless they otherwise agree among themselves) be determined by lot.

31. If the Charity at the meeting at which a trustee retires by rotation, does not fill the vacancy the retiring trustee shall, if willing to act, be deemed to have been reappointed unless at the meeting it is resolved not to fill the vacancy or unless a resolution for the reappointment of the trustee is put to the meeting and lost.

32. No person other than a trustee retiring by rotation shall be appointed or reappointed a trustee at any general meeting unless:

(1) he is recommended by the trustees; or
(2) not less than fourteen nor more than thirty-five clear days before the date appointed for the meeting, notice executed by a member qualified to vote at the meeting has been given to the Charity of the intention to propose that person for appointment or reappointment stating the particulars which would, if he were so appointed or reappointed, be required to be included in the Charity's register of trustees together with a notice executed by that person of his willingness to be appointed or reappointed.

33. No person may be appointed as a trustee:

(1) unless he has attained the age of 18 years; or
(2) in circumstances such that, had he already been a trustee, he would have been disqualified from acting under the provisions of Article 38.

34. Not less than seven nor more than twenty-eight clear days before the date appointed for holding a general meeting notice shall be given to all persons who are entitled to receive notice of the meeting of any person (other than a trustee retiring by rotation at the meeting) who is recommended by the trustees for appointment or reappointment as a trustee at the meeting or in respect of whom notice has been duly given to the Charity of the intention to propose him at the meeting for appointment or reappointment as a trustee. The notice shall give the particulars of that person which would, if he were so appointed or re-appointed, be required to be included in the Charity's register of trustees.

35. Subject as aforesaid, the Charity may by ordinary resolution appoint a person who is willing to act to be a trustee either to fill a

vacancy or as an additional trustee and may also determine the rotation in which any additional trustees are to retire.

36. The trustees may appoint a person who is willing to act to be a trustee either to fill a vacancy or as an additional trustee provided that the appointment does not cause the number of trustees to exceed any number fixed by or in accordance with the articles as the maximum number of trustees. A trustee so appointed shall hold office only until the next following annual general meeting and shall not be taken into account in determining the trustees who are to retire by rotation at the meeting. If not reappointed at such annual general meeting, he shall vacate office at the conclusion thereof.

37. Subject as aforesaid, a trustee who retires at an annual general meeting may, if willing to act, be reappointed.

## Disqualification and removal of trustees

38. A trustee shall cease to hold office if he

(1) ceases to be a trustee by virtue of any provision in the Act or is disqualified from acting as a trustee by virtue of section 72 of the Charities Act 1993 (or any statutory re-enactment or modification of that provision);

(2) becomes incapable by reason of mental disorder, illness or injury of managing and administering his own affairs;

(3) resigns his office by notice to the Charity (but only if at least two trustees will remain in office when the notice of resignation is to take effect); or

(4) is absent without the permission of the trustees from all their meetings held within a period of six months and the trustees resolve that his office be vacated.

## Trustees' expenses

39. The trustees may be paid all reasonable travelling, hotel and other expenses properly incurred by them in connection with their attendance at meetings of trustees or committees of trustees or general meetings or otherwise in connection with the discharge of their duties, but shall otherwise be paid no remuneration.

## Trustees' appointments

40. Subject to the provisions of the Act and to Clause 5 of the memorandum, the trustees may appoint one or more of their number to the unremunerated office of managing director or to any other unremunerated executive office under the Charity. Any such appointment may be made upon such terms as the trustees determine. Any appointment of a trustee to an executive office shall terminate if he ceases to be a trustee. A managing director and a trustee holding any other executive office shall not be subject to retirement by rotation.

41. Except to the extent permitted by clause 5 of the memorandum, no trustee shall take or hold any interest in property belonging to the Charity or receive remuneration or be interested

otherwise than as a trustee is any other contract to which the Charity is a party.

## Proceedings of trustees

42. Subject to the provisions of the articles, the trustees may regulate their proceedings as they think fit. A trustee may, and the secretary at the request of a trustee shall, call a meeting of the trustees. It shall not be necessary to give notice of a meeting to a trustee who is absent from the United Kingdom. Questions arising at a meeting shall be decided by a majority of votes. In the case of an equality of votes, the chairman shall have a second or casting vote.

43. The quorum for the transaction of the business of the trustees may be fixed by the trustees but shall not be less than one third of their number or two trustees, whichever is the greater.

44. The trustees may act notwithstanding any vacancies in their number, but, if the number of trustees is less than the number fixed as the quorum, the continuing trustees or trustee may act only for the purpose of filling vacancies or of calling a general meeting.

45. The trustees may appoint one of their number to be the chairman of their meetings and may at any time remove him from that office. Unless he is unwilling to do so, the trustee so appointed shall preside at every meeting of trustees at which he is present. But if there is no trustee holding that office, or if the trustee holding it is unwilling to preside or is not present within five minutes after the time appointed for the meeting, the trustees present may appoint one of their number to be chairman of the meeting.

46. The trustees may appoint one or more sub-committees consisting of three or more trustees for the purpose of making any inquiry or supervising or performing any function or duty which in the opinion of the trustees would be more conveniently undertaken or carried out by a sub-committee: provided that all acts and proceedings of any such sub-committees shall be fully and promptly reported to the trustees.

47. All acts done by a meeting of trustees, or of a committee of trustees, shall, notwithstanding that it be afterwards discovered that there was a defect in the appointment of any trustee or that any of them were disqualified from holding office, or had vacated office, or were not entitled to vote, be as valid as if every such person had been duly appointed and was qualified and had continued to be a trustee and had been entitled to vote.

48. A resolution in writing, signed by all the trustees entitled to receive notice of a meeting of trustees or of a committee of trustees, shall be as valid and effective as if it had been passed at a meeting of trustees or (as the case may be) a committee of trustees duly convened and held. Such a resolution may consist of several documents in the same form, each signed by one or more of the trustees.

49. Any bank account in which any part of the assets of the Charity is deposited shall be operated by the trustees and shall indicate the name of the Charity. All cheques and orders for the payment of money from such account shall be signed by at least two trustees.

## Secretary

50. Subject to the provisions of the Act, the secretary shall be appointed by the trustees for such term, at such remuneration (if not a trustee) and upon such conditions as they may think fit; and any secretary so appointed may be removed by them.

## Minutes

51. The trustees shall keep minutes in books kept for the purpose:

    (1) of all appointments of officers made by the trustees; and
    (2) of all proceedings at meetings of the Charity and of the trustees and of committees of trustees including the names of the trustees present at each such meeting.

## The Seal

52. The seal shall only be used by the authority of the trustees or of a committee of trustees authorised by the trustees. The trustees may determine who shall sign any instrument to which the seal is affixed and unless otherwise so determined it shall be signed by a trustee and by the secretary or by a second trustee.

## Accounts

53. Accounts shall be prepared in accordance with the provisions of Part VII of the Act.

## Annual Report

54. The trustees shall comply with their obligations under the Charities Act 1993 (or any statutory re-enactment or modification of that Act) with regard to the preparation of an annual report and its transmission to the Commissioners.

## Annual Return

55. The trustees shall comply with their obligations under the Charities Act 1993 (or any statutory re-enactment or modification of that Act) with regard to the preparation of an annual return and its transmission to the Commissioners.

## Notices

56. Any notice to be given to or by any person pursuant to the articles shall be in writing except that a notice calling a meeting of the trustees need not be in writing.

57. The Charity may give any notice to a member either personally or by sending it by post in a prepaid envelope addressed to the member at his registered address or by leaving it at that address. A member whose registered address is not within the United Kingdom and who gives to the company an address within the United Kingdom at which notices may be given to him shall be entitled to have notices given to him at that address, but otherwise no such member shall be entitled to receive any notice from the Charity.

58. A member present in person at any meeting of the Charity shall be deemed to have received notice of the meeting and, where necessary, of the purposes for which it was called.

59. Proof that an envelope containing a notice was properly addressed, prepaid and posted shall be conclusive evidence that the notice was given. A notice shall be deemed to be given at the expiration of 48 hours after the envelope containing it was posted.

## Indemnity

60. Subject to the provisions of the Act every trustee or other officer or auditor of the Charity shall be indemnified out of the assets of the Charity against any liability incurred by him in that capacity in defending any proceedings, whether civil or criminal, in which judgment is given in his favour or in which he is acquitted or in connection with any application in which relief is granted to him by the court from liability for negligence, default, breach of duty or breach of trust in relation to the affairs of the Charity.

## Rules

61. (1) The trustees may from time to time make such rules or bye laws as they may deem necessary or expedient or convenient for the proper conduct and management of the Charity and for the purposes of prescribing classes of and conditions of membership, and in particular but without prejudice to the generality of the foregoing, they may by such rules or bye laws regulate:

    (i) the admission and classification of members of the Charity (including the admission of organisations to membership) and the rights and privileges of such members, and the conditions of membership and the terms on which members may resign or have their membership terminated and the entrance fees, subscriptions and other fees or payments to be made by members;

    (ii) the conduct of members of the Charity in relation to one another, and to the Charity's servants;

    (iii) the setting aside of the whole or any part or parts of the Charity's premises at any particular time or times or for any particular purpose or purposes;

    (iv) the procedure at general meetings and meetings of the trustees and committees of the trustees in so far as such procedure is not regulated by the articles;

    (v) generally, all such matters as are commonly the subject

matter of company rules.

(2) The Charity in general meeting shall have power to alter, add to or repeal the rules or bye laws and the trustees shall adopt such means as they think sufficient to bring to the notice of members of the Charity all such rules or bye laws, which shall be binding on all members of the Charity. Provided that no rule or bye law shall be inconsistent with, or shall affect or repeal anything contained in, the memorandum or the articles.

---

Signatures, Names and Addresses of Subscribers

---

Dated:

Witness to the above Signatures:

Name:

Address:

Occupation:

## PRECEDENT 3

# Model constitution for charitable unincorporated association

### Constitution

adopted on the ...... days of ............ 19 ......

## A   Name

**Clause A**   The name of the Association is .......................................

...................................................................................

........................................................... ("the Charity")

## B   Administration

**Clause B**   Subject tot he matters set out below the Charity and its property shall be administered and managed in accordance with this constitution by the members of the Executive Committee, constituted by clause . . . . . . of this constitution ("the Executive Committee").

## C  Objects

**Clause C**    The Charity's objects ("the objects") are . . . . . . . . . . . . . . . . . . . . . . . . . . . . .

. . . . . . . . . . . . . . . . . . . . . . . . . . . . . . . . . . . . . . . . . . . . . . . . . . . . . . . . . . . . . . . . . . . .

. . . . . . . . . . . . . . . . . . . . . . . . . . . . . . . . . . . . . . . . . . . . . . . . . . . . . . . . . . . . . . . . . . . .

. . . . . . . . . . . . . . . . . . . . . . . . . . . . . . . . . . . . . . . . . . . . . . . . . . . . . . . . . . . . . . . . . . . .

. . . . . . . . . . . . . . . . . . . . . . . . . . . . . . . . . . . . . . . . . . . . . . . . . . . . . . . . . . . . . . . . . . . .

. . . . . . . . . . . . . . . . . . . . . . . . . . . . . . . . . . . . . . . . . . . . . . . . . . . . . . . . . . . . . . . . . . . .

. . . . . . . . . . . . . . . . . . . . . . . . . . . . . . . . . . . . . . . . . . . . . . . . . . . . . . . . . . . . . . . . . . . .

## D  Powers

**Clause D**    In furtherance of the objects but not otherwise the Executive Committee may exercise the following powers:

    (i) power to raise funds and to invite and receive contributions provided that in raising funds the Executive Committee shall not undertake any substantial permanent trading activities and shall conform to any relevant requirements of the law;

    (ii) power to buy, take on lease or in exchange any property necessary for the achievement of the objects and to maintain and equip it for use;

    (iii) power subject to any consents required by law to sell, lease or dispose of all or any part of the property of the Charity;

    (iv) power subject to any consents required by law to borrow money and to charge all or any part of the property of the Charity with repayment of the money so borrowed;

    (v) power to employ such staff (who shall not be members of the Executive Committee) as are necessary for the proper pursuit of the objects and to make all reasonable and necessary provision for the payment of pensions and superannuation for staff and their dependants;

    (vi) power to co-operate with other charities, voluntary bodies and statutory authorities operating in furtherance of the objects or of similar charitable purposes and to exchange information and advice with them;

    (vii) power to establish or support any charitable trusts, associations or institutions formed for all or any of the objects;

    (viii) power to appoint and constitute such advisory committees as the Executive Committee may think fit;

    (ix) power to do all such other lawful things as are necessary for the achievement of the objects.[5]

---

[5] Additional powers may be included to authorise accumulation of income, payment of premiums on trustee insurance policies etc.

## E Membership (Option 1)

**Clause E** (1) Membership of the Charity shall be open to any person over the age of 18 years interested in furthering the objects and who has paid the annual subscription laid down from time to time by the Executive Committee.

(2) Every member shall have one vote.

(3) The Executive Committee may by unanimous vote and for good reason terminate the membership of any individual: Provided that the individual concerned shall have the right to be heard by the Executive Committee, accompanied by a friend, before a final decision is made.

## F Membership (Option 2)

**Clause F** (1) Membership of the Charity shall be open to:

(i) individuals (over the age of 18 years) who are interested in furthering the work of the Charity and who have paid any annual subscription laid down from time to time by the Executive Committee, and

(ii) any body corporate or unincorporated association which is interested in furthering the Charity's work and has paid an annual subscription (any such body being called in this constitution a "member organisation").

(2) Every member shall have one vote.

(3) Each member organisation shall appoint an individual to represent it and to vote on its behalf at meetings of the Charity; and may appoint an alternate to replace its appointed representative at any meeting of the Charity if the appointed representative is unable to attend.

(4) Each member organisation shall notify the name of the representative appointed by it and of any alternate to the secretary. If the representative or alternate resigns from or otherwise leaves the member organisation, he or she shall forthwith cease to be the representative of the member organisation.

(5) The Executive Committee may unanimously and for good reason terminate the membership of any individual or member organisation: Provided that the individual concerned or the appointed representative of the member organisation concerned (as the case may be) shall have the right to be heard by the Executive Committee, accompanied by a friend, before a final decision is made.

## G Honorary Officers

**Clause G** At the annual general meeting of the Charity the members shall elect from amongst themselves a chairman, a secretary and a treasurer, who shall hold office from the conclusion of that meeting.

## H    Executive Committee

**Clause H**    (1) The Executive Committee shall consist of not less than ......
members nor more than ...... members being:

- (a)  the honorary officers specified in the preceding clause;
- (b)  not less than ...... and not more than ...... members
  elected at the annual general meeting who shall hold
  office from the conclusion of that meeting;
- (c)  ...... nominated members appointed as follows:

.................................................................................

.................................................................................

.................................................................................

.................................................................................

.................................................................................

.................................................................................

.................................................................................

.................................................................................

.................................................................................

.................................................................................

.................................................................................

.................................................................................

(2) The Executive Committee may in addition appoint not
more than ...... co-opted members but so that no-one may be
appointed as a co-opted member if, as a result, more than one
third of the members of the Executive Committee would be
co-opted members. Each appointment of a co-opted member
shall be made at a special meeting of the Executive Committee
called under clause ...... and shall take effect from the end of
that meeting unless the appointment is to fill a place which has
not then been vacated in which case the appointment shall run
from the date when the post becomes vacant.

(3) All the members of the Executive Committee shall retire
from office together at the end of the annual general meeting next
after the date on which they came into force but they may be
re-elected or re-appointed.

(4) The proceedings of the Executive Committee shall not
be invalidated by any vacancy among their number or by any
failure to appoint or any defect in the appointment or qualification of a member.

(5) Nobody shall be appointed as a member of the Executive
Committee who is aged under 18 or who would if appointed be
disqualified under the provisions of the following clause.

(6) No person shall be entitled to act as a member of the
Executive Committee whether on a first or on any subsequent
entry into office until after signing in the minute book of the
Executive Committee a declaration of acceptance and of willingness to act in the trusts of the Charity.

## I Determination of Membership of Executive Committee

**Clause I**  A member of the Executive Committee shall cease to hold office if he or she:

(1) is disqualified from acting as a member of the Executive Committee by virtue of section 72 of the Charities Act 1993 (or any statutory re-enactment or modification of that provision);

(2) becomes incapable by reason of mental disorder, illness or injury of managing and administering his or her own affairs;

(3) is absent without the permission of the Executive Committee from all their meetings held within a period of six months and the Executive Committee resolve that his or her office be vacated; or

(4) notifies to the Executive Committee a wish to resign (but only if at least three members of the Executive Committee will remain in office when the notice of resignation is to take effect).

## J Executive Committee Members not to be personally interested

**Clause J**  (1) [Subject to the provisions of sub-clause 92) of this clause] no member of the Executive Committee shall acquire any interest in property belonging to the Charity (otherwise than as a trustee for the Charity) or receive remuneration or be interested (otherwise than as a member of the Executive Committee) in any contract entered into by Executive Committee.

[(2) Any member of the Executive Committee for the time being who is a solicitor, accountant or other person engaged in a profession may charge and be paid all the usual professional charges for business done by him or her or his or her firm when instructed by the other members of the Executive Committee to act in a professional capacity on behalf of the Charity: Provided that at no time shall a majority of the members of the Executive Committee benefit under this provision and that a member of the Executive Committee shall withdraw from any meeting at which his or her own instruction or remuneration, or that of his or her firm, is under discussion.]

## K Meetings and proceedings of the Executive Committee

**Clause K**  (1) The Executive Committee shall hold at least two ordinary meetings each year. A special meeting may be called at any time by the chairman or by any two members of the Executive Committee upon not less than 4 days' notice being given to the other members of the Executive Committee of the matters to be discussed but if the matters include an appointment of a co-opted member then not less than 21 days' notice must be given.

(2) The chairman shall act as chairman at meetings of the Executive Committee. If the chairman is absent from any meeting, the members of the Executive Committee present shall choose one of their number to be chairman of the meeting before any other business is transacted.

(3) There shall be a quorum when at least one third of the number of members of the Executive Committee for the time being or three members of the Executive Committee, whichever is the greater, are present at a meeting.

(4) Every matter shall be determined by a majority of votes of the members of the Executive Committee present and voting on the question but in the case of equality of votes the chairman of the meeting shall have a second or casting vote.

(5) The Executive Committee shall keep minutes, in books kept for the purpose, of the proceedings at meetings of the Executive Committee and any sub-committee.

(6) The Executive Committee may from time to time make and alter rules for the conduct of their business, the summoning and conduct of their meetings and the custody of documents. No rule may be made which is inconsistent with this constitution.

(7) The Executive Committee may appoint one or more sub-committees consisting of three or more members of the Executive Committee for the purpose of making any inquiry or supervising or performing any function or duty which in the opinion of the Executive Committee would be more conveniently undertaken or carried out by a sub-committee: provided that all acts and proceedings of any such sub-committees shall be fully and promptly reported to the Executive Committee.

## L  Receipts and expenditure

**Clause L**  (1) The funds of the Charity, including all donations, contributions and bequests, shall be paid into an account operated by the Executive Committee in the name of the Charity at such bank as the Executive Committee shall from time to time decide. All cheques drawn on the account must be signed by at least two members of the Executive Committee.

(2) The funds belonging to the Charity shall be applied only in furthering the objects.

## M  Property

**Clause M**  (1) Subject to the provisions of sub-clause (2) of this clause, the Executive Committee shall cause the title to:

(a) all land held by or in trust for the charity which is not vested in the Official Custodian for Charities; and
(b) all investments held by or on behalf of the charity;

to be vested either in a corporation entitled to act as custodian trustee or in not less than three individuals appointed by them as holding trustees. Holding trustees may be removed by the Executive Committee at their pleasure and shall act in accordance with the lawful directions of the Executive Committee. Provided they act only in accordance with the lawful directions of the Executive Committee, the holding trustees shall not be liable for the acts and defaults of its members.

(2) If a corporation entitled to act as custodian trustee has not been appointed to hold the property of the charity, the Executive Committee may permit any investments held by or in

trust for the charity to be held in the name of a clearing bank, trust corporation or any stockbroking company which is a member of the International Stock Exchange (or any subsidiary of any such stockbroking company) as nominee for the Executive Committee, and may pay such a nominee reasonable and proper remuneration for acting as such.[6]

## N   Accounts

**Clause N**   The Executive Committee shall comply with their obligations under the Charities Act 1993 (or any statutory re-enactment or modification of that Act) with regard to:

    (1) the keeping of accounting records for the Charity;

    (2) the preparation of annual statements of account for the charity;

    (3) the auditing or independent examination of the statements of account of the Charity; and

    (4) the transmission of the statements of account of the Charity to the Commissioners.

## O   Annual Report

**Clause O**   The Executive Committee shall comply with their obligations under the Charities Act 1993 (or any statutory re-enactment or modification of that Act) with regard to the preparation of an annual report and its transmission to the Commissioners.

## P   Annual Return

**Clause P**   The Executive Committee shall comply with their obligations under the Charities Act 1993 (or any statutory re-enactment or modification of that Act) with regard to the preparation of an annual return and its transmission to the Commissioners.

## Q   Annual General Meeting

**Clause Q**   (1) There shall be an annual general meeting of the Charity which shall be held in the month of . . . . . . in each year or as soon as practicable thereafter.

(2) Every annual general meeting shall be called by the Executive Committee. The Secretary shall give at least 21 days' notice of the annual general meeting to all the members of the Charity. All the members of the Charity shall be entitled to attend and vote at the meeting.

(3) Before any other business is transacted at the first annual general meeting the persons present shall appoint a chairman of the meeting. The chairman shall be the chairman of subsequent annual general meetings, but if he or she is not present, before any other business is transacted, the persons present shall appoint a chairman of the meeting.

[6] It is wise to include an indemnity here to provide that trustees may be reimbursed their expenses and liabilities which are properly incurred.

(4) The Executive Committee shall present to each annual general meeting the report and accounts of the Charity for the preceding year.

(5) Nominations for election to the Executive Committee must be made by members of the Charity in writing and must be in the hands of the secretary of the Executive Committee at least 14 days before the annual general meeting. Should nominations exceed vacancies, election shall be by ballot.

## R    Special General Meetings

**Clause R**    The Executive Committee may call a special general meeting of the Charity at any time. It at least ten members request such a meeting in writing stating the business to be considered the secretary shall call such a meeting. At least 21 days' notice must be given. The notice must state the business to be discussed.

## S    Procedure at General Meetings

**Clause S**    (1) The secretary or other person specially appointed by the Executive Committee shall keep a full record of proceedings at every general meeting of the Charity.

(2) There shall be a quorum when at least one tenth of the number of members of the Charity for the time being or ten members of the Charity, whichever is the greater, are present at any general meeting.

## T    Notices

**Clause T**    Any notice required to be served on any member of the Charity shall be in writing and shall be served by the secretary or the Executive Committee on any member either personally or by sending it through the post in a prepaid letter addressed to such member at his or her last known address in the United Kingdom, and any letter so sent shall be deemed to have been received within 10 days of posting.

## U    Alterations to the Constitution

**Clause U**    (1) Subject to the following provisions of this clause the Constitution may be altered by a resolution passed by not less than two thirds of the members present and voting at a general meeting. The notice of the general meeting must include notice of the resolution, setting out the terms of the alteration proposed.

(2) No amendment may be made to clause . . . . . . (the name of charity clause), clause . . . . . . (the objects clause), clause . . . . . . (Executive Committee members not to be personally interested clause), clause . . . . . . (the dissolution clause) or this clause without the prior consent in writing of the Commissioners.

(3) No amendment may be made which would have the effect of making the Charity cease to be a charity at law.

(4) The Executive Committee should promptly send to the Commissioners a copy of any amendment made under this clause.

## V   Dissolution

**Clause V**   If the Executive Committee decides that it is necessary or advisable to dissolve the Charity it shall call a meeting of all members of the Charity, of which not less than 21 days' notice (stating the terms of the resolution to be proposed) shall be given. If the proposal is confirmed by a two-thirds majority of those present and voting the Executive Committee shall have power to realise any assets held by or on behalf of the Charity. Any assets remaining after the satisfaction of any proper debts and liabilities shall be given or transferred to such other charitable institution or institutions having objects similar to the objects of the Charity as the members of the Charity may determine or failing that shall be applied for some other charitable purpose. A copy of the statement of accounts, or account and statement, for the final accounting period of the Charity must be sent to the Commissioners.

## W   Arrangements until first Annual General Meeting

**Clause W**   Until the first annual general meeting takes place this constitution shall take effect as if references in it to the Executive Committee were references to the persons whose signatures appear at the bottom of this document.

This constitution was adopted on the date mentioned above by the persons whose signatures appear at the bottom of this document.

**Signed** ................................................................................

# APPENDIX B

## Sample Objects Clauses

It is best (see Chapter 4) for the principal objects clause of a charity to be expressed in wide terms. The particular field in which the charity is intended to operate can then be specified as one method by which its general purposes are to be achieved. This pattern is followed here. Examples are given of a variety of specific purposes coming within each of the four heads of charity. In some cases it may be desirable for more than one to be included.

## 1. The relief of poverty, sickness, disablement and old age

(a) the relief of financial need among [people resident in ] [employees and former employees of Limited and their families and dependants] and in particular but not so as to limit the generality of the foregoing:—
* the provision of financial assistance, goods and services
* the provision of residential accommodation at low cost and its maintenance and improvement
* assisting young people who are in financial need to receive training to enable them to earn their living
* the provision of free legal services and assistance for poor people which they would not otherwise be able to obtain through lack of means

(b) The relief of sickness generally and in particular but not so as to limit the generality of the foregoing:—
* the provision, maintenance and improvement of a hospital/nursing home/hospice/clinic at
* the improvement of nursing care at through the provision of training/accommodation/ recreational facilities/a library/transport/a rest room for nurses working at
* the improvement of conditions for patients at by providing shopping facilities/library services/transport to enable their relatives and friends who are in financial need to make hospital visits/such services as hairdressing and chiropody/ additional or improved equipment or amenities in connection with their care and treatment
* promoting research into the causes and treatment of and publishing the useful results thereof
* providing counselling services for persons suffering from and their families

* the preservation and protection of the health of the public by educating them and conducting research into the causes and prevention of
* the education/training/rehabilitation of people suffering from        to enable them to earn their living and develop their full potential as members of society

(c) The relief of aged/blind/deaf people/people suffering from      and in particular but not so as to limit the generality of the foregoing:—

* the provision, maintenance and improvement of residential accommodation/sheltered housing for such persons on terms appropriate to their means
* the alleviation of loneliness and isolation of such people by running day centres and providing recreational and social facilities
* supplying special aids and equipment for such people in order to help them to live independent lives
* providing counselling and support for such people or their families.

## 2. The advancement of education

The advancement of the education of the public and in particular but not so as to limit the generality of the foregoing:—

* providing and maintaining a school for young persons under the age of
* promoting the education and training of members of the public in music/drama/the study of
* providing scholarships, exhibitions and bursaries for young persons under the age of      to enable them to further their education
* promoting the mental, moral and physical development and improvement of young people under the age of      through the provision of [recreational facilities]
* promoting the advancement of public education in the study of and research into wildlife and its conservation with particular reference to and the dissemination of the useful results of such research
* the advancement of education in and understanding the works of
* the promotion of research into      and the publication of the useful results of such research
* the education of young people under the age of      /people suffering from      /young people over the statutory school leaving age who are in need of education so as to develop their full capacities and enable them to become responsible members of society and so that their conditions of life may be improved
* the education, training and rehabilitation of persons who [are mentally or physically handi-

capped] [through their social or economic circumstances are in need and are unable to obtain employment]

* the advancement of the education of the public by promoting artistic activities including art exhibitions, performances of drama, music, opera and ballet, film shows and poetry readings
* to advance the education of the public in the knowledge of [plant or animal species] which are rare or in danger of extinction and to preserve such [species] for the benefit of the public.

## 3. The promotion of religion

The advancement of the                religion and in particular but not so as to limit the generality of the foregoing:—

* the advancement of the religious and other charitable work of the                church in the parish of

* the maintenance of the fabric and furnishings of the parish church of
* the production, publication and dissemination of religious works
* the advancement of religious education in accordance with the doctrines and practice of                by means of Sunday Schools, classes, seminars, lectures and conferences
* the advancement of education of children in accordance with the doctrines of the religion.

## 4. General benefit of the public

For the general benefit of [persons resident in                ] [the public] in such manner as may be charitable
And in particular but not so as to limit the generality of the foregoing:—

* the provision of such amenities and facilities for the benefit of the public [resident in                ] as are not provided from public funds
* the preservation for the benefit of the public of buildings of aesthetic, historic, architectural, constructional or scientific interest or importance
* the conservation and protection of land or other property which is of aesthetic or scientific value;
* the protection of dogs/cats/[other domestic animals] from ill usage, suffering and distress by providing for their rescue, care and treatment;
* the promotion of high standards of craftsmanship and design;
* the improvement of safety standards [among drivers] [in the home] [at work] through conducting research and publishing the useful results of such research/instituting tests and examinations/ promoting high standards of conduct/good working practices among

* the promotion of good relations between people of different races;
* the protection and safeguarding of the environment/countryside and the control and reduction of pollution.

## 5. Recreational purposes for racial minorities (Approved by the Charity Commission[1])

"The objects of the Association are to:

(a) promote the benefit of the inhabitants and primarily the [racial minority group] inhabitants of ... ... and the neighbourhood together defined by ... ... (hereafter called "the area of benefit") without distinction of sex or sexual orientation [or race] or of political [or religious] or other opinions by associating together the said inhabitants and the local authorities voluntary and other organisations in a common effort to:

(i) advance the education of the said inhabitants; and
(ii) provide facilities for recreation or other leisure-time occupation for the said inhabitants in the interests of social welfare with the object of improving their conditions of life.

(b) establish or secure the establishment of a Community Centre (hereinafter called "the Centre") and to maintain and manage the same (whether alone or in co-operation with any local or other person or body) in furtherance of the above object.

(c) promote such charitable purposes as may from time to time be determined."

## 6. General charitable purposes

For such charitable purposes as the Trustees in their absolute discretion think fit.

[1] *Decisions of the Charity Commissioners*, Vol. 4, pp. 18–21.

# APPENDIX C

## Additional Precedents

### 1. Useful Clauses acceptable to the Charity Commission.

### Power of amendment

For a trust:

"(1) The trustees may amend the provisions of this deed provided that:

    (a) no amendment may be made to clause ...... (the objects clause) clause ...... (trustees not to have a personal interest clause) [clause ... ... (remuneration of trustees clause)] [clause ... ... (trustee indemnity clause)] clause ... ... (the dissolution clause), this clause or the trustees' power of investment [and no amendment may be made which would allow the trustees to spend permanent endowment]; without the prior written approval of the Commissioners;

    (b) no amendment may be made which has the effect of the charity ceasing to be a charity at law.

(2) The trustees must:

    (a) promptly send to the Commissioners a copy of any amendment made; and

    (b) keep a copy of any such amendment with this deed."

For an unincorporated association:

"(1) Subject to the following provisions of this clause the Constitution/Rules may be amended by a resolution passed by not less than two-thirds of the members present and voting at a general meeting. The notice of the general meeting must include notice of the resolution setting out the terms of the amendment proposed.

(2) No amendment may be made to clause ... ... (the objects clause) clause ... ... (trustees not to have a personal interest clause) [clause ...... (remuneration of trustees clause)] [clause ... ... (trustee indemnity insurance clause), clause ...... (the dissolution clause), this clause or the trustees' power of investment [and no amendment may be made which would allow the trustees to spend permanent endowment of the charity] without the prior written approval of the Commissioners.

(3) No amendment may be made which would have the effect of making the charity cease to be a charity at law.

(4) The trustees must:

    (a) promptly send to the Commissioners a copy of any amendment made; and

    (b) keep a copy of any such amendment with this Constitution/these Rules."

    (See Decisions of the Charity Commissioners Volume 2 (1994) pages 24–27)

## Power to pay premiums on trustee indemnity policies

Power to pay any premium in respect of any indemnity insurance to cover the liability of the trustees (or any of them) which by virtue of any rule of law would otherwise attach to them in respect of any negligence, default, breach of duty or breach of trust of which they may be guilty in relation to the Charity; Provided that any such insurance or indemnity shall not extend to any claim arising from any act or omission which the trustees (or any of them) knew to be a breach of trust or breach of duty or which was committed in reckless disregard of whether it was a breach of trust or breach of duty or not.

## Remuneration of Trustees

(See Charity Commission leaflet CC11 "Remuneration of Charity Trustees")

Any Trustee for the time being hereof shall be entitled to charge and be paid reasonable charges for necessary work done by him on behalf of the charity Provided that

(1) such trustee shall not be present at or take part in any discussions relating to any such proposed remuneration or the conferring of other benefits

(2) any decision or resolution to remunerate or confer other benefits on such Trustee shall be taken or made unanimously by all the remaining trustees

(3) the Trustees are satisfied that the level of the remuneration or the nature and scale of the benefits conferred upon such Trustee is reasonable and proper having regard to all the circumstances of the work carried out by such Trustee for the charity

(4) the Trustees are satisfied that the services to be rendered to the charity by such Trustee and his ability to provide those services in fulfilment of the objects of the charity have a special value to the Trust and it is also necessary for the said person to serve as a Trustee

(5) if any Trustee is remunerated for services to the charity the number of such Trustees receiving remuneration shall never be a majority of the trustees.

## Delegation

(1) The Trustees may establish sub-committees consisting of such persons as the Trustees may decide and may delegate to such sub-committees any of their powers and the implementation of any of their resolutions provided that any such delegation may be revoked at any time.

(2) The members of each sub-committee shall be appointed by the Trustees to hold office for such period as the Trustees shall decide.

(3) The Trustees shall specify the financial limits within which any sub-committee shall function and shall make such regulations and impose such terms and conditions on any such sub-committee as they from time to time think fit.

(4) The meetings and proceedings of each sub-committee shall be governed by the provisions of this Deed/these Articles regulating the meetings and proceedings of the Trustees in so far as the same are applicable.

(5) Every sub-committee shall ensure that its deliberations and decisions are reported as soon as possible to the Trustees and shall appoint a secretary with responsibility for making such reports.

(6) The Trustees may authorise a sub-committee to operate any bank account of the Charity and to decide upon the manner in which such account shall be operated provided that the signature of a member of the Trustees shall always be required.

There shall not be a quorum at a meeting of a sub-committee unless at least one member of the Trustees is present and no resolution of a sub-committee shall be passed unless a majority of the members of the Trustees present shall vote in favour in addition to a majority of the sub-committee as a whole.

## 2. Memorandum recording the Appointment of new trustees

(s.83 of the Charities Act 1993)

At a meeting of the trustees held on          it was resolved, in exercise of the power contained in Clause          of the trust deed/constitution of the charity, that the following persons should be appointed as trustees:

[ name ]
of   [ address ]

and [ name ]
of   [ address ]

in place of
[ name ]
of   [ address ]who has died/wished to retire

and [ name ]
of   [ address ]who has died/wished to retire

Dated                                         19

SIGNED and DELIVERED
by
the chairman/person
presiding at the said
meeting in our presence                    [ signature ]
(being persons who were

present at the said meeting)

signature of first witness:

address

occupation

signature of second witness:

address:

occupation:

### 3.    **Inland Revenue Model Deed of Covenant**

by an individual to a charity for use in England and Wales from 31 July 1990.[1]

## DEED OF COVENANT

| | NOTES |
|---|---|
| To ................................................ | |
| [Name of Charity] | |

| | |
|---|---|
| I promise to pay you for ... years, or during my lifetime, if shorter, such a sum as after deduction of income tax at the basic rate amounts to | 1 |
| £ ............ | 2 |
| each [week] [month] [quarter] [year] | 3 |
| from [the date shown below] [.....]. | 4 |
| Signed & Delivered ........................... | 5 |
| Date ..................................... | |
| Full Name ..................................... | |
| Address ..................................... | |

Witnessed by:

Signed    .....................................

Full Name .....................................

Address    .....................................

*NOTES*

1. Enter the period of the covenant, which must be longer than **three** years.

2. Enter the amount you will be paying to the charity.

3. Delete as appropriate to show how often you will make the payment.

4. Delete as appropriate. If you choose to enter an actual date **it must not be earlier than the date you sign the deed**.

5. You must sign the form and enter the date you actually sign it in the presence of the witness, who should also sign where shown.

[1] See pp. 131–133 for details of the requirements for tax relief.

# APPENDIX D

## Statutes

### Charities Act 1993

An Act to consolidate the Charitable Trustees Incorporation Act 1872 and, except for certain spent or transitional provisions, the Charities Act 1960 and Part I of the Charities Act 1992.

BE IT ENACTED by the Queen's most Excellent Majesty, by and with the advice and consent of the Lords Spiritual and Temporal, and Commons, in this present Parliament assembled, and by the authority of the same, as follows:—

## PART I

### THE CHARITY COMMISSIONERS AND THE OFFICIAL CUSTODIAN FOR CHARITIES

**The Charity Commissioners**

1.—(1) There shall continue to be a body of Charity Commissioners for England and Wales, and they shall have such functions as are conferred on them by this Act in addition to any functions under any other enactment for the time being in force.

(2) The provisions of Schedule 1 to this Act shall have effect with respect to the constitution and proceeding of the Commissioners and other matters relating to the Commissioners and their officers and employees.

(3) The Commissioners shall (without prejudice to their specific powers and duties under other enactments) have the general function of promoting the effective use of charitable resources by encouraging the development of better methods of administration, by giving charity trustees information or advice on any matter affecting the charity and by investigating and checking abuses.

(4) It shall be the general object of the Commissioners so to act in the case of any charity (unless it is a matter of altering its purposes) as best to promote and make effective the work of the charity in meeting the needs designated by its trusts; but the Commissioners shall not themselves have power to act in the administration of a charity.

(5) The Commissioners shall, as soon as possible after the end of every year, make to the Secretary of State a report on their operations during that year, and he shall lay a copy of the report before each House of Parliament.

**The official custodian for charities**

2.—(1) There shall continue to be an officer known as the official custodian for charities (in this Act referred to as "the official custodian") whose function it shall be to act as trustee for charities in the cases provided for by this Act; and the official custodian shall be by that name a corporation sole having perpetual succession and using an official seal which shall be officially and judicially noticed.

(2) Such officer of the Commissioners as they may from time to time designate shall be the official custodian.

(3) The official custodian shall perform his duties in accordance with such general or special directions as may be given him by the Commissioners, and his expenses (except those reimbursed to him or recovered by him as trustee for any charity) shall be defrayed by the Commissioners.

(4) Anything which is required to or may be done by, to or before the official custodian may be done by, to or before any officer of the Commissioners generally or specially authorised by them to act for him during a vacancy in his office or otherwise.

(5) The official custodian shall not be liable as trustee for any charity in respect of any loss or of the mis-application of any property unless it is occasioned by or through the wilful neglect or default of the custodian or of any person acting for him; but the Consolidated Fund shall be liable to make good to a charity any sums for which the custodian may be liable by reason of any such neglect or default.

(6) The official custodian shall keep such books of account and such records in relation thereto as may be directed by the Treasury and shall prepare accounts in such form, in such manner and at such times as may be so directed.

(7) The accounts so prepared shall be examined and certified by the Comptroller and Auditor General, and the report to be made by the Commissioners to the Secretary of State for any year shall include a copy of the accounts so prepared for any period ending in or with the year and of the certificate and report of the Comptroller and Auditor General with respect to those accounts.

PART II

REGISTRATION AND NAMES OF CHARITIES

*Registration of charities*

**The register of**
**charities**

3.—(1) The Commissioners shall continue to keep a register of charities, which shall be kept by them in such manner as they think fit.

(2) There shall be entered in the register every charity not excepted by subsection (5) below; and a charity so excepted (other than one excepted by paragraph (*a*) of that subsection) may be entered in the register at the request of the charity, but (whether or not it was excepted at the time of registration) may at any time, and shall at the request of the charity, be removed from the register.

(3) The register shall contain—

(*a*) the name of every registered charity; and
(*b*) such other particulars of, and such other information relating to, every such charity as the Commissioners think fit.

(4) Any institution which no longer appears to the Commissioners to be a charity shall be removed from the register, with effect, where the removal is due to any change in its purposes or trusts, from the date of that change; and there shall also be removed from the register any charity which ceases to exist or does not operate.

(5) The following charities are not required to be registered—

(*a*) any charity comprised in Schedule 2 to this Act (in this Act referred to as an "exempt charity");
(*b*) any charity which is excepted by order or regulations;
(*c*) any charity which has neither—
    (i) any permanent endowment, nor
    (ii) the use or occupation of any land,
        and whose income from all sources does not in aggregate amount to more than £1,000 a year;

and no charity is required to be registered in respect of any registered place of worship.

(6) With any application for a charity to be registered there shall be supplied to the Commissioners copies of its trusts (or, if they are not set out in any extant document, particulars of them), and such other documents or information as may be prescribed by regulations made by the Secretary of State or as the Commissioners may require for the purpose of the application.

(7) It shall be the duty—

(*a*) of the charity trustees of any charity which is not registered nor excepted from registration to apply for it to be registered, and to supply the documents and information required by subsection (6) above; and
(*b*) of the charity trustees (or last charity trustees) of any institution which is for the time being registered to notify the Commissioners if it ceases to exist, or if there is any

change in its trusts or in the particulars of it entered in the register, and to supply to the Commissioners particulars of any such change and copies of any new trusts or alterations of the trusts.

(8) The register (including the entries cancelled when institutions are removed from the register) shall be open to public inspection at all reasonable times; and copies (or particulars) of the trusts of any registered charity as supplied to the Commissioners under this section shall, so long as it remains on the register, be kept by them and be open to public inspection at all reasonable times, except in so far as regulations made by the Secretary of State otherwise provide.

(9) Where any information contained in the register is not in documentary form, subsection (8) above shall be construed as requiring the information to be available for public inspection in legible form at all reasonable times.

(10) If the Commissioners so determine, subsection (8) above shall not apply to any particular information contained in the register and specified in their determination.

(11) Nothing in the foregoing subsections shall require any person to supply the Commissioners with copies of schemes for the administration of a charity made otherwise than by the court, or to notify the Commissioners of any change made with respect to a registered charity by such a scheme, or require a person, if he refers the Commissioners to a document or copy already in the possession of the Commissioners, to supply a further copy of the document; but where by virtue of this subsection a copy of any document need not be supplied to the Commissioners, a copy of it, if it relates to a registered charity, shall be open to inspection under subsection (8) above as if supplied to the Commissioners under this section.

(12) If the Secretary of State thinks it expedient to do so—

(a) in consequence of changes in the value of money, or
(b) with a view to extending the scope of the exception provided for by subsection (5)(c) above,

he may by order amend subsection (5)(c) by substituting a different sum for the sum for the time being specified there.

(13) The reference in subsection (5)(b) above to a charity which is excepted by order or regulations is to a charity which—

(a) is for the time being permanently or temporarily excepted by order of the Commissioners; or
(b) is of a description permanently or temporarily excepted by regulations made by the Secretary of State,

and which complies with any conditions of the exception.

(14) In this section "registered place of worship" means any land or building falling within section 9 of the Places of Worship Registration Act 1855 (that is to say, the land and buildings which if the Charities Act 1960 had not been passed, would by virtue of that section as amended by subsequent enactments be partially excepted from the operation of the Charitable Trusts Act 1853), and for the purposes of this subsection "building" includes part of a building.

**Effect of, and claims and objections to, registration**

4.—(1) An institution shall for all purposes other than rectification of the register be conclusively presumed to be or to have been a charity at any time when it is or was on the register of charities.

(2) Any person who is or may be affected by the registration of an institution as a charity may, on the ground that it is not a charity, object to its being entered by the Commissioners in the register, or apply to them for it to be removed from the register; and provision may be made by regulations made by the Secretary of State as to the manner in which any such objection or application is to be made, prosecuted or dealt with.

(3) An appeal against any decision of the Commissioners to enter or not to enter an institution in the register of charities, or to remove or not to remove an institution from the register, may be brought in the High Court by the Attorney General, or by the persons who are or claim to be the charity trustees of the institution, or by any person whose objection or application under subsection (2) above is disallowed by the decision.

(4) If there is an appeal to the High Court against any decision of the Commissioners to enter an institution in the register, or not to remove an institution from the register, then until the Commissioners are satisfied whether the decision of the Commissioners is or is not to stand, the entry in the register shall be maintained, but shall be in suspense and marked to indicate that it is in suspense; and for the purposes of subsection (1) above an institution shall be deemed not to be on the register during any period when the entry relating to it is in suspense under this subsection.

(5) Any question affecting the registration or removal from the register of an institution may, notwithstanding that it has been determined by a decision on appeal under subsection (3) above, be considered afresh by the Commissioners and shall not be concluded by that decision, if it appears to the Commissioners that there has been a change of circumstances or that the decision is inconsistent with a later judicial decision, whether given on such an appeal or not.

**Status of registered charity (other than small charity) to appear on official publications etc.**

5.—(1) This section applies to a registered charity if its gross income in its financial year exceeded £5,000.

(2) Where this section applies to a registered charity, the fact that it is a registered charity shall be stated in English in legible characters—

(a) in all notices, advertisements and other documents issued by or on behalf of the charity and soliciting money or other property for the benefit of the charity;

(b) in all bills of exchange, promissory notes, endorsements, cheques and orders for money or goods purporting to be signed on behalf of the charity; and

(c) in all bills rendered by it and in all its invoices, receipts and letters of credit.

(3) Subsection (2)(a) above has effect whether the solicitation is express or implied, and whether the money or other property is to be given for any consideration or not.

(4) If, in the case of a registered charity to which this section applies, any person issues or authorises the issue of any document

falling within paragraph (*a*) or (*c*) of subsection (2) above in which the fact that the charity is a registered charity is not stated as required by that subsection, he shall be guilty of an offence and liable on summary conviction to a fine not exceeding level 3 on the standards scale.

(5) If, in the case of any such registered charity, any person signs any document falling within paragraph (*b*) of subsection (2) above in which the fact that the charity is a registered charity is not stated as required by that subsection, he shall be guilty of an offence and liable on summary conviction to a fine not exceeding level 3 on the standard scale.

(6) The Secretary of State may by order amend subsection (1) above by substituting a different sum for the sum for the time being specified there.

*Charity names*

**Power of Commissioners to require charity's name to be changed**

6.—(1) Where this subsection applies to a charity, the Commissioners may give a direction requiring the name of the charity to be changed, within such period as is specified in the direction, to such other name as the charity trustees may determine with the approval of the Commissioners.

(2) Subsection (1) above applies to a charity if—

(*a*) it is a registered charity and its name ("the registered name")—
    (i) is the same as, or
    (ii) is in the opinion of the Commissioners too like, the name, at the time when the registered name was entered in the register in respect of the charity, of any other charity (whether registered or not);

(*b*) the name of the charity is in the opinion of the Commissioners likely to mislead the public as to the true nature—
    (i) of the purposes of the charity as set out in its trusts, or
    (ii) of the activities which the charity carries on under its trusts in pursuit of those purposes;

(*c*) the name of the charity includes any word or expression for the time being specified in regulations made by the Secretary of State and the inclusion in its name of that word or expression is in the opinion of the Commissioners likely to mislead the public in any respect as to the status of the charity;

(*d*) the name of the charity is in the opinion of the Commissioners likely to give the impression that the charity is connected in some way with Her Majesty's Government or any local authority, or with any body of persons or any individual, when it is not so connected; or

(*e*) the name of the charity is in the opinion of the Commissioners offensive;

and in this subsection any reference to the name of the charity is, in relation to a registered charity, a reference to the name by which it is registered.

(3) Any direction given by virtue of subsection (2)(*a*) above

must be given within twelve months of the time when the registered name was entered in the register in respect of the charity.

(4) Any direction given under this section with respect to a charity shall be given to the charity trustees; and on receiving any such direction the charity trustees shall give effect to it notwithstanding anything in the trusts of the charity.

(5) Where the name of any charity is changed under this section, then (without prejudice to section 3(7)(b) above) it shall be the duty of the charity trustees forthwith to notify the Commissioners of the charity's new name and of the date on which the change occurred.

(6) A change of name by a charity under this section does not affect any rights or obligations of the charity; and any legal proceedings that might have been continued or commenced by or against it in its former name may be continued or commenced by or against it in its new name.

(7) Section 26(3) of the Companies Act 1985 (minor variations in names to be disregarded) shall apply for the purposes of this section as if the reference to section 26(1)(c) of that Act were a reference to subsection (2)(a) above.

(8) Any reference in this section to the charity trustees of a charity shall, in relation to a charity which is a company, be read as a reference to the directors of the company.

(9) Nothing in this section applies to an exempt charity.

**Effect of direction under s.6 where charity is a company** 7.—(1) Where any direction is given under section 6 above with respect to a charity which is a company, the direction shall be taken to require the name of the charity to be changed by resolution of the directors of the company.

(2) Section 380 of the Companies Act 1985 (registration etc. of resolutions and agreements) shall apply to any resolution passed by the directors in compliance with any such direction.

(3) Where the name of such a charity is changed in compliance with any such direction, the registrar of companies—

(a) shall, subject to section 26 of the Companies Act 1985 (prohibition on registration of certain names), enter the new name on the register of companies in place of the former name, and

(b) shall issue a certificate of incorporation altered to meet the circumstances of the case;

and the change of name has effect from the date on which the altered certificate is issued.


PART III

COMMISSIONERS' INFORMATION POWERS

**General power to institute inquiries** 8.—(1) The Commissioners may from time to time institute inquiries with regard to charities or a particular charity or class of charities, either generally or for particular purposes, but no such inquiry shall extend to any exempt charity.

(2) The Commissioners may either conduct such an inquiry themselves or appoint a person to conduct it and make a report to them.

(3) For the purposes of any such inquiry the Commissioners, or a person appointed by them to conduct it, may direct any person (subject to the provisions of this section)—

(*a*) to furnish accounts and statements in writing with respect to any matter in question at the inquiry, being a matter on which he has or can reasonably obtain information, or to return answers in writing to any questions or inquiries addressed to him on any such matter, and to verify any such accounts, statements or answers by statutory declaration;

(*b*) to furnish copies of documents in his custody or under his control which relate to any matter in question at the inquiry, and to verify any such copies by statutory declaration;

(*c*) to attend at a specified time and place and give evidence or produce any such documents.

(4) For the purposes of any such inquiry evidence may be taken on oath, and the person conducting the inquiry may for that purpose administer oaths, or may instead of administering an oath require the person examined to make and subscribe a declaration of the truth of the matters about which he is examined.

(5) The Commissioners may pay to any person the necessary expenses of his attendance to give evidence or produce documents for the purpose of an inquiry under this section, and a person shall not be required in obedience to a direction under paragraph (*c*) of subsection (3) above to go more than ten miles from his place of residence unless those expenses are paid or tendered to him.

(6) Where an inquiry has been held under this section, the Commissioners may either—

(*a*) cause the report of the person conducting the inquiry, or such other statement of the results of the inquiry as they think fit, to be printed and published, or

(*b*) publish any such report or statement in some other way which is calculated in their opinion to bring it to the attention of persons who may wish to make representations to them about the action to be taken.

(7) The council of a country or district, the Common Council of the City of London and the council of a London borough may contribute to the expenses of the Commissioners in connection with inquiries under this section into local charities in the council's area.

**Power to call for documents and search records**

9.—(1) The Commissioners may by order—

(*a*) require any person to furnish them with any information in his possession which relates to any charity and is relevant to the discharge of their functions or of the functions of the official custodian;

(*b*) require any person who has in his custody or under his control any document which relates to any charity and is relevant to the discharge of their functions or of the functions of the official custodian—

(i) to furnish them with a copy of or extract from the document, or

(ii) (unless the document forms part of the records or other documents of a court or of a public or local authority) to transmit the document itself to them for their inspection.

(2) Any officer of the Commissioners, if so authorised by them, shall be entitled without payment to inspect and take copies of or extracts from the records or other documents of any court, or of any public registry or office of records, for any purpose connected with the discharge of the functions of the Commissioners or of the official custodian.

(3) The Commissioners shall be entitled without payment to keep any copy or extract furnished to them under subsection (1) above; and where a document transmitted to them under that subsection for their inspection relates only to one or more charities and is not held by any person entitled as trustee or otherwise to the custody of it, the Commissioners may keep it or may deliver it to the charity trustees or to any other person who may be so entitled.

(4) No person properly having the custody of documents relating only to an exempt charity shall be required under subsection (1) above to transmit to the Commissioners any of those documents, or to furnish any copy of or extract from any of them.

(5) The rights conferred by subsection (2) above shall, in relation to information recorded otherwise than in legible form, include the right to require the information to be made available in legible form for inspection or for a copy or extract to be made of or from it.

**Disclosure of information to and by Commissioners**
10.—(1) Subject to subsection (2) below and to any express restriction imposed by or under any other enactment, a body or person to whom this section applies may disclose to the Charity Commissioners any information received by that body or person under or for the purpose of any enactment, where the disclosure is made by the body or person for the purpose of enabling or assisting the Commissioners to discharge any of their functions.

(2) Subsection (1) above shall not have effect in relation to the Commissioners of Customs and Excise or the Commissioners of Inland Revenue; but either of those bodies of Commissioners ("the relevant body") may disclose to the Charity Commissioners the following information—

(a) the name and address of any institution which has for any purpose been treated by the relevant body as established for charitable purposes;

(b) information as to the purposes of an institution and the trusts under which it is established or regulated, where the disclosure is made by the relevant body in order to give or obtain assistance in determining whether the institution ought for any purpose to be treated as established for charitable purposes; and

(c) information with respect to an institution which has for any purpose been treated as so established but which appears to the relevant body—

(i) to be, or to have been, carrying on activities which are not charitable, or

(ii) to be, or to have been, applying any of its funds for purposes which are not charitable.

(3) In subsection (2) above, any reference to an institution shall, in relation to the Commissioners of Inland Revenue, be construed as a reference to an institution in England and Wales.

(4) Subject to subsection (5) below, the Charity Commissioners may disclose to a body or person to whom this section applies any information received by them under or for the purposes of any enactment, where the disclosure is made by the Commissioners—

(a) for any purpose connected with the discharge of their functions, and

(b) for the purpose of enabling or assisting that body or person to discharge any of its or his functions.

(5) Where any information disclosed to the Charity Commissioners under subsection (1) or (2) above is so disclosed subject to any express restriction on the disclosure of the information by the Commissioners, the Commissioners' power of disclosure under subsection (4) above shall, in relation to the information, be exercisable by them subject to any such restriction.

(6) This section applies to the following bodies and persons—

(a) any government department (including a Northern Ireland department);

(b) any local authority;

(c) any constable; and

(d) any other body or person discharging functions of a public nature (including a body or person discharging regulatory functions in relation to any description of activities).

(7) In subsection (6)(d) above the reference to any such body or person as is there mentioned shall, in relation to a disclosure by the Charity Commissioners under subsection (4) above, be construed as including a reference to any such body or person in a country or territory outside the United Kingdom.

(8) Nothing in this section shall be construed as affecting any power of disclosure exercisable apart from this section.

(9) In this section "enactment" includes an enactment comprised in subordinate legislation (within the meaning of the Interpretation Act 1978).

**Supply of false or misleading information to Commissioners, etc.**

11.—(1) Any person who knowingly or recklessly provides the Commissioners with information which is false or misleading in a material particular shall be guilty of an offence if the information—

(a) is provided in purported compliance with a requirement imposed by or under this Act; or

(b) is provided otherwise than as mentioned in paragraph (a) above but in circumstances in which the person providing the information intends, or could reasonably be expected to know, that it would be used by the Commissioners for the purpose of discharging their functions under this Act.

(2) Any person who wilfully alters, suppresses, conceals or destroys any document which he is or is liable to be required, by or under this Act, to produce to the Commissioners shall be guilty of an offence.

(3) Any person guilty of an offence under this section shall be liable—

(*a*) on summary conviction, to a fine not exceeding the statutory maximum;

(*b*) on conviction on indictment, to imprisonment for a term not exceeding two years or to a fine, or both.

(4) In this section references to the Commissioners include references to any person conducting an inquiry under section 8 above.

**12.** An order under section 30 of the Data Protection Act 1984 (exemption from subject access provisions of data held for the purpose of discharging designated functions in connection with the regulation of financial services etc.) may designate for the purposes of that section, as if they were functions conferred by or under such an enactment as is there mentioned, any functions of the Commissioners appearing to the Secretary of State to be—

(*a*) connected with the protection of charities against misconduct or mismanagement (whether by trustees or other persons) in their administration; or

(*b*) connected with the protection of the property of charities from loss or misapplication or with the recovery of such property.

## PART IV

### APPLICATION OF PROPERTY CY-PRÈS AND ASSISTANCE AND SUPERVISION OF CHARITIES BY COURT AND COMMISSIONERS

*Extended powers of court and variation of charters*

**Occasions for applying property *cy-près***   **13.**—(1) Subject to subsection (2) below, the circumstances in which the original purposes of a charitable gift can be altered to allow the property given or part of it to be applied cy-près shall be as follows—

(*a*) where the original purposes, in whole or in part—
(i) have been as far as may be fulfilled; or
(ii) cannot be carried out, or not according to the directions given and to the spirit of the gift; or

(*b*) where the original purposes provide a use for part only of the property available by virtue of the gift; or

(*c*) where the property available by virtue of the gift and other property applicable for similar purposes can be more effectively used in conjunction, and to that end can suitably, regard being had to the spirit of the gift, be made applicable to common purposes; or

(*d*) where the original purposes were laid down by reference to an area which then was but has since ceased to be a unit for some other purpose, or by reference to a class of persons or to an area which has for any reason since ceased to be suitable, regard being had to the spirit of the gift, or to be practical in administering the gift; or

(*e*) where the original purposes, in whole or in part, have, since they were laid down—

    (i) been adequately provided for by other means; or

    (ii) ceased, as being useless or harmful to the community or for other reasons, to be in law charitable; or

    (iii) ceased in any other way to provide a suitable and effective method of using the property available by virtue of the gift, regard being had to the spirit of the gift.

(2) Subsection (1) above shall not affect the conditions which must be satisfied in order that property given for charitable purposes may be applied cy-près except in so far as those conditions require a failure of the original purposes.

(3) References in the foregoing subsections to the original purpose of a gift shall be construed, where the application of the property given has been altered or regulated by a scheme or otherwise, as referring to the purposes for which the property is for the time being applicable.

(4) Without prejudice to the power to make schemes in circumstances falling within subsection (1) above, the court may by scheme made under the court's jurisdiction with respect to charities, in any case where the purposes for which the property is held are laid down by reference to any such area as is mentioned in the first column in Schedule 3 to this Act, provide for enlarging the area to any such area as is mentioned in the second column in the same entry in that Schedule.

(5) It is hereby declared that a trust for charitable purposes places a trustee under a duty, where the case permits and requires the property or some part of it to be applied cy-près, to secure its effective use for charity by taking steps to enable it to be so applied.

**Application *cy-près* of gifts of donors unknown or disclaiming**

14.—(1) Property given for specific charitable purposes which fail shall be applicable cy-près as if given for charitable purposes generally, where it belongs—

(*a*) to a donor who after—

    (i) the prescribed advertisements and inquiries have been published and made, and

    (ii) the prescribed period beginning with the publication of those advertisements has expired,

    cannot be identified or cannot be found; or

(*b*) to a donor who has executed a disclaimer in the prescribed form of his right to have the property returned.

(2) Where the prescribed advertisements and inquiries have been published and made by or on behalf of trustees with respect to any such property, the trustees shall not be liable to any person in respect of the property if no claim by him to be interested in it is received by them before the expiry of the period mentioned in subsection (1)(*a*)(ii) above.

(3) For the purposes of this section property shall be conclusively presumed (without any advertisement or inquiry) to belong to donors who cannot be identified, in so far as it consists—

(*a*) of the proceeds of cash collections made by means of collecting boxes or by other means not adapted for distinguishing one gift from another; or

(*b*) of the proceeds of any lottery, competition, entertainment, sale or similar money-raising activity, after allowing for property given to provide prizes or articles for sale or otherwise to enable the activity to be undertaken.

(4) The court may by order direct that property not falling within subsection (3) above shall for the purposes of this section be treated (without any advertisement or inquiry) as belonging to donors who cannot be identified where it appears to the court either—

(*a*) that it would be unreasonable, having regard to the amounts likely to be returned to the donors, to incur expense with a view to returning the property; or

(*b*) that it would be unreasonable, having regard to the nature, circumstances and amounts of the gifts, and to the lapse of time since the gifts were made, for the donors to expect the property to be returned.

(5) Where property is applied cy-près by virtue of this section, the donor shall be deemed to have parted with all his interest at the time when the gift was made; but where property is so applied as belonging to donors who cannot be identified or cannot be found, and is not so applied by virtue of subsection (3) or (4) above—

(*a*) the scheme shall specify the total amount of that property, and

(*b*) the donor of any part of that amount shall be entitled, if he makes a claim not later than six months after the date on which the scheme is made, to recover from the charity for which the property is applied a sum equal to that part, less any expenses properly incurred by the charity trustees after that date in connection with claims relating to his gift; and

(*c*) the scheme may include directions as to the provision to be made for meeting any such claim.

(6) Where—

(*a*) any sum is, in accordance with any such directions, set aside for meeting any such claims; but

(*b*) the aggregate amount of any such claims actually made exceeds the relevant amount, then, if the Commissioners so direct, each of the donors in question shall be entitled only to such proportions of the relevant amount as the amount of his claim bears to the aggregate amount referred to in paragraph (*b*) above; and for this purpose "the relevant amount" means the amount of the sum so set aside after deduction of any expenses properly incurred by the charity trustees in connection with claims relating to the donors' gifts.

(7) For the purpose of this section, charitable purposes shall be deemed to "fail" where any difficulty in applying property to those purposes makes that property or the part not applicable cy-près available to be returned to the donors.

(8) In this section "prescribed" means prescribed by regulations made by the Commissioners; and such regulations may, as respects the advertisements which are to be published for the purposes of subsection (1)(*a*) above, make provision as to the form and content of such advertisements as well as the manner in which they are to be published.

(9) Any regulations made by the Commissioners under this section shall be published by the Commissioners in such manner as they think fit.

(10) In this section, except in so far as the context otherwise requires, references to a donor include persons claiming through or under the original donor, and references to property given include the property for the time being representing the property originally given or property derived from it.

(11) This section shall apply to property given for charitable purposes, notwithstanding that it was given before the commencement of this Act.

**Charities governed by charter, or by or under statute**

15.—(1) Where a Royal charter establishing or regulating a body corporate is amendable by the grant and acceptance of a further charter, a scheme relating to the body corporate or to the administration of property held by the body (including a scheme for the cy-près application of any such property) may be made by the court under the court's jurisdiction with respect to charities notwithstanding that the scheme cannot take effect without the alteration of the charter, but shall be so framed that the scheme, or such part of it as cannot take effect without the alteration of the charter, does not purport to come into operation unless or until Her Majesty thinks fit to amend the charter in such manner as will permit the scheme or that part of it to have effect.

(2) Where under the court's jurisdiction with respect to charities or the corresponding jurisdiction of a court in Northern Ireland, or under powers conferred by this Act or by any Northern Ireland legislation relating to charities, a scheme is made with respect to a body corporate, and it appears to Her Majesty expedient, having regard to the scheme, to amend any Royal charter relating to that body, Her Majesty may, on the application of that body, amend the charter accordingly by Order in Council in any way in which the charter could be amended by the grant and acceptance of a further charter; and any such Order in Council may be revoked or varied in like manner as the charter it amends.

(3) The jurisdiction of the court with respect to charities shall not be excluded or restricted in the case of a charity of any description mentioned in Schedule 4 to this Act by the operation

of the enactments or instruments there mentioned in relation to that description, and a scheme established for any such charity may modify or supersede in relation to it the provision made by any such enactment or instrument as if made by a scheme of the court, and may also make any such provision as is authorised by that Schedule.

*Powers of Commissioners to make schemes and act for protection of charities etc.*

**Concurrent jurisdiction with High Court for certain purposes**

**16.**—(1) Subject to the provisions of this Act, the Commissioners may by order exercise the same jurisdiction and powers as are exercisable by the High Court in charity proceedings for the following purposes—

(*a*) establishing a scheme for the administration of a charity;

(*b*) appointing, discharging or removing a charity trustee or trustee for a charity, or removing an officer or employee;

(*c*) vesting or transferring property, or requiring or entitling any person to call for or make any transfer of property or any payment.

(2) Where the court directs a scheme for the administration of a charity to be established, the court may by order refer the matter to the Commissioners for them to prepare or settle a scheme in accordance with such directions (if any) as the court sees fit to give, and any such order may provide for the scheme to be put into effect by order of the Commissioners as if prepared under subsection (1) above and without any further order of the court.

(3) The Commissioners shall not have jurisdiction under this section to try or determine the title at law or in equity to any property as between a charity or trustee for a charity and a person holding or claiming the property or an interest in it adversely to the charity, or to try or determine any question as to the existence or extent of any charge or trust.

(4) Subject to the following subsections, the Commissioners shall not exercise their jurisdiction under this section as respects any charity, except—

(*a*) on the application of the charity; or

(*b*) on an order of the court under subsection (2) above; or

(*c*) in the case of a charity other than an exempt charity, on the application of the Attorney General.

(5) In the case of a charity which is not an exempt charity and whose income from all sources does not in aggregate exceed £500 a year, the Commissioners may exercise their jurisdiction under this section on the application—

(*a*) of any one or more of the charity trustees; or

(*b*) of any person interested in the charity; or

(*c*) of any two or more inhabitants of the area of the charity if it is a local charity.

(6) Where in the case of a charity, other than an exempt charity, the Commissioners are satisfied that the charity trustees ought in the interests of the charity to apply for a scheme, but have

unreasonably refused or neglected to do so and the Commissioners have given the charity trustees an opportunity to make representations to them, the Commissioners may proceed as if an application for a scheme had been made by the charity but the Commissioners shall not have power in a case where they act by virtue of this subsection to alter the purposes of the charity, unless forty years have elapsed from the date of its foundation.

(7) Where—

(a) a charity cannot apply to the Commissioners for a scheme by reason of any vacancy among the charity trustees or the absence or incapacity of any of them, but

(b) such an application is made by such number of the charity trustees as the Commissioners consider appropriate in the circumstances of the case,

the Commissioners may nevertheless proceed as if the application were an application made by the charity.

(8) The Commissioners may on the application of any charity trustee or trustee for a charity exercise their jurisdiction under this section for the purpose of discharging him from his trusteeship.

(9) Before exercising any jurisdiction under this section otherwise than on an order of the court, the Commissioners shall give notice of their intention to do so to each of the charity trustees, except any that cannot be found or has no known address in the United Kingdom or who is party or privy to an application for the exercise of the jurisdiction; and any such notice may be given by post, and, if given by post, may be addressed to the recipient's last known address in the United Kingdom.

(10) The Commissioners shall not exercise their jurisdiction under this section in any case (not referred to them by order of the court) which, by reason of its contentious character, or of any special question of law or of fact which it may involve, or for other reasons, the Commissioners may consider more fit to be adjudicated on by the court.

(11) An appeal against any order of the Commissioners under this section may be brought in the High Court by the Attorney General.

(12) An appeal against any order of the Commissioners under this section may also, at any time within the three months beginning with the day following that on which the order is published, be brought in the High Court by the charity or any of the charity trustees, or by any person removed from any office or employment by the order (unless he is removed with the concurrence of the charity trustees or with the approval of the special visitor, if any, of the charity).

(13) No appeal shall be brought under subsection (12) above except with a certificate of the Commissioners that it is a proper case for an appeal or with the leave of one of the judges of the High Court attached to the Chancery Division.

(14) Where an order of the Commissioners under this section establishes a scheme for the administration of a charity, any person interested in the charity shall have the like right of appeal under subsection (12) above as a charity trustee, and so

also, in the case of a charity which is a local charity in any area, shall any two or more inhabitants of the area and the council of any parish or (in Wales) any community comprising the area or any part of it.

(15) If the Secretary of State thinks it expedient to do so—

(a) in consequence of changes in the value of money, or

(b) with a view to increasing the number of charities in respect of which the Commissioners may exercise their jurisdiction under this section in accordance with subsection (5) above,

he may by order amend that subsection by substituting a different sum for the sum for the time being specified there.

**Further powers to make schemes or alter application of charitable property**

17.—(1) Where it appears to the Commissioners that a scheme should be established for the administration of a charity, but also that it is necessary or desirable for the scheme to alter the provision made by an Act of Parliament establishing or regulating the charity or to make any other provision which goes or might go beyond the powers exercisable by them apart from this section, or that it is for any reason proper for the scheme to be subject to parliamentary review, then (subject to subsection (6) below) the Commissioners may settle a scheme accordingly with a view to its being given effect under this section.

(2) A scheme settled by the Commissioners under this section may be given effect by order of the Secretary of State, and a draft of the order shall be laid before Parliament.

(3) Without prejudice to the operation of section 6 of the Statutory Instruments Act 1946 in other cases, in the case of a scheme which goes beyond the powers exercisable apart from this section in altering a statutory provision contained in or having effect under any public general Act of Parliament, the order shall not be made unless the draft has been approved by resolution of each House of Parliament.

(4) Subject to subsection (5) below, any provision of a scheme brought into effect under this section may be modified or superseded by the court or the Commissioners as if it were a scheme brought into effect by order of the Commissioners under section 16 above.

(5) Where subsection (3) above applies to a scheme, the order giving effect to it may direct that the scheme shall not be modified or superseded by a scheme brought into effect otherwise than under this section, and may also direct that that subsection shall apply to any scheme modifying or superseding the scheme to which the order gives effect.

(6) The Commissioners shall not proceed under this section without the like application and the like notice to the charity trustees, as would be required if they were proceeding (without an order of the court) under section 16 above; but on any application for a scheme, or in a case where they act by virtue of subsection (6) or (7) of that section, the Commissioners may proceed under this section or that section as appears to them appropriate.

(7) Notwithstanding anything in the trusts of a charity, no expenditure incurred in preparing or promoting a Bill in Parliament shall without the consent of the court or the Commissioners

be defrayed out of any moneys applicable for the purposes of a charity but this subsection shall not apply in the case of an exempt charity.

(8) Where the Commissioners are satisfied—

(*a*) that the whole of the income of a charity cannot in existing circumstances be effectively applied for the purposes of the charity; and

(*b*) that, if those circumstances continue, a scheme might be made for applying the surplus cy-près; and

(*c*) that it is for any reason not yet desirable to make such a scheme;

then the Commissioners may by order authorise the charity trustees at their discretion (but subject to any conditions imposed by the order) to apply any accrued or accruing income for any purposes for which it might be made applicable by such a scheme, and any application authorised by the order shall be deemed to be within the purposes of the charity.

(9) An order under subsection (8) above shall not extend to more than £300 out of income accrued before the date of the order, nor to income accruing more than three years after that date, nor to more than £100 out of the income accruing in any of those three years.

**Power to act for protection of charities**

18.—(1) Where, at any time after they have instituted an inquiry under section 8 above with respect to any charity, the Commissioners are satisfied—

(*a*) that there is or has been any misconduct or mis-management in the administration of the charity; or

(*b*) that it is necessary or desirable to act for the purpose of protecting the property of the charity or securing a proper application for the purposes of the charity of that property or of property coming to the charity,

the Commissioners may of their own motion to one or more of the following things—

(i) by order suspend any trustee, charity trustee, officer, agent or employee of the charity from the exercise of his office or employment pending consideration being given to his removal (whether under this section or otherwise);

(ii) by order appoint such number of additional charity trustees as they consider necessary for the proper administration of the charity;

(iii) by order vest any property held by or in trust for the charity in the official custodian, or require the persons in whom any such property is vested to transfer it to him, or appoint any person to transfer any such property to him;

(iv) order any person who holds any property on behalf of the charity, or of any trustee for it, not to part with the property without the approval of the Commissioners;

(v) order any debtor of the charity not to make any payment in or towards the discharge of his liability to the charity without the approval of the Commissioners;

(vi) by order restrict (notwithstanding anything in the trusts of the charity) the transactions which may be entered into, or the nature or amount of the payments which may be made, in the administration of the charity without the approval of the Commissioners;

(vii) by order permit (in accordance with section 19 below) a receiver and manager in respect of the property and affairs of the charity.

(2) Where, at any time after they have instituted an inquiry under section 8 above with respect to any charity, the Commissioners are satisfied—

(a) that there is or has been any misconduct or mismanagement in the administration of the charity; and

(b) that it is necessary or desirable to act for the purpose of protecting the property of the charity or securing a proper application for the purposes of the charity of that property or of property coming to the charity,

the Commissioners may of their own motion do either or both of the following things—

(i) by order remove any trustee, charity trustee, officer, agent or employee of the charity who has been responsible for or privy to the misconduct or mismanagement or has by his conduct contributed to it or facilitated it;

(ii) by order establish a scheme for the administration of the charity.

(3) The references in subsection (1) or (2) above to misconduct or mismanagement shall (notwithstanding anything in the trusts of the charity) extend to the employment for the remuneration or reward of persons acting in the affairs of the charity, or for other administrative purposes, of sums which are excessive in relation to the property which is or is likely to be applied or applicable for the purposes of the charity.

(4) The Commissioners may also remove a charity trustee by order made by their own motion—

(a) where, within the last five years, the trustee—
   (i) having previously been adjudged bankrupt or had his estate sequestrated, has been discharged, or
   (ii) having previously made a composition or arrangement with, or granted a trust deed for, his creditors, has been discharged in respect of it;

(b) where the trustee is a corporation in liquidation;

(c) where the trustee is incapable of acting by reason or mental disorder within the meaning of the Mental Health Act 1983;

(d) where the trustee has not acted, and will not declare his willingness or unwillingness to act;

(e) where the trustee is outside England and Wales or cannot be found or does not act, and his absence or failure to act impedes the proper administration of the charity.

(5) The Commissioners may by order of their own motion appoint a person to be a charity trustee—

    (a) in place of a charity trustee removed by them under this section or otherwise;

    (b) where there are no charity trustees, or where by reason of vacancies in their number or the absence or incapacity of any of their number the charity cannot apply for the appointment;

    (c) where there is a single charity trustee, not being a corporation aggregate, and the Commissioners are of opinion that it is necessary to increase the number for the proper administration of the charity;

    (d) where the Commissioners are of opinion that it is necessary for the proper administration of the charity to have an additional charity trustee because one of the existing charity trustees who ought nevertheless to remain charity trustee either cannot be found or does not act or is outside England and Wales.

(6) The powers of the Commissioners under this section to remove or appoint charity trustees of their own motion shall include power to make any such order with respect to the vesting in or transfer to the charity trustees of the property as the Commissioners could make on the removal or appointment of a charity trustee by them under section 16 above.

(7) Any order under this section for the removal or appointment of a charity trustee or trustee for a charity, or for the vesting or transfer of any property, shall be of the like effect as an order made under section 16 above.

(8) Subject to subsection (9) below, subsections (11) to (13) of section 16 above shall apply to orders under this section as they apply to orders under that section.

(9) The requirement to obtain any such certificate or leave as is mentioned in section 16(13) above shall not apply to—

    (a) an appeal by a charity or any of the charity trustees of a charity against an order under subsection (1)(vii) above appointing a receiver and manager in respect of the charity's property and affairs, or

    (b) an appeal by a person against an order under subsection (2)(i) or (4)(a) above removing him from his office or employment.

(10) Subsection (14) of section 16 above shall apply to an order under this section which establishes a scheme for the administration of a charity as it applies to such an order under that section.

(11) The power of the Commissioners to make an order under subsection (1)(i) above shall not be exercisable so as to suspend any person from the exercise of his office or employment for a period of more than twelve months; but (without prejudice to the generality of section 89(1) below), any such order made in the case of any person may make provision as respects the period of his suspension for matters arising out of it, and in particular for enabling any person to execute any instrument in his name or otherwise act for him and, in the case of a charity trustee, for

adjusting any rules governing the proceedings of the charity trustees to take account of the reduction in number capable of acting.

(12) Before exercising any jurisdiction under this section otherwise than by virtue of subsection (1) above, the Commissioners shall give notice of their intention to do so to each of the charity trustees, except any that cannot be found or has no known address in the United Kingdom; and any such notice may be given by post and, if given by post, may be addressed to the recipient's last known address in the United Kingdom.

(13) The Commissioners shall, at such intervals as they think fit, review any order made by them under paragraph (i), or any of paragraphs (iii) to (vii), of subsection (1) above; and, if on any such review it appears to them that it would be appropriate to discharge the order in whole or in part, they shall so discharge it (whether subject to any savings or other transitional provisions or not).

(14) If any person contravenes an order under subsection (1)(iv), (v) or (vii) above, he shall be guilty of an offence and liable on summary conviction to a fine not exceeding level 5 on the standard scale.

(15) Subsection (14) above shall not be taken to preclude the bringing of proceedings for breach of trust against any charity trustee or trustee for a charity in respect of a contravention of an order under subsection (1)(iv) or (vi) above (whether proceedings in respect of the contravention are brought against him under subsection (14) above or not).

(16) This section shall not apply to an exempt charity.

**Supplementary provisions relating to receiver and manager appointed for a charity**

19.—(1) The Commissioners may under section 18(1)(vii) above appoint to be receiver and manager in respect of the property and affairs of a charity such person (other than an officer or employee of theirs) as they think fit.

(2) Without prejudice to the generality of section 89(1) below, any order made by the Commissioners under section 18(1)(vii) above may make provision with respect to the functions to be discharged by the receiver and manager appointed by the order; and those functions shall be discharged by him under the supervision of the Commissioners.

(3) In connection with the discharge of those functions any such order may provide—

    (a) for the receiver and manager appointed by the order to have such powers and duties of the charity trustees of the charity concerned (whether arising under this Act or otherwise) as are specified in the order;

    (b) for any powers or duties exercisable or falling to be performed by the receiver and manager by virtue of paragraph (a) above to be exercisable or performed by him to the exclusion of those trustees.

(4) Where a person has been appointed receiver and manager by any such order—

    (a) section 29 below shall apply to him and to his functions as a person so appointed as it applies to a charity trustee of the charity concerned and to his duties as such; and

(b) the Commissioners may apply to the High Court for directions in relation to any particular matter arising in connection with the discharge of those functions.

(5) The High Court may on an application under subsection (4)(b) above—

(a) give such directions, or
(b) make such orders declaring the rights of any persons (whether before the court or not),

as it thinks just; and the costs of any such application shall be paid by the charity concerned.

(6) Regulations made by the Secretary of State may make provision with respect to—

(a) the appointment and removal of persons appointed in accordance with this section;
(b) the remuneration of such persons out of the income of the charities concerned;
(c) the making of reports to the Commissioners by such persons.

Regulations under subsection (6) above may, in particular, authorise the Commissioners—

(a) to require security for the due discharge of his functions to be given by a person so appointed;
(b) to determine the amount of such a person's remuneration;
(c) to disallow any amount of remuneration in such circumstances as are prescribed by the regulations.

**Publicity for proceedings under ss.16 to 18**

20.—(1) The Commissioners shall not make any order under this Act to establish a scheme for the administration of a charity, or submit such a scheme to the court or the Secretary of State for an order giving it effect, unless not less than one month previously there has been given public notice of their proposals, inviting representations to be made to them within a time specified in the notice, being no less than one month from the date of such notice, and, in the case of a scheme relating to a local charity, other than on ecclesiastical charity, in a parish or (in Wales) a community, a draft of the scheme has been communicated to the parish or community council or, in the case of a parish not having a council, to the chairman of the parish meeting.

(2) The Commissioners shall not make any order under this Act to appoint, discharge or remove a charity trustee or trustee for a charity (other than the official custodian), unless not less than one month previously there has been given the like public notice as is required by subsection (1) above for an order establishing a scheme but this subsection shall not apply in the case of—

(a) an order under purpose 18(1)(ii) above; or
(b) an order discharging or removing a trustee if the Commissioners are of opinion that it is unnecessary and not in his interest to give publicity to the proposal to discharge or remove him.

(3) Before the Commissioners make an order under this Act to remove without his consent a charity trustee or trustee for a charity, or an officer, agent or employee of a charity, the Commissioners shall, unless he cannot be found or has no known address in the United Kingdom, give him not less than one month's notice of their proposal, inviting representations to be made to them within a time specified in the notice.

(4) Where notice is given of any proposals as required by subsections (1) to (3) above, the Commissioners shall take into consideration any representations made to them about the proposals within the time specified in the notice, and may (without further notice) proceed with the proposals either without modification or with such modifications as appear to them to be desirable.

(5) Where the Commissioners make an order which is subject to appeal under subsection (12) of section 16 above the order shall be published either by giving public notice of it or by giving notice of it to all persons entitled to appeal against it under that subsection, as the Commissioners think fit.

(6) Where the Commissioners make an order under this Act to establish a scheme for the administration of a charity, a copy of the order shall, for not less than one month after the order is published, be available for public inspection at all reasonable times at the Commissioners' office and also at some convenient place in the area of the charity, if it is a local charity.

(7) Any notice to be given under this section of any proposals or order shall give such particulars of the proposals or order, or such directions for obtaining information about them, as the Commissioners think sufficient and appropriate, and any public notice shall be given in such manner as they think sufficient and appropriate.

(8) Any notice to be given under this section, other than a public notice, may be given by post and, if given by post, may be addressed to the recipient's last known address in the United Kingdom.

*Property vested in official custodian*

**Entrusting charity property to official custodian, and termination of trust**

21.—(1) The court may by order—

(*a*) vest in the official custodian any land held by or in trust for a charity;

(*b*) authorise or require the persons in whom any such land is vested to transfer it to him; or

(*c*) appoint any person to transfer any such land to him;

but this subsection does not apply to any interest in land by way of mortgage or other security.

(2) Where property is vested in the official custodian in trust for a charity, the court may make an order discharging him from the trusteeship as respects all or any of that property.

(3) Where the official custodian is discharged from his trusteeship of any property, or the trusts on which he holds any property come to an end, the court may make such vesting orders and give such directions as may seem to the court to be necessary or expedient in consequence.

(4) No person shall be liable for any loss occasioned by his acting in conformity with an order under this section or by his giving effect to anything done in pursuance of such an order, or be excused from so doing by reason of the order having been in any respect improperly obtained.

**Supplementary provisions as to property vested in official custodian**

22.—(1) Subject to the provisions of this Act, where property is vested in the official custodian in trust for a charity, he shall not exercise any powers of management, but he shall as trustee of any property have all the same powers, duties and liabilities, and be entitled to the same rights and immunities, and be subject to the control and orders of the court, as a corporation appointed custodian trustee under section 4 of the Public Trustee Act 1906 except that he shall have no power to charge fees.

(2) Subject to subsection (3) below, where any land is vested in the official custodian in trust for a charity, the charity trustees shall have power in his name and on his behalf to execute and do all assurances and things which they could properly execute or do in their own name and on their own behalf if the land were vested in them.

(3) If any land is so vested in the official custodian by virtue of an order under section 18 above, the power conferred on the charity trustees by subsection (2) above shall not be exercisable by them in relation to any transaction affecting the land, unless the transaction is authorised by order of the court or of the Commissioners.

(4) Where any land is vested in the official custodian in trust for a charity, the charity trustees shall have the like power to make obligations entered into by them binding on the land as if it were vested in them; and any covenant, agreement or condition which is enforceable by or against the custodian by reason of the land being vested in him shall be enforceable by or against the charity trustees as if the land were vested in them.

(5) In relation to a corporate charity, subsections (2), (3) and (4) above shall apply with the substitution of references to the charity for references to the charity trustees.

(6) Subsections (2), (3) and (4) above shall not authorise any charity trustees or charity to impose any personal liability on the official custodian.

(7) Where the official custodian is entitled as trustee for a charity to the custody of securities or documents of title relating to the trust property, he may permit them to be in the possession or under the control of the charity trustees without thereby incurring any liability.

**Divestment in the case of land subject to Reverter of Sites Act 1987**

23.—(1) Where—

(a) any land vested in the official custodian in trust for a charity, and

(b) it appears to the Commissioners that section 1 of the Reverter of Sites Act 1987 (right of reverter replaced by trust for sale) will, or is likely to, operate in relation to the land at a particular time or in particular circumstances,

the jurisdiction which, under section 16 above, is exercisable by the Commissioners for the purpose of discharging a trustee for a charity may, at any time before section 1 of that Act ("the 1987

Act") operates in relation to the land, be exercised by them of their own motion for the purpose of—

   (i)   making an order discharging the official custodian from his trusteeship of the land, and

   (ii)   making such vesting orders and giving such directions as appear to them to be necessary or expedient in consequence.

(2) Where—

   (a)   section 1 of the 1987 Act has operated in relation to any land which, immediately before the time when that section so operated, was vested in the official custodian in trust for a charity, and

   (b)   the land remains vested in him but on the trust arising under that section,

the court or the Commissioners (of their own motion) may—

   (i)   make an order discharging the official custodian from his trusteeship of the land, and

   (ii)   (subject to the following provisions of this section) make such vesting orders and give such directions as appear to it or them to be necessary or expedient in consequence.

(3) Where any order discharging the official custodian from his trusteeship of any land—

   (a)   is made by the court under section 21(2) above, or by the Commissioners under section 16 above, on the grounds that section 1 of the 1987 Act will, or is likely to, operate in relation to the land, or

   (b)   is made by the court or the Commissioners under subsection (2) above,

the persons in whom the land is to be vested on the discharge of the official custodian shall be the relevant charity trustees (as defined in subsection (4) below), unless the court or (as the case may be) the Commissioners is or are satisfied that it would be appropriate for it to be vested in some other persons.

(4) In subsection (3) above "the relevant charity trustees" means—

   (a)   in relation to an order made as mentioned in paragraph (a) of that subsection, the charity trustees of the charity in trust for which the land is vested in the official custodian immediately before the time when the order takes effect, or

   (b)   in relation to an order made under subsection (2) above, the charity trustees of the charity in trust for which the land was vested in the official custodian immediately before the time when section 1 of the 1987 Act operated in relation to the land.

(5) Where—

(*a*) section 1 of the 1987 Act has operated in relation to any such land as is mentioned in subsection (2)(*a*) above, and

(*b*) the land remains vested in the official custodian as mentioned in subsection (2)(*b*) above,

then (subject to subsection (6) below), all the powers, duties and liabilities that would, apart from this section, be those of the official custodian as trustee for sale of the land shall instead be those of the charity trustees of the charity concerned; and those trustees shall have power in his name and on his behalf to execute and do all assurances and things which they could properly execute or do in their own name and on their own behalf if the land were vested in them.

(6) Subsection (5) above shall not be taken to require or authorise those trustees to sell the land at a time when it remains vested in the official custodian.

(7) Where—

(*a*) the official custodian has been discharged from his trusteeship of any land by an order under subsection (2) above, and

(*b*) the land has, in accordance with subsection (3) above, been vested in the charity trustees concerned or (as the case may be) in any persons other than those trustees,

the land shall be held by those trustees, or (as the case may be) by those persons, as trustees for sale on the terms of the trust arising under section 1 of the 1987 Act.

(8) The official custodian shall not be liable to any person in respect of any loss or misapplication of any land vested in him in accordance with that section unless it is occasioned by or through any wilful neglect or default of his or of his person acting for him; but the Consolidated Fund shall be liable to make good to any person any sums for which the official custodian may be liable by reason of any such neglect or default.

(9) In this section any reference to section 1 of the 1987 Act operating in relation to any land is a reference to a trust for sale arising in relation to the land under that section.

*Establishment of common investment or deposit funds*

**Schemes to establish common investment funds**

24.—(1) The court or the Commissioners may by order make and bring into effect schemes (in this section referred to as "common investment schemes") for the establishment of common investment funds under trusts which provide—

(*a*) for property transferred to the fund by or on behalf of a charity participating in the scheme to be invested under the control of trustees appointed to manage the fund; and

(*b*) for the participating charities to be entitled (subject to the provisions of the scheme) to the capital and income of the funds in shares determined by reference to the amount or value of the property transferred to it by or on behalf of each of them and to the value of the fund at the time of the transfers.

(2) The court or the Commissioners may make a common investment scheme on the application of any two or more charities.

(3) A common investment scheme may be made in terms admitting any charity to participate, or the scheme may restrict the right to participate in any manner.

(4) A common investment scheme may make provision for, and for all matters connected with, the establishment, investment, management and winding up of the common investment fund, and may in particular include provision—

(a) for remunerating persons appointed trustees to hold or manage the fund or any part of it, with or without provision authorising a person to receive the remuneration notwithstanding that he is also a charity trustee of or trustee for a participating charity;

(b) for restricting the size of the fund, and for regulating as to time, amount or otherwise the right to transfer property to or withdraw it from the fund, and for enabling sums to be advanced out of the fund by way of loan to a participating charity pending the withdrawal of property from the fund by the charity;

(c) for enabling income to be withheld from distribution with a view to avoiding fluctuations in the amounts distributed, and generally for regulating distributions of income;

(d) for enabling money to be borrowed temporarily for the purpose of meeting payments to be made out of the funds;

(e) for enabling questions arising under the scheme as to the right of a charity to participate, or as to the rights of participating charities, or as to any other matter, to be conclusively determined by the decision of the trustees managing the fund or in any other manner;

(f) for regulating the accounts and information to be supplied to participating charities.

(5) A common investment scheme, in addition to the provision for property to be transferred to the fund on the basis that the charity shall be entitled to a share in the capital and income of the fund, may include provision for enabling sums to be deposited by or on behalf of a charity on the basis that (subject to the provisions of the scheme) the charity shall be entitled to repayment of the sums deposited and to interest thereon at a rate determined by or under the scheme; and where a scheme makes any such provision it shall also provide for excluding from the amount of capital and income to be shared between charities participating otherwise than by way of deposit such amounts (not exceeding the amounts properly attributable to the making of deposits) as are from time to time reasonably required in respect of the liabilities of the fund for the repayment of deposits and for the interest on deposits, including amounts required by way of reserve.

(6) Except in so far as a common investment scheme provides to the contrary, the rights under it of a participating charity shall not be capable of being assigned or charged, nor shall

any trustee or other person concerned in the management of the common investment fund be required or entitled to take account of any trust or other equity affecting a participating charity or its property or rights.

(7) The powers of investment of every charity shall include power to participate in common investment schemes unless the power is excluded by a provision specifically referring to common investment schemes in the trusts of the charity.

(8) A common investment fund shall be deemed for all purposes to be a charity; and if the scheme admits only exempt charities, the fund shall be an exempt charity for the purposes of this Act.

(9) Subsection (8) above shall apply not only to common investment funds established under the powers of this section, but also to any similar fund established for the exclusive benefit of charities by or under any enactment relating to any particular charities or class of charity.

**Schemes to establish common deposit funds**

25.—(1) The court of the Commissioners may by order make and bring into effect schemes (in this section referred to as "common deposit schemes") for the establishment of common deposit funds under trusts which provide—

(a) for sums to be deposited by or on behalf of a charity participating in the scheme and invested under the control of trustees appointed to manage the fund; and

(b) for any such charity to be entitled (subject to the provisions of the scheme) to repayment of any sums so deposited and to interest thereon at a rate determined under the scheme.

(2) Subject to subsection (3) below, the following provisions of section 24 above, namely—

(a) subsections (2) to (4), and

(b) subsections (6) to (9),

shall have effect in relation to common deposit schemes and common deposit funds as they have effect in relation to common investment schemes and common investment funds.

(3) In its application in accordance with subsection (2) above, subsection (4) of that section shall have effect with the substitution for paragraphs (b) and (c) of the following paragraphs—

"(b) for regulating as to time, amount or otherwise the right to repayment of sums deposited in the fund;

(c) for authorising a part of the income for any year to be credited to a reserve account maintained for the purpose of counteracting any losses accruing to the fund, and generally for regulating the manner in which the rate of interest on deposits is to be determined from time to time;".

Additional powers of Commissioners

**Power to authorise dealings with charity property, etc.**

26.—(1) Subject to the provisions of this section, where it appears to the Commissioners that any action proposed or contemplated in the administration of a charity is expedient in the interests of the charity, they may by order sanction that action, whether or not it would otherwise be within the powers exercisable by the charity trustees in the administration of the charity; and anything done under the authority of such an order shall be deemed to be properly done in the exercise of those powers.

(2) An order under this section may be made so as to authorise a particular transaction, compromise or the like, or a particular application of property, or so as to give a more general authority, and (without prejudice to the generality of subsection (1) above) may authorise a charity to use common premises, or employ a common staff, or otherwise combine for any purposes of administration, with any other charity.

(3) An order under this section may give directions as to the manner in which any expenditure is to be borne and as to other matters connected with or arising out of the action thereby authorised; and where anything is done in pursuance of an authority given by any such order, any directions given in connection therewith shall be binding on the charity trustees for the time being as if contained in the trusts of the charity; but any such directions may on the application of the charity be modified or superseded by a further order.

(4) Without prejudice to the generality of subsection (3) above, the directions which may be given by an order under this section shall in particular include directions for meeting any expenditure out of a specified fund, for charging any expenditure to capital or to income, for requiring expenditure charged to capital to be recouped out of income within a specified period, for restricting the costs to be incurred at the expense of the charity, or for the investment of moneys arising from any transaction.

(5) An order under this section may authorise any act notwithstanding that it is prohibited by any of the disabling Acts mentioned in subsection (6) below or that the trusts of the charity provide for the act to be done by or under the authority of the court; but no such order shall authorise the doing of any act expressly prohibited by Act of Parliament other than the disabling Acts or by the trusts of the charity or shall extend or alter the purposes of the charity.

(6) The Acts referred to in subsection (5) above as the disabling Acts are the Ecclesiastical Leases Act 1571, the Ecclesiastical Leases Act 1572, the Ecclesiastical Leases Act 1575 and the Ecclesiastical Leases Act 1836.

(7) An order under this section shall not confer any authority in relation to a building which has been consecrated and of which the use or disposal is regulated, and can be further regulated, by a scheme having effect under the Union of Benefices Measures 1923 to 1952, the Reorganisation Areas Measures 1944 and 1954, the Pastoral Measure 1968 or the Pastoral Measure 1983, the reference to a building being taken to include part of a building and any land which under such a scheme is to be used or disposed of with a building to which the scheme applies.

**Power to authorise ex gratia payments, etc.**

27.—(1) Subject to subsection (3) below, the Commissioners may by order exercise the same power as is exercisable by the Attorney General to authorise the charity trustees of a charity—

(*a*) to make any application of property of the charity, or (*b*) to waive to any extent, on behalf of the charity, its entitlement to receive any property,

in a case where the charity trustees—

(i) (apart from this section) have no power to do so, but
(ii) in all the circumstances regard themselves as being under a moral obligation to do so.

(2) The power conferred on the Commissioners by subsection (1) above shall be exercisable by them under the supervision of, and in accordance with such directions as may be given by, the Attorney General; and any such directions may in particular require the Commissioners, in such circumstances as are specified in the directions—

(*a*) to refrain from exercising that power; or
(*b*) to consult the Attorney General before exercising it.

(3) Where—

(*a*) an application is made to the Commissioners for them to exercise that power in a case where they are not precluded from doing so by any such directions, but
(*b*) they consider that it would nevertheless be desirable for the application to be entertained by the Attorney General rather than by them.

they shall refer the application to the Attorney General.

(4) It is hereby declared that where, in the case of any application made to them as mentioned in subsection (3)(*a*) above, the Commissioners determine the application by refusing to authorise charity trustees to take any action falling within subsection (1)(*a*) or (*b*) above, that refusal shall not preclude the Attorney General, on an application subsequently made to him by the trustees, from authorising the trustees to take that action.

**Power to give directions about dormant bank accounts of charities**

28.—(1) Where the Commissioners—

(*a*) are informed by a relevant institution—
    (i) that it holds one or more accounts in the name of or on behalf of a particular charity ("the relevant charity"), and
    (ii) that the account, or (if it so holds two or more accounts) each of the accounts, is dormant, and
(*b*) are unable, after making reasonable inquiries, to locate that charity or any of its trustees.

they may give a direction under subsection (2) below.

(2) A direction under this subsection is a direction which—

(*a*) requires the institution concerned to transfer the amount, or (as the case may be) the aggregate amount, standing to the credit of the relevant charity in the account or accounts in question to such other charity as is specified in the direction in accordance with subsection (3) below; or
(*b*) requires the institution concerned to transfer to each of two or more other charities so specified in the direction

such part of that amount or aggregate amount as is there specified in relation to that charity.

(3) The Commissioners may specify in a direction under subsection (2) above such other charity or charities as they consider appropriate, having regard, in a case where the purposes of the relevant charity are known to them, to those purposes and to the purposes of the other charity or charities; but the Commissioners shall not so specify any charity unless they have received from the charity trustees written confirmation that those trustees are willing to accept the amount proposed to be transferred to the charity.

(4) Any amount received by a charity by virtue of this section shall be received by the charity on terms that—

(a) it shall be held and applied by the charity for the purposes of the charity, but

(b) it shall, as property of the charity, nevertheless be subject to any restrictions on expenditure to which it was subject as property of the relevant charity.

(5) Where—

(a) the Commissioners have been informed as mentioned in subsection (1)(a) above by any relevant institution, and

(b) before any transfer is made by the institution in pursuance of a direction under subsection (2) above, the institution has, by reason of any circumstances, cause to believe that the account or (as the case may be) any of the accounts, held by it in the name of or on behalf of the relevant charity is no longer dormant,

the institution shall forthwith notify those circumstances in writing to the Commissioners; and, if it appears to the Commissioners that the account or accounts in question is or are no longer dormant, they shall revoke any direction under subsection (2) above which has previously been given by them to the institution with respect to the relevant charity.

(6) The receipt of any charity trustees or trustee for a charity in respect of any amount received from a relevant institution by virtue of this section shall be a complete discharge of the institution in respect of that amount.

(7) No obligation as to secretary or other restriction on disclosure (however imposed) shall preclude a relevant institution from disclosing any information to the Commissioners for the purpose of enabling them to discharge their functions under this section.

(8) For the purposes of this section—

(a) an account is dormant if no transaction, other than—

(i) a transaction consisting in a payment into the account, or

(ii) a transaction which the institution holding the account has itself caused to be effected,

has been effected in relation to the account within the period of five years immediately preceding the date when the Commissioners are informed as mentioned in paragraph (*a*) of subsection (1) above;

(*b*) a "relevant institution" means—

(i) the Bank of England;

(ii) an institution which is authorised by the Bank of England to operate a deposit-taking business under Part I of the Banking Act 1987;

(iii) a European deposit-taker as defined in regulation 82(3) of the Banking Coordination (Second Council Directive) Regulations 1992;

(iv) a building society which is authorised by the Building Societies Commission under section 9 of the Building Societies Act 1986 to raise money from its members; or

(v) such other institution mentioned in Schedule 2 to the Banking Act 1987 as the Secretary of State may prescribe by regulations; and

(*c*) references to the transfer of any amount to a charity are references to its transfer—

(i) to the charity trustees, or

(ii) to any trustee for the charity,

as the charity trustees may determine (and any reference to any amount received by a charity shall be construed accordingly).

(9) For the purpose of determining the matters in respect of which any of the powers conferred by section 8 or 9 above may be exercised it shall be assumed that the Commissioners have no functions under this section in relation to accounts to which this subsection applies (with the result that, for example, a relevant institution shall not, in connection with the functions of the Commissioners under this section, be required under section 8(3)(*a*) above to furnish any statements, or answer any questions or inquiries, with respect to any such accounts held by the institution).

This subsection applies to accounts which are dormant accounts by virtue of subsection (8)(*a*) above but would not be such accounts if subparagraph (i) of that provision were omitted.

(10) Subsection (1) above shall not apply to any account held in the name of or on behalf of an exempt charity.

**Power to advise charity trustees**
29.—(1) The Commissioners may on the written application of any charity trustee give him their opinion or advice on any matter affecting the performance of his duties as such.

(2) A charity trustee or trustee for a charity acting in accordance with the opinion or advice of the Commissioners given under this section with respect to the charity shall be deemed, as regards his responsibility for so acting, to have acted in accordance with his trust, unless, when he does so, either—

(*a*) he knows or has reasonable cause to suspect that the opinion or advice was given in ignorance of material facts; or

(*b*) the decision of the court has been obtained on the matter or proceedings are pending to obtain one.

**Powers for preservation of charity documents**

30.—(1) The Commissioners may provide books in which any deed, will or other document relating to a charity may be enrolled.

(2) The Commissioners may accept for safe keeping any document of or relating to a charity, and the charity trustees or other persons having the custody of documents of or relating to a charity (including a charity which has ceased to exist) may with the consent of the Commissioners deposit them with the Commissioners for safe keeping, except in the case of documents required by some other enactment to be kept elsewhere.

(3) Where a document is enrolled by the Commissioners or is for the time being deposited with them under this section, evidence of its contents may be given by means of a copy certified by any officer of the Commissioners generally or specially authorised by them to act for this purpose; and a document purporting to be such a copy shall be received in evidence without proof of the official position, authority or handwriting of the person certifying it or of the original document being enrolled or deposited as aforesaid.

(4) Regulations made by the Secretary of State may make provision for such documents deposited with the Commissioners under this section as may be prescribed by the regulations to be destroyed or otherwise disposed of after such period or in such circumstances as may be so prescribed.

(5) Subsections (3) and (4) above shall apply to any document transmitted to the Commissioners under section 9 above and kept by them under subsection (3) of that section, as if the document had been deposited with them for safe keeping under this section.

**Power to order taxation of solicitor's bill**

31.—(1) The Commissioners may order that a solicitor's bill of costs for business done for a charity, or for charity trustees or trustees for a charity, shall be taxed, together with the costs of the taxation, by a taxing officer in such division of the High Court as may be specified in the order, or by the taxing officer of any other court having jurisdiction to order the taxation of the bill.

(2) On any order under this section for the taxation of a solicitor's bill the taxation shall proceed, and the taxing officer shall have the same powers and duties, and the costs of the taxation shall be borne, as if the order had been made, on the application of the person chargeable with the bill, by the court in which the costs are taxed.

(3) No order under this section for the taxation of a solicitor's bill shall be made after payment of the bill unless the Commissioners are of opinion that it contains exorbitant charges; and no such order shall in any case be made where the solicitor's costs are not subject to taxation on an order of the High Court by reason either of an agreement as to his remuneration or the lapse of time since payment of the bill.

*Legal proceedings relating to charities*

**Proceedings by Commissioners**

32.—(1) Subject to subsection (2) below, the Commissioners may exercise the same powers with respect to—

(*a*) the taking of legal proceedings with reference to charities or the property or affairs of charities, or (*b*) the compromise of claims with a view to avoiding or ending such proceedings,

as are exercisable by the Attorney General acting ex officio.

(2) Subsection (1) above does not apply to the power of the Attorney General under section 63(1) below to present a petition for the winding up of a charity.

(3) The practice and procedure to be followed in relation to any proceedings taken by the Commissioners under subsection (1) above shall be the same in all respects (and in particular as regards costs) as if they were proceedings taken by the Attorney General acting ex officio.

(4) No rule of law or practice shall be taken to require the Attorney General to be a party to any such proceedings.

(5) The powers exercisable by the Commissioners by virtue of this section shall be exercisable by them of their own motion, but shall be exercisable only with the agreement of the Attorney General on each occasion.

**Proceedings by other persons**    33.—(1) Charity proceedings may be taken with reference to a charity either by the charity, or by any of the charity trustees, or by any person interested in the charity, or by any two or more inhabitants of the area of the charity if it is a local charity, but not by any other person.

(2) Subject to the following provisions of this section, no charity proceedings relating to a charity (other than an exempt charity) shall be entertained or proceeded with in any court unless the taking of the proceedings is authorised by order of the Commissioners.

(3) The Commissioners shall not, without special reasons, authorise the taking of charity proceedings where in their opinion the case can be dealt with by them under the power of this Act other than those conferred by section 32 above.

(4) This section shall not require any order for the taking of proceedings in a pending cause or matter or for the bringing of any appeal.

(5) Where the foregoing provisions of this section require the taking of charity proceedings to be authorised by an order of the Commissioners, the proceedings may nevertheless be entertained or proceeded with if, after the order had been applied for and refused, leave to take the proceedings was obtained from one of the judges of the High Court attached to the Chancery Division.

(6) Nothing in the foregoing subsections shall apply to the taking of proceedings by the Attorney General, with or without a relator, or to the taking of proceedings by the Commissioners in accordance with section 32 above.

(7) Where it appears to the Commissioners, on an application for an order under this section or otherwise, that it is desirable for legal proceedings to be taken with reference to any charity (other than an exempt charity) or its property or affairs, and for the proceedings to be taken by the Attorney General, the Commissioners shall so inform the Attorney General, and send him such statements and particulars as they think necessary to explain the matter.

(8) In this section "charity proceedings" means proceedings in any court in England or Wales brought under the court's

jurisdiction with respect to charities, or brought under the court's jurisdiction with respect to trusts in relation to the administration of a trust for charitable purposes.

**Report of s.8 inquiry to be evidence in certain proceedings**

**34.**—(1) A copy of the report of the person conducting an inquiry under section 8 above shall, if certified by the Commissioners to be a true copy, be admissible in any proceedings to which this section applies—

    (*a*) as evidence of any fact stated in the report; and

    (*b*) as evidence of the opinion of that person as to any matter referred to in it.

(2) This section applies to—

    (*a*) any legal proceedings instituted by the Commissioners under this Part of the Act; and

    (*b*) any legal proceedings instituted by the Attorney General in respect of a charity.

(3) A document purporting to be a certificate issued for the purposes of subsection (1) above shall be received in evidence and be deemed to be such a certificate, unless the contrary is proved.

*Meaning of "trust corporation"*

**Application of provisions to trust corporations appointed under s.16 or 18**

**35.**—(1) In the definition of "trust corporation" contained in the following provisions—

    (*a*) section 117(xxx) of the Settled Land Act 1925,

    (*b*) section 68(18) of the Trustees Act 1925,

    (*c*) section 205(xxviii) of the Law of Property Act 1925,

    (*d*) section 55(xxvi) of the Administration of Estates Act 1925, and

    (*e*) section 128 of the Supreme Court Act 1981,

the reference to a corporation appointed by the court in any particular case to be a trustee includes a reference to a corporation appointed by the Commissioners under this Act to be a trustee.

(2) This section shall be deemed always to have had effect; but the reference to section 128 of the Supreme Court Act 1981 shall, in relation to any time before January 1, 1982, be construed as a reference to section 175(1) of the Supreme Court of Judicature (Consolidation) Act 1925.

## PART V

### CHARITY LAND

**Restrictions on dispositions**

**36.**—(1) Subject to the following provisions of this section and section 40 below, no land held by or in trust for a charity shall be sold, leased or otherwise disposed of without an order of the court or of the Commissioners.

(2) Subsection (1) above shall not apply to a disposition of such land if—

(*a*) the disposition is made to a person who is not—
  (i) a connected person (as defined in Schedule 5 to this Act), or
  (ii) a trustee for, or nominee of, a connected person; and
(*b*) the requirements of subsection (3) or (5) below have been complied with in relation to it.

(3) Except where the proposed disposition is the granting of such a lease as is mentioned in subsection (5) below, the charity trustees must, before entering into an agreement for the sale, or (as the case may be) for a lease or other disposition, of the land—

(*a*) obtain and consider a written report on the proposed disposition from a qualified surveyor instructed by the trustees and acting exclusively for the charity;
(*b*) advertise the proposed disposition for such period and in such manner as the surveyor has advised in his report (unless he has there advised that it would not be in the best interests of the charity to advertise the proposed disposition); and
(*c*) decide that they are satisfied, having considered the surveyor's report, that the terms on which the disposition is proposed to be made are the best that can reasonably be obtained for the charity.

(4) For the purpose of subsection (3) above a person is a qualified surveyor if—

(*a*) he is a fellow or professional associate of the Royal Institution of Chartered Surveyors or of the Incorporated Society of Valuers and Auctioneers or satisfies such other requirement or requirements as may be prescribed by regulations made by the Secretary of State; and
(*b*) he is reasonably believed by the charity trustees to have ability in, and experience of, the valuation of land of the particular kind, and in the particular area, in question;

and any report prepared for the purposes of that subsection shall contain such information and deal with such matters, as may be prescribed by regulations so made.

(5) Where the proposed disposition is the granting of a lease for a term ending not more than seven years after it is granted (other than one granted wholly or partly in consideration of a fine), the charity trustees must, before entering into an agreement for the lease—

(*a*) obtain and consider the advice on the proposed disposition of a person who is reasonably believed by the trustees to have the requisite ability and practical experience to provide them with competent advice on the proposed disposition; and
(*b*) decide that they are satisfied, having considered that person's advice, that the terms on which the disposition is proposed to be made are the best that can reasonably be obtained for the charity.

(6) Where—

(a) any land is held by or in trust for a charity, and
(b) the trusts on which it is so held stipulate that it is to be used for the purposes, or any particular purposes, of the charity,

then (subject to subsections (7) and (8) below and without prejudice to the operation of the preceding provisions of this section) the land shall not be sold, leased or otherwise disposed of unless the charity trustees have previously—

(i) given public notice of the proposed disposition, inviting representations to be made to them within a time specified in the notice, being not less than one month from the date of the notice; and
(ii) taken into consideration any representations made to them within that time about the proposed disposition.

(7) Subsection (6) above shall not apply to any such disposition of land as is there mentioned if—

(a) the disposition is to be effected with a view to acquiring by way of replacement other property which is to be held on the trusts referred to in paragraph (b) of that subsection; or
(b) the disposition is the granting of a lease for a term ending not more than two years after it is granted (other than one granted wholly or partly in consideration of a fine).

(8) The Commissioners may direct—

(a) that subsection (6) above shall not apply to dispositions of land held by or in trust for a charity or class of charities (whether generally or only in the case of a specified class of dispositions or land, or otherwise as may be provided in the direction), or
(b) that that subsection shall not apply to a particular disposition of land held by or in trust for a charity,

if, on an application made to them in writing by or on behalf of the charity or charities in question, the Commissioners are satisfied that it would be in the interests of the charity or charities for them to give the direction.

(9) The restrictions on disposition imposed by this section apply notwithstanding anything in the trusts of a charity; but nothing in this section applies—

(a) to any disposition for which general or special authority is expressly given (without the authority being made subject to the sanction of an order of the court) by any statutory provision contained in or having effect under an Act of Parliament or by any scheme legally established; or
(b) to any disposition of land held by or in trust for a charity which—
(i) is made to another charity otherwise than for the best price that can reasonably be obtained, and
(ii) is authorised to be so made by the trusts of the first-mentioned charity; or

(c) to the granting, by or on behalf of a charity and in accordance with its trusts, of a lease to any beneficiary under those trusts where the lease—

(i) is granted otherwise than for the best rent that can reasonably be obtained; and

(ii) is intended to enable the demised premises to be occupied for the purposes, or any particular purposes, of the charity.

(10) Nothing in this section applies—

(a) to any disposition of land held by or in trust for an exempt charity;

(b) to any disposition of land by way of mortgage or other security; or

(c) to any disposition of an advowson.

(11) In this section "land" means land in England or Wales.

**Supplementary provisions relating to dispositions**

37.—(1) Any of the following instruments, namely—

(a) any contract for the sale, or for a lease or other disposition, of land which is held by or in trust for a charity, and

(b) any conveyance, transfer, lease or other instrument effecting a disposition of such land,

shall state—

(i) that the land is held by or in trust for a charity,

(ii) whether the charity is an exempt charity and whether the disposition is one falling within paragraph (a), (b) or (c) of subsection (9) of section 36 above, and

(iii) if it is not an exempt charity and the disposition is not one falling within any of those paragraphs, that the land is land to which the restrictions on disposition imposed by that section apply.

(2) Where any land held by or in trust for a charity is sold, leased or otherwise disposed of by a disposition to which subsection (1) or (2) of section 36 above applies, the charity trustees shall certify in the instrument by which the disposition is effected—

(a) (where subsection (1) of that section applies) that the disposition has been sanctioned by an order of the court or of the Commissioners (as the case may be), or

(b) (where subsection (2) of that section applies) that the charity trustees have power under the trusts of the charity to effect the disposition, and that they have complied with the provisions of that section so far as applicable to it.

(3) Where subsection (2) above has been complied with in relation to any disposition of land, then in favour of a person who (whether under the disposition or afterwards) acquires an interest in the land for money or money's worth, it shall be conclusively presumed that the facts were as stated in the certificate.

(4) Where—

(a) any land held by or in trust for a charity is sold, leased or otherwise disposed of by a disposition to which subsection (1) or (2) of section 36 above applies, but

(b) subsection (2) above has not been complied with in relation to the disposition,

then in favour of a person who (whether under the disposition or afterwards) in good faith acquires an interest in the land for money or money's worth, the disposition shall be valid whether or not—

(i) the disposition has been sanctioned by an order of the court or of the Commissioners, or

(ii) the charity trustees have power under the trusts of the charity to effect the disposition and have complied with the provisions of that section so far as applicable to it.

(5) Any of the following instruments, namely—

(a) any contract for the sale, or for a lease or other disposition, of land which will, as a result of the disposition, be held by or in trust for a charity, and

(b) any conveyance, transfer, lease or other instrument effecting a disposition of such land,

shall state—

(i) that the land will, as a result of the disposition, be held by or in trust for a charity,

(ii) whether the charity is an exempt charity, and

(iii) if it is not an exempt charity, that the restrictions on disposition imposed by section 36 above will apply to the land (subject to subsection (9) of that section).

(6) In section 29(1) of the Settled Land Act 1925 (charitable and public trusts)—

(a) the requirement for a conveyance of land held on charitable ecclesiastical or public trusts to state that it is held on such trusts shall not apply to any instrument to which subsection (1) above applies; and

(b) the requirement imposed on a purchaser, in the circumstances mentioned in section 29(1) of that Act, to see that any consents or orders requisite for authorising a transaction have been obtained shall not apply in relation to any disposition in relation to which subsection (2) above has been complied with;

and expressions used in this subsection which are also used in that Act have the same meaning as in that Act.

(7) Where—

(a) the disposition to be effected by any such instrument as is mentioned in subsection (1)(b) of (5)(b) above will be registered disposition, or

(b) any such instrument will on taking effect be an instrument to which section 123(1) of the Land Registration Act 1925 (compulsory registration of title) applies, the statement which, by virtue of subsection (1) or (5) above, is to be contained in the instrument shall be in such form as may be prescribed.

(8) Where—

    (a) an application duly made—
        (i) for registration of a disposition of registered land, or
        (ii) for registration of a person's title under a disposition of unregistered land, and
    (b) the instrument by which the disposition is effected contains a statement complying with subsections (5) and (7) above, and
    (c) the charity by or in trust for which the land is held as a result of the disposition is not an exempt charity,

the registrar shall enter in the register, in respect of the land, a restriction in such form as may be prescribed.

(9) Where—

    (a) any such restriction is entered in the register in respect of any land, and
    (b) the charity by or in trust for which the land is held becomes an exempt charity,

the charity trustees shall apply to the registrar for the restriction to be withdrawn; and on receiving any application duly made under this subsection the registrar shall withdraw the restriction.

(10) Where—

    (a) any registered land is held by or in trust for an exempt charity and the charity ceases to be an exempt charity, or
    (b) any registered land becomes, as a result of a declaration of trust by the registered proprietor, land held in trust for a charity (other than an exempt charity),

the charity trustees shall apply to the registrar for such a restriction as is mentioned in subsection (8) above to be entered in the register in respect of the land; and on receiving any application duly made under this subsection the registrar shall enter such a restriction in the register in respect of the land.

(11) In this section—

    (a) references to a disposition of land do not include references to—
        (i) a disposition of land by way of mortgage or other security,
        (ii) any disposition of an advowson, or
        (iii) any release of a rentcharge falling within section 40(1) below; and
    (b) "land" means land in England or Wales;

and subsections (7) to (10) above shall be construed as one with the Land Registration Act 1925.

**Restrictions on mortgaging**     **38.**—(1) Subject to subsection (2) below, no mortgage of land held by or in trust for a charity shall be granted without an order of the court or of the Commissioners.

(2) Subsection (1) above shall not apply to a mortgage of any such land by way of security for the repayment of a loan where the charity trustees have, before executing the mortgage, obtained and considered proper advice, given to them in writing, on the matters mentioned in subsection (3) below.

(3) Those matters are—

(a) whether the proposed loan is necessary in order for the charity trustees to be able to pursue the particular course of action in connection with which the loan is sought by them;

(b) whether the terms of the proposed loan are reasonable having regard to the status of the charity as a prospective borrower; and

(c) the ability of the charity to repay on those terms the sum proposed to be borrowed.

(4) For the purposes of subsection (2) above proper advice is the advice of a person—

(a) who is reasonably believed by the charity trustees to be qualified by his ability in and practical experience of financial matters; and

(b) who has no financial interest in the making of the loan in question;

and such advice may constitute proper advice for those purposes notwithstanding that the person giving it does so in the course of his employment as an officer or employee of the charity or of the charity trustees.

(5) This section applies notwithstanding anything in the trusts of a charity; but nothing in this section applies to any mortgage for which general or special authority is given as mentioned in section 36(9)(a) above.

(6) In this section—

"land" means land in Europe or Wales;
"mortgage" includes a charge.

(7) Nothing in this section applies to an exempt charity.

**Supplementary provisions relating to mortgaging**

39.—(1) Any mortgage of land held by or in trust for a charity shall state—

(a) that the land is held by or in trust for a charity,

(b) whether the charity is an exempt charity and whether the mortgage is one falling within subsection (5) of section 38 above, and

(c) if it is not an exempt charity and the mortgage is not one falling within that subsection, that the mortgage is one to which the restrictions imposed by that section apply;

and where the mortgage will be a registered disposition any such statement shall be in such form as may be prescribed.

(2) Where subsection (1) or (2) of section 38 above applies to any mortgage of land held by or in trust for a charity, the charity trustees shall certify in the mortgage—

(a) (where subsection (1) of that section applies) that the mortgage has been sanctioned by an order of the court or of the Commissioners (as the case may be), or

(b) (where subsection (2) of that section applies) that the charity trustees have power under the trusts of the charity to grant the mortgage, and that they have obtained and considered such advice as is mentioned in that subsection.

(3) Where subsection (2) above has been complied with in relation to any mortgage, then in favour of a person who (whether under the mortgage or afterwards) acquires an interest in the land in question for money or money's worth, it shall be conclusively presumed that the facts were as stated in the certificate.

(4) Where—

(a) subsection (1) or (2) of section 38 above applies to any mortgage of land held by or in trust for a charity, but

(b) subsection (2) above has not been complied with in relation to the mortgage,

then in favour of a person who (whether under the mortgage or afterwards) in good faith acquires an interest in the land for money or money's worth, the mortgage shall be valid whether or not—

(i) the mortgage has been sanctioned by an order of the court or of the Commissioners, or

(ii) the charity trustees have power under the trusts of the charity to grant the mortgage and have obtained and considered such advice as is mentioned in subsection (2) of that section.

(5) In section 29(1) of the Settled Land Act 1925 (charitable and public trusts)—

(a) the requirement for a mortgage of land held on charitable, ecclesiastical or public trusts (as a "conveyance" of such land for the purposes of that Act) to state that it is held on such trusts shall not apply to any mortgage to which subsection (1) above applies; and

(b) the requirement imposed on a mortgagee (as a "purchaser" for those purposes), in the circumstances mentioned in section 29(1) of that Act, to see that any consents or orders requisite for authorising a transaction have been obtained shall not apply in relation to any mortgage in relation to which subsection (2) above has been complied with;

and expressions used in this subsection which are also used in that Act have the same meaning as in that Act.

(6) In this section—

"mortgage" includes a charge, and "mortgagee" shall be construed accordingly;

"land" means land in England or Wales;

"prescribed" and "registered disposition" have the same meaning as in the Land Registration Act 1925.

**Release of charity rentcharges**  40.—(1) Section 36(1) above shall not apply to the release by a charity of a rentcharge which is entitled to receive if the release is given in consideration of the payment of an amount which is not less than 10 times the annual amount of the rentcharge.

(2) Where a charity which is entitled to receive a rentcharge releases it in consideration of the payment of an amount not exceeding £500, any costs incurred by the charity in connection with proving its title to the rentcharge shall be recoverable by the charity from the person or persons in whose favour the rentcharge is being released.

(3) Neither section 36(1) or subsection (2) above applies where a rentcharge which a charity is entitled to receive is redeemed under sections 8 to 10 of the Rentcharges Act 1977.

(4) The Secretary of State may by order amend subsection (2) above by substituting a different sum for the sum for the time being specified there.

PART VI

CHARITY ACCOUNTS, REPORTS AND RETURNS

**Duty to keep accounting records**
41.—(1) The charity trustees of a charity shall ensure that accounting records are kept in respect of the charity which are sufficient to show and explain all the charity's transactions, and which are such as to—

(a) disclose at any time, with reasonable accuracy, the financial position of the charity at that time, and

(b) enable the trustees to ensure that, where any statements of accounts are prepared by them under section 42(1) below, those statements of accounts comply with the requirements of regulations under that provision.

(2) The accounting records shall in particular contain—

(a) entries showing from day to day all sums of money received and expended by the charity, and the matters in respect of which the receipt and expenditure takes place; and

(b) a record of the assets and liabilities of the charity.

(3) The charity trustees of a charity shall preserve any accounting records made for the purposes of this section in respect of the charity for at least six years from the end of the financial year of the charity in which they are made.

(4) Where a charity ceases to exist within the period of six years mentioned in subsection (3) above as it applies to any accounting records, the obligation to preserve those records in accordance with that subsection shall continue to be discharged by the last charity trustees of the charity, unless the Commissioners consent in writing to the records being destroyed or otherwise disposed of.

(5) Nothing in this section applies to a charity which is a company.

**Annual statements of accounts**
42.—(1) The charity trustees of a charity shall (subject to subsection (3) below) prepare in respect of each financial year of the charity a statement of account complying with such require-

ments as to its form and contents as may be prescribed by regulations made by the Secretary of State.

(2) Without prejudice to the generality of subsection (1) above, regulations under that subsection may make provision—

   (a) for any such statement to be prepared in accordance with such methods and principles as are specified or referred to in the regulations;

   (b) as to any information to be provided by way of notes to the accounts;

and regulations under that subsection may also make provision for determining the financial years of a charity for the purposes of this Act and any regulations made under it.

(3) Where a charity's gross income in any financial year does not exceed £25,000, the charity trustees may, in respect of that year, elect to prepare the following, namely—

   (a) a receipts and payments account, and

   (b) a statement of assets and liabilities,

instead of a statement of accounts under subsection (1) above.

(4) The charity trustees of a charity shall preserve—

   (a) any statement of accounts prepared by them under subsection (1) above, or

   (b) any account and statement prepared by them under subsection (3) above,

for at least six years from the end of the financial year to which any such statement relates or (as the case may be) to which any such account and statement relate.

(5) Subsection (4) of section 41 above shall apply in relation to the preservation of any such statement or account and statement as it applies in relation to the preservation of any accounting records (the references to subsection (3) of that section being read as references to subsection (4) above).

(6) The Secretary of State may by order amend subsection (3) above by substituting a different sum for the sum for the time being specified there.

(7) Nothing in this section applies to a charity which is a company.

**Annual audit or examination of charity accounts**

43.—(1) Subsection (2) below applies to a financial year of a charity ("the relevant year") if the charity's gross income or total expenditure in any of the following, namely—

   (a) the relevant year,

   (b) the financial year of the charity immediately preceding the relevant year (if any), and

   (c) the financial year of the charity immediately preceding the year specified in paragraph (b) above (if any),

exceeds £100,000.

(2) If this subsection applies to a financial year of a charity, the accounts of the charity for that year shall be audited by a person who—

(a) is, in accordance with section 25 of the Companies Act 1989 (eligibility for appointment), eligible for appointment as a company auditor, or

(b) he is a member of a body for the time being specified in regulations under section 44 below and is under the rules of that body eligible for appointment as auditor of the charity.

(3) If subsection (2) above does not apply to a financial year of a charity, then (subject to subsection (4) below) the accounts of the charity for that year shall, at the election of the charity trustees, either—

(a) be examined by an independent examiner, that is to say an independent person who is reasonably believed by the trustees to have the requisite ability and practical experience to carry out a competent examination of the accounts, or

(b) be audited by such a person as is mentioned in subsection (2) above.

(4) Where it appears to the Commissioners—

(a) that subsection (2), or (as the case may be) subsection (3) above, has not been complied with in relation to a financial year of a charity within 10 months from the end of that year, or

(b) that, although subsection (2) above does not apply to a financial year of a charity, it would nevertheless be desirable for the accounts of the charity for that year to be audited by such a person as is mentioned in that subsection,

the Commissioners may by order require the accounts of the charity for that year to be audited by such a person as is mentioned in that subsection.

(5) If the Commissioners make an order under subsection (4) above with respect to a charity, then unless—

(a) the order is made by virtue of paragraph (b) of that subsection, and

(b) the charity trustees themselves appoint an auditor in accordance with the order,

the auditor shall be a person appointed by the Commissioners.

(6) The expenses of any audit carried out by an auditor appointed by the Commissioners under subsection (5) above, including the auditor's remuneration, shall be recoverable by the Commissioners—

(a) from the charity trustees of the charity concerned, who shall be personally liable, jointly and severally, for those expenses; or

(b) to the extent that it appears to the Commissioners not to be practical to seek recovery of those expenses in accordance with paragraph (a) above, from the funds of the charity.

(7) The Commissioners may—

(*a*) give guidance to charity trustees in connection with the selection of a person for appointment as an independent examiner;

(*b*) give such directions as they think appropriate with respect to the carrying out of an examination in pursuance of subsection (3)(*a*) above;

and any such guidance or directions may either be of general application or apply to a particular charity only.

(8) The Secretary of State may by order amend subsection (1) above by substituting a different sum for the sum for the time being specified there.

(9) Nothing in this section applies to a charity which is a company.

**Supplementary provisions relating to audits, etc.**

44.—(1) The Secretary of State may by regulations make provision—

(*a*) specifying one or more bodies for the purposes of section 43(2)(*b*) above;

(*b*) with respect to the duties of an auditor carrying out an audit under section 43 above, including provision with respect to the making by him of a report on—

   (i) the statement of accounts prepared for the financial year in question under section 42(1) above, or

   (ii) the account and statement so prepared under section 42(3) above,

   as the case may be;

(*c*) with respect to the making by an independent examiner of a report in respect of an examination carried out by him under section 43 above;

(*d*) conferring on such an auditor or on an independent examiner a right of access with respect to books, documents and other records (however kept) which relate to the charity concerned;

(*e*) entitling such an auditor or an independent examiner to require, in the case of a charity, information and explanations from past or present charity trustees or trustees for the charity, or from past or present officers or employees of the charity;

(*f*) enabling the Commissioners, in circumstances specified in the regulations, to dispense with the requirements of section 43(2) or (3) above in the case of a particular charity or in the case of any particular financial year of a charity.

(2) If any person fails to afford an auditor or an independent examiner any facility to which he is entitled by virtue of subsection (1)(*d*) or (*e*) above, the Commissioners may by order give—

(*a*) to that person, or

(*b*) to the charity trustees for the time being of the charity concerned,

such directions as the Commissioners think appropriate for securing that the default is made good.

(3) Section 727 of the Companies Act 1985 (power of court to grant relief in certain cases) shall have effect in relation to an auditor or independent examiner appointed by a charity in pursuance of section 43 above as it has effect in relation to a person employed as auditor by a company within the meaning of that Act.

**Annual reports**

45.—(1) The charity trustees of a charity shall prepare in respect of each financial year of the charity an annual report containing—

(a) such a report by the trustees on the activities of the charity during that year, and
(b) such other information relating to the charity or to its trustees or officers,

as may be prescribed by regulations made by the Secretary of State.

(2) Without prejudice to the generality of subsection (1) above, regulations under that subsection may make provision—

(a) for any such report as is mentioned in paragraph (a) of that subsection to be prepared in accordance with such principles as are specified or referred to in the regulations;
(b) enabling the Commissioners to dispense with any requirement prescribed by virtue of subsection (1)(b) above in the case of a particular charity or a particular class of charities, or in the case of a particular financial year of a charity or of any class of charities.

(3) The annual report required to be prepared under this section in respect of any financial year of a charity shall be transmitted to the Commissioners by the charity trustees—

(a) within 10 months from the end of that year, or
(b) within such longer period as the Commissioners may for any special reason allow in the case of that report.

(4) Subject to subsection (5) below, any such annual report shall have attached to it the statement of accounts prepared for the financial year in question under section 42(1) above or (as the case may be) the account and statement so prepared under section 42(3) above, together with—

(a) where the accounts of the charity for that year have been audited under section 43 above, a copy of the report made by the auditor on that statement of accounts or (as the case may be) on that account and statement;
(b) where the accounts of the charity for that year have been examined under section 43 above, a copy of the report made by the independent examiner in respect of the examination carried out by him under that section.

(5) Subsection (4) above does not apply to a charity which is a company, and any annual report transmitted by the charity trustees of such a charity under subsection (3) above shall instead have attached to it a copy of the charity's annual accounts prepared for the financial year in question under Part VII of the

Companies Act 1985, together with a copy of the auditors' report on those accounts.

(6) Any annual report transmitted to the Commissioners under subsection (3) above, together with the documents attached to it, shall be kept by the Commissioners for such period as they think fit.

**Special provision as respects accounts and annual reports of exempt and other excepted charities**

46.—(1) Nothing in sections 41 to 45 above applies to any exempt charity; but the charity trustees of an exempt charity shall keep proper books of accounts with respect to the affairs of the charity, and if not required by or under the authority of any other Act to prepare periodical statements of account shall prepare consecutive statements of account consisting on each occasion of an income and expenditure account relating to a period of not more than 15 months and a balance sheet relating to the end of that period.

(2) The books of accounts and statements of account relating to an exempt charity shall be preserved for a period of six years at least unless the charity ceases to exist and the Commissioners consent in writing to their being destroyed or otherwise disposed of.

(3) Nothing in sections 43 to 45 above applies to any charity which—

(a) falls within section 3(5)(c) above, and
(b) is not registered.

(4) Except in accordance with subsection (7) below, nothing in section 45 above applies to any charity (other than an exempt charity or a charity which falls within section 3(5)(c) above) which—

(a) is excepted by section 3(5) above, and
(b) is not registered.

(5) If requested to do so by the Commissioners, the charity trustees of any such charity as is mentioned in subsection (4) above shall prepare an annual report in respect of such financial year of the charity as is specified in the Commissioners' request.

(6) Any report prepared under subsection (5) above shall contain—

(a) such a report by the charity trustees on the activities of the charity during the year in question, and
(b) such other information relating to the charity or to its trustees or officers,

as may be prescribed by regulations made under section 45(1) above in relation to annual reports prepared under that provision.

(7) Subsections (3) to (6) of section 45 above shall apply to any report required to be prepared under subsection (5) above as if it were an annual report required to be prepared under subsection (1) of that section.

(8) Any reference in this section to a charity which falls within section 3(5)(c) above includes a reference to a charity which falls within that provision but is also excepted from registration by section 3(5)(b) above.

**Public inspection of annual reports, etc.**

47.—(1) Any annual report or other document kept by the Commissioners in pursuance of section 45(6) above shall be open to public inspection at all reasonable times—

(a) during the period for which it is so kept; or

(b) if the Commissioners so determine, during such lesser period as they may specify.

(2) Where any person—

(a) requests the charity trustees of a charity in writing to provide him with a copy of the charity's most recent accounts, and

(b) pays them such reasonable fee (if any) as they may require in respect of the costs of complying with the request,

those trustees shall comply with the request within the period of two months beginning with the date on which it is made.

(3) In subsection (2) above the reference to a charity's most recent accounts is—

(a) in the case of a charity other than one falling within any of paragraphs (b) to (d) below, a reference to the statement of accounts or account and statement prepared in pursuance of section 42(1) or (3) above in respect of the last financial year of the charity the accounts for which have been audited or examined under section 43 above;

(b) in the case of such a charity as is mentioned in section 46(3) above, a reference to the statement of accounts or account and statement prepared in pursuance of section 42(1) or (3) above in respect of the last financial year of the charity in respect of which a statement of accounts or account and statement has or have been so prepared;

(c) in the case of a charity which is a company, a reference to the annual accounts of the company most recently audited under Part VII of the Companies Act 1985; and

(d) in the case of an exempt charity, a reference to the accounts of the charity most recently audited in pursuance of any statutory or other requirement or, if its accounts are not required to be audited, the accounts most recently prepared in respect of the charity.

**Annual returns by registered charities**

48.—(1) Every registered charity shall prepare in respect of each of its financial years an annual return in such form, and containing such information, as may be prescribed by regulations made by the Commissioners.

(2) Any such return shall be transmitted to the Commissioners by the date by which the charity trustees are, by virtue of section 45(3) above, required to transmit to them the annual report required to be prepared in respect of the financial year in question.

(3) The Commissioners may dispense with the requirements of subsection (1) above in the case of a particular charity or a particular class of charities, or in the case of a particular financial year of a charity or of any class of charities.

**Offences**        49. Any person who, without reasonable excuse, is persistently in default in relation to any requirement imposed—

(a)  by section 45(3) above (taken with section 45(4) or (5), as the case may require), or

(b)  by section 47(2) or 48(2) above,

shall be guilty of an offence and liable on summary conviction to a fine not exceeding level 4 on the standard scale.

## PART VII

### INCORPORATION OF CHARITY TRUSTEES

**Incorporation of trustees of a charity**        50.—(1) Where—

(a)  the trustees of a charity, in accordance with section 52 below, apply to the Commissioners for a certificate of incorporation of the trustees as a body corporate, and

(b)  the Commissioners consider that the incorporation of the trustees would be in the interests of the charity,

the Commissioners may grant such a certificate, subject to such conditions or directions as they think fit to insert in it.

(2) The Commissioners shall not, however, grant such a certificate in a case where the charity appears to them to be required to be registered under section 3 above but is not so registered.

(3) On the grant of such a certificate—

(a)  the trustees of the charity shall become a body corporate by such name as is specified in the certificate; and

(b)  (without prejudice to the operation of section 54 below) any relevant rights or liabilities of those trustees shall become rights or liabilities of that body.

(4) After the incorporation the trustees—

(a)  may sue and be sued in their corporate name; and

(b)  shall have the same powers, as respects the holding, acquisition and disposal of property for or in connection with the purposes of the charity as they had or were subject to while unincorporated;

and any relevant legal proceedings that might have been continued or commenced by or against the trustees may be continued or commenced by or against them in their corporate name.

(5) A body incorporated under this section need not have a common seal.

(6) In this section—

"relevant rights or liabilities" means rights or liabilities in connection with any property vesting in the body in question under section 51 below; and

"relevant legal proceedings" means legal proceedings in connection with any such property.

**Estate to vest in body corporate**

**51.** The certificate of incorporation shall vest in the body corporate all real and personal estate, of whatever nature or tenure, belonging to or held by any person or persons in trust for the charity, and thereupon any person or persons in whose name or names any stocks, funds or securities are standing in trust for the charity, shall transfer them into the name of the body corporate, except that the foregoing provisions shall not apply to property vested in the official custodian.

**Applications for incorporation**

**52.**—(1) Every application to the Commissioners for a certificate of incorporation under this Part of this Act shall—

(a) be in writing and signed by the trustees of the charity concerned; and

(b) be accompanied by such documents or information as the Commissioners may require for the purpose of the application.

(2) The Commissioners may require—

(a) any statement contained in any such application, or

(b) any document or information supplied under subsection (1)(b) above,

to be verified in such manner as they may specify.

**Nomination of trustees, and filling up vacancies**

**53.**—(1) Before a certificate of incorporation is granted under this Part of this Act, trustees of the charity must have been effectually appointed to the satisfaction of the Commissioners.

(2) Where a certificate of incorporation is granted vacancies in the number of the trustees of the charity shall from time to time be filled up so far as required by the constitution or settlement of the charity, or by any conditions or directions in the certificate, by such legal means as would have been available for the appointment of new trustees of the charity if no certificate of incorporation had been granted, or otherwise as required by such conditions or directions.

**Liability of trustees and others, notwithstanding incorporation**

**54.** After a certificate of incorporation has been granted under this Part of this Act all trustees of the charity, notwithstanding their incorporation, shall be chargeable for such property as shall come into their hands, and shall be answerable and accountable for their own acts, receipts, neglects, and defaults, and for the due administration of the charity and its property, in the same manner and to the same extent as if no such incorporation had been effected.

**Certificate to be evidence of compliance with requirements for incorporation**

**55.** A certificate of incorporation granted under this Part of this Act shall be conclusive evidence that all the preliminary requirements for incorporation under this Part of this Act have been complied with, and the date of incorporation mentioned in the certificate shall be deemed to be the date at which incorporation has taken place.

**Power of Commissioners to amend certificate of incorporation**

**56.**—(1) The Commissioners may amend a certificate of incorporation either on the application of the incorporated body to which it relates or of their own motion.

(2) Before making any such amendment of their own motion, the Commissioners shall by notice in writing—

(a) inform the trustees of the relevant charity of their proposals, and

(b) invite those trustees to make representations to them within a time specified in the notice, being not less than one month from the date of the notice.

(3) The Commissioners shall take into consideration any representations made by those trustees within the time so specified, and may then (without further notice) proceed with their proposals either without modification or with such modifications as appear to them to be desirable.

(4) The Commissioners may amend a certificate of incorporation either—

(a) by making an order specifying the amendment; or

(b) by issuing a new certificate of incorporation taking account of the amendment.

**Records of applications and certificates**

57.—(1) The Commissioners shall keep a record of all applications for, and certificates of, incorporation under this Part of this Act and shall preserve all documents sent to them under this Part of this Act.

(2) Any person may inspect such documents, under the direction of the Commissioners, and any person may require a copy or extract of any such document to be certified by a certificate signed by the secretary of the Commissioners.

**Enforcement of orders and directions**

58. All conditions and directions inserted in any certificate of incorporation shall be binding upon and performed or observed by the trustees as trusts of the charity, and section 88 below shall apply to any trustee who fails to perform or observe any such condition or direction as it applies to a person guilty of disobedience to any such order of the Commissioners as is mentioned in that section.

**Gifts to charity before incorporation to have same effect afterwards**

59. After the incorporation of the trustees of any charity under this Part of this Act every donation, gift and disposition of property, real or personal, lawfully made before the incorporation but not having actually taken effect, or thereafter lawfully made, by deed, will or otherwise to or in favour of the charity, or the trustees of the charity, or otherwise for the purposes of the charity, shall take effect as if made to or in favour of the incorporated body or otherwise for the like purposes.

**Execution of documents by incorporated body**

60.—(1) This section has effect as respects the execution of documents by an incorporated body.

(2) If an incorporated body has a common seal, a document may be executed by the body by the affixing of its common seal.

(3) Whether or not it has a common seal, a document may be executed by an incorporated body either—

(a) by being signed by a majority of the trustees of the relevant charity and expressed (in whatever form of words) to be executed by the body; or

(b) by being executed in pursuance of an authority given under subsection (4) below.

(4) For the purposes of subsection (3)(b) above the trustees of the relevant charity in the case of an incorporated body may,

subject to the trusts of the charity, confer on any two or more of their number—

(*a*) a general authority, or

(*b*) an authority limited in such manner as the trustees think fit,

to execute in the name and on behalf of the body documents for giving effect to transactions to which the body is a party.

(5) An authority under subsection (4) above—

(*a*) shall suffice for any document if it is given in writing or by resolution of a meeting of the trustees of the relevant charity, notwithstanding the want of any formality that would be required in giving an authority apart from that subsection;

(*b*) may be given so as to make the powers conferred exercisable by any of the trustees, or may be restricted to named persons or in any other way;

(*c*) subject to any such restriction, and until it is revoked, shall, notwithstanding any change in the trustees of the relevant charity, have effect as a continuing authority given by the trustees from time to time of the charity and exercisable by such trustees.

(6) In any authority under subsection (4) above to execute a document in the name and on behalf of an incorporated body there shall, unless the contrary intention appears, be implied authority also to execute it for the body in the name and on behalf of the official custodian or of any other person, in any case in which the trustees could do so.

(7) A document duly executed by an incorporated body which makes it clear on its face that it is intended by the person or persons making it to be a deed has effect, upon delivery, as a deed; and it shall be presumed, unless a contrary intention is proved, to be delivered upon its being so executed.

(8) In favour of a purchaser a document shall be deemed to have been duly executed by such a body if it purports to be signed—

(*a*) by a majority of the trustees of the relevant charity, or

(*b*) by such of the trustees of the relevant charity as are authorised by the trustees of that charity to execute it in the name and on behalf of the body,

and, where the document makes it clear on its face that it is intended by the person or persons making it to be a deed, it shall be deemed to have been delivered upon its being executed.

For this purpose "purchaser" means a purchaser in good faith for valuable consideration and includes a lessee, mortgagee or other person who for valuable consideration acquires an interest in property.

**Power of Commissioners to dissolve incorporated body**

61.—(1) Where the Commissioners are satisfied—

(*a*) that an incorporated body has no assets or does not operate, or

(*b*) that the relevant charity in the case of an incorporated body has ceased to exist, or

(c) that the institution previously constituting, or treated by them as constituting, any such charity has cased to be, or (as the case may be) was not at the time of the body's incorporation, a charity, or

(d) that the purposes of the relevant charity in the case of an incorporated body have been achieved so far as is possible or are in practice incapable of being achieved,

they may of their own motion make an order dissolving the body as from such date as is specified in the order.

(2) Where the Commissioners are satisfied, on the application of the trustees of the relevant charity in the case of an incorporated body, that it would be in the interests of the charity for that body to be dissolved, the Commissioners may make an order dissolving the body as from such date as is specified in the order.

(3) Subject to subsection (4) below, an order made under this section with respect to an incorporated body shall have the effect of vesting in the trustees of the relevant charity, in trust for that charity, all property for the time being vested—

(a) in the body, or

(b) in any other person (apart from the official custodian),

in trust for that charity.

(4) If the Commissioners so direct in the order—

(a) all or any specified part of that property shall, instead of vesting in the trustees of the relevant charity, vest—
  (i) in a specified person as trustee for, or nominee of, that charity, or
  (ii) in such persons (other than the trustees of the relevant charity) as may be specified;

(b) any specified investments, or any specified class or description of investments, held by any person in trust for the relevant charity shall be transferred—
  (i) to the trustees of that charity, or
  (ii) to any such person or persons as is or are mentioned in paragraph (a)(i) or (ii) above;

and for this purpose "specified" means specified by the Commissioners in the order.

(5) Where an order to which this subsection applies is made with respect to an incorporated body—

(a) any rights or liabilities of the body shall become rights or liabilities of the trustees of the relevant charity; and

(b) any legal proceedings that might have been continued or commenced by or against the body may be continued or commenced by or against those trustees.

(6) Subsection (5) above applies to any order under this section by virtue of which—

(a) any property vested as mentioned in subsection (3) above is vested—
  (i) in the trustees of the relevant charity, or
  (ii) in any person as trustee for, or nominee of, that charity; or

(*b*) any investments held by any person in trust for the relevant charity are required to be transferred—

    (i) to the trustees of that charity, or

    (ii) to any person as trustee for, or nominee of, that charity.

(7) Any order made by the Commissioners under this section may be varied or revoked by a further order so made.

**Interpretation of Part VII**

**62.** In this Part of this Act—

"incorporated body" means a body incorporated under section 50 above;

"the relevant charity", in relation to an incorporated body, means the charity the trustees of which have been incorporated as that body;

"the trustees", in relation to a charity, means the charity trustees.


PART VIII

CHARITABLE COMPANIES

**Winding up**

**63.**—(1) Where a charity may be wound up by the High Court under the Insolvency Act 1986, a petition for it to be wound up under that Act by any court in England or Wales having jurisdiction may be presented by the Attorney General, as well as by any person authorised by that Act.

(2) Where a charity may be so wound up by the High Court, such a petition may also be presented by the Commissioners if, at any time after they have instituted an inquiry under section 8 above with respect to the charity, they are satisfied as mentioned in section 18(1)(*a*) or (*b*) above.

(3) Where a charitable company is dissolved, the Commissioners may make an application under section 651 of the Companies Act 1985 (power of court to declare dissolution of company void) for an order to be made under that section with respect to the company; and for this purpose subsection (1) of that section shall have effect in relation to a charitable company as if the reference to the liquidator of the company included a reference to the Commissioners.

(4) Where a charitable company's name has been struck off the register of companies under section 652 of the Companies Act 1985 (power of registrar to strike defunct company off register), the Commissioners may make an application under section 653(2) of that Act (objection to striking off by person aggrieved) for an order restoring the company's name to that register; and for this purpose section 653(2) shall have effect in relation to a charitable company as if the reference to any such person aggrieved as is there mentioned included a reference to the Commissioners.

(5) The powers exercisable by the Commissioners by virtue of this section shall be exercisable by them of their own motion,

but shall be exercisable only with the agreement of the Attorney General on each occasion.

(6) In this section "charitable company" means a company which is a charity.

**Alteration of objects clause**

64.—(1) Where a charity is a company or other body corporate having power to alter the instruments establishing or regulating it as a body corporate, no exercise of that power which has the effect of the body ceasing to be a charity shall be valid so as to affect the application of—

(a) any property acquired under any disposition or agreement previously made otherwise than for full consideration in money or money's worth, or any property representing property so acquired,

(b) any property representing income which has accrued before the alteration is made, or

(c) the income from any such property as aforesaid.

(2) Where a charity is a company, any alteration by it—

(a) of the objects clause in its memorandum of association, or

(b) of any other provision in its memorandum of association, or any provision in its articles of association, which is a provision directing or restricting the manner in which property of the company may be used or applied,

is ineffective without the prior written consent of the Commissioners.

(3) Where a company has made any such alteration in accordance with subsection (2) above and—

(a) in connection with the alteration is required by virtue of—

(i) section 6(1) of the Companies Act 1985 (delivery of documents following alteration of objects), or

(ii) that provision as applied by section 17(3) of that Act (alteration of condition in memorandum which could have been contained in articles), to deliver to the registrar of companies a printed copy of its memorandum, as altered, or

(b) is required by virtue of section 380(1) of that Act (registration etc. of resolutions and agreements) to forward to the registrar a printed or other copy of the special resolution effecting the alteration,

the copy so delivered or forwarded by the company shall be accompanied by a copy of the Commissioner's consent.

(4) Section 6(3) of that Act (offences) shall apply to any default by a company in complying with subsection (3) above as it applies to any such default as is mentioned in that provision.

**Invalidity of certain transactions**

65.—(1) Sections 35 and 35A of the Companies Act 1985 (capacity of company not limited by its memorandum; power of directors to bind company) do not apply to the acts of a company which is a charity except in favour of a person who—

(a) gives full consideration in money or money's worth in relation to the act in question, and

(b) does not know that the act is not permitted by the company's memorandum or, as the case may be, is beyond the powers of the directors,

or who does not know at the time the act is done that the company is a charity.

(2) However, where such a company purports to transfer or grant an interest in property, the fact that the act was not permitted by the company's memorandum or, as the case may be, that the directors in connection with the act exceeded any limitation on their powers under the company's constitution, does not affect the title of a person who subsequently acquires the property or any interest in it for full consideration without actual notice of any such circumstances affecting the validity of the company's act.

(3) In any proceedings arising out of subsection (1) above the burden of proving—

(a) that a person knew that an act was not permitted by the company's memorandum or was beyond the powers of the directors, or

(b) that a person knew that the company was a charity,

lies on the person making the allegation.

(4) Where a company is a charity, the ratification of an act under section 35(3) of the Companies Act 1985, or the ratification of a transaction to which section 322A of that Act applies (invalidity of certain transactions to which directors or their associates are parties), is ineffective without the prior written consent of the Commissioners.

**Requirement of consent of Commissioners to certain acts**

66.—(1) Where a company is a charity—

(a) any approval given by the company for the purposes of any of the provisions of the Companies Act 1985 specified in subsection (2) below, and

(b) any affirmation by it for the purposes of section 322(2)(c) of that Act (affirmation of voidable arrangements under which assets are acquired by or from a director or person connected with him),

is ineffective without the prior written consent of the Commissioners.

(2) The provisions of the Companies Act 1985 referred to in subsection (1)(a) above are—

(a) section 312 (payment to director in respect of loss of office or retirement);

(b) section 313(1) (payment to director in respect of loss of office or retirement made in connection with transfer of undertaking or property of company);

(c) section 319(3) (incorporation in director's service contract of term whereby his employment will or may continue for a period of more than five years);

(d) section 320(1) (arrangement whereby assets are acquired by or from director or person connected with him);

(e)  section 337(3)(a) (provision of funds to meet certain expenses incurred by director).

**Name to appear on correspondence, etc.**

67. Section 30(7) of the Companies Act 1985 (exemption from requirements relating to publication of name etc.) shall not, in its application to any company which is a charity, have the effect of exempting the company from the requirements of section 349(1) of that Act (company's name to appear in its correspondence etc.)

**Status to appear on correspondence, etc.**

68.—(1) Where a company is a charity and its name does not include the word "charity" or the word "charitable", the fact that the company is a charity shall be stated in English in legible characters—

(a)  in all business letters of the company,
(b)  in all its notices and other official publications,
(c)  in all bills of exchange, promissory notes, endorsements, cheques and orders for money or goods purporting to be signed on behalf of the company,
(d)  in all conveyances purporting to be executed by the company, and
(d)  in all bills rendered by it and in all its invoices, receipts, and letters of credit.

(2) In subsection (1)(d) above "conveyance" means any instrument creating, transferring, varying or extinguishing an interest in land.

(3) Subsections (2) to (4) of section 349 of the Companies Act 1985 (offences in connection with failure to include required particulars in business letters etc.) shall apply in relation to a contravention of subsection (1) above, taking the reference in subsection (3)(b) of that section to a bill of parcels as a reference to any such bill as is mentioned in subsection (1)(e) above.

**Investigation of accounts**

69.—(1) In the case of a charity which is a company the commissioners may by order require that the condition and accounts of the charity for such period as they think fit shall be investigated and audited by an auditor appointed by them, being a person eligible for appointment as a company auditor under section 25 of the Companies Act 1989.

(2) An auditor acting under subsection (1) above—

(a)  shall have a right of access to all books, accounts and documents relating to the charity which are in the possession or control of the charity trustees or to which the charity trustees have access;
(b)  shall be entitled to require from any charity trustee, past or present, and from any past or present officer or employee of the charity such information and explanation as he thinks necessary for the performance of his duties;
(c)  shall at the conclusion or during the progress of the audit make such reports to the Commissioners above the audit or about the accounts or affairs of the charity as he thinks the case requires, and shall send a copy of any such report to the charity trustees.

(3) The expenses of any audit under subsection (1) above, including the remuneration of the auditor, shall be paid by the Commissioners.

(4) If any person fails to afford an auditor any facility to which he is entitled under subsection (2) above the Commissioners may by order give to that person or to the charity trustees for the time being such directions as the Commissioners think appropriate for securing that the default is made good.

## PART IX

### MISCELLANEOUS

#### *Powers of investment*

**Relaxation of restrictions on wider-range investments** 70.—(1) The Secretary of State may by order made with the consent of the Treasury—

 (*a*) direct that, in the case of a trust fund consisting of property held by or in trust for a charity, any division of the fund in pursuance of section 2(1) of the Trustee Investments Act 1961 (trust funds to be divided so that wider-range and narrower-range investments are equal in value) shall be made so that the value of the wider-range part the time of the division bears to the then value of the narrower-range part such properties as is specified in the order;

 (*b*) provide that, in its application in relation to such a trust fund, that Act shall have effect subject to such modifications so specified as the Secretary of State considers appropriate in consequence of, or in connection with, any such direction.

(2) Where, before the coming into force of an order under this section, a trust fund consisting of property held by or in trust for a charity has already been divided in pursuance of section 2(1) of that Act, the fund may, notwithstanding anything in that provision, be again divided (once only) in pursuance of that provision during the continuance in force of the order.

(3) No order shall be made under this section unless a draft of the order has been laid before and approved by a resolution of each House of Parliament.

(4) Expressions used in this section which are also used in the Trustee Investments Act 1961 have the same meaning as in that Act.

(5) In the application of this section to Scotland, "charity" means a recognised body with the meaning of section 1(7) of the Law Reform (Miscellaneous Provisions) (Scotland) Act 1990.

**Extension of powers of investment** 71.—(1) The Secretary of State may by regulations made with the consent of the Treasury make, with respect to property held by or in trust for a charity, provision authorising a trustee to invest such property in a manner specified in the regulations, being a manner of investment not for the time being included in any Part of Schedule 1 to the Trustee Investments Act 1961.

(2) Regulations under this section may make such provision—

(*a*) regulating the investment of property in any manner authorised by virtue of subsection (1) above, and

(*b*) with respect to the variation and retention of investments so made,

as the Secretary of State considers appropriate.

(3) Such regulations may, in particular, make provision—

(*a*) imposing restrictions with respect to the proportion of the property held by or in trust for a charity which may be invested in any manner authorised by virtue of subsection (1) above, being either restrictions applying to investment in any such manner generally or restrictions applying to investment in any particular such manner;

(*b*) imposing the like requirements with respect to the obtaining and consideration of advice as are imposed by any of the provisions of section 6 of the Trustee Investments Act 1961 (duty of trustees in choosing investments).

(4) Any power of investment conferred by any regulations under this section—

(*a*) shall be in addition to, and not in derogation from, any power conferred otherwise than by such regulations; and

(*b*) shall not be limited by the trusts of a charity (in so far as they are not contained in any Act or instrument made under an enactment) unless it is excluded by those trusts in express terms;

but any such power shall only be exercisable by a trustee in so far as a contrary intention is not expressed in any Act or in any instrument made under an enactment and relating to the powers of the trustee.

(5) No regulations shall be made under this section unless a draft of the regulations has been laid before and approved by a resolution of each House of Parliament.

(6) In this section "property"—

(*a*) in England and Wales, means real or personal property of any description, including money and things in action, but does not include an interest in expectancy; and

(*b*) in Scotland, means property of any description (whether heritable or moveable, corporeal or incorporeal) which is presently enjoyable, but does not include a future interest, whether vested or contingent;

and any reference to property held by or in trust for a charity is a reference to property so held, whether it is for the time being in a state of investment or not.

(7) In application of this section to Scotland, "charity" means a recognised body within the meaning of section 1(7) of

the Law Reform (Miscellaneous Provisions) (Scotland) Act
1990.

*Disqualification for acting as charity trustee*

**Persons**
**disqualified for**
**being trustees of**
**a charity**

72.—(1) Subject to the following provisions of this section, a
person shall be disqualified for being a charity trustee or trustee
for a charity if—

(a)  he has been convicted of any offence involving dishonesty or deception;

(b)  he has been adjudged bankrupt or sequestration of his
estate has been awarded and (in either case) he has not
been discharged;

(c)  he has made a composition or arrangement with, or
granted a trust deed for, his creditors and has not been
discharged in respect of it;

(d)  he has been removed from the office of charity trustee or
trustee for a charity by an order made—

(i)  by the Commissioners under section 18(2)(i)
above, or

(ii)  by the Commissioners under section 20(1A)(i) of
the Charities Act 1960 (power to act for protection
of charities) or under section 20(1)(i) of that Act
(as in force before the commencement of section 8
of the Charities Act 1992), or

(iii)  by the High Court,

on the grounds of any misconduct or mismanagement in
the administration of the charity for which he was
responsible or to which he was privy, or which he by his
conduct contributed to or facilitated;

(e)  he has been removed, under section 7 of the Law Reform
(Miscellaneous Provisions) (Scotland) Act 1990 (powers of
Court of Session to deal with management of charities), from
being concerned in the management or control of any body;

(f)  he is subject to a disqualification order under the Company
Directors Disqualification Act 1986 or to an order made
under section 429(2)(b) of the Insolvency Act 1986 (failure
to pay under county court administration order).

(2) In subsection (1) above—

(a)  paragraph (a) applies whether the conviction occurred
before or after the commencement of that subsection,
but does not apply in relation to any conviction which is
a spent conviction for the purposes of the Rehabilitation
of Offenders Act 1974;

(b)  paragraph (b) applies whether the adjudication of bankruptcy or the sequestration occurred before or after the
commencement of that subsection;

(c)  paragraph (c) applies whether the composition or arrangement was made, or the trust deed was granted,
before or after the commencement of that subsection;
and

(*d*)  paragraphs (*d*) to (*f*) apply in relation to orders made and removals effected before or after the commencement of that subsection.

(3) Where (apart from this subsection) a person is disqualified under subsection (1)(*b*) above for being a charity trustee or trustee for any charity which is a company, he shall not be so disqualified if leave has been granted under section 11 of the Company Directors Disqualification Act 1986 (undischarged bankrupts) for him to act as director of the charity; and similarly a person shall not be disqualified under subsection (1)(*f*) above for being a charity trustee or trustee for such a charity if—

(*a*)in the case of a person subject to a disqualification order, leave under the order has been granted for him to act as director of the charity, or
(*b*)  in the case of a person subject to an order under section 429(2)(*b*) of the Insolvency Act 1986, leave has been granted by the court which made the order for him to so act.

(4) The Commissioners may, on the application of any person disqualified under subsection (1) above, waive his disqualification either generally or in relation to a particular charity or a particular class of charities; but no such waiver may be granted in relation to any charity which is a company if—

(*a*)  the person concerned is for the time being prohibited, by virtue of—
  (i) a disqualification order under the Company Directors Disqualification Act 1986, or
  (ii) section 11(1) or 12(2) of that Act (undischarged bankrupts; failure to pay under county court administration order),
  from acting as director of the charity; and
(*b*)  leave has not been granted for him to act as director of any other company.

(5) Any waiver under subsection (4) above shall be notified in writing to the person concerned.
(6) For the purposes of this section the Commissioners shall keep, in such manner as they think fit, a register of all persons who have been removed from office as mentioned in subsection (1)(*d*) above either—

(*a*)  by an order of the Commissioners made before or after the commencement of subsection (1) above, or
(*b*)  by an order of the High Court made after the commencement of section 45(1) of the Charities Act 1992;

and, where any person is so removed from office by an order of the High Court, the court shall notify the Commissioners of his removal.
(7) The entries in the register kept under subsection (6) above shall be available for public inspection in legible form at all reasonable times.

**Person acting as charity trustee while disqualified**

73.—(1) Subject to subsection (2) below, any person who acts as a charity trustee or trustee for a charity while he is disqualified for being such a trustee by virtue of section 72 above shall be guilty of an offence and liable—

(a) on summary conviction, to imprisonment for a term not exceeding six months or to a fine not exceeding the statutory maximum, or both;

(b) on conviction on indictment, to imprisonment for a term not exceeding two years or to a fine, or both.

(2) Subsection (1) above shall not apply where—

(a) the charity concerned is a company; and

(b) the disqualified person is disqualified by virtue only of paragraph (b) or (f) of section 72(1) above.

(3) Any acts done as charity trustee or trustee for a charity by a person disqualified for being such a trustee by virtue of section 72 above shall not be invalid by reason only of that disqualification.

(4) Where the Commissioners are satisfied—

(a) that any person has acted as charity trustee or trustee for a charity (other than an exempt charity) while disqualified for being such a trustee by virtue of section 72 above, and

(b) that, while so acting, he has received from the charity any sums by way of remuneration or expenses, or any benefit in kind, in connection with his acting as charity trustee or trustee for the charity,

they may by order direct him to repay to the charity the whole or part of any such sums, or (as the case may be) to pay to the charity the whole or part of the monetary value (as determined by them) of any such benefit.

(5) Subsection (4) above does not apply to any sums received by way of remuneration or expenses in respect of any time when the person concerned was not disqualified for being a charity trustee or trustee for the charity.

## Small charities

**Power to transfer all property, modify objects etc.**

74.—(1) This section applies to a charity if—

(a) its gross income in its last financial year did not exceed £5,000, and

(b) it does not hold any land on trusts which stipulate that the land is to be used for the purposes, or any particular purposes, of the charity,

and it is neither an exempt charity nor a charitable company.

(2) Subject to the following provisions of this section, the charity trustees of a charity to which this section applies may resolve for the purposes of this section—

(a) that all the property of the charity should be transferred to such other charity as is specified in the resolution, being either a registered charity or a charity which is not required to be registered;

(*b*)  that all the property of the charity should be divided, in such manner as is specified in the resolution, between such two or more other charities as are so specified, being in each case either a registered charity or a charity which is not required to be registered;

(*c*)  that the trusts of the charity should be modified by replacing all or any of the purposes of the charity with such other purposes, being in law charitable, as are specified in the resolution;

(*d*)  that any provision of the trusts of the charity—

(i)  relating to any of the powers exercisable by the charity trustees in the administration of the charity, or

(ii)  regulating the procedure to be followed in any respect in connection with its administration,

should be modified in such manner as is specified in the resolution.

(3) Any resolution passed under subsection (2) above must be passed by a majority of not less than two-thirds of such charity trustees as vote on the resolution.

(4) The charity trustees of a charity to which this section applies ("the transferor charity") shall not have power to pass a resolution under subsection (2)(*a*) or (*b*) above unless they are satisfied—

(*a*)  that the existing purposes of the transferor charity have ceased to be conducive to a suitable and effective application of the charity's resources; and

(*b*)  that the purposes of the charity or charities specified in the resolution are as similar in character to the purposes of the transferor charity as is reasonably practicable;

and before passing the resolution they must have received from the charity trustees of the charity, or (as the case may be) of each of the charities, specified in the resolution written confirmation that those trustees are willing to accept a transfer of property under this section.

(5) The charity trustees of any such charity shall not have power to pass a resolution under subsection (2)(*c*) above unless they are satisfied—

(*a*)  that the existing purposes of the charity (or, as the case may be, such of them as it is proposed to replace) have ceased to be conducive to a suitable and effective application of the charity's resources; and

(*b*)  that the purposes specified in the resolution are as similar in character to those existing purposes as is practical in the circumstances.

(6) Where charity trustees have passed a resolution under subsection (2) above, they shall—

(*a*)  give public notice of the resolution in such manner as they think reasonable in the circumstances; and

(*b*)  send a copy of the resolution to the Commissioners, together with a statement of their reasons for passing it.

(7) The Commissioners may, when considering the resolution, require the charity trustees to provide additional information or explanation—

(a) as to the circumstances in and by reference to which they have determined to act under this section, or

(b) relating to their compliance with this section in connection with the resolution;

and the Commissioners shall take into account any representations made to them by persons appearing to them to be interested in the charity where those representations are made within the period of six weeks beginning with the date when the Commissioners receive a copy of the resolution by virtue of subsection (6)(b) above.

(8) Where the Commissioners have so received a copy of a resolution from any charity trustees and it appears to them that the trustees have complied with this section in connection with the resolution, the Commissioners shall, within the period of three months beginning with the date when they receive the copy of the resolution, notify the trustees in writing either—

(a) that the Commissioners concur with the resolution; or

(b) that they do not concur with it.

(9) Where the Commissioners so notify their concurrence with the resolution, then—

(a) if the resolution was passed under subsection (2)(a) or (b) above, the charity trustees shall arrange for all the property of the transferor charity to be transferred in accordance with the resolution and on terms that any property so transferred—

(i) shall be held and applied by the charity to which it is transferred ("the transferee charity") for the purposes of that charity, but

(ii) shall, as property of the transferee charity, nevertheless be subject to any restrictions on expenditure to which it is subject as property of the transferor charity,

and those trustees shall arrange for it to be so transferred by such date as may be specified in the notification; and

(b) if the resolution was passed under subsection (2)(c) or (d) above, the trusts of the charity shall be deemed, as from such date as may be specified in the notification, to have been modified in accordance with the terms of the resolution.

(10) For the purpose of enabling any property to be transferred to a charity under this section, the Commissioners shall have power, at the request of the charity trustees of that charity, to make orders vesting in any property of the transferor charity—

(a)
in the charity trustees of the first-mentioned charity or in any trustee for that charity, or

(b) in any other person nominated by those charity trustees to hold the property in trust for that charity.

(11) The Secretary of State may by order amend subsection (1) above by substituting a different sum for the sum for the time being specified there.

(12) In this section—

(*a*) "charitable company" means a charity which is a company or other body corporate; and

(*b*) references to the transfer of property to a charity are references to its transfer—

(i) to the charity trustees, or

(ii) to any trustee for the charity, or

(iii) to a person nominated by the charity trustees to hold it in trust for the charity,

as the charity trustees may determine.

**Power to spend capital**

75.—(1) This section applies to a charity if—

(*a*) it has a permanent endowment which does not consist of or comprise any land, and

(*b*) its gross income in its last financial year did not exceed £1,000, and it is neither an exempt charity nor a charitable company.

(2) Where the charity trustees of a charity to which this section applies are of the opinion that the property of the charity is too small, in relation to its purposes, for any useful purpose to be achieved by the expenditure of income alone, they may resolve for the purposes of this section that the charity ought to be freed from the restrictions with respect to expenditure of capital to which its permanent endowment is subject.

(3) Any resolution passed under subsection (2) above must be passed by a majority of not less than two-thirds of such charity trustees as vote on the resolution.

(4) Before passing such a resolution the charity trustees must consider whether any reasonable possibility exists of effecting a transfer or division of all the charity's property under section 74 above (disregarding any such transfer or division as would, in their opinion, impose on the charity an unacceptable burden of costs).

(5) Where charity trustees have passed a resolution under subsection (2) above, they shall—

(*a*) give public notice of the resolution in such manner as they think reasonable in the circumstances; and

(*b*) send a copy of the resolution to the Commissioners, together with a statement of their reasons for passing it.

(6) The Commissioners may, when considering the resolution, require the charity trustees to provide additional information or explanation—

(*a*) as to the circumstances in and by reference to which they have determined to act under this section, or

(*b*) relating to their compliance with this section in connection with the resolution;

and the Commissioners shall take into account any representations made to them by persons appearing to them to be interested

interested in the charity where those representations are made within the period of six weeks beginning with the date when the Commissioners receive a copy of the resolution by virtue of subsection (5)(*b*) above.

(7) Where the Commissioners have so received a copy of a resolution from any charity trustees and it appears to them that the trustees have complied with this section in connection with the resolution, the Commissioners shall, within the period of three months beginning with the date when they receive the copy of the resolution, notify the trustees in writing either—

(*a*)  that the Commissioners concur with the resolution; or

(*b*)  that they do not concur with it.

(8) Where the Commissioners so notify their concurrence with the resolution, the charity trustees shall have, as from such date as may be specified in the notification, power by virtue of this section to expend any property of the charity without regard to any such restrictions as are mentioned in subsection (2) above.

(9) The Secretary of State may by order amend subsection (1) above by substituting a different sum for the sum for the time being specified there.

(10) In this section "charitable company" means a charity which is a company or other body corporate.

*Local charities*

**Local authority's index of local charities**

76.—(1) The council of a county or of a district or London borough and the Common Council of the City of London may maintain an index of local charities or of any class of local charities in the council's area, and may publish information contained in the index, or summaries or extracts taken from it.

(2) A council proposing to establish or maintaining under this section an index of local charities or of any class of local charities shall, on request, be supplied by the Commissioners free of charge with copies of such entries in the register of charities as are relevant to the index or with particulars of any changes in the entries of which copies have been supplied before; and the Commissioners may arrange that they will without further request supply a council with particulars of any such changes.

(3) An index maintained under this section shall be open to public inspection at all reasonable times.

(4) A council may employ any voluntary organisation as their agent for the purposes of this section, on such terms and within such limits (if any) or in such cases as they may agree; and for this purpose "voluntary organisation" means any body of which the activities are carried on otherwise than for profit, not being a public or local authority.

(5) A joint board discharging any of a council's functions shall have the same powers under this section as the council as respects local charities in the council's area which are established for purposes similar or complementary to any services provided by the board.

**Reviews of local charities by local authority**

77.—(1) The council of a county or of a district or London borough and the Common Council of the City of London may, subject to the following provisions of this section, initiate, and carry out in co-operation with the charity trustees, a review of the working of any group of local charities with the same or similar purposes in the council's area, and may make to the Commissioners such report on the review and such recommendations arising from it as the council after consultation with the trustees think fit.

(2) A council having power to initiate reviews under this section may co-operate with other persons in any review by them of the working of local charities in the council's area (with or without other charities), or may join with other persons in initiating and carrying out such a review.

(3) No review initiated by a council under this section shall extend to any charity without the consent of the charity trustees, nor to any ecclesiastical charity.

(4) No review initiated under this section by the council of a district shall extend to the working in any county of a local charity established for purposes similar or complementary to any services provided by county councils unless the review so extends with the consent of the council of that county.

(5) Subsections (4) and (5) of section 76 above shall apply for the purposes of this section as they apply for the purposes of that section.

**Co-operation between charities, and between charities and local authorities**

78.—(1) Any local council and any joint board discharging any functions of such a council—

(a) may make, with any charity established for purposes similar or complementary to services provided by the council or board, arrangements for co-ordinating the activities of the council or board and those of the charity in the interests of persons who may benefit from those services or from the charity; and

(b) shall be at liberty to disclose any such charity in the interests of those persons any information obtained in connection with the services provided by the council or board, whether or not arrangements have been made with the charity under this subsection.

In this subsection "local council" means the council of a county, or of a district, London borough, parish or (in Wales) community, and includes also the Common Council of the City of London and the Council of the Isles of Scilly.

(2) Charity trustees shall, notwithstanding anything in the trusts of the charity, have power by virtue of this subsection to do all or any of the following things, where it appears to them likely to promote or make more effective the work of the charity, and may defray the expense of so doing out of any income or money applicable as income of the charity, that is to say—

(a) they may co-operate in any view undertaken under section 77 above or otherwise of the working of charities or any class of charities;

(b) they may make arrangements with an authority acting under subsection (1) above or with another charity for co-ordinating their activities and those of the authority or of the other charity;

(c)  they may publish information of other charities with a
view to bringing them to the notice of those for whose
benefit they are intended.

**Parochial**       **79.**—(1) Where trustees hold any property for the purposes
**charities**    of a public recreation ground, or of allotments (whether under
inclosure Acts or otherwise), for the benefit of inhabitants of a
parish having a parish council, or for other charitable purposes
connected with such a parish, except for an ecclesiastical charity,
they may with the approval of the commissioners and with the
consent of the parish council transfer the property to the parish
council or to persons appointed by the parish council; and the
council or their appointees shall hold the property on the same
trusts and subject to the same conditions as the trustees did.

This subsection shall apply to property held for any public
purposes as it applies to property held for charitable purposes.

(2) Where the charity trustees of a parochial charity in a
parish, not being an ecclesiastical charity nor a charity founded
within the preceding forty years, do not include persons elected
by the local government electors, ratepayers or inhabitants of the
parish or appointed by the parish council or parish meeting, the
parish council or parish meeting may appoint additional charity
trustees, to such members as the Commissioners may allow; and
if there is a sole charity trustee not elected or appointed as
aforesaid of any such charity, the number of the charity trustees
may, with the approval of the Commissioners, be increased to
three of whom one may be nominated by the person holding the
office of the sole trustee and one by the parish council or parish
meeting.

(3) Where, under the trusts of a charity other than an
ecclesiastical charity, the inhabitants of a rural parish (whether in
vestry or not) or a select vestry were formerly (in 1894) entitled to
appoint charity trustees for, or trustees or beneficiaries of, the
charity, then—

(a)  in a parish having a parish council, the appointment
shall be made by the parish council or, in the case of
beneficiaries, by persons appointed by the parish council; and
(b)  in a parish not having a parish council, the appointment
shall be made by the parish meeting.

(4) Where overseers as such or, except in the case of an
ecclesiastical charity, churchwardens as such were formerly (in
1894) charity trustees of or trustees for a parochial charity in a
rural parish, either alone or jointly with other persons, then
instead of the former overseer or church warden trustees there
shall be trustees (to a number not greater than that of the former
overseer or churchwarden trustees) appointed by the parish
council or, if there is no parish council, by the parish meeting.

(5) Where, outside Greater London (other than the outer
London boroughs), overseers of a parish as such were formerly
(in 1927) charity trustees of or trustees for any charity, either
alone or jointly with other persons, then instead of the former
overseer trustees there shall be trustees (to a number not greater

than that of the former overseer trustees) appointed by the parish council or, if there is no parish council, by the parish meeting.

(6) In the case of an urban parish existing immediately before the passing of the Local Government Act 1972 which after 1st April 1974 is not comprised in a parish, the power of appointment under subsection (5) above shall be exercisable by the district council.

(7) In the application of the foregoing provisions of this section to Wales—

(a) for references in subsections (1) and (2) to a parish or a parish council there shall be substituted respectively references to a community or a community council;

(b) for references in subsections (3)(a) and (b) to a parish, a parish council or a parish meeting there shall be substituted respectively references to a community, a community council or the district council;

(c) in subsections (4) and (5) for references to a parish council or a parish meeting there shall be substituted respectively references to a community council or the district council.

(8) Any appointment of a charity trustee or trustee for a charity which is made by virtue of this section shall be for the term of four years, and a retiring trustee shall be eligible for re-appointment but—

(a) on an appointment under subsection (2) above, where no previous appointments have been made by virtue of that subsection or of the corresponding provision of the Local Government Act, 1894 or the Charities Act 1960, and more than one trustee is appointed, half of those appointed (or as nearly as may be) shall be appointed for a term of two years; and

(b) an appointment made to fill a casual vacancy shall be for the remainder of the term of the previous appointment.

(9) This section shall not affect the trusteeship, control or management of any voluntary school within the meaning of the Education Act 1944 or of any grant-maintained school.

(10) The provisions of this section shall not extend to the Isles of Scilly, and shall have effect subject to any order (including any future order) made under any enactment relating to local government with respect to local government areas or the powers of local authorities.

(11) In this section the expression "formerly (in 1894)" relates to the period immediately before the passing of the Local Government Act 1894, and the expression "formerly (in 1927)" to the period immediately before 1st April 1927; and the word "former" shall be construed accordingly.

*Scottish charities*

**Supervision by Commissioners of certain Scottish charities**

80.—(1) The following provisions of this Act, namely—

(a) sections 8 and 9,

(b) section 18 (except subsection (2)(ii)), and

(c) section 19,

shall have effect in relation to any recognised body which is managed or controlled wholly or mainly in or from England or Wales as they have effect in relation to a charity.

(2) Where—

(a) a recognised body is managed or controlled wholly or mainly in or from Scotland, but

(b) any person in England and Wales holds any property on behalf of the body or of any person concerned in its management or control,

then, if the Commissioners are satisfied as to the matters mentioned in subsection (3) below, they may make an order requiring the person holding the property not to part with it without their approval.

(3) The matters referred to in subsection (2) above are—

(a) that there has been any misconduct or mismanagement in the administration of the body; and

(b) that it is necessary or desirable to make an order under that subsection for the purpose of protecting the property of the body or securing a proper application of such property for the purposes of the body;

and the reference in that subsection to the Commissioners being satisfied as to those matters is a reference to their being so satisfied on the basis of such information as may be supplied to them by the Lord Advocate.

(4) Where—

(a) any person in England and Wales holds any property on behalf of a recognised body or of any person concerned in the management or control of such a body, and

(b) the Commissioners are satisfied (whether on the basis of such information as may be supplied to them by the Lord Advocate or otherwise)—

(i) that there has been any misconduct or mismanagement in the administration of the body, and

(ii) that it is necessary or desirable to make an order under this subsection for the purpose of protecting the property of the body or securing a proper application of such property for the purposes of the body,

the Commissioners may by order vest the property in such recognised body or charity as is specified in the order in accordance with subsection (5) below, or require any persons in whom the property is vested to transfer it to any such body or charity, or appoint any person to transfer the property to any such body or charity.

(5) The Commissioners may specify in an order under subsection (4) above such other recognised body or such charity as they consider appropriate, being a body or charity whose purposes are, in the opinion of the Commissioners, as similar in character to those of the body referred to in paragraph (a) of that subsection as is reasonably practicable; but the Commissioners shall not so specify any body or charity unless they have received—

(*a*) from the persons concerned in the management or control of the body, or

(*b*) from the charity trustees of the charity,

as the case may be, written confirmation that they are willing to accept the property.

(6) In this section "recognised body" has the same meaning as in Part I of the Law Reform (Miscellaneous Provisions) (Scotland) Act 1990 (Scottish charities).

*Administrative provisions about charities*

**Manner of giving notice of charity meetings, etc.**

81.—(1) All notices which are required or authorised by the trusts of a charity to be given to a charity trustee, member or subscriber may be sent by post, and, if sent by post, may be addressed to any address given as his in the list of charity trustees, members or subscribers for the time being in use at the office or principal office of the charity.

(2) Where any such notice required to be given as aforesaid is given by post, it shall be deemed to have been given by the time at which the letter containing it would be delivered in the ordinary course of post.

(3) No notice required to be given as aforesaid of any meeting, or election need be given to any charity trustee, member or subscriber, if in the list above mentioned he has no address in the United Kingdom.

**Manner of executing instruments**

82.—(1) Charity trustees may, subject to the trusts of the charity, confer on any of their body (not being less than two in number) a general authority, or an authority limited in such manner as the trustees think fit, to execute in the names and on behalf of the trustees assurances or other deeds or instruments for giving effect to transactions to which the trustees are a party; and any deed or instrument executed in pursuance of an authority so given shall be of the same effect as if executed by the whole body.

(2) An authority under subsection (1) above—

(*a*) shall suffice for any deed or instrument if it is given in writing or by resolution of a meeting of the trustees, notwithstanding the want of any formality that would be required in giving an authority apart from that sub-section;

(*b*) may be given so as to make the powers conferred exercisable by any of the trustees, or may be restricted to named persons or in any other way;

(*c*) subject to any such restriction, and until it is revoked, shall, notwithstanding any change in the charity trustees, have effect as a continuing authority given by the charity trustees from time to time of the charity and exercisable by such trustees.

(3) In any authority under this section to execute a deed or instrument in the names and on behalf of charity trustees there shall, unless the contrary intention appears, be implied authority also to execute it for them in the name and on behalf of the official custodian or of any other person, in any case in which the charity trustees could do so.

(4) Where a deed or instrument purports to be executed in pursuance of this section, then in favour of a person who (then or afterwards) in good faith acquires for money or money's worth an interest in or charge on property for the benefit of any covenant or agreement expressed to be entered into by the charity trustees, it shall be conclusively presumed to have been duly exercised by virtue of this section.

(5) The powers conferred by this section shall be in addition to and not in derogation of any other powers.

**Transfer and evidence of title to property vested in trustees**

**83.**—(1) Where, under the trusts of a charity, trustees of property held for the purposes of the charity may be appointed or discharged by resolution of a meeting of the charity trustees, members or other persons, a memorandum declaring a trustee to have been so appointed or discharged shall be sufficient evidence of that fact if the memorandum is signed either at the meeting by the person presiding or in some other manner directed by the meeting and is attested by two persons present at the meeting.

(2) A memorandum, evidencing the appointment or discharge of a trustee under subsection (1) above, if executed as a deed, shall have the like operation under section 40 of the Trustee Act 1925 (which relates to vesting declarations as respects trust property in deeds appointing or discharging trustees) as if the appointment or discharge were effected by the deed.

(3) For the purposes of this section, where a document purports to have been signed and attested as mentioned in subsection (1) above, then on proof (whether by evidence or as a matter of presumption) of the signature the document shall be presumed to have been so signed and attested, unless the contrary is shown.

(4) This section shall apply to a memorandum made at any time, except that subsection (2) shall apply only to those made after the commencement of the Charities Act 1960.

(5) This section shall apply in relation to any institution to which the Literary and Scientific Institutions Act 1854 applies as it applies in relation to a charity.

## PART X

### SUPPLEMENTARY

**Supply by Commissioners of copies of documents open to public inspection**

**84.** The Commissioners shall, at the request of any person, furnish him with copies of, or extracts from, any document in their possession which is for the time being open to inspection under Parts II to VI of this Act.

**Fees and other amounts payable to Commissioners**

**85.**—(1) The Secretary of State may by regulations require the payment to the Commissioners of such fees as may be prescribed by the regulations in respect of—

 (*a*) the discharge by the Commissioners of such functions under the enactments relating to charities as may be so prescribed;

 (*b*) the inspection of the register of charities or of other material kept by them under those enactments, or the furnishing of copies of or extracts from documents so kept.

(2) Regulations under this section may—

(*a*) confer, or provide for the conferring of, exemptions from liability to pay a prescribed fee;

(*b*) provide for the remission or refunding of a prescribed fee (in whole or in part) in circumstances prescribed by the regulations.

(3) Any regulation under this section which require the payment of a fee in respect of any matter for which no fee was previously payable shall not be made unless a draft of the regulations has been laid before and approved by a resolution of each House of Parliament.

(4) The Commissioners may impose charges of such amounts as they consider reasonable in respect of any publications produced by them.

(5) Any fees and other payments received by the Commissioners by virtue of this section shall be paid into the Consolidated Fund.

**Regulations and orders**

**86.**—(1) Any regulations or order of the Secretary of State under this Act—

(*a*) shall be made by statutory instrument; and

(*b*) (subject to subsection (2) below) shall be subject to annulment in pursuance of a resolution of either House of Parliament.

(2) Subsection (1)(*b*) above does not apply—

(*a*) to an order under section 17(2), 70 or 99(2);

(*b*) to any regulations under section 71; or

(*c*) to any regulations to which section 85(3) applies.

(3) Any regulations of the Secretary of State or the Commissioners and any order of the Secretary of State under this Act may make—

(*a*) different provision for different cases; and

(*b*) such supplemental, incidental, consequential or transitional provision or savings as the Secretary of State or, as the case may be, the Commissioners consider appropriate.

(4) Before making any regulations under section 42, 44 or 45 above the Secretary of State shall consult such persons or bodies of persons as he considers appropriate.

**Enforcement of requirements by order of Commissioners**

**87.**—(1) If a person fails to comply with any requirement imposed by or under this Act then (subject to subsection (2) below) the Commissioners may by order give him such directions as they consider appropriate for securing that the default is made good.

(2) Subsection (1) above does not apply to any such requirement if—

(*a*) a person who fails to comply with, or is persistently in default in relation to, the requirement is liable to any criminal penalty; or

(b) the requirement is imposed—

    (i) by an order of the Commissioners to which section 88 below applies, or

    (ii) by a direction of the Commissioners to which that section applies by virtue of section 90(2) below.

**Enforcement of orders of Commissioners**

88. A person guilty of disobedience—

(a) to an order of the Commissioners under section 9(1), 44(2), 61, 73 or 80 above; or

(b) to an order of the Commissioners under section 16 or 18 above requiring a transfer of property or payment to be called for or made; or

(c) to an order of the Commissioners requiring a default under this Act to be made good;

may on the application of the Commissioners to the High Court be dealt with as for disobedience to an order of the High Court.

**Other provisions as to orders of Commissioners**

89.—(1) Any order made by the Commissioners under this Act may include such incidental or supplementary provisions as the Commissioners think expedient for carrying into effect the objects of the order, and where the Commissioners exercise any jurisdiction to make such an order or an application or reference to them, they may insert any such provisions in the order notwithstanding that the application or reference does not propose their insertion.

(2) Where the Commissioners make an order under this Act, then (without prejudice to the requirements of this Act where the order is subject to appeal) they may themselves give such public notice as they think fit of the making or contents of the order, or may require it to be given by any person on whose application the order is made or by any charity affected by the order.

(3) The Commissioners at any time within twelve months after they have made an order under any provision of this Act other than section 61 if they are satisfied that the order was made by mistake or on misrepresentation or otherwise than in conformity with this Act, may with or without any application or reference to them discharge the order in whole or in part, and subject or not to any savings or other transitional provisions.

(4) Except for the purposes of subsection (3) above or of an appeal under this Act, an order made by the Commissioners under this Act shall be deemed to have been duly and formally made and not be called in question on the ground only of irregularity or informality, but (subject to any further order) have effect according to its tenor.

90.—(1) Any direction given by the Commissioners under any provision contained in this Act—

**Directions of the Commissioners**

(a) may be varied or revoked by a further direction given under that provision; and

(b) shall be given in writing.

(2) Sections 88 and 89(1), (2) and (4) above shall apply to any such directions as they apply to an order of the Commissioners.

(3) In subsection (1) above the reference to the Commissioners includes, in relation to a direction under subsection (3) of

section 8 above, a reference to any person conducting an inquiry under that section.

(4) Nothing in this section shall be read as applying to any directions contained in an order made by the Commissioners under section 87(1) above.

**Service of orders and directions**

91.—(1) This section applies to any order or direction made or given by the Commissioners under this Act.

(2) An order or direction to which this section applies may be served on a person (other than a body corporate)—

(a) by delivering it to that person;

(b) by leaving it as his last known address in the United Kingdom; or

(c) by sending it by post to him at that address.

(3) An order or direction to which this section applies may be served on a body corporate by delivering it or selling it by post—

(a) to the registered or principal office of the body in the United Kingdom, or

(b) if it has no such office in the United Kingdom, to any place in the United Kingdom where it carries on business or conducts its activities (as the case may be).

(4) Any such order or direction may also be served on a person (including a body corporate) by sending it by post to that person at an address notified by that person to the Commissioners for the purposes of this subsection.

(5) In this section any reference to the Commissioners includes, in relation to a direction given under subsection (3) of section 8 above, a reference to any person conducting an inquiry under that section.

**Appeals from Commissioners**

92.—(1) Provision shall be made by rules of court for regulating appeals to the High Court under this Act against orders or decisions of the Commissioners.

(2) On such an appeal the Attorney General shall be entitled to appear and be heard, and such other persons as the rules allow or as the court may direct.

**Miscellaneous provisions as to evidence**

93.—(1) Where, in any proceedings to recover or compel payment of any rentcharge or other periodical payment claimed by or on behalf of a charity out of land or of the rents, profits or other income of land, otherwise than as rent incident to a reversion, it is shown that the rentcharge or other periodical payment has at any time been paid for twelve consecutive years to or for the benefit of the charity, that shall be prima facie evidence of the perpetual liability to it of the land or income, and no proof of its origin shall be necessary.

(2) In any proceedings, the following documents, that is to say,—

(a) the printed copies of the reports of the Commissioners for enquiring concerning charities, 1818 to 1837, who were appointed under the Act 58 Geo. 3. c. 91, and subsequent Acts; and

(b) the printed copies of the reports which were made for various counties and county boroughs to the Charity

Commissioners by their assistant commissioners and presented to the House of Commons as returns to orders of various dates beginning with 8th December 1890, and ending with 9th September 1909,

shall be admissible as evidence of the documents and facts stated in them.

(3) Evidence of any order, certificate or other document issued by the Commissioners may be given by means of a copy retained by them, or taken from a copy so retained, and certified to be a true copy by any officer of the Commissioners generally or specially authorised by them to act for this purpose; and a document purporting to be such a copy shall be received in evidence without proof of the official position, authority or handwriting of the person certifying it.

**Restriction on institution of proceedings for certain offences**

**94.**—(1) No proceedings for an offence under this Act to which this section applies shall be instituted except by or with the consent of the Director of Public Prosecutions.

(2) This section applies to any offence under—

(*a*)  section 5;
(*b*)  section 11;
(*c*)  section 18(14);
(*d*)  section 49; or
(*e*)  section 73(1).

**Offences by bodies corporate**

**95.** Where any offence under this Act is committed by a body corporate and is proved to have been committed with the consent or connivance of, or to be attributable to any neglect on the part of, any director, manager, secretary or other similar officer of the body corporate, or any person who was purporting to act in any such capacity, he as well as the body corporate shall be guilty of that offence and shall be liable to be proceeded against and punished accordingly.

In relation to a body corporate whose affairs are managed by its members, "director" means a member of the body corporate

**Construction of references to a "charity" or to particular classes of charity**

**96.**—(1) In this Act, except in so far as the context otherwise requires—

"charity" means any institution, corporate or not, which is established for charitable purposes and is subject to the control of the High Court in the exercise of the court's jurisdiction with respect to charities;

"ecclesiastical charity" has the same meaning as in the Local Government Act 1894;

"exempt charity" means (subject to section 24(8) above) a charity comprised in Schedule 2 to this Act;

"local charity" means, in relation to any area, a charity established for purposes which are by their nature or by the trusts of a charity directed wholly or mainly to the benefit of that area or of part of it;

"parochial charity" means, in relation to any parish or (in Wales) community, a charity the benefits of which are, or the separate distribution of the benefits of which is, confined to inhabitants of the parish or community, or of a single ancient ecclesiastical parish which included that parish or community or part of it, or of an area consisting of that parish or community with not more than four neighbouring parishes or communities.

(2) The expression "charity" is not in this Act applicable—

(a) to any ecclesiastical corporation (that is to say, any corporation in the Church of England, whether sole or aggregate, which is established for spiritual purposes) in respect of the corporate property of the corporation, except to a corporation aggregate having some purposes which are not ecclesiastical in respect of its corporate property held for those purposes; or

(b) to any Diocesan Board of Finance within the meaning of the Endowments and Glebe Measure 1976 for any diocese in respect of the diocesan glebe land of that diocese within the meaning of that Measure; or

(c) to any trust of property for purposes for which the property has been consecrated.

(3) A charity shall be deemed for the purposes of this Act to have a permanent endowment unless all property held for the purposes of the charity may be expended for those purposes without distinction between capital and income, and in this Act "permanent endowment" means, in relation to any charity, property held subject to a restriction on its being expended for the purposes of the charity.

(4) References in this Act to a charity whose income from all sources does not in aggregate amount to more than a specified amount shall be construed—

(a) by reference to the gross revenues of the charity, or

(b) if the Commissioners so determine, by reference to the amount which they estimate to be the likely amount of those revenues,

but without (in either case) bringing into account anything for the yearly value of land occupied by the charity apart from the pecuniary income (if any) received from that land; and any question as to the application of any such reference to a charity shall be determined by the Commissioners, whose decision shall be final.

(5) The Commissioners may direct that for all or any of the purposes of this Act an institution established for any special purposes of or in connection with a charity (being charitable purposes) shall be treated as forming part of that charity or as forming a distinct charity.

**General interpretation**     97.—(1) In this Act, except in so far as the context otherwise requires—

"charitable purposes" means purposes which are exclusively charitable according to the law of England and Wales;

"charity trustees" means the persons having the general control and management of the administration of a charity;

"the Commissioners" means the Charity Commissioners for England and Wales;

"company" means a company formed and registered under the Companies Act 1985 or to which the provisions of that Act apply as they apply to such a company;

"the court" means the High Court and, within the limits of its jurisdiction, any other court in England and Wales having a jurisdiction in respect of charities concurrent (within any limit of area or amount) with that of the High Court, and includes any judge or officer of the court exercising the jurisdiction of the court;

"financial year"—

(a) in relation to a charity which is a company, shall be construed in accordance with section 223 of the Companies Act 1985; and

(b) in relation to any other charity shall be construed in accordance with regulations made by virtue of section 42(2) above;

but this definition is subject to the transitional provisions in section 99(4) below and Part II of Schedule 8 to this Act;

"gross income", in relation to charity, means its gross recorded income from all sources including special trusts;

"independent examiner", in relation to a charity, means such a person as is mentioned in section 43(3)(a) above;

"institution" includes any trust or undertaking;

"the official custodian" means the official custodian for charities;

"permanent endowment" shall be construed in accordance with section 96(3) above;

"the register" means the register of charities kept under section 3 above and "registered" shall be construed accordingly;

"special trust" means property which is held and administered by or on behalf of a charity for any special purposes of the charity, and is so held and administered on separate trusts relating only to that property but a special trust shall not, by itself, constitute a charity for the purposes of Part VI of this Act;

"trusts" in relation to a charity, means the provisions establishing it as a charity and regulating its purposes and administration, whether those provisions take effect by way of trust or not, and in relation to other institutions has a corresponding meaning.

(2) In this Act, except in so far as the context otherwise requires, "document" includes information recorded in any form, and, in relation to information recorded otherwise that in legible form—

(a) any reference to its production shall be construed as a reference to the furnishing of a copy of it in legible form; and

(b) any reference to the furnishing of a copy of, or extract from, it shall accordingly be construed as a reference to the furnishing of a copy of, or extract from, it in legible form.

(3) No vesting or transfer of any property in pursuance of any provision of Part IV or IX of this Act shall operate as a breach of a covenant or condition against alienation of give rise to a forfeiture.

**Consequential amendments and repeals**

**98.**—(1) The enactments mentioned in Schedule 6 to this Act shall be amended as provided in that Schedule.

(2) The enactments mentioned in Schedule 7 to this Act are hereby repealed to the extent specified in the third column of the Schedule.

**Commencement and transitional provisions**

**99.**—(1) Subject to subsection (2) below this Act shall come into force on 1st August 1993.

(2) Part IV, section 69 and paragraph 21(3) of Schedule 6 shall not come into force until such day as the Secretary of State may by order appoint; and different days may be appointed for different provisions or different purposes.

(3) Until the coming into force of all the provisions mentioned in subsection (2) above the provisions mentioned in Part I of Schedule 8 to this Act shall continue in force notwithstanding their repeal.

(4) Part II of Schedule 8 to this Act shall have effect until the coming into force of the first regulations made by virtue of section 42(2) above for determining the financial year of a charity for the purposes of the provisions mentioned in that Part.

**Short title and extent**

**100.**—(1) This Act may be cited as the Charities Act 1993.

(2) Subject to the subsection (3) to (6) below, this Act extends only to England and Wales.

(3) Section 10 above and this section extend to the whole of the United Kingdom.

(4) Section 15(2) extends also to Northern Ireland.

(5) Sections 70 and 71 and so much of section 86 as relates to those sections extended also to Scotland.

(6) The amendments in Schedule 6 and the repeals in Schedule 7 have the same extent as the enactments to which they refer and section 98 above extends accordingly.

## SCHEDULES

### SCHEDULE 1

#### CONSTITUTION ETC. OF CHARITY COMMISSIONERS

1.—(1) There shall be a Chief Charity Commissioner and two other commissioners.

(2) Two at least of the commissioners shall be persons who have a seven year general qualification within the meaning of section 71 of the Courts and Legal Services Act 1990.

(3) The chief commissioner and the other commissioners shall be appointed by the Secretary of State, and shall be deemed for all purposes to be employed in the civil service of the Crown.

(4) There may be paid to each of the commissioners such salary and allowances as the Secretary of State may with the approval of the Treasury determine.

(5) If at any time it appears to the Secretary of State that there should be more than three commissioners, he may with the approval of the Treasury appoint not more than two additional commissioners.

2.—(1) The chief commissioner may, with the approval of the Treasury as to number and conditions of service, appoint such assistant commissioners and other officers and such employees as he thinks necessary for the proper discharge of the functions of the Commissioners and of the official custodian.

(2) There may be paid to officers and employees so appointed such salaries or remuneration as the Treasury may determine.

3.—(1) The Commissioners may use an official seal for authentication of documents, and their seal shall be officially and judicially noticed.

(2) The Documentary Evidence Act 1868, as amended by the Documentary Evidence Act 1882, shall have effect as if in the Schedule to the Act of 1868 the Commissioners were included in the first column and any commissioner or assistant commissioner and any officer authorised to act on behalf of the commissioners were mentioned in the second column.

(3) The Commissioners shall have power to regulate their own procedure and, subject to any such regulations and to any directions of the chief commissioner, any one commissioner or any assistant commissioner may act for and in the name of the Commissioners.

(4) Where the Commissioners act as a board, then—

(a) if not more than four commissioners hold office for the time being, the quorum shall be two commissioners (of whom at least one must be a person having a qualification such as is mentioned in paragraph 1(2) above; and

(b) if five commissioners so hold office, the quorum shall be three commissioners (of whom at least one must be a person having such a qualification);

and in the case of an equality of votes the chief commissioner or in his absence the commissioner presiding shall have a second or casting vote.

(5) The Commissioners shall have power to act notwithstanding any vacancy in their number.

(6) It is hereby declared that the power of a commissioner or assistant commissioner to act for and in the name of the Commissioners in accordance with sub-paragraph (3) above may, in particular, be exercised in relation to functions of the Commissioners under sections 8, 18, 19 and 63 of this Act, including functions under sections 8, 18 and 19 as applied by section 80(1).

4. Legal proceedings may be instituted by or against the Commissioners by the name of the Charity Commissioners for England and Wales, and shall not abate or be affected by any change in the persons who are the commissioners.

## SCHEDULE 2

### EXEMPT CHARITIES

The following institutions, so far as they are charities, are exempt charities within the meaning of this Act, that is to say—

(a) any institution which, if the Charities Act 1960 had not been passed, would be exempted from the powers and jurisdiction, under the Charitable Trusts Acts 1853 to 1939, of the commissioners or Minister of Education (apart from any power of the commissioners or Minister to apply those Acts in whole or in part to charities otherwise exempt) by the terms of any enactment not contained in those Acts other than section 9 of the Places of Worship Registration Act 1855;

(b) the universities of Oxford, Cambridge, London, Durham and Newcastle, the colleges and halls of the universities of Oxford, Cambridge, Durham and Newcastle, Queen Mary and Westfield College in the University of London and the colleges of Winchester and Eton;

(c) any university, university college, or institution connected with a university or university college, which Her Majesty declares by Order in Council to be an exempt charity for the purposes of this Act;

(d) a grant-maintained school;

(e) the National Curriculum Council;

(f) the Curriculum Council for Wales;

(g) the School Examinations and Assessment Council;

(h) the higher education corporation;

(i) a successor company to a higher education corporation (within the meaning of section 129(5) of the Education Reform Act 1988) at a time when an institution conducted by the company is for the time being designated under that section;

(j) a further education corporation;

(k) the Board of Trustees of the Victoria and Albert Museum;

(l) the Board of Trustees of the Science Museum;

(m) the Board of Trustees of the Armouries;

(n) the Board of Trustees of the Royal Botanic Gardens, Kew;

(o) the Board of Trustees of the National Museums and Galleries on Merseyside;

(p) the trustees of the British Museum and the trustees of the Natural History Museum;

(q) the Board of Trustees of the National Gallery;

(r) the Board of Trustees of the Tate Gallery;

(s) the Board of Trustees of the National Portrait Gallery;

(t) the Board of Trustees of the Wallace Collection;

(u) the Trustees of the Imperial War Museum;

(v) the Trustees of the National Maritime Museum;

(w) any institution which is administered by or on behalf of an institution included above and is established for the general purposes of, or for any special purpose of or in connection with, the last-mentioned institution;

(x) the Church Commissioners and any institution which is administered by them;

(y) any registered society within the meaning of the Industrial and Provident Societies Act 1965 and any registered society or branch within the meaning of the Friendly Societies Act 1974;

(z) the Board of Governors of the Museum of London;

(za) the British Library Board.

## SCHEDULE 3

### ENLARGEMENT OF AREAS OF LOCAL CHARITIES

| Existing area | Permissible enlargement |
| --- | --- |
| 1. Greater London. | Any area comprising Greater London. |
| 2. Any area in Greater London and not in, or partly in, the City of London. | (i) Any area in Greater London and not in, or partly in, the City of London; <br> (ii) the area of Greater London exclusive of the City of London; <br> (iii) any area comprising the area of Greater London, exclusive of the City of London; <br> (iv) any area partly in Greater London and partly in any adjacent parish or parishes (civil or ecclesiastical), and not partly in the City of London. |
| 3. A district. | Any area comprising the district. |
| 4. Any area in a district. | (i) Any area in the district; <br> (ii) the district; <br> (iii) any area comprising the district; <br> (iv) area partly in the district and partly in any adjacent district. |
| 5. A parish (civil or ecclesiastical), or two or more parishes, or an area in a parish, or partly in each of two or more parishes. | Any area not extending beyond the parish or parishes comprising or adjacent to the area in column 1. |

| *Existing area* | *Permissible enlargement* |
|---|---|
| 6. In Wales, a community, or two or more communities, or an area in a community, or partly in each of two or more communities. | Any area not extending beyond the community or communities comprising or adjacent to the area in column 1. |

## SCHEDULE 4

COURT'S JURISDICTION OVER CERTAIN CHARITIES GOVERNED BY OR UNDER STATUTE

1. The court may by virtue of section 15(3) of this Act exercise its jurisdiction with respect to charities—

(a) in relation to charities established or regulated by any provision of the Seamen's Fund Winding-up Act 1851 which is repealed by the Charities Act 1960;

(b) in relation to charities established or regulated by schemes under the Endowed Schools Act 1869 to 1948, or section 75 of the Elementary Education Act 1870 or by schemes given effect under section 2 of the Education Act 1973;

(c) in relation to allotments regulated by sections 3 to 9 of the Poor Allotments Management Act 1873;

(d) in relation to fuel allotments, that is to say, land which, by any enactment relating to inclosure or any instrument having effect under such an enactment, is vested in trustees upon trust that the land or the rents and profits of the land shall be used for the purpose of providing poor persons with fuel;

(e) in relation to charities established or regulated by any provision of the Municipal Corporations Act 1883 which is repealed by the Charities Act 1960 or by a scheme having effect under any such provision;

(f) in relation to charities regulated by schemes under the London Government Act 1899;

(g) in relation to charities established or regulated by orders or regulations under section 2 of the Regimental Charitable Funds Act 1935;

(h) in relation to charities regulated by section 79 of this Act, or by any such order as is mentioned in that section.

2. Notwithstanding anything in section 19 of the Commons Act 1876 a scheme for the administration of a fuel allotment (within the meaning of the foregoing paragraph) may provide—

(a) for the sale or letting of the allotment or any part thereof, for the discharge of the land sold or let from any restrictions as to the use thereof imposed by or under any enactment relating to inclosure and for the application of the sums payable to the trustees of the allotment in respect of the sale or lease; or

(b) for the exchange of the allotment or any part thereof for other land, for the discharge as aforesaid of the land given in exchange by the said trustees, and for the application of any money payable to the said trustees for equality of exchange; or

(c) for the use of the allotment or any part thereof for any purposes specified in the scheme.

## SCHEDULE 5

MEANING OF "CONNECTED PERSON" FOR PURPOSES OF SECTION 36(2)

1. In section 36(2) of this Act "connected person", in relation to a charity, means—

    (*a*)   a charity trustee or trustee for the charity;
    (*b*)   a person who is the donor of any land to the charity (whether the gift was made on or after the establishment of the charity);
    (*c*)   a child, parent, grandchild, grandparent, brother or sister of any such trustee or donor;
    (*d*)   an officer, agent or employee of the charity;
    (*e*)   the spouse of any person falling within any of sub-paragraphs (*a*) to (*d*) above;
    (*f*)   an institution which is controlled—
        (i)   by any person falling within any of sub-paragraphs (*a*) to (*e*) above, or
        (ii)   by two or more persons taken together; or
    (*g*)   a body corporate in which—
        (i)   any connected person falling within any of sub-paragraphs (*a*) to (*f*) above has a substantial interest, or
        (ii)   two or more such persons, taken together, have a substantial interest.

2.—(1) In paragraph 1(*c*) above "child" includes a stepchild and an illegitimate child.

(2) For the purposes of paragraph 1(*e*) above a person living with another as that person's husband or wife shall be treated as that person's spouse.

3. For the purposes of paragraph 1(*f*) above a person controls an institution if he is able to secure that the affairs of the institution are conducted in accordance with his wishes.

4.—(1) For the purposes of paragraph 1(*g*) above any such connected person as is there mentioned has a substantial interest in a body corporate if the person or institution in question—

    (*a*)   is interested in shares comprised in the equity share capital of that body of a nominal value of more than one-fifth of that share capital, or
    (*b*)   is entitled to exercise, or control the exercise of, more than one-fifth of the voting power at any general meeting of that body.

(2) The rules set out in Part I of Schedule 13 to the Companies Act 1985 (rules for interpretation of certain provisions of that Act) shall apply for the purposes of sub-paragraph (1) above as they apply for the purposes of section 346(4) of that Act ("connected persons" etc.).

(3) In this paragraph "equity share capital" and "share" have the same meaning as in that Act.

## SCHEDULE 6

CONSEQUENTIAL AMENDMENTS

*The Places of Worship Registration Act 1855 (c.81)*

1.—(1) Section 9 of the Places of Worship Registration Act 1855 shall be amended as follows.

(2) For "subsection (4) of section four of the Charities Act 1960" there shall be substituted "subsection (5) of section 3 of the Charities Act 1993".

(3) At the end there shall be added—

"(2) Section 89 of the said Act of 1993 (provisions as to orders under that Act) shall apply to any order under paragraph (*b*) above as it applies to orders under that Act."

*The Open Spaces Act 19096 (c.25)*

2. At the end of section 4 of the Open Spaces Act 1906 there shall be added—

"(4) Section 89 of the Charities Act 1993 (provisions as to orders under this Act) shall apply to any order of the Charity Commissioners under this section as it applies to orders made by them under that Act."

*The New Parishes Measure 1943 (No. 1)*

3.—(1) The New Parishes Measure 1943 shall be amended as follows—
(2) In subsection 1(*b*) of section 14 for "the Charities Act 1960" there shall be substituted "the Charities Act 1993".
(3) At the end of that section there shall be added—

"(4) Section 89 of the Charities Act 1993 (provisions as to orders under that Act) shall apply to any order under section (1)(*b*) above as it applies to orders under that Act."

(4) In section 31 for "the Charities Act 1960" there shall be substituted "the Charities Act 1993".

*The Clergy Pensions Measure 1961 (No. 3)*

4. In section 33 of the Clergy Pensions Measure 1961 for "section 32 of the Charities Act 1992" and "the Charities Act 1960" there shall be substituted respectively "section 36 of the Charities Act 1993" and "that Act".

*The Finance Act 1963 (c.25)*

5. In section 65(2) of the Finance Act 1963 at the end of paragraph (*a*) there shall be added "or to any common investment scheme under section 24 or any common deposit scheme under section 25 of the Charities Act 1993,".

*The Cathedrals Measure 1963 (No. 2)*

6.—(1) The Cathedrals Measure 1963 shall be amended as follows.
(2) In section 20(2)(iii) for "section 32 of the Charities Act 1992" there shall be substituted "section 36 of the Charities Act 1993".
(3) In section 51 for "the Charities Act 1960" there shall be substituted "the Charities Act 1993".

*The Incumbents and Churchwardens (Trusts) Measure 1964 (No. 2)*

7. In section 1 of the Incumbents and Churchwardens (Trusts) Measure 1964 for "subsection (3) of section forty-five of the Charities Act 1960" there shall be substituted "section 96(3) of the Charities Act 1993".

*The Leasehold Reform Act 1967 (c.88)*

8. In section 23(4) of the Leasehold Reform Act 1967 for "section 32 of the Charities Act 1992" there shall be substituted "section 36 of the Charities Act 1993".

*The Greater London Council (General Powers) Act 1968 (c.xxxix)*

9. In section 43 of the Greater London Council (General Powers) Act 1968, in the definition of "night café", for "section 4 of the Charities Act 1960" and "subsection (4) thereof" there shall be substituted respectively "section 3 of the Charities Act 1993" and "subsection (5) thereof".

*The Redundant Churches and other Religious Buildings Act 1969 (c.22)*

10.—(1) The Redundant Churches and other Religious Buildings Act 1969 shall be amended as follows.
(2) In subsection (6) of section 4 for "section 18 of the Charities Act 1960" there shall be substituted "section 16 of the Charities Act 1993".

(3) In subsection (7) of that section for "subsection (4) of section 18 of that Act" there shall be substituted "subsection (4) of section 16 of that Act".

(4) In subsection (8) of that section for "section 18 of the Charities Act 1960" and (where next occurring) "section 18" there shall be substituted respectively "section 16 of the Charities Act 1993" and "section 16" and for "section 21" there shall be substituted "section 20".

(5) In subsection (13) of that section for "sections 45 and 46 of the Charities Act 1960" there shall be substituted "sections 96 and 97 of the Charities Act 1993".

(6) In section 7(2) for "the Charities Act 1960" and "section 23" there shall be substituted respectively "the Charities Act 1993" and "section 26".

*The Sharing of Church Buildings Act 1969 (c.38)*

11.—(1) The Sharing of Church Buildings Act 1969 shall be amended as follows.

(2) In section 2(4) for "the Charities Act 1960" there shall be substituted "the Charities Act 1993".

(3) In section (1) of section 8 for "the Charities Act 1960" there shall be substituted "the Charities Act 1993".

(4) In subsection (2) of that section for "section 45(2) of the Charities Act 1960" there shall be substituted "section 96(2) of the Charities Act 1993".

(5) In subsection (3) of that section for "Section 32 of the Charities Act 1992" there shall be substituted "Section 36 of the Charities Act 1993".

*The Local Government Act 1972 (c.70)*

12.—(1) The Local Government Act 1972 shall be amended as follows.

(2) In sections 11(3)(*c*) and 29(3)(*c*) for "section 37 of the Charities Act 1960" there shall be substituted "section 79 of the Charities Act 1993".

(3) In sections 123(6) and 127(4) for "the Charities Act 1960" there shall be substituted "the Charities Act 1993".

(4) In section 131(3) for "section 32 of the Charities Act 1993" and "section 32(9)(*a*) of that Act" there shall be substituted respectively "section 36 of the Charities Act 1993" and "section 36(9)(*a*) of that Act".

*The Fire Precautions (Loans) Act 1973 (c.11)*

13. In section 1(7) of the Fire Precautions (Loans) Act 1973 for "Section 34 of the Charities Act 1992" there shall be substituted "Section 38 of the Charities Act 1993".

*The Theatres Trust Act 1976 (c.27)*

14. In section 2(2)(*d*) of the Theatres Trust Act 1976 for "sections 32 and 34 of the Charities Act 1992" there shall be substituted "sections 36 and 38 of the Charities Act 1993".

*The Interpretation Act 1978 (c.30)*

16. In Schedule 1 to the Interpretation Act 1978, in the definition of "Charity Commissioners" for "section 1 of the Charities Act 1960" there shall be substituted "section 1 of the Charities Act 1993".

*The Reserve Forces Act 1980 (c.9)*

16.—(1) Section 147 of the Reserve Forces Act 1980 shall be amended as follows.

(2) In subsection (4) for "section 28 of the Charities Act 1960" there shall be substituted "section 33 of the Charities Act 1933".

(3) In subsection (5) for "section 28(5) of that Act of 1960" there shall be substituted "section 33(5) of that Act of 1993".

(4) In subsection (7) for "section 18 of the Charities Act 1960" there shall be substituted "section 16 of the Charities Act 1993".

(5) In subsection (10)(*b*) for "the Charities Act 1960" there shall be substituted "the Charities Act 1993".

*The Disused Burial Grounds (Amendment) Act 1981 (c.18)*

17. In section 6 of the Disused Burial Grounds (Amendment) Act 1981 for "section 13(5) of the Charities Act 1960" there shall be substituted "section 13(5) of the Charities Act 1993".

*The Pastoral Measure 1983 (No. 1)*

18.—(1) The Pastoral Measure 1983 shall be amended as follows.

(2) In section 55(1) for "the Charities Act 1960" and "section 456(2)(*b*)" there shall be substituted "the Charities Act 1993" and "section 96(2)(*c*)".

(3) In section 63(3) for "the Charities Act 1960" there shall be substituted "the Charities Act 1993".

(4) In section 87(1) for "section 45 of the Charities Act 1960" there shall be substituted "section 96 of the Charities Act 1993".

(5) In paragraphs 11(6) and 16(1)(*e*) of Schedule 3 for "section 18 of the Charities Act 1960" there shall be substituted "section 16 of the Charities Act 1993".

*The Rates Act 1984 (c.33)*

19. In section 3(9) of the Rates Act 1984 for "section 4 of the Charities Act 1960" there shall be substituted "section 3 of the Charities Act 1993".

*The Companies Act 1985 (c.6)*

20.—(1) The Companies Act 1985 shall be amended as follows.

(2) In sections 35(4) and 35A(6) for "section 30B(1) of the Charities Act 1960" there shall be substituted "section 65(1) of the Charities Act 1993".

(3) In section 209(1)(*c*) and paragraph 11(*b*) of Schedule 13 after "the Charities Act 1960" there shall be inserted "or section 24 or 25 of the Charities Act 1993".

*The Housing Associations Act 1985 (c.69)*

21.—(1) The Housing Associations Act 1985 shall be amended as follows.

(2) In section 10(1) for "sections 32 and 34 of the Charities Act 1992" there shall be substituted "sections 36 and 38 of the Charities Act 1993".

(3) In section 26(2) for the words from "section 8" onwards there shall be substituted "section 41 to 45 of the Charities Act 1993 (charity accounts)".

(4) In section 35(2)(*c*) for "section 32 of the Charities Act 1992" there shall be substituted "section 36 of the Charities Act 1993".

(5) In section 38—

(*a*) in paragraph (*a*) for "the Charities Act 1960" there shall be substituted "the Charities Act 1993";

(*b*) in paragraph (*b*) for "section 4 of that Act" there shall be substituted "section 3 of that Act".

*The Financial Services Act 1986 (c.60)*

22. In section 45(1)(j) of the Financial Services Act 1986 after "the Charities Act 1960" there shall be inserted ", section 24 or 25 of the Charities Act 1993".

*The Coal Industry Act 1987 (c.3)*

23.—(1) In section 5 of the Coal Industry Act 1987 for subsection (8) there shall be substituted—

"(8) Sections 16(3), (9), (11) to (14), 17(1) to (5) and (7) and 20 of the Charities Act 1993 shall apply in relation to the powers of the Charity Commissioners and the making of schemes under this section as they apply in relation to their powers and the making of schemes under that Act and sections 89, 91 and 92 of that Act shall apply to orders and decisions under this section as they apply to orders and decisions under that Act."

(2) In subsection (8A) of that section for "section 29" (in both places) there shall be substituted "section 17".

*The Reverter of Sites Act 1987 (c.15)*

24. In section 4(4) of the Reverter of Sites Act 1987 for "sections 40, 40A and 42 of the Charities Act 1960" there shall be substituted "sections 89, 91 and 92 of the Charities Act 1993".

*The Income and Corporation Taxes Act 1988 (c.1)*

25. In Schedule 20 to the Income and Corporation Taxes Act 1988—

(*a*) in paragraph 3 after "the Charities Act 1960" there shall be inserted ", section 24 of the Charities Act 1993";
(*b*) in paragraph 3A after "the Charities Act 1960" there shall be inserted "or section 25 of the Charities Act 1993".

*The Courts and Legal Services Act 1990 (c.41)*

26. In Schedule 11 to the Courts and Legal Services Act 1990, in the reference to a Charity Commissioner, for "under the First Schedule to the Charities Act 1960" there shall be substituted "as provided in Schedule 1 to the Charities Act 1993".

*The London Local Authorities Act 1990 (c.vii)*

27. In section 4 of the London Local Authorities Act 1990, in the definition of "night café", for "section 4 of the Charities Act 1960" and "subsection (4) thereof" there shall be substituted respectively "section 3 of the Charities Act 1993" and "subsection (5) thereof".

*The London Local Authorities Act 1991 (c.xiii)*

28. In section 4 of the London Local Authorities Act 1991, in the definition of "establishment for special treatment", for "section 4 of the Charities Act 1960" and "subsection (4) of that section" there shall be substituted respectively "section 3 of the Charities Act 1993" and "subsection (5) of that section".

*The Charities Act 1992 (c.41)*

29.—(1) The Charities Act 1992 shall be amended as follows.
(2) In section 29(2)(*b*) after "Act" there shall be inserted "or section 18 of the Charities Act 1993".
(3) In section 30(1)(*b*) after "Act" there shall be inserted "or section 22(1) of the Charities Act 1993".
(4) In section 30(3)(*a*) after "Act" there shall be inserted "or section 18 of the Charities Act 1993".
(5) In section 58(1), in the definition of "charity" for "the Charities Act 1960" there shall be substituted "the Charities Act 1993" and in the definition of "company" for the words after "section" there shall be substituted "97 of the Charities Act 1993".
(6) In section 63(2) for "section 4 of the Charities Act 1960" there shall be substituted "section 3 of the Charities Act 1993".
(7) In section 72 for subsection (5) there shall be substituted—

"(5) Section 89(1), (2) and (4) of the Charities Act 1993 (provisions as to orders made by the Commissioners) shall apply to an order made by them under this section as it applies to an order made by them under that Act.
(6) In this section "charity" and "charitable purposes" have the same meaning as in that Act."

(8) In section 74, after subsection (3) there shall be inserted—

"(3A) Any person who knowingly or recklessly provides the Commissioners with information which is false or misleading in a material particular shall be guilty of an offence if the information is provided in circumstances in which he intends, or could reasonably be expected to know, that it would be used by them for the purpose of discharging their functions under section 72.

(3B) A person guilty of an offence under subsection (3A) shall be liable—

 (*a*) on summary conviction, to a fine not exceeding the statutory maximum;
 (*b*) on conviction or indictment, to imprisonment for a term not exceeding two years or to a fine or both."

*Other amendments*

30. In the following provisions for "the Charities Act 1960" there shall be substituted "the Charities Act 1993"—

The National Health Service Reorganisation Act 1973 section 30(5).
The Consumer Credit Act 1974 section 189(1).
The Rent (Agriculture) Act 1976 section 5(3)(*f*).
The Rent Act 1977 section 15(2)(*b*).
The National Health Service Act 1977 section 96(2).
The Dioceses Measure 1978 section 19(4).
The Ancient Monuments and Archaeological Areas Act 1979 section 49(3).
The Greater London Council (General Powers) Act 1984 section 10(2)(n).
The Local Government Act 1985 section 90(4).
The Housing Act 1985 sections 525 and 622.
The Landlord and Tenant Act 1987 section 60(1).
The Education Reform Act 1988 sections 128(5) and 192(11).
The Copyright, Designs and Patents Act 1988 Schedule 6 paragraph 7.
The Housing Act 1988 Schedule 2 Part I Ground 6.
The University of Wales College of Cardiff Act 1988 section 9.
The Imperial College Act 1988 section 10.
The Local Government and Housing Act 1989 section 138(1).

## SCHEDULE 7

### REPEALS

| Chapter | Short title | Extent of repeal |
|---|---|---|
| 35 & 36 Vic. c.24. | The Charitable Trustees Incorporation Act 1972. | The whole Act so far as unrepealed. |
| 10 & 11 Geo. 5 c.16. | The Imperial War Museum Act 1920. | Section 5. |
| 24 & 25 Geo. 5 c.43. | The National Maritime Museum Act 1934. | Section 7. |
| 8 & 9 Eliz. 2 c.58. | The Charities Act 1960. | The whole Act so far as unrepealed except— section 28(9) section 35(6) section 38(3) to (5) section 39(2) sections 48 and 49 Schedule 6. |
| 1963 c.33. | The London Government Act 1963. | Section 81(9)(*b*) and (*c*). |
| 1963 c.xi. | The Universities of Durham and Newcastle-upon-Tyne Act 1963. | Section 10. |
| 1965 c.17. | The Museum of London Act 1965. | Section 11. |
| 1972 c.54. | The British Library Act 1972. | Section 4(2). |
| 1972 c.70. | The Local Government Act 1972. | Section 210(9). |

| Chapter | Short title | Extent of repeal |
|---|---|---|
| 1973 c.16. | The Education Act 1973. | In section 2(7) the words from "but" onwards.<br>In Schedule 1, paragraph 1(1) and (3). |
| 1976 No. 4. | The Endowments and Glebe Measure 1976. | Section 44. |
| 1983 c.47. | The National Heritage Act 1983. | In Schedule 5, paragraph 4. |
| 1985 c.9. | The Companies Consolidation (Consequential Provisions) Act 1985. | In Schedule 2 the entry relating to the Charities Act 1960. |
| 1985 c.20. | The Charities Act 1985. | Section 1. |
| 1986 c.60 | The Financial Services Act 1986. | In Schedule 16, paragraph 1. |
| 1988 c.40. | The Education Reform Act 1988. | In Schedule 12, paragraphs 9, 10, 63 and 64. |
| 1989 c.40. | The Companies Act 1989. | Section 111. |
| 1989 c.xiii. | The Queen Mary and Westfield College Act 1989. | Section 10. |
| 1990 c.41. | The Courts and Legal Services Act 1990. | In Schedule 10, paragraph 14. |
| 1992 c.13. | The Further and Higher Education Act 1992. | In Schedule 8, paragraph 69. |
| 1992 c.41. | The Charities Act 1992. | The whole of Part I except—<br>section 1(1) and (4)<br>sections 29 and 30<br>section 36<br>sections 49 and 50.<br>Section 75(*b*).<br>Section 76(1)(*a*).<br>In section 77, subsections 2(*a*), (*b*) and (*c*) and in subsection (4) the figures 20, 22 and 23.<br>Section 79(4) and (5).<br>Schedules 1 to 4.<br>In Schedule 6, paragraph 13(2).<br>In Schedule 7, the entries relating to section 8 of the Charities Act 1960 and (so far as not in force at the date specified in section 99(1) of this Act) the Charities Act 1985. |
| 1992 c.44. | The Museum and Galleries Act 1992. | In Schedule 8, paragraphs 4 and 10.<br>In Schedule 9, the entry relating to the Charities Act 1960. |

## SCHEDULE 8

TRANSITIONAL PROVISIONS

### PART I

PROVISIONS APPLYING PENDING COMING INTO FORCE OF PART IV ETC.

1. In the Charities Act 1960—

section 8
section 32
Part V so far as relevant to those sections.

2. In the Charities Act 1985

section 1
sections 6 and 7 so far as relevant to section 1.

### PART II

PROVISIONS APPLYING PENDING COMING INTO FORCE OF "FINANCIAL YEAR" REGULATIONS

*Section 5*

In section 5(1) of this Act "financial year"—

(a) in relation to a charity which is a company, shall be construed in accordance with section 223 of the Companies Act 1985;
(b) in relation to any other charity, means any period in respect of which an income and expenditure account is required to be prepared whether under section 32 of the Charities Act 1960 or by or under the authority of any other Act, whether that period is a year or not.

*Sections 74 and 75*

In sections 74(1)(a) and 75(1)(b) of this Act "financial year" means any period in respect of which an income and expenditure account is required to be prepared whether under section 32 of the Charities Act 1960 or by or under the authority of any other Act, whether that period is a year or not.

# TRUSTEE INVESTMENTS ACT 1961

## SCHEDULES

**Section 1**               FIRST SCHEDULE

MANNER OF INVESTMENT

### PART I

NARROWER-RANGE INVESTMENTS NOT REQUIRING ADVICE

1. In Defence Bonds, National Savings Certificates and Ulster Savings Certificates, Ulster Development Bonds, National Development Bonds, British Savings Bonds, National Savings Income Bonds, National Savings Deposit Bonds, National Savings Indexed-Income Bonds.

2. In deposits in the National Savings Bank, and deposits in a bank or department thereof certified under subsection (3) of section nine of the Finance Act 1956.

## PART II

### NARROWER-RANGE INVESTMENTS REQUIRING ADVICE

1. In securities issued by Her Majesty's Government in the United Kingdom, the Government of Northern Ireland or the Government of the Isle of Man, not being securities falling within Part I of this Schedule and being fixed-interest securities registered in the United Kingdom or the Isle of Man, Treasury Bills or Tax Reserve Certificates or any variable interest securities issued by her Majesty's Government in the United Kingdom and registered in the United Kingdom.

2. In any securities the payment of interest on which is guaranteed by Her Majesty's Government in the United Kingdom or the Government of Northern Ireland.

3. In fixed-interest securities issued in the United Kingdom by any public authority or nationalised industry or undertaking in the United Kingdom.

4. In fixed-interest securities issued in the United Kingdom by the government of any overseas territory within the Commonwealth or by any public or local authority within such a territory, being securities registered in the United Kingdom.

References in this paragraph to an overseas territory or to the government of such a territory shall be construed as if they occurred in the Overseas Services Act 1958.

4A. In securities issued in the United Kingdom by the government of an overseas territory within the Commonwealth or by any public or local authority within such a territory, being securities registered in the United Kingdom and in respect of which the rate of interest is variable by reference to one or more of the following:—

(*a*) the Bank of England's minimum lending rate;
(*b*) the average rate of discount on allotment on 91-day Treasury bills;
(*c*) a yield on 91-day Treasury bills;
(*d*) a London sterling inter-bank offered rate;
(*e*) a London sterling certificate of deposit rate.

References in this paragraph to an overseas territory or to the government of such a territory shall be construed as if they occurred in the Overseas Services Act 1958.

5. In fixed-interest securities issued in the United Kingdom by the African Development Bank, the Asian Development Bank, the Caribbean Development Bank, the International Finance Corporation, the International Monetary Fund or by the International Bank for Reconstruction and Development, being securities registered in the United Kingdom.

In fixed-interest securities issued in the United Kingdom by the Inter-American Development Bank.

In fixed-interest securities issued in the United Kingdom by the European Atomic Energy Community, the European Economic Community, the European Investment Bank or by the European Coal and Steel Community, being securities registered in the United Kingdom.

5A. In securities issued in the United Kingdom by

(i) the International Bank for Reconstruction and Development or by the European Investment Bank or by the European Coal and Steel Community, being securities registered in the United Kingdom or

(ii) the Inter-American Development Bank

being securities in respect of which the rate of interest is variable by reference to one or more of the following:—

(a) the Bank of England's minimum lending rate;
(b) the average rate of discount on allotment on 91-day Treasury bills;
(c) a yield on 91-day Treasury bills;
(d) a London sterling inter-bank offered rate;
(e) a London sterling certificate of deposit rate.

5B. In securities issued in the United Kingdom by the African Development Bank, the Asian Development Bank, the Caribbean Development Bank, the European Atomic Energy Community, the European Economic Community, the International Finance Corporation or by the International Monetary Fund, being securities registered in the United Kingdom and in respect of which the rate of interest is variable by reference to one or more of the following:—

(a) The average rate of discount on allotment on 91-day Treasury Bills;
(b) a yield on 91-day Treasury Bills;
(c) a London sterling inter-bank offered rate;
(d) a London sterling certificate of deposit rate.

6. In debentures issued in the United Kingdom by a company incorporated in the United Kingdom, being debentures registered in the United Kingdom.

7. In stock of the Bank of Ireland.

In Bank of Ireland 7 per cent Loan Stock 1986/91.

8. In debentures issued by the Agricultural Mortgage Corporation Limited or the Scottish Agricultural Securities Corporation Limited.

9. In loans to any authority to which this paragraph applies charged on all or any of the revenues of the authority or on a fund into which all or any of those revenues are payable, in any fixed-interest securities issued in the United Kingdom by any such authority for the purpose of borrowing money so charged, and in deposits with any such authority by way of temporary loan made on the giving of a receipt for the loan by the treasurer or other similar officer of the authority and on the giving of an undertaking by that authority the, if requested to charge the loan as aforesaid, it will either comply with the request or repay the loan.

This paragraph applies to the following authorities, that is to say—

(a)  any local authority in the United Kingdom;
(b)  any authority all the members of which are appointed or elected by one or more local authorities in the United Kingdom;
(c)  any authority the majority of the members of which are appointed or elected by one or more local authorities in the United Kingdom, being an authority which by virtue of any enactment has power to issue a precept to a local authority in England and Wales, or a requisition to a local authority in Scotland, or to the expenses of which, by virtue of any enactment, a local authority in the United Kingdom is or can be required to contribute;
(d)  the Receiver for the Metropolitan Police District or a combined police authority (within the meaning of the Police Act 1946);
(e)  the Belfast City and District Water Commissioners;
(f)  the Great Ouse Water Authority;
(g)  any district council in Northern Ireland;
(h)  the Inner London Education Authority;
(i)  any residuary body established by section 57 of the Local Government Act 1985.

9A. In any securities issued in the United Kingdom by any authority to which paragraph 9 applies for the purpose of borrowing money charged on all or any of the revenues of the authority or on a fund into which all or any of those revenues are payable and being securities in respect of which the rate of interest is variable by reference to one or more of the following—

(a)  the Bank of England's minimum rate;
(b)  the average rate of discount on allotment on 91-day Treasury bills;
(c)  a yield on 91-day Treasury bills;
(d)  a London sterling inter-bank offered rate;
(e)  a London sterling certificate of deposit rate.

10. In debentures or in the guaranteed or preference stock of any incorporated company, being statutory water undertakers within the meaning of the Water Act 1945, or any corresponding enactment in force in Northern Ireland, and having during each of the ten years immediately preceding the calendar year in which the investment was made paid a dividend of not less than $3\frac{1}{2}$ per cent. on its ordinary shares.

10A. In any units, or other shares of the investments subject to the trusts, of a unit trust scheme which, at the time of investment, is an authorised unit trust, within the meaning of subsection (1) of section 468 of the Income and Corporation Taxes Act 1988, in relation to which that subsection does not, by virtue of subsection (5) of that section, apply.

11. [Repealed.]

12. In deposits with a building society within the meaning of the Building Societies Act 1986.

13. In mortgages of freehold property in England and Wales or Northern Ireland and of leasehold property in those countries

of which the unexpired term at the time of investment is not less than sixty years, and in loans on heritable security in Scotland.

14. In perpetual rent-charges charged on land in England and Wales or Northern Ireland and fee-farm rents (not being rent-charges) issuing out of such land, and in feu-duties or ground annuals in Scotland.

15. In certificates of Tax Deposit.

## PART III

### WIDER-RANGE INVESTMENTS

1. In any securities issued in the United Kingdom by a company incorporated in the United Kingdom, being securities registered in the United Kingdom and not being securities falling within Part II of this Schedule.

2. In shares in a building society within the meaning of the Building Societies Act 1986.

3. In any units of an authorised unit trust scheme within the meaning of the Financial Services Act 1986.

## PART IV

### SUPPLEMENTAL

1. The securities mentioned in Parts I to III of this Schedule do not include any securities where the holder can be required to accept repayment of the principal, or the payment of any interest, otherwise than in sterling.

2. The securities mentioned in paragraphs 1 to 8 of Part II, other than Treasury Bills or Tax Reserve Certificates, securities issued before the passing of this Act by the Government of the Isle of Man, securities falling within paragraph 4 of the said Part II issued before the passing of this Act or securities falling within paragraph 9 of that Part, and the securities mentioned in paragraph 1 of Part III of this Schedule, do not include—

(a) securities the price of which is not quoted on a recognised investment exchange within the meaning of the Financial Services Act 1986;

(b) shares or debenture stock not fully paid up (except shares or debenture stock which by the terms of issue are required to be fully paid up within nine months of the date of issue).

3. The securities mentioned in paragraph 6 of Part II and paragraph 1 of Part III of this Schedule do not include—

(a) shares or debentures of an incorporated company of which the total issued and paid up share capital is less than one million pounds;

(b) shares or debentures of an incorporated company which has not in each of the five years immediately preceding the calendar year in which the investment is made paid a dividend on all the shares issued by the company, excluding any shares issued after the dividend was declared and any shares which by their terms of issue did not rank for the dividend for that year.

For the purposes of sub-paragraph (*b*) of this paragraph a company formed—

(i)    to take over the business of another company or other companies, or

(ii)   to acquire the securities of, or control of, another company or other companies,

or for either of those purposes and for other purposes shall be deemed to have paid a dividend as mentioned in that sub-paragraph in any year in which such a dividend has been paid by the other company or all the other companies, as the case may be.

4. In this Schedule, unless the context otherwise requires, the following expressions have the meanings hereby respectively assigned to them, that is to say—

"debenture" includes debenture stock and bonds, whether constituting a charge on assets or not, and loan stock or notes;

"enactment" includes an enactment of the Parliament of Northern Ireland;

"fixed-interest securities" means securities which under their terms of issue bear a fixed rate of interest;

"local authority" in relation to the United Kingdom, means any of the following authorities—

(*a*)   in England and Wales, the council of a county, a borough, an urban or rural district or a parish, the Common Council of the City of London, the Greater London Council and the Council of the Isles of Scilly;

(*b*)   in Scotland, a local authority within the meaning of the Local Government (Scotland) Act 1947;

(*c*)   [*Repealed.*]

"securities" includes shares, debentures, units within paragraph 3 of Part III of this Schedule, Treasury Bills and Tax Reserve Certificates;

"share" includes stock;

"Treasury Bills" includes bills issued by Her Majesty's Government in the United Kingdom and Northern Ireland Treasury Bills.

5. It is hereby declared that in this Schedule "mortgage," in relation to freehold or leasehold property in Northern Ireland, includes a registered charge which, by virtue of subsection (4) of section forty of the Local Registration of Title (Ireland) Act 1891 or any other enactment, operates as a mortgage by deed.

6. References in this Schedule to an incorporated company are references to a company incorporated by or under any enactment and include references to a body of persons established for the purpose of trading for profit and incorporated by Royal Charter.

7. [*Repealed by the Building Societies Act* 1986, *s.*120(2), *Sched.* 19, *Pt.* I.]

# CHARITIES ACT 1992

## PART II

### CONTROL OF FUND-RAISING FOR CHARITABLE INSTITUTIONS

#### *Preliminary*

**58.**—(1) In this Part—

"charitable contributions", in relation to any representation made by any commercial participator or other person, means—

(a) the whole or part of—
   (i) the consideration given for goods or services sold or supplied by him, or
   (ii) any proceeds (other than such consideration) of a promotional venture undertaken by him, or
(b) sums given by him by way of donation in connection with the safe or supply of any such goods or services (whether the amount of such sums is determined by reference to the value of any such goods or services or otherwise);

"charitable institution" means a charity or an institution (other than a charity) which is established for charitable, benevolent or philanthropic purposes;

"charity" means a charity within the meaning of the Charities Act 1960;

"commercial participator", in relation to any charitable institution, means any person who—

(a) carries on for gain a business other than a fund-raising business, but
(b) in the course of that business, engages in any promotional venture in the course of which it is represented that charitable contributions are to be given to or applied for the benefit of the institution;

"company" has the meaning given by section 46 of the Charities Act 1960 (as amended by the Companies Act 1989);

"the court" means the High Court or a county court;

"credit card" means a card which is a credit-token within the meaning of the Consumer Credit Act 1974;

"debit card" means a card the use of which by its holder to make a payment results in a current account of his at a bank, or at any other institution providing banking services, being debited with the payment;

"fund-raising business" means any business carried on for gain and wholly or primarily engaged in soliciting or otherwise procuring money or other property for charitable, benevolent or philanthropic purposes;

"institution" includes any trust or undertaking;

"professional fund-raiser" means—

(a) any person (part from a charitable institution) who carries on a fund-raising business, or

(b) any other person (apart from a person excluded by virtue of subsection (2) or (3)) who for reward solicits money or other property for the benefit of a charitable institution, if he does so otherwise than in the course of any fund-raising venture undertaken by a person falling within paragraph (a) above;

"promotional venture" means any advertising or sales campaign or any other venture undertaken for promotional purposes;

"radio or television programme" includes any item included in a programme service within the meaning of the Broadcasting Act 1990.

(2) In subsection (1), paragraph (b) of the definition of "professional fund-raiser" does not apply to any of the following, namely—

(a) any charitable institution or any company connected with any such institution;

(b) any officer or employee of any such institution or company, or any trustee of any such institution, acting (in each case) in his capacity as such;

(c) any person acting as a collector in respect of a public charitable collection (apart from a person who is to be treated as a promoter of such a collection by virtue of section 65(3));

(d) any person who in the course of a relevant programme, that is to say a radio or television programme in the course of which a fund-raising venture is undertaken by—

(i) a charitable institution, or
(ii) a company connected with such an institution,

makes any solicitation at the instance of that institution or company; or

(e) any commercial participator;

and for this purpose "collector" and "public charitable collection" have the same meaning as in Part III of this Act.

(3) In addition, paragraph (b) of the definition of "professional fund-raiser" does not apply to a person if he does not receive—

(a) more than—

(i) £5 per day, or
(ii) £500 per year,

by way of remuneration in connection with soliciting money or other property for the benefit of the charitable institution referred to in that paragraph; or

(b) more than £500 by way of remuneration in connection with any fund-raising venture in the course of which he solicits money or other property for the benefit of that institution.

(4) In this Part any reference to charitable purposes, where occurring in the context of a reference to charitable, benevolent

or philanthropic purposes, is a reference to charitable purposes whether or not the purposes are charitable within the meaning of any rule of law.

(5) For the purposes of this Part a company is connected with a charitable institution if—

(a) the institution, or

(b) the institution and one or more other charitable institutions, taken together,

is or are entitled (whether directly, or through one or more nominees) to exercise, or control the exercise of, the whole of the voting power at any general meeting of the company.

(6) In this Part—

(a) "represent" and "solicit" mean respectively represent and solicit in any manner whatever, whether expressly or impliedly and whether done—

(i) by speaking directly to the person or persons to whom the representation or solicitation is addressed (whether when in his or their presence or not), or

(ii) by means of a statement published in any newspaper, film or radio or television programme,

or otherwise, and references to a representation or solicitation shall be construed accordingly; and

(b) any reference to soliciting or otherwise procuring money or other property is a reference to soliciting or otherwise procuring money or other property whether any consideration is, or is to be, given in return for the money or other property or not.

(7) Where—

(a) any solicitation of money or other property for the benefit of a charitable institution is made in accordance with arrangements between any person and that institution, and

(b) under those arrangements that person will be responsible for receiving on behalf of the institution money or other property given in response to the solicitation,

then (if he would not be so regarded apart from this subsection) that person shall be regarded for the purposes of this Part as soliciting money or other property for the benefit of the institution.

(8) Where any fund-raising venture is undertaken by a professional fund-raiser in the course of a radio or television programme, any solicitation which is made by a person in the course of the programme at the instance of the fund-raiser shall be regarded for the purposes of this Part as made by the fund-raiser and not by that person (and shall be so regarded whether or not the solicitation is made by that person for any reward).

(9) In this Part "services" includes facilities, and in particular—

(a) access to any premises or event;

(b) membership of any organisation;

(c)  the provision of any advertising space; and

(d)  the provision of any financial facilities;

and references to the supply of services shall be construed accordingly.

(10) The Secretary of State may by order amend subsection (3) by substituting a different sum for the time being specified there.

### Control of fund-raising

**59.**—(1) It shall be unlawful for a professional fund-raiser to solicit money or other property for the benefit of a charitable institution unless he does so in accordance with an agreement with the institution satisfying the prescribed requirements.

(2) It shall be unlawful for a commercial participator to represent that charitable contributions are to be given to or applied for the benefit of a charitable institution unless he does so in accordance with an agreement with the institution satisfying the prescribed requirements.

(3) Where on the application of a charitable institution the court is satisfied—

(a)  that any person has contravened or is contravening subsection (1) or (2) in relation to the institution, and

(b)  that, unless restrained, any such contravention is likely to continue or be repeated,

the court may grant an injunction restraining the contravention; and compliance with subsection (1) or (2) shall not be enforceable otherwise than in accordance with this subsection.

(4) Where—

(a)  a charitable institution makes any agreement with a professional fund-raiser or a commercial participator by virtue of which—

(i) the professional fund-raiser is authorised to solicit money or other property for the benefit of the institution, or

(ii) the commercial participator is authorised to represent that charitable contributions are to be given to or applied for the benefit of the institution.

as the case may be, but

(b)  the agreement does not satisfy the prescribed requirements in any respect,

the agreement shall not be enforceable against the institution except to such extent (if any) as may be provided by an order of the court.

(5) A professional fund-raiser or commercial participator who is a party to such an agreement as is mentioned in subsection (4)(a) shall not be entitled to receive any amount by way of remuneration or expenses in respect of anything done by him in pursuance of the agreement unless—

(a)  he is so entitled under any provision of the agreement, and

(b)  either—

(i) the agreement satisfies the prescribed requirements, or

(ii) any such provision has effect by virtue of an order of
the court under subsection (4).

(6) In this section "the prescribed requirements" means
such requirements as are prescribed by regulations made by
virtue of section 64(2)(*a*).

**60.**—(1) Where a professional fund-raiser solicits money or
other property for the benefit of one or more particular charitable
institutions, the solicitation shall be accompanied by a statement
clearly indicating—

(*a*) the name or names of the institution or institutions
concerned;

(*b*) if there is more than one institution concerned, the
proportions in which the institutions are respectively to
benefit; and

(*c*) (in general terms) the method by which the fund-raiser's
remuneration in connection with the appeal is to be
determined.

(2) Where a professional fund-raiser solicits money or other
property for charitable, benevolent or philanthropic purposes of
any description (rather than for the benefit of one or more
particular charitable institutions), the solicitation shall be
accompanied by a statement clearly indicating—

(*a*) the fact that he is soliciting money or other property for
those purposes and not for the benefit of any particular
charitable institution or institutions;

(*b*) the method by which it is to be determined how the
proceeds of the appeal are to be distributed between
different charitable institutions; and

(*c*) (in general terms) the method by which his remuneration in connection with the appeal is to be determined.

(3) Where any representation is made by a commercial
participator to the effect that charitable contributions are to be
given to or applied for the benefit of one or more particular
charitable institutions, the representation shall be accompanied
by a statement clearly indicating—

(*a*) the name or names of the institution or institutions
concerned;

(*b*) if there is more than one institution concerned, the
proportions in which the institutions are respectively to
benefit; and

(*c*) (in general terms) the method by which it is to be
determined—

(i) what proportion of the consideration given for
goods or services sold or supplied by him, or of any
other proceeds of a promotional venture undertaken by him, is to be given to or applied for the
benefit of the institution or institutions concerned,
or

        (ii) what sums by way of donations by him in connection with the sale or supply of any such goods or services are to be so given or applied,

as the case may require.

(4) If any such solicitation or representation as is mentioned in any of subsections (1) to (3) is made—

    (*a*)  in the course of a radio or television programme, and

    (*b*)  in association with an announcement to the effect that payment may be made, in response to the solicitation or representation, by means of a credit or debit card,

the statement required by virtue of subsection (1), (2) or (3) (as the case may be) shall include full details of the right to have refunded under section 61(1) any payment of £50 or more which is so made.

(5) If any such solicitation or representation as is mentioned in any of subsections (1) to (3) is made orally but is not made—

    (*a*)  by speaking directly to the particular person or persons to whom it is addressed and in his or their presence, or

    (*b*)  in course of any radio or television programme,

the professional fund-raiser or commercial participator concerned shall, within seven days of any payment of £50 or more being made to him in response to the solicitation or representation, give to the person making the payment a written statement—

    (i)  of the matters specified in paragraphs (*a*) to (*c*) of that subsection; and

    (ii)  including full details of the right to cancel under section 61(2) an agreement made in response to the solicitation or representation, and the right to have refunded under section 61(2) or (3) any payment of £50 or more made in response thereto.

(6) In subsection (5) above the reference to the making of a payment is a reference to the making of a payment of whatever nature and by whatever means, including a payment made by means of a credit card or a debit card; and for the purposes of that subsection—

    (*a*)  where the person making any such payment makes it in person, it shall be regarded as made at the time it is so made;

    (*b*)  where the person making any such payment sends it by post, it shall be regarded as made at the time when it is posted; and

    (*c*)  where the person making any such payment makes it by giving, by telephone or by means of any other telecommunication apparatus, authority for an account to be debited with the payment, it shall be regarded as made at the time when any such authority is given.

(7) Where any requirement of subsections (1) to (5) is not complied with in relation to any solicitation or representation, the professional fund-raiser or commercial participator concerned shall be guilty of an offence and liable on summary conviction to a fine not exceeding the fifth level on the standard scale.

(8) It shall be a defence for a person charged with any such offence to prove that he took all reasonable precautions and exercised all due diligence to avoid the commission of the offence.

(9) Where the commission by any person of an offence under subsection (7) is due to the act or default of some other person, that other person shall be guilty of the offence; and a person may be charged with and convicted of the offence by virtue of this subsection whether or not proceedings are taken against the first-mentioned person.

(10) In this section—

"the appeal", in relation to any solicitation by a professional fund-raiser, means the campaign or other fund-raising venture in the course of which the solicitation is made;
"telecommunication apparatus" has the same meaning as in the Telecommunications Act 1984.

**61.**—(1) Where—

(a) a person ("the donor"), in response to any such solicitation or representation as is mentioned in any of subsections (1) to (3) of section 60 which is made in the course of a radio or television programme, makes any payment of £50 or more to the relevant fund-raiser by means of a credit card or a debit card, but

(b) before the end of the period of seven days beginning with the date of the solicitation or representation, the donor serves on the relevant fund-raiser a notice in writing which, however expressed, indicates the donor's intention to cancel the payment,

the donor shall (subject to subsection (4) below) be entitled to have the payment refunded to him forthwith by the relevant fund-raiser.

(2) Where—

(a) a person ("the donor"), in response to any solicitation or representation falling within subsection (5) of section 60, enters into an agreement with the relevant fund-raiser under which the donor is, or may be, liable to make any payment or payments to the relevant fund-raiser, and the amount or aggregate amount which the donor is, or may be, liable to pay to him under the agreement is £50 or more, but

(b) before the end of the period of seven days beginning with the date when he is given any such written statement as is referred to in that subsection, the donor serves on the relevant fund-raiser a notice in writing which, however expressed, indicates the donor's intention to cancel the agreement,

the notice shall operate, as from the time when it is so served, to cancel the agreement and any liability of any person other than the donor in connection with the making of any such payment or payments, and the donor shall (subject to subsection (4) below) be entitled to have any payment of £50 or more made by him under the agreement refunded to him forthwith by the relevant fund-raiser.

(3) Where, in response to any solicitation or representation falling within subsection (5) of section 60, a person ("the donor")—

(a) makes any payment of £50 or more to the relevant fund-raiser, but

(b) does not enter into any such agreement as is mentioned in subsection (2) above,

then, if before the end of the period of seven days beginning with the date when the donor is given any such written statement as is referred to in subsection (5) of that section, the donor serves on the relevant fund-raiser a notice in writing which, however expressed, indicates the donor's intention to cancel the payment, the donor shall (subject to subsection (4) below) be entitled to have the payment refunded to him forthwith by the relevant fund-raiser.

(4) The right of any person to have a payment refunded to him under any of subsections (1) to (3) above—

(a) is a right to have refunded to him the amount of the payment less any administrative expenses reasonably incurred by the relevant fund-raiser in connection with—

(i) the making of the refund, or

(ii) (in the case of a refund under subsection (2)) dealing with the notice of cancellation served by that person; and

(b) shall, in the case of a payment for goods already received, be conditional upon restitution being made by him of the goods in question.

(5) Nothing in subsections (1) to (3) above has effect in relation to any payment made or to be made in respect of services which have been supplied at the time when the relevant notice is served.

(6) In this section any reference to the making of a payment is a reference to the making of a payment of whatever nature and (in the case of subsection (2) or (3)) a payment made by whatever means, including a payment made by means of a credit card or a debit card; and subsection (6) of section 60 shall have effect for determining when a payment is made for the purposes of this section as it has effect for determining when a payment is made for the purposes of subsection (5) of that section.

(7) In this section "the relevant fund-raiser", in relation to any solicitation or representation, means the professional fund-raiser or commercial participator by whom it is made.

(8) The Secretary of State may by order—

(a) amend any provision of this section by substituting a different sum for the sum for the time being specified there; and

(b) make such consequential amendments in section 60 as he considers appropriate.

**62.**—(1) Where on the application of any charitable institu-tion—

(a) the court is satisfied that any person has done or is doing either of the following, namely—
  (i) soliciting money or other property for the benefit of the institution, or
  (ii) representing that charitable contributions are to be given to or applied for the benefit of the institution,
  and that, unless restrained, he is likely to do further acts of that nature, and
(b) the court is also satisfied as to one or more of the matters specified in subsection (2),

then (subject to subsection (3)) the court may grant an injunction restraining the doing of any such acts.

(2) The matters referred to in subsection (1)(b) are—

(a) that the person in question is using methods of fund-raising to which the institution objects;
(b) that the person is not a fit and proper person to raise funds for the institution; and
(c) where a conduct complained of is the making of such representation as are mentioned in subsection (1)(a)(ii), that the institution does not wish to be associated with the particular promotional or other fund-raising venture in which the person is engaged.

(3) The power to grant an injunction under subsection (1) shall not be exercisable on the application of a charitable institution unless the institution has, not less than 28 days before making the application, served on the person in question a notice in writing—

(a) requesting him to cease forthwith—
  (i) soliciting money or other property for the benefit of the institution, or
  (ii) representing that charitable contributions are to be given to or applied for the benefit of the institution,
  as the case may be; and
(b) stating that, if he does not comply with the notice, the institution will make an application under this section for an injunction.

(4) Where—

(a) a charitable institution has served on any person a notice under subsection (3) ("the relevant notice") and that person has complied with the notice, but
(b) that person has subsequently begun to carry on activities which are the same, or substantially the same, as those in respect of which the relevant notice was served,

the institution shall not, in connection with an application made by it under this section in respect of the activities carried on by that person, be required by virtue of that subsection to serve a further notice on him, if the application is made not more than 12 months after the date of service of the relevant notice.

(5) This section shall not have the effect of authorising a charitable institution to make an application under this section in respect of anything done by a professional fund-raiser or commercial participator in relation to the institution.

**63.**—(1) Where—

(*a*)  a person solicits money or other property for the benefit of an institution in association with a representation that the institution is a registered charity, and

(*b*)  the institution is not such a charity,

he shall be guilty of an offence and liable on summary conviction to a fine not exceeding the fifth level on the standard scale.

(2) In subsection (1) "registered charity" means a charity which is for the time being registered in the register of charities kept under section 4 of the Charities Act 1960.

*Supplementary*

**64.**—(1) The Secretary of State may make such regulations as appear to him to be necessary or desirable for any purposes connected with any of the preceding provisions of this Part.

(2) Without prejudice to the generality of subsection (1), any such regulations may—

(*a*)  prescribe the form and content of—
   (i)  agreements made for the purposes of section 59, and
   (ii)  notices served under section 62(3);

(*b*)  require professional fund-raisers or commercial participators who are parties to such agreements with charitable institutions to make available to the institutions books, documents or other records (however kept) which relate to the institutions;

(*c*)  specify the manner in which money or other property acquired by professional fund-raisers or commercial participators for the benefit of, or otherwise falling to be given to or applied by such persons for the benefit of, charitable institutions is to be transmitted to such institutions;

(*d*)  provide for any provisions of section 60 or 61 having effect in relation to solicitations or representations made in the course of radio or television programmes to have effect, subject to any modifications specified in the regulations, in relation to solicitations or representations made in the course of such programmes—
   (i)  by charitable institutions, or
   (ii)  by companies connected with such institutions,
   and, in that connection, provide for any other provisions of this Part to have effect for the purposes of the regulations subject to any modifications so specified;

(*e*)  make other provision regulating the raising of funds for charitable, benevolent or philanthropic purposes (whether by professional fund-raisers or commercial participators or otherwise).

(3) In subsection (2)(*c*) the reference to such money or other property as is there mentioned includes a reference to money or other property which, in the case of a professional fund-raiser or commercial participator—

(a) has been acquired by him otherwise than in accordance with an agreement with a charitable institution, but

(b) by reason of any solicitation or representation in consequence of which it has been acquired, is held by him on trust for such an institution.

(4) Regulations under this section may provide that any failure to comply with a specified provision of the regulations shall be an offence punishable on summary conviction by a fine not exceeding the second level on the standard scale.

# PART III

## PUBLIC CHARITABLE COLLECTIONS

### *Preliminary*

**65.**—(1) In this Part—

(a) "public charitable collection" means (subject to subsection (2)) a charitable appeal which is made—
  (i) in any public place, or
  (ii) by means of visits from house to house; and

(b) "charitable appeal" means an appeal to members of the public to give money or other property (whether for consideration or otherwise) which is made in association with a representation that the whole or any part of its proceeds is to be applied for charitable, benevolent or philanthropic purposes.

(2) Subsection (1)(a) does not apply to a charitable appeal which—

(a) is made in the course of a public meeting; or

(b) is made—
  (i) on land within a churchyard or burial ground contiguous or adjacent to a place of public worship, or
  (ii) on other land occupied for the purposes of a place of public worship and contiguous or adjacent to it,
  being (in each case) land which is enclosed or substantially enclosed (whether by any wall or building or otherwise); or

(c) is an appeal to members of the public to give money or other property by placing it in an unattended receptacle;

and for the purposes of paragraph (c) above a receptacle is unattended if it is not in the possession or custody of a person acting as a collector.

(3) In this Part, in relation to a public charitable collection—

(a) "promoter" means a person who (whether alone or with others and whether for remuneration or otherwise) organises or controls the conduct of the charitable appeal in question, and associated expressions shall be construed accordingly; and

(b) "collector" means any person by whom that appeal is made (whether made by him alone or with others and whether made by him for remuneration or otherwise);

but where no person acts in the manner mentioned in paragraph (a) above in respect of a public charitable collection, any person who acts as a collector in respect of it shall for the purposes of this Part be treated as a promoter of it as well.

(4) In this Part—

"local authority" means the council of the district or of a London borough, the Common Council of the City of London, or the Council of the Isles of Scilly; and

"proceeds", in relation to a public charitable collection, means all money or other property given (whether for consideration or otherwise) in response to the charitable appeal in question.

(5) In this Part any reference to charitable purposes, where occurring in the context of a reference to charitable, benevolent or philanthropic purposes, is a reference to charitable purposes whether or not the purposes are charitable within the meaning of any rule of law.

(6) The functions exercisable under this Part by a local authority shall be exercisable—

(a) as respects the Inner Temple, by its Sub-Treasurer, and
(b) as respects the Middle Temple, by its Under Treasurer;

and references in this Part to a local authority or to the area of a local authority shall be construed accordingly.

(7) It is hereby declared that an appeal to members of the public (other than one falling within subsection (2)) is a public charitable collection for the purposes of this Part if—

(a) it consists in or includes the making of an offer to sell goods or to supply services, or the exposing of goods for sale, to members of the public, and
(b) it is made as mentioned in sub-paragraph (i) or (ii) of subsection (1)(a) and in association with a representation that the whole or any part of its proceeds is to be applied for charitable, benevolent or philanthropic purposes.

This subsection shall not be taken as prejudicing the generality of subsection (1)(b).

(8) In this section—

"house" includes any part of a building constituting a separate dwelling;

"public place", in relation to a charitable appeal, means—

(a) any highway, and
(b) (subject to subsections (9)) any other place to which, at any time when the appeal is made, members of the public have or are permitted to have access and which either—
    (i) is not within a building, or
    (ii) if within a building, is a public area within any station, airport or shopping precinct or any other similar public area.

(9) In subsection (8), paragraph (*b*) of the definition of "public place" does not apply to—

(*a*) any place to which members of the public are permitted to have access only if any payment or ticket required as a condition of access has been made or purchased; or

(*b*) any place to which members of the public are permitted to have access only by virtue of permission given for the purposes of the appeal in question.

*Prohibition on conducting unauthorised collections*

**66.**—(1) No public charitable collection shall be conducted in the area of any local authority except in accordance with—

(*a*) a permit issued by the authority under section 68; or

(*b*) an order made by the Charity Commissioners under section 72.

(2) Where a public charitable collection is conducted in contravention of subsection (1), any promoter of that collection shall be guilty of an offence and liable on summary conviction to a fine not exceeding the fourth level on the standard scale.

*Permits*

**67.**—(1) An application for a permit to conduct a public charitable collection in the area of a local authority shall be made to the authority by the person or persons proposing to promote that collection.

(2) Any such application—

(*a*) shall specify the period for which it is desired that the permit, if issued, should have effect, being a period not exceeding 12 months; and

(*b*) shall contain such information as may be prescribed by regulations under section 73.

(3) Any such application—

(*a*) shall be made at least one month before the relevant day or before such later date as the local authority may in the case of that application allow, but

(*b*) shall not be made more than six months before the relevant day;

and for this purpose "the relevant day" means the day on which the collection is to be conducted or, where it is to be conducted on more than one day, the first of those days.

(4) Before determining any application duly made to them under this section, a local authority shall consult the chief officer of police for the police area which comprises or includes their area and may make such other inquiries as they think fit.

**68.**—(1) Where an application for a permit is duly made to a local authority under section 67 in respect of a public charitable collection, the authority shall either—

    (*a*)  issue a permit in respect of the collection, or

    (*b*)  refuse the application on one or more of the grounds specified in section 69,

and, where they issue such a permit, it shall (subject to section 70) have effect for the period specified in the application in accordance with section 67(2)(*a*).

(2) A local authority may, at the time of issuing a permit under this section, attach to it such conditions as they think fit, having regard to the local circumstances of the collection; but the authority shall secure that the terms of any such conditions are consistent with the provisions of any regulations under section 73.

(3) Without prejudice to the generality of subsection (2), a local authority may attach conditions—

    (*a*)  specifying the day of the week, date, time or frequency of the collection;

    (*b*)  specifying the locality or localities within their area in which the collection may be conducted;

    (*c*)  regulating the manner in which the collection is to be conducted.

(4) Where a local authority—

    (*a*)  refuse to issue a permit, or

    (*b*)  attach any condition to a permit under subsection (2),

they shall serve on the applicant written notice of their decision to do so and of the reasons for their decision; and that notice shall also state the right of appeal conferred by section 71(1) or (as the case may be) section 71(2), and the time within such an appeal must be brought.

**69.**—(1) A local authority may refuse to issue a permit to conduct a public charitable collection on any of the following grounds, namely—

    (*a*)  that it appears to them that the collection would cause undue inconvenience to members of the public by reason of—

        (i)  the day of the week or date on which,

        (ii)  the time at which,

        (iii)  the frequency with which, or

        (iv)  the locality or localities in which,
           it is proposed to be conducted;

    (*b*)  that the collection is proposed to be conducted on a day on which another public charitable collection is already authorised (whether under section 68 or otherwise) to be conducted in the authority's area, or on the day falling immediately before, or immediately after, any such day;

    (*c*)  that it appears to them that the amount likely to be applied for charitable, benevolent or philanthropic purposes in consequence of the collection would be inadequate, having regard to the likely amount of the proceeds of the collection;

(*d*) that it appears to them the applicant or any other person would be likely to receive an excessive amount by way of remuneration in connection with the collection;

(*e*) that the applicant has been convicted—

    (i) of an offence under section 5 of the 1916 Act, under the 1939 Act, under section 119 of the 1982 Act or regulations made under it, or under this Part or regulations made under section 73 below, or

    (ii) of any offence involving dishonesty or of a kind the commission of which would in their opinion be likely to be facilitated by the issuing to him of a permit under section 68 above;

(*f*) where the applicant is a person other than a charitable, benevolent or philanthropic institution for whose benefit the collection is proposed to be conducted, that they are not satisfied that the applicant is authorised (whether by any such institution or by any person acting on behalf of any such institution) to promote the collection ; or

(*g*) that it appears to them that the applicant, in promoting any other collection authorised under this Part or under section 119 of the 1982 Act, failed to exercise due diligence—

    (i) to secure that persons authorised by him to act as collectors for the purposes of the collection were fit and proper persons;

    (ii) to secure that such persons complied with the provisions of regulations under section 73 below or (as the case may be) section 119 of the 1982 Act; or

    (iii) to prevent badges or certificates of authority being obtained by persons other than those he had so authorised.

(2) A local authority shall not, however, refuse to issue such a permit on the ground mentioned in subsection (1)(*b*) if it appears to them—

(*a*) that the collection would be conducted only in one location, which is on land to which members of the public would have access only by virtue of the express or implied permission of the occupier of the land; and

(*b*) that the occupier of the land consents to the collection being conducted there;

and for this purpose "the occupier", in relation to unoccupied land, means the person entitled to occupy it.

(3) In subsection (1)—

(*a*) in the case of a collection in relation to which there is more than one applicant, any reference to the applicant shall be construed as a reference to any of the applicants; and

(*b*) (subject to subsection (4)) the reference in paragraph (*g*)(iii) to badges or certificates of authority is a reference to badges or certificates of authority in the form prescribed by regulations under section 73 below or (as the case may be) under section 119 of the 1982 Act.

(4) Subsection (1)(*g*) applies to the conduct of the applicant (or any of the applicants) in relation to any public charitable collection authorised under regulations made under section 5 of the 1916 Act (collection of money or sale of articles in a street or other public place), or authorised under the 1939 Act (collection of money or other property by means of visits from house to house), as it applies to his conduct in relation to a collection authorised under this Part, subject to the following modifications, namely—

(*a*) in the case of a collection authorised under regulations made under the 1916 Act—

  (i) the reference in sub-paragraph (ii) to regulations under section 73 below shall be construed as a reference to the regulations under which the collection in question was authorised, and

  (ii) the reference in sub-paragraph (iii) to badges or certificates of authority shall be construed as a reference to any written authority provided to a collector pursuant to those regulations; and

(*b*) in the case of a collection authorised under the 1939 Act—

  (i) the reference in sub-paragraph (ii) to regulations under section 73 below shall be construed as a reference to regulations under section 4 of that Act, and

  (ii) the reference in sub-paragraph (iii) to badges or certificates of authority shall be construed as a reference to badges or certificates of authority in a form prescribed by such regulations.

(5) In this section—

"the 1916 Act" means the Police, Factories &c. (Miscellaneous Provisions) Act 1916;

"the 1939 Act" means the House to House Collection Act 1939; and

"the 1982 Act" means the Civil Government (Scotland) Act 1982.

**70.**—(1) Where a local authority who have issued a permit under section 68—

(*a*) have reason to believe that there has been a change in the circumstances which prevailed at the time when they issued the permit, and are of the opinion that, if the application for the permit had been made in the new circumstances of the case, the permit would not have been issued by them, or

(*b*) have reason to believe that any information furnished to them by the promoter (or, in the case of a collection in relation to which there is more than one promoter, by any of them) for the purposes of the application for the permit was false in a material particular,

then (subject to subsection (2)) they may—

  (i) withdraw the permit;

  (ii) attach any condition to the permit; or

(iii) vary any existing condition of the permit.

(2) Any condition imposed by the local authority under subsection (1) (whether by attaching a new condition to the permit or by varying an existing condition) must be one that could have been attached to the permit under section 68(2) at the time when it was issued, assuming for this purpose—

(a) that the new circumstances of the case had prevailed at that time, or
(b) (in a case falling within paragraph (b) of subsection (1) above) that the authority had been aware of the true circumstances of the case at that time.

(3) Where a local authority who have issued a permit under section 68 have reason to believe that there has been or is likely to be a breach of any condition of it, or that a breach of such a condition is continuing, they may withdraw the permit.

(4) Where under this section a local authority withdraw, attach any condition to, or vary in existing condition of, a permit, they shall serve on the promoter written notice of their decision to do so and of the reasons for their decision; and that notice shall also state the right of appeal conferred by section 71(2) and the time within which such an appeal must be brought.

(5) Where a local authority so withdraw, attach any condition to, or vary an existing condition of, a permit, the permit shall nevertheless continue to have effect as if it had not been withdrawn or (as the case may be) as if the condition had not been attached or the variation had not been made—

(a) until the time for bringing an appeal under section 71(2) has expired, or
(b) if such an appeal is duly brought, until the determination or abandonment of the appeal.

**71.**—(1) A person who has duly applied to a local authority under section 67 for a permit to conduct a public charitable collection in the authority's area may appeal to a magistrates' court against a decision of the authority to refuse to issue a permit to him.

(2) A person to whom a permit has been issued under section 68 may appeal to a magistrates' court against—

(a) a decision of the local authority under that section or section 70 to attach any condition to the permit; or
(b) a decision of the local authority under section 70 to vary any condition so attached or to withdraw the permit.

(3) An appeal under subsection (1) or (2) shall be by way of complaint for an order, and the Magistrates' Courts Act 1980 shall apply to the proceedings; and references in this section to a magistrates' court are to a magistrates' court acting for the petty sessions area in which is situated the office or principal office of the local authority against whose decision the appeal is brought.

(4) Any such appeal shall be brought within 14 days of the date of service on the person in question of the relevant notice under section 68(4) or (as the case may be) section 70(4); and for

the purposes of this subsection an appeal shall be taken to be brought when the complaint is made.

(5) An appeal against the decision of a magistrates' court on an appeal under subsection (1) or (2) may be brought to the Crown Court.

(6) On an appeal to a magistrates' court or the Crown Court under this section, the court may confirm, vary or reverse the local authority's decision and generally give such directions as it thinks fit, having regard to the provisions of this Part and of regulations under section 73.

(7) It shall be the duty of the local authority to comply with any directions given by the court under subsection (6); but the authority need not comply with any directions given by a magistrates' court—

(a) until the time for bringing an appeal under subsection (5) has expired, or

(b) if such an appeal is duly brought, until the determination or abandonment of the appeal.

### *Orders made by Charity Commissioners*

72.—(1) Where the Charity Commissioners are satisfied, on the application of the charity, that that charity proposes—

(a) to promote public charitable collections—
  (i) throughout England and Wales, or
  (ii) throughout a substantial part of England and Wales,
  in connection with any charitable purposes pursued by the charity, or

(b) to authorise other persons to promote public charitable collections as mentioned in paragraph (a),

the Commissioners may make an order under this subsection in respect of the charity.

(2) Such an order shall have the effect of authorising public charitable collections with—

(a) are promoted by the charity in respect of which the order is made, or by persons authorised by the charity, and

(b) are so promoted in connection with the charitable purposes mentioned in subsection (1),

to be conducted in such area or areas as may be specified in the order.

(3) An order under subsection (1) may—

(a) include such conditions as the Commissioners think fit;

(b) be expressed (without prejudice to paragraph (c)) to have effect without limit of time, or for a specified period only;

(c) be revoked or varied by a further order of the Commissioners.

(4) Where the Commissioners, having made an order under subsection (1) in respect of a charity, make any further order revoking or varying that order, they shall serve on the charity

written notice of their reasons for making the further order, unless it appears to them that the interests of the charity would not be prejudiced by the further order.

(5) In this section "charity" and "charitable purposes" have the same meaning as in the Charities Act 1960.

*Supplementary*

**73.**—(1) The Secretary of State may make regulations—

(a) prescribing the information which is to be contained in applications made under section 67;
(b) for the purposes of regulating the conduct of public charitable collections authorised under—
   (i) permits issued under section 68; or
   (ii) orders made by the Charity Commissioners under section 72.

(2) Regulations under subsection (1)(b) may, without prejudice to the generality of that provision, make provision—

(a) about the keeping and publication of accounts;
(b) for the prevention of annoyance to members of the public;
(c) with respect to the use by collectors of badges and certificates of authority, or badges incorporating such certificates, and to other matters relating to such badges and certificates, including, in particular, provision—

   (i) prescribing the form of such badges and certificates;
   (ii) requiring a collector, on request, to permit his badge, or any certificate of authority held by him for the purposes of the collection, to be inspected by a constable or a duly authorised officer of a local authority, or by an occupier of any premises visited by him in the course of the collection;
(d) for prohibiting persons under a prescribed age from acting as collectors, and prohibiting others from causing them so to act.

(3) Regulations under this section may provide that any failure to comply with a specified provision of the regulations shall be an offence punishable on summary conviction by a fine not exceeding the second level on the standard scale.

**74.**—(1) A person shall be guilty of an offence if, in connection with any charitable appeal, he displays or uses—

(a) a prescribed badge or a prescribed certificate of authority which is not for the time being held by him for the purposes of the appeal pursuant to regulations under section 73, or
(b) any badge or article, or any certificate or other document, so nearly resembling a prescribed badge or (as the case may be) a prescribed certificate of authority as to be likely to deceive a member of the public

(2) A person guilty of an offence under subsection (1) shall be liable on summary conviction to a fine not exceeding the fourth level on the standard scale.

(3) Any person who, for the purposes of an application made under section 67, knowingly or recklessly furnishes any information which is false in a material particular shall be guilty of an offence and liable on summary conviction to a fine not exceeding the fourth level on the standard scale.

(4) In subsection (1) "prescribed badge" and "prescribed certificate of authority" mean respectively a badge and a certificate of authority in such form as may be prescribed by regulations under section 73.

# APPENDIX E

## Some useful addresses

**Charity Commission**
**London Office**
St. Alban's House
57/60 Haymarket
London SW1Y 4QX
Tel. 0171 210 4477

**Liverpool Office**
2nd Floor
20 Kings Parade
Queens Dock
Liverpool L3 4DQ
Tel. 0151 703 1500

**Taunton Office**
Woodfield House
Tangier
Taunton
Somerset TA1 4BL
Tel. 01823 345000
Internet:   http://www.charity-commission.gov.uk

**Inland Revenue**
Financial Intermediaries & Claims Branch
Trusts and Charities
St. Johns House
Merton Road
Bootle
Merseyside L69 9BB
Tel. General enquiries 0151 472 6043
Covenant Helpline 0151 472 6037
Gift Aid Helpline 0151 472 6036

Inland Revenue Claims (Scotland)
Trinity Park House
South Trinity Road
Edinburgh EH5 3SD
Tel. 0131 551 8127

**Charities Official Investment Fund**
**Charities Deposit Fund**
St. Alphage House
2 Fore Street
London EC2Y 5AQ
Tel. 0171 588 1615

These are common investment funds for charities, which operate
in a similar way to unit trusts. (See Chapter 10.)

### Charities Aid Foundation
Kings Hill
West Malling
Kent ME19 4TA

Tel. 01732 520033

Provides services to help donors to charity and covenant administration services for charities; conducts research and publishes
information on funding for charities.

### Charities Tax Reform Group
c/o 12 Little College Street
London SW1P 3SH

Tel. 0171 222 1265

Membership open to charities. Provides advice and representation on fiscal treatment of charities and VAT in particular.

### The Charity Law Association
c/o Paisner & Co
Bouverie House
154 Fleet Street
London EC4A 2DQ

Tel. 0171 353 0299

Professional association for lawyers and accountants dealing with
charities.

### Institute of Charity Fundraising Managers
Rooms 208–210
Market Towers
1 Nine Elms Lane
London SW8 5NQ

Tel. 0171 627 3436

Professional body for fundraisers; aims to improve standards of
practice and ethics in fund-raising; provides training and guidelines for fund-raising practitioners.

### The Directory of Social Change
24 Stephenson Way
London NW1 2DP

Tel. 0171 209 0902

Information and Training for Voluntary Sector

### National Association of Almhouses
Billingbear Lodge
Wokingham
Berks

Tel. 01344 52922

Provides information, advice and practical assistance to
almhouse charities.

### National Playing Fields Association
25 Ovington Square
London SW3 1LQ

Tel. 0171 584 6445

Promotes the preservation, improvement and provision of playing fields and playgrounds by advice and practical assistance and publishing information.

### National Council for Voluntary Organisations
Regents Wharf
8 All Saints Street
London N1 9RL

Tel. 0171 713 6161

Umbrella organisation for voluntary sector: provides advice and information for charities and voluntary bodies; publishes guides and books.

### Scottish Charities Office
Crown Office
25 Chambers Street
Edinburgh EH1 1LA

Tel. 0131 226 2626
Fax 0131 226 6912

### Wales Council for Voluntary Action
Llys Ifor
Crescent Road
Caerffili
Wales CF8 1XL

Tel. 01222 869224

Carries out similar functions to NCVO in Wales.

### Legislation Monitoring Service for Charities
7 Market Street
Woodstock
Oxfordshire OX7 1SU

Tel. 01993 811357

Provides information to subscribers on legislation and policy affecting charities and organises representations where appropriate.

### The Data Protection Registrar
Springfield House
Water Lane
Wilmslow
Cheshire SK9 5AX

Tel. 01625 545700

### Treasury Solicitors Department
Queen Anne's Chambers
28 Broadway
London SW1

Tel. 0171 210 3000

**British Red Cross**
Disaster Appeal Scheme
(United Kingdom)
9 Grosvenor Crescent
London SW1X 7EJ

Tel. 0171 235 5454
Emergency Service:—
Tel. 0800 777100
    Ask for DAS Duty Officer

# APPENDIX F

## Charity Commission Publications

| Explanatory Leaflets | | Date of issue |
|---|---|---|
| CC43 | Incorporation of Charity Trustees | 9/95 |
| CC44 | Small Charities: Alteration of Trusts, Transfer of Property, Expenditure of Capital | 9/95 |
| CC45 | Central Register of Charities: Services Available | 11/95 |
| CC47 | Investigating Charities | 3/95 |
| CC49 | Charities and Insurance | 10/96 |
| CC50 | Getting in Touch with the Charity Commission | 11/95 |
| CC51 | Charity Accounts: The New Framework | 11/95 |

Leaflet marked (*) is available in Welsh


**Audio-cassettes**
Available from the Charity Commission Taunton office:—

- AC2 **Charities and the Charity Commission†**
- AC3 **Responsibilities of Charity Trustees†**
- AC3(a) **Responsibilities of Charity Trustees: A Summary†**
- AC9 **Political Activities and Campaigning by Charities†**
- AC20 **Charities and Fund-raising†**
- AC28 **Disposing of Charity Land**
- AC44 **Small Charities: Alteration of Trusts, Transfer of Property, Expenditure of Capital†**
- AC50 **Getting in Touch with the Charity Commission**
- AC51 **Charity Accounts: The New Framework**
- **Charity Commission News** (Twice yearly)

Those marked (†) are also available in Braille.

Information issued by the Charity Commission is also available on the Internet. The address is on the CCTA's site at http:/www.open.gov.uk/Charity/ccintro.htm


Other publications
Available from HMSO:—

- **Charity Commissioners for England and Wales: Annual Report** (published in May of each year).

- **Decisions of the Charity Commissioners** (published twice yearly).

- **Charity Accounts and Reports: Core Guide** (produced by the Home Office). This includes a copy of the Regulations, relevant extracts from the legislation and a commentary. Copies available from HMSO (telephone 0171 873 9090. Fax 0171 873 8200).

Available from Charity Commission:—

- **Accounting by Charities – Statement of Recommended Practice** (the Charities SORP) available from the London office

- **The Carrying Out of an Independent Examination: Directions and Guidance Notes**

- **Accounting for the Smaller Charity**

- **Accruals Accounting for the Smaller Charity**

- A standard accounts form (**ACC–1371**).

## Video

- **It's for Charity,** which explains the work of the Commission, is available on loan to local charities and community groups free of charge from the Press and Information Office at the Charity Commission London office.

# APPENDIX G

## List of approved agencies for payroll deduction schemes—I.C.T.A. 1988, s.202

**Barnardo's**
Barkingside
Tanners Lane
Ilford
Essex IG6 1QG
Tel. 0181-550-8822
(An independent payroll deduction scheme for all charities)

**British Sugar Foundation**
British Sugar plc
PO Box 26
Oundle Road
Peterborough PE2 9QU
Tel. 01733-63171
(The Foundation intends to act for British Sugar plc employees only)

**Charities Aid Foundation (Give As You Earn)**
Foundation House
Coach and Horses Passage
The Pantiles
Tunbridge Wells
Kent TN2 5TZ
Tel. 01892-512244

**Scottish Council for Voluntary Organisations**
18/19 Claremont Crescent
Edinburgh EH7 4QD
Tel. 0131-556-3882

**United Way Payroll Giving Service**
PO Box 14
8 Nelson Road
Edge Hill
Liverpool L69 7AA
Tel. 0151-709-8252

**Wales Council for Voluntary Action**
c/o Charities Aid Foundation
Foundation House
Coach and Horses Passage
The Pantiles
Tunbridge Wells
Kent TN2 5TZ
Tel. 01892-512244

**Promotion Officer**
**Northern Ireland Council for Voluntary Action**
127–131 Ormeau Road
Belfast BT7 1SH

Tel. 01232-321224

**South West Charitable Trust**
Churchtown
Peter Tavy
Tavistock
Devon PL19 9NN

Tel. 01822-614679

**Director and Secretary**
**(Ben) Motor and Allied Trades Benevolent Fund**
Lynwood
Sunninghill
Ascot
Berkshire SL5 0AJ

Tel. 01344-20191

(The Fund acts for motor and cycle trades employees only)

**Chest, Heart and Stroke Association**
65 North Castle Street
Edinburgh EH2 3LT

Tel. 0131-225-6963

**Minet Employees' Charitable Trust**
Rose Cottage
Pond Lane
Hatfield Heath
Nr. Bishop's Stortford
Herts CM22 7AB

Tel. 01279-730210

(The Trust acts for Minet companies only)

**Lankro Employee Charity Fund (Lankro Chemicals Ltd.)**
PO Box 1
Eccles
Manchester M30 0BH

Tel. 0161-789-7300

(The Fund acts for Lankro Chemicals Ltd. employees only)

**Charities Trust**
PO Box 15
Liverpool L23 0UU

Tel. 0151-949-1900

# INDEX